Genocide & Human Rights

Lessons from the Armenian Experience

A Special Issue of
the Journal of Armenian Studies
Volume IV, Nos. 1 and 2 (1992)

NAASR

Armenian Heritage Press
National Association for Armenian Studies and Research
Belmont, Massachusetts

*Papers presented at the National Conference
Organized and Sponsored by Bentley College and
the National Association for Armenian Studies and Research*

JOURNAL OF ARMENIAN STUDIES (ISSN 0883-9948) is a publication of the National Association for Armenian Studies and Research, Inc., Armenian Heritage Press, 395 Concord Ave., Belmont, Mass. 02178. Telephone: (617) 489-1610.

Library of Congress Cataloging-in-Publication Data

Genocide & human rights: lessons from the Armenian experience.
    p. cm.
  "A special issue of the Journal of Armenian studies, volume IV, nos. 1 and 2 (1992)."
  "Papers presented at the national conference, organized and sponsored by Bentley College and the National Association for Armenian Studies and Research."
  Includes bibliographical references.
  ISBN 0-935411-11-9: $25.00
  1. Armenian massacres, 1915-1923--Congresses. 2. Holocaust, Jewish (1939-1945)--Congresses. 3. Genocide--Congresses.
I. Bentley College. II. National Association for Armenian Studies and Research (U.S.) III. Journal of Armenian studies. IV. Title: Genocide and human rights.
DS195.5.G345 1993
956.6'2015--dc20   93-19321
                                    CIP

Publication of this special issue of the
Journal of Armenian Studies
was underwritten in part by a grant from the
AGBU-Alex Manoogian Cultural Fund of Southfield, Michigan

Contents

POLITICAL IMPLICATIONS OF GENOCIDE

EDITOR'S NOTE: The National Conference on Genocide and Human Rights ("Seventy Years after the Genocide: Lessons from the Armenian Experience") held at Bentley College in Waltham, Massachusetts, on April 18, 19, and 20, 1985, created widespread interest in the media and academic circles both because of the insights it provided into the causes and effects of genocide and also because of its emphasis on identifying the means to prevent future outbreaks of genocide. The observations of several participants concerning minority rights, human rights, and the responsibilities of governments and the worldwide community to secure these rights are especially pertinent today, in the post cold-war era, as nations search for new methods to deal with ethnic strife and international conflicts.

The National Association for Armenian Studies and Research is therefore pleased to make these papers now available to a wider audience. Although it has been impossible to include all of the papers and commentary presented in the two-and-a-half day conference,* the present collection provides ample material dealing with the major themes and issues raised by the participants concerning genocide in the twentieth century.

Thanks are due to a number of individuals who helped to make this publication possible. These include Bentley College faculty members David A. Fedo (English, now dean of students at Gordon College), Richard Geehr (history), and Herbert Sawyer (government), who were active members of the conference organizing committee and provided initial review of several of the papers. Roger W. Smith, author of the Foreword and the Appendix, was of immeasurable assistance in editing the papers for publication.

In order to secure the widest possible distribution, this collection is being issued both as a separate publication and as a special double issue of NAASR's *Journal of Armenian Studies*. Customary *Journal* features, such as book reviews, will be resumed with the *Journal's* next regular issue.

---

*The papers which were published elsewhere in modified form and/or were not submitted for publication include the following: Levon Z. Boyajian and Haigaz M. Grigorian, "Children of Survivors of the Armenian Genocide: A Psychological Study"; Lucy Der Manuelian, "The Impact of the Armenian Genocide on Armenian Art and Scholarship"; Marilyn B. Feingold, "The Status of Education on the Holocaust and Genocide in the United States"; Gerard Libaridian, "The Armenian Genocide as a Paradigm for 'Political' Genocide"; Levon Marashlian, "Population Statistics, Politics, and the Armenian Question"; Donald E. Miller, "The Impact of the Turkish Massacres on the Survivors"; Allen J. Salerian, "Long-Term Psychological Effects of the 1915 Genocide on Armenian Survivors"; and Puzant Yeghiayan, "Historical References and Comparative Statistics of the Armenian Population in Turkey."

Foreword

Roger W. Smith

Milan Kundera, the exiled Czech writer, tells us that "the struggle of man against power is the struggle of memory against forgetting." By memory, Kundera does not mean remembrance alone, but remembrance that is accompanied by understanding, and understanding that leads to commitment and action. It is commendable, therefore, that a National Conference on Genocide and Human Rights was held at Bentley College in Waltham, Massachusetts, on April 18 to 20, 1985, a conference that coincided with the world-wide observances of the seventieth anniversary of the Armenian Genocide. The program, which was jointly organized by Bentley College and the National Association for Armenian Studies and Research, took as its overall theme: "Seventy Years after the Genocide: Lessons from the Armenian Experience."

The goals of the conference were to foster greater awareness and understanding of genocide and to promote further study of its causes, effects, and potential for recurrence. Emphasizing human rights and the responsibilities of governments and the international community, it also sought to build bridges between victims of genocide in order that they might work together in an attempt to end, to use the language of the United Nations Convention, the "odious scourge" of genocide.

I went to the conference on the Armenian Genocide as a relative innocent, though perhaps I was not "wholly innocent," since I later received a letter from the Turkish Ambassador to the United States rebuking my scholarship. My "mistake" was that I had mentioned the Armenian Genocide, something, he said, that never happened. But as I read these papers again, many vivid moments from the conference came back to me. It was there that I met Helen Fein, Israel Charny, and Richard Hovannisian, scholars whom I hold in the highest regard. It was there too that I met, for the first time, survivors of the Genocide, their children and grandchildren, all of whom shared their stories with me, bearing witness to a proud and tragic history. And it was there that the first evening of the conference I sat at the banquet table with a group of Armenians who began to sing in Armenian, a language I had never heard before, songs of home and long ago, songs sad yet sweet, coming from the heart, and accompanied with tears. Little did I know then that on April 24, 1990, I would stand before the Martyrs' Memorial in Yerevan, Armenia, and I too would weep. But, in the end, tears of sadness and anger are not enough; they must also become tears of resolution and action.

Many of you will be pleased, as I am, that the *Journal of Armenian Studies* is now making available to a wider audience many of the papers from the conference. Of course, not all the papers will appeal to every reader, but the collection does allow us to hear different voices and learn from different perspectives. We hear the survivors speak, listen to the voices of social scientists as they seek to understand why the Genocide occurred, why it has been denied, and what roles and responsibilities governments have in the prevention of possible future atrocities; we listen to the statesman who spoke out every day for more than twenty years on the floor of the United States Senate in support of American ratification of the Genocide Convention; we hear scholars draw parallels between the Armenian Genocide and the present; and we learn about both the importance of teaching about genocide and human rights and how we might go about that. Ironically, there is contained within these pages the voice of one who artfully denies the Genocide, claiming that there are two sides to the Genocide, that the Armenians were not "wholly innocent," that both sides suffered, that the Armenian deaths were not intentional, but rather the result of the breakdown of governmental control ("things got terribly out of hand in 1915"), and who writes euphemistically of deaths "suffered by" rather than "inflicted upon" Armenians. But let it stand as an exhibit of the continuing attempt to deny, rationalize, and trivialize the Genocide, and as a pointed reminder of the truth of Kundera's words.

The studies presented here go some way toward answering a number of questions about the Genocide, and more recent work (some of it listed in the Appendix) has taken our understanding further in certain respects. But of equal importance, and despite the persistence of the conditions that allow genocide to take place (deep social and political conflict, nationalism and other ideologies, dehumanization of others, obedience to orders regardless of consequences, indifference to the destruction of other groups and peoples, and the cynical pursuit of narrowly conceived ideas of national interest at the expense of human rights and truths), these studies help to jar us out of our indifference to the plight of others and to overcome the feeling of powerlessness to affect the decisions of governments.

Scholarship, of course, bears the mark of the conditions under which it is produced and it also reflects the temperaments of its authors. Thus, the author of one of the papers published here asserted that: "As ethnic past and present collide, international political dynamics move ever further from circumstances favorable to the emergence of an Armenian state." In 1985 that was a statement that sounded reasonable enough, but today it reminds us that history is not the same as nature: that nothing in human history, except our individual mortality, is inevitable, least of all genocide; rather, choice and will play decisive roles in shaping society and its future. Can we not choose to act in non-genocidal ways? Can we not purge ourselves of stereotypes, hate, and indifference? Can we not find ways to insist that governments protect human rights and not align themselves with states that violate them? Can we not build bridges (a common theme in this volume) between victims of genocide, or must every group appropriate suffering for itself and turn its back on the tragedies of other peoples? Can we not insist that students be taught about human rights and citizenship, about how to overcome the tendency to be the passive bystander who watches as injustice is carried out, and about how one can resist obedience to orders when obedience means harming innocent persons? Can we not ask: What can *I* do to protect human rights and how may I do it?

Belief in fate and determinism can be comforting since it relieves us of responsibility. The openness of the future provokes anxiety in some, but, I believe, it also offers us hope, since it suggests that we can shape the kind of world we live in: whether human rights are protected, whether genocide claims new victims, depends upon what *we become* and what *we do*. Remembrance, understanding, commitment—these are what Kundera had in mind when he wrote, to say it once again, that "the struggle of man against power is the struggle of memory against forgetting." Yet there is no doubt that the struggle for truth, for the healing power that recognition of the Armenian

Genocide can bring to the survivors and their descendants, and for the prevention of atrocities against yet another people place heavy responsibilities upon us all.

The Armenian people have known tragedy and injustice in the extreme, but they have also known rebirth. The existence of men and women who care about the past, but are committed to defending human rights—above all, the right to life—in the present and future, provides grounds for cautious optimism.

Preface

Gregory H. Adamian[*]

Our coming together today constitutes a profession of faith. Although the subject of our Conference compels us to confront the darkest, most shameful chapters in the history of this century, we bring to our task the shared conviction that *knowledge* and *history* have the power to affect human behavior.

We recognize that justice and liberty can thrive only in an atmosphere of unflinching self-awareness—and we therefore propose to examine the moral blight that is genocide and to analyze it, much as a biologist might probe a mysterious and complex virus in an attempt to discover the secret of its deadly contagion.

That same confidence in the human capacity to understand the nature of our universe motivates us here today. Our task is to study the terrible facts of this infectious moral disease, to make sure they are acknowledged and understood in a public forum, and to develop working hypotheses that might lead to prevention or cure.

It takes courage to remind the world that, along with a noble striving for peace and justice and beauty, the horror of genocide has been a recurrent element of our human heritage. History teaches us that our human race carries within it a seemingly unlimited potential for good *and* for evil. As educators, scholars, statesmen and leading citizens, we are sometimes called upon to acknowledge the darkest side of our shared human nature in order to explore the means of overcoming—or at least *controlling*—the most hateful and destructive of human instincts.

---

[*]Statement delivered by the President of Bentley College to open the Conference on Genocide and Human Rights.

We *must* believe that moral progress is attainable, that the best that is within us will ultimately triumph over hatred, injustice, and violence. This and hope, I think, is the shared assumption that brings us together today.

The seventieth anniversary of the Armenian Genocide is the immediate occasion of the quest for recognition generated by this Conference. Because genocide leaves its terrible mark on both its perpetrators and its survivors, neither the guilt nor the pain can ever be eradicated. It will be visited upon the children and the children's children. In fact, the pain worsens as the inflictors rub salt in the wounds by not acknowledging the perpetration of the unthinkable crime, the massacres and the deportation of the Armenian people, and thus the wounds never heal, but continue to fester and to pain.

The world today is more and more an *interdependent* society. Certainly more so than between 1915 and 1920, when the Armenian people were practically annihilated and the international community for reasons best known to themselves could not or would not take any action and then negotiated a treaty to establish an independent Armenian nation, but did not have the commitment, the integrity or the courage to implement it. It is no longer possible for people to live in isolation one from the other or from the truth. The claims of the Armenians and the denials of the Turks must be resolved—and this resolution can only be achieved through public awareness and honest dialogue.

As you all know, such dialogue is no easy matter. It is full of risks and requires great wisdom and courage. But this is precisely the responsibility that the international community must confront: not only public declarations acknowledging the reality of the Armenian extermination, but a genuine political commitment to compel the present government of Turkey to join at last into a meaningful international dialogue, and to abide by the consequences of that dialogue.

This is one of the goals we set before us today. But our ambitions reach out even further. The Armenian debacle was the first genocide of the twentieth century. Tragically, it was not the last. The Jewish Holocaust with its six million victims, and most recently the Cambodian Genocide served to remind us that inhumanity persists with unparalleled regularity. An awful unlearned lesson weighs upon us and our humanity demands that we struggle to comprehend the reasons, to recognize the signs, and to resist the inevitability of racial extermination.

We have no choice but to accept responsibility for the fate of potential future victims. Their innocence and their utter powerlessness demand our protection.

Let us work together then, to devote our strength, our intelligence, and our compassion to a cause that we cannot afford to ignore. Our challenge is to safeguard society by exposing genocide and insuring greater multicultural and ethnic understanding.

The Stereotype as a Prelude to Genocide

Sol Gittleman

This is not a routine conference, not merely a gathering of scholars for the purpose of reviewing the past, checking footnotes, arguing about theories. This conference has set for itself an extraordinary mission, one which is challenged by the historical events of the past centuries—particularly the last century—and which the events of the next century will attempt to refute and deny. The conference has set for itself no less a task than changing the course of history. For it believes that it is indeed possible, through the study of the phenomenon of genocide, and particularly the Armenian tragedy of this century, to make future genocides impossible.

Let me start out with a terribly pessimistic contention. Unless future generations dramatically alter human patterns of behavior, unless those yet unborn somehow manage to come to grips with the nature and fundamental causes of genocides which have already taken place, it is as certain as I am standing in front of you this evening that either in our lifetimes or the lifetimes of our children we will experience the horrors of genocide once again. This is, alas, the nature of the beast within us. For as much as we have the divine spark of the Almighty within each of us, we each also possess the capacity to dehumanize, delegitimize; and as much as we would deny it, we are all capable of creating a mental state in which we might, with complete dispassion, destroy another group of human beings. That human beings have the capacity to create beauty and at the same time possess the potential for total beastiality is one of the great mysteries of the human condition.

If that is a keynote agenda, if that is an opening remark, then I throw down the gauntlet and challenge us as civilized individuals to try to make a difference with this conference, to change this inevitable course of human events, to say to ourselves that in the next three days we can do something which will make a difference. It is my intent this evening to set a tone in which this might occur. This has been a century without parallel in the history of genocide. We have advanced the state of this horrific art to a point of sufficient sophistication that numerically now we are capable of extraordinary feats which were impossible at an earlier time. This century does indeed have a special relationship to genocide. It has provided us with the possibility of mass murder unknown, inconceivable, and beyond the imagination of any previous era. We have discovered the economy of technology.

But technology is not enough. Poison gas, Zyklon-B, atomic bombs, thermonuclear devices yet uninvented are, strange as it may sound, not enough. The ability provided by technology to slaughter millions is in and of itself insufficient. What is required in addition is the will, the special feeling, the psychological disposition to murder millions. This is the essential quality of the genocidal act. This, too, is a product of the twentieth century. I would suggest that never before in mankind's history have we been able to create, through the mass media, the total hypnosis of a population which could then be bent to the idea of genocide. It is not enough for the leaders to want to kill. It must also be the will of the people; and for that special state of mind to occur, we must have the means to communicate on a scale which only the twentieth century could provide. Such is the benefit of progress.

An absolutely essential ingredient for genocide in our time is the capacity to dehumanize the victim. The history of genocide has been inevitably accompanied by an ability not merely to turn the good guys into heroes, but by our need to turn the enemy into monsters, or worse: vermin, lice, bacilli. We can examine the great genocides in this century, and in each case the population representing the oppressor was placed in a state of mind where the "target" enemy was significantly less than human, so that one could say with certainty that one was eliminating nothing human, but rather was discarding some putrescence, some less than human specimen of which the world was better rid.

This, I am suggesting, is the stereotype, the preparation of the state of mind. Today, the means are at our disposal in literature for those who read, in film for the illiterate, on radio, television, and in print. For Americans our preparation began with our initial confrontation with the indigenous Indian population. Even without the sophisticated modern media, we were able to shape the image of the Indian to suit our purpose, which was to eliminate him. What was, after all, the American Indian to the average settler? Or to the reader of pulp literature? He was a drunken heathen, a rapist of white women, a scalper of men, a beast, and sub-human. This was the prevailing image for centuries. Not until the 1970s and our increasing awareness of our racial prejudice did we take off the mask of General Custer and reveal what we did to the Red Man. The stereotype disappeared; we Americans learned something, and changed our image of the native American. It is possible. There is hope. Our image of the black man is too complex and would be the subject of another symposium.

The American context of the stereotyped Japanese in the Second World War is a vivid example of our capacity to dehumanize, less we delude ourselves into thinking that we as Americans might be incapable of genocide, or lacking the state of mind required to commit genocide. If we examine the war movies coming out of Hollywood from 1942 to 1945, we discover a race of yellow men whose evil was of such enormity that we could scarcely control our hatred. I remember, if I may be anecdotal for a moment, my personal feelings as a ten-year-old boy leaving a movie house in Hoboken, N.J., after seeing a triple feature of *Objective Burma, Guadalcanal Diary*, and *The Purple Heart*, and asking God only to permit me to live long enough to kill Japanese. To my pre-adolescent mind, these were not human beings, clearly; and when we dropped the atomic bomb a few years later, I applauded. I would not have cared had we killed another million "Japs," as we called them. My own psychological disposition to genocide was complete and in place. What Americans were prepared to accept concerning the Japanese during World War II is an indication of the effect of stereotyping. We were conditioned to believe that every Japanese we met was a spy or agent of Imperial Japan; someone who, like the sneak attack at Pearl Harbor, would stab us in the back.

It is almost inconceivable today, but in 1942 we took 100,000 Japanese Americans—*not* aliens, not Issei, but *Nissei*, American-born Japanese Americans, and placed them in isolated detention or concentration camps in Oregon, California, Utah, and Arkansas. Their only crime was that they were yellow and had eyes which slanted differently from the Chinese, who were then still our allies. We had effectively dehumanized the Japanese American, whose sons were fighting with extraordinary bravery with the 442nd tactical brigade in Italy, dying, and having posthumous medals of honor presented to grieving parents behind the barbed wire of the internment camps. Can one imagine taking Joe DiMaggio's parents or Babe Ruth's parents—Italians and Germans—and placing them in detention camps? They, too, after all, were the enemy. But we did not dehumanize the Italians or even the Germans in a similar fashion. We did stereotype the Italian, but only as a charming, laughable, not very fighting man who always seemed to have a relative in Brooklyn. The Germans, at least in American films, were of two kinds; brown uniforms of a military cut meant army and were acceptable. We did, after all, make a war hero out of Gen. Rommel. But a black uniform meant gestapo, and these were villains.

Of course the greatest example of linguistic dehumanization and stereotyping occurred in Nazi Germany, where the entire weight of the propaganda machine of Dr. Josef Goebbels was aimed at turning the Jew, the negro, the Slav (Russians and Poles) into a non-human which should for the health of the state be systematically eradicated. It was an act of heroism to eliminate these creatures. From the outset, beginning in 1933, and even before his coming to power, Hitler effectively made those target enemies into sub-humans, and the language of the Nazi press bombarded the German people with cartoons, language, and image which reinforced the stereotype. Jewish men raping Aryan women; Jewish businessmen stealing from Aryan customers; Jewish diseases infecting Aryan children. But it was with the coming to power after 1933 that the total mobilization of the state could be shaped by Goebbels who, when asked by Hitler what ministery he wanted, said: "If you make me Minister of Propaganda, I will hand you the German people forever." Every script of every film and radio play, every novel and short story, every work of literature was read by Goebbels and his associates, and the stereotypes were beaten into the hearts and minds of the German people. The motion picture became a particularly effective device. Jews were generally shown in juxtaposition with rats or creeping animals. Blacks were shown with apes and monkeys, and slavs with other animals of a lower form. The stereotypes prepared the way for the mass killings.

When the killing began of those who had not been stereotyped, there was public outcry. In 1940 Hitler ordered through his ministry of Hereditary Diseases the elimination of the mentally retarded, the mentally ill, epileptics, and victims of Down's Syndrome (many of them children). Within six months nearly 100,000 Germans had been killed with injections of oxygen. The public rumblings began almost immediately, but did not culminate until late in 1940, when the Bishop of Munster, Bishop Galen, mounted the pulpit of this cathedral and informed his congregation that anyone participating in the liquidation of the mentally retarded would forthwith be excommunicated from the Catholic Church. The order was revoked within a week, and the killing stopped. The Germans had not been prepared for the murder of their own kind, Aryans, even if they were mentally retarded. But no voice was raised in Germany or elsewhere for the Jew, the Gypsy, or the Slav, who were among the 20 million killed by Hitler's horde.

The other great genocide in this century is the main subject of this symposium; and the Armenian tragedy has not drawn the attention of many scholars to the conditions of stereotyping which can be found in Turkish culture and in the Turkish language, as well as in the Muslim faith. But the campaign of villification and dehumanization which preceded the destruction of hundreds of thousands of Armenians in 1895-1896 and again in 1915 was, in subtlety and in preparation, just as carefully orchestrated as was the preparation of Dr. Goebbels. The religious alienation of the Jew from the German was never emphasized. The Muslim rhetoric, however, effectively make it an act of honor to kill an infidel. Turkish propaganda directed against the Armenian minority was particularly effective in the hands of the Muslim preachers, who described the Christians as dogs and vermin. The language of the Turkish press enflamed the semi-literate, and the preachers enflamed the illiterate. The effect was the same. The Armenians were categorized according to the stereotype. Therefore they were less than human, and killing men, women, and children was not an act of brutality, but rather an act of heroism necessary to free the country from an infection.

Everywhere in this century where we can document genocidal slaughter we find the same phenomenon: dehumanization and brutal stereotyping. On a smaller but no less horrible scale, the language of Charles Manson when he slaughtered Sharon Tate attempted the same effect as does the Ayatollah when he sends young children into mine fields in order to die fighting the quintessential evil of the Iraqis, who are described as the angels of death.

But we are faced now with a new imperative to mend our ways. We stand on the edge of a deep, deep precipice. We possess the means to destroy the world. If our stereotyping and hatred becomes as explosive as the means in our possession to incinerate this earth, if our ability to hate continues to be channeled toward the ultimate act of aggression, genocide, there seems to be little doubt that someone will come along with the urge to kill his enemies and to eradicate a people to a state of total obliteration. In other words, the next Hitler *will have the bomb*, of that there is little doubt. Are we capable of doing this ultimate act, we Americans, who up to now are the only people who have ever dropped an atomic device in anger? It is today inconceivable, yet one wonders how close we came in Vietnam. Certainly there was the potential for dehumanization, if we recall Vice President Agnew's comment about the war dissenters, who, he said, "should be separated from our society with no more regret than we should feel over discarding rotten apples." We did dehumanize each other in that time. Today, if one examines the language associated with the abortion argument, we can understand why blowing up buildings becomes for some an act of heroic necessity. The pro-choice people are looked upon as child murderers.

But the most potentially dangerous situation confronting all of us today, with the potential for stereotyping and genocide, is in the Middle East once again. We can be grateful that the Ayatollah does not have a thermo-nuclear device, given the level of rhetoric and his hypnotic power to create an image of his enemies as infidels who should be liquidated in the name of Allah. Also, think what the phrase Palestinian Liberation Organization has come to mean to an Israeli; or what Zionist has come to mean to an Arab. The enemy is evil; the enemy, whoever he may be, does not deserve to live. We are brutalizing ourselves again, as we brutalize each other.

What next? Where next? Where are those stereotypes which are being formed now. In Africa, with its tribal hatreds? Is the Soviet Union really the Kingdom of Evil? Our Students for a Democratic Society in the sixties called the police "pigs." The critic Haig Basmajian has stated that words and language can be used to inspire us and to motivate us to acts of great humanity, and they can also be used to dehumanize human beings and to justify extermination.

This, then, is what I leave you with as a keynote to this conference. Watch out, be on the alert for the language and images of dehumanization; the stereotype defined by those who would seek to destroy first creates a language of hatred. We humans are capable of extraordinary acts of barbarism, but we are also gifted with blessing of speech and therefore will provide hints, signals, and a preface for our acts of violence: "Nuke the gukes," "Kill a queer," "Flame a fag,"

"Don't burn oil, burn Jews"—these are bumper stickers found while casually driving through Boston. We can see in the hearts of our neighbors the potential for genocide. How to alert ourselves? How to alert our children? How to deal with the language of hate and with the stereotype which prepares us to dehumanize?

If we answer these and other similar questions in the next three days, this conference will indeed be a tribute to mankind's humanity, not to his inhumanity.

The Historical Dimensions of the Armenian Question, 1878-1923*

Richard G. Hovannisian

The genocide of the Armenian minority in the Ottoman Empire during World War I may be viewed in the context of the broader Armenian Question, which had both internal and international aspects. Indeed, it was to rid themselves of this question and to create a new, homogeneous order that the Turkish dictators organized the deportations and massacres of the Armenian population. Through death and destruction they eliminated the Armenians from most of the Ottoman Empire, including all of the historic Armenian homelands, and radically altered the racial and religious character of the region. An overview of the Armenian Question in the Ottoman Empire should help to place the following presentations concerning the Armenian Genocide into perspective.

Although tracing their lineage, according to epical-biblical traditions, to Noah, whose ark was said to have rested on Mount Ararat, the Armenians actually passed through a long era of formation and emerged as an identifiable people sometime around the sixth century before Christ. Their lands lay between the Black, Caspian, and Mediterranean seas, in an area now referred to as Eastern Anatolia and Transcaucasia, on both sides of the current Soviet-Turkish frontier. For the next two thousand years, they were led by their kings, nobles, and patriarchs, sometimes independently and often under the sway of powerful, neighboring empires of the East and West. Located on perhaps the most strategic crossroads of the ancient and medieval worlds, the Armenians managed not only to survive but

---

*Reprinted, with permission, from *The Armenian Genocide in Perspective*, Richard G. Hovannisian, ed. (New Brunswick, N.J.: Transaction Publishers, 1986).

also to develop a rich, distinctive culture by maintaining a delicate balance between Orient and Occident. Adopting Christianity as the state religion at the turn of the fourth century A.D., however, the Armenians were often persecuted because of their faith by invaders and alien overlords. By the end of the fourteenth century, the last Armenian kingdom had collapsed, the nobility had been decimated in constant warfare, and the Armenian plateau had fallen under foreign subjugation. Most of the country ultimately came under Turkish rule, except for the eastern sector, which came first under Persian and then in the nineteenth century under Russian dominion.

In the Ottoman Empire, which by the seventeenth century pressed to the gates of Vienna, the Armenians were included in a multi-national and multi-religious realm, but as a Christian minority they had to endure official discrimination and second-class citizenship. Inequality, including special taxes, the inadmissibility of legal testimony, and the prohibition on bearing arms, was the price paid to maintain their religion and sense of community. Down through the centuries, many thousands eventually converted in order to be relieved of these disabilities as well as the sporadic violence that fell most heavily upon the defenseless Armenian peasantry. The *devshirme* or child levy was occasionally imposed, and in many districts in Western Anatolia the Armenians were not allowed to speak their own language except in recitation of prayers. This is not to say that there were not prosperous merchants, traders, artisans, and professional persons throughout the empire, for it is well known that the minority populations played a most important role in international commerce, as interpreters and intermediaries, and in the highly skilled professions. Nonetheless, most of the Armenian population remained rooted in its historic homeland, becoming, in large part, tenant formers or sharecroppers under the dominant Muslin feudal-military elite.

Despite their second-class status, most Armenians lived in relative peace so long as the Ottoman Empire was strong and expanding. But as the empire's administrative, financial, and military structure crumbled under the weight of internal corruption and external challenges in the eighteenth and nineteenth centuries, intolerance and exploitation increased. The breakdown of order was accelerated by Ottoman inability to compete with the growing capitalistic system in the West and to modernize and reform. The legal and practical superiority of one element over the other groups continued, and the lavish and uncontrolled spending of the Ottoman court led to even more oppressive taxation, including the infamous method of tax farming, that is, the sale of the privilege to exact as much tax as possible from a particular district in return for an advance lump-sum payment. The wasteful ways of the ruling elite drew the empire into bankruptcy in the 1870s and opened the way for direct European financial supervision, beginning in 1881.

The decay of the Ottoman Empire was paralleled by cultural and political revival among many of the subject nationalities, which were swept by the European winds of romanticism and revolt. The national liberation struggles, supported at times by certain European powers, contributed to Ottoman loss of most Balkan provinces in the nineteenth century and constituted one aspect of the Eastern Question, namely, what was to become of the decrepit empire. The rivalry among the European powers and their economic exploitation of the Ottoman Empire led to efforts to preserve it as a weak buffer state and a lucrative marketplace. The British, in particular, fearing that dissolution of the empire would threaten their mastery of the seas, came to the conclusion that it could be saved only if the worst abuses of government were eliminated and fundamental administrative changes implemented. A growing circle of Ottoman liberals was also persuaded that survival depended on reform. These men became the movers behind the several major reform edicts issued during the so-called *tanzimat* period from 1839 to 1876.[1] Yet time and again the supporters of reform became disappointed and disillusioned in the face of the entrenched vested interest that resisted change. The *tanzimat* era, for all its fanfare, brought virtually no improvement in the daily life of the common person.

Of the various subject peoples, the Armenians perhaps sought the least. Unlike the Balkan Christians, they were dispersed throughout the empire and no longer constituted a majority in much of their historic homelands. Hence, Armenian leaders did not think in terms of separation or independence, but, professing loyalty to the sultan and renouncing any separatist aspirations, they petitioned for the protection of their people and property from corrupt officials and from marauding bands often linked with those officials. It was not inappropriate, therefore, that the Ottoman sultans should have referred to the Armenians as their "faithful community." The Armenians nonetheless also passed through a long period of cultural revival. Thousands of youngsters enrolled in schools established in the nineteenth century by U.S. and European missionaries and hundreds of middle-class youth traveled to Europe for higher education. Many of these men returned home, imbued with the social and political philosophies of contemporary Europe, to engage in teaching, journalism, and literary criticism. Gradually a network of Armenian schools and newspapers spread from Constantinople (Istanbul) and Smyrna (Izmir) to Cilicia, and eventually to many towns in the primitive eastern provinces, that is, Turkish Armenia. As it happened, however, this Armenian self-discovery was paralleled by heightened administrative corruption, economic exploitation, and physical insecurity. It was this dual development—the conscious demand for security of life and property on the one hand, and the growing insecurity of both life and property on the other—that gave rise to the Armenian Question as a part of the larger Eastern Question.

Widespread dissatisfaction with inadequate implementation of the several reform edicts of the *tanzimat* period, the aggravated plight of the Asiatic Christians, and, above all, the severe Turkish reprisals against a rebellious Balkan Christian population renewed European pressure on the Sublime Porte [Ottoman government] in 1876. In a maneuver to undermine the international conference summoned to deal with the crisis, Sultan Abdul-Hamid II (1876-1909) promulgated a liberal constitution drafted by sincere advocates of reform.[2] Had the sultan been as sincere in implementing the constitution, it could have removed the major grievances of the subject peoples, the Armenians included. But having warded off the European diplomats, Abdul-Hamid soon suspended the constitution and the parliament for which it had provided. Instead of abating, the tribulations of the Armenians multiplied. Robbery, murder, and kidnapping became commonplace in a land where even the traditional feudal protective system had broken down.

In the aftermath of the Russo-Turkish war of 1877-78, the leaders of the Armenian community, or *millet*, put aside their customary caution and conservatism and appealed to the victorious Russian commander-in-chief to include provisions for the protection of the Armenians in the forthcoming peace treaty.[3] That treaty, which was signed at San Stefano in March 1878, granted independence to Serbia, Montenegro, and Romania, and autonomy to a large Bulgarian state. No such provision was either sought or executed for the Armenians. On the contrary, the Russians agreed to withdraw their armies from most of Turkish Armenia, while annexing the border districts of Batum, Ardahan, Kars, Alashkert, and Bayazid. The Armenian leaders were not entirely disappointed, however, because

Article 16 of the treaty stipulated that Russian withdrawal would be contingent upon the implementation of effective reforms in Turkish Armenia:

> As the evacuation by the Russian troops of the territory which they occupy in Armenia, and which is to be restored to Turkey, might give rise to conflicts and complications detrimental to the maintenance of good relations between the two countries, the Sublime Porte undertakes to carry out into effect, without further delay, the improvements and reforms demanded by local requirements in the provinces inhabited by the Armenians, and to guarantee their security from Kurds and Circassians.[4]

General M. T. Loris-Melikov was to stand firm in Erzurum until this condition was met.

The aftermath of the Treaty of San Stefano is familiar to students of European history. Prime Minister Benjamin Disraeli and especially Foreign Secretary Robert Salisbury believed that the interests of the British Empire were jeopardized by the treaty. Enlisting the support of other European powers, they intimidated Russia with threats of joint action, not excluding war. The outcome was the convening of a European congress in Berlin in mid-1878 to review and revise the treaty. An Armenian delegation also traveled to Berlin with the goal of persuading the six European powers to arrange for a specific Armenian reform program, rather than simply general reforms, past instances of which had proved most disappointing. Using the administrative statute for Lebanon as a model, the Armenians asked that Turkish Armenia be granted a Christian governor, local self-government, civil courts of law, mixed Christian-Muslim militias, voting privileges for all tax-paying adult males, and the allocation of most local tax revenues for local improvements.[5]

The sympathetic expressions of the European diplomats aside, the Berlin congress revised the Treaty of San Stefano in conformity with the guidelines of the British negotiators. Several provinces were taken back from the newly independent and autonomous states in the Balkans, and on the Caucasus frontier the districts of Alashkert and Bayazid were restored to Ottoman rule. Moreover, insofar as Armenian reforms were concerned, the coercive aspect of Article 16 in the Treaty of San Stefano was superseded by the stipulation of Article 61 of the Treaty of Berlin that the Russian armies should withdraw immediately, and that the sultan would simply pledge to take it upon himself to implement the necessary reforms and to report to the European powers collectively about the progress.[6] The effect of the inversion of Article 16 at San Stefano to Article 61 at Berlin was trenchantly caught in the Duke of Argyll's cryptic observation, "What was everybody's business was nobody's business."[7]

As payment for services rendered to the sultan, Great Britain exacted, through secret agreement, control over the strategic island of Cyprus, and Austria-Hungary gained the right to administer Bosnia and Herzegovina, which had been taken back from Serbia. In the eastern provinces, meanwhile, horrified Armenian peasants witnessed the evacuation of Loris-Melikov's army. As had been the case during the Russian withdrawal from Erzurum in 1829, thousands of Armenians departed with the Russian troops to resettle in the Caucasus. Yet, despite the setback, the Armenian religious leaders did not lose hope and declared that they still had faith in the Ottoman government and in its introduction of the necessary reforms. Armenian patriarch Nerses Varzhapetian swore fidelity to the sultan and emphasized that efforts to overcome Armenian misfortunes would be made within the established legal framework of the Ottoman homeland. At a time when several of the Balkan nationalities had won independence, the Armenians still shunned talk of separatism.[8]

The Treaty of Berlin elevated the Armenian Question to the level of international diplomacy, but the Armenians gained no advantage from that status. On the contrary, Kurdish tribesmen, organized and armed by the sultan's government, spread havoc over the eastern provinces, particularly in the districts from which the Russian army had recently withdrawn. Neither the petitions of the Armenian patriarch nor the establishment of more European consular posts in Turkish Armenia helped to improve the situation. European consuls at Kharpert, Erzurum, Van, and other interior centers could do little more than relay frequent dispatches describing the rapacious acts to which the Armenians were subjected. For two years the European powers, outwardly cooperating under the joint responsibility of Article 61, issued collective and identic notes reminding the Sublime Porte of its treaty obligations. But by 1881, these powers had become too involved in the scramble for empire elsewhere to worry further about the Armenians. They silently shelved the Armenian Question and turned away from Armenian troubles.[9]

Feeling abandoned and betrayed, a growing number of Armenians began to espouse extralegal means to achieve what they now regarded as the right and moral duty to resist tyrannical rule. Instead of meeting its obligation to protect its subjects, the Ottoman government had become the instrument of exploitation and suppression. Some Armenians came to believe that, like the Balkan Christians, they too would have to organize, perhaps even take arms. Local self-defense groups that had coalesced in the 1880s gradually gave way to several broadly based secret political societies in the 1890s. Still, few among those who called themselves revolutionaries were prepared to expound national independence as a goal. Rather, they sought cultural freedom and regional autonomy, equality before the law, freedom of speech, press, and assembly, unhindered economic opportunity, and the right to bear arms.[10]

Thus, while the patriarch of Constantinople continued supplications to the Sublime Porte, exponents of the new political mentality preached resistance. Under such influence the rugged villagers of the Sassun district in the province of Bitlis refused to continue paying an extortionary protection tax to Kurdish chieftains. In 1894 the Kurds, unable to subdue their former clients, accused Sassun of sedition and appealed to Ottoman officials. Regular Turkish regiments joined the irregular Kurdish Hamidiye cavalry units and, after weeks of siege and combat, forced the Armenians to lay down their arms in return for the promise of amnesty. Instead, however, Sassun was plundered and several thousand Armenians were put to the sword without regard to age or sex. European consuls and Christian missionaries raised their voices against the outrage and soon the newspapers of Europe and the United States were again demanding intercession on behalf of the Armenians. After nearly fifteen years of silence, the European powers were drawn back to the Armenian Question, but now only Great Britain, France, and Russia were willing to address the Sublime Porte on the subject. European representatives attached to an Ottoman commission of inquiry reported that the Armenians of Sassun had been forced to take arms for their own protection and that the gratuitous acts of cruelty by the sultan's regular and irregular troops and the irresponsibility of the Ottoman officials and commanders were reprehensible. There had been no rebellion, and even if the facts had proved otherwise, the unbridled, indiscriminate brutality could in no measure be justified.[11]

The Sassun crisis revived the European call for Armenian reforms. In May 1895 a joint British, French, and Russian plan was submitted for the consolidation of the Armenian provinces into a single administrative region, the release of political prisoners and the repatriation of exiles, the making of reparations to the people of Sassun and other victims, the disarming of the Hamidiye corps in time of peace, and the creation of a permanent control commission to oversee the reforms. Diplomatic exchanges continued through the summer and autumn of

1895 until at last, in October, Sultan Abdul-Hamid assented to a reform program based on, but far less inclusive than, that proposed by the three European governments. Once again, a ripple of optimism emanated from Constantinople.[12]

As before, however, European intercession unsustained by force only compounded the troubles of the Armenians. Even as Abdul-Hamid seemed to acquiesce in the reform program in October 1895, the Armenians in Trebizond were in the throes of massacre. In the following months, systematic pogroms swept over every district of Turkish Armenia. The slaughter of between 100,000 and 200,000 Armenians, the forced religious conversion of the population of scores of villages, the looting and burning of hundreds of other settlements, and the coerced flight into exile of countless Armenians were Abdul-Hamid's actual response to European meddling.[13] His use of violent methods was a desperate attempt to preserve the weakening status quo in the face of enormous external and internal challenges to it. In this regard, the major difference between Abdul-Hamid and his Young Turk successors was that he unleashed massacres in an effort to maintain a state structure in which the Armenians would be kept in their place without the right to resist corrupt and oppressive government, whereas the Young Turks were to employ the same tactic in 1915 on a grander scale to bring about fundamental and far-reaching changes in the status quo and to create an entirely new frame of reference that did not include the Armenians at all.

In the years following the calamities of 1894-96, disillusion weighed heavily upon the Armenians, yet some comfort was found in the fact that other elements, too, were organizing against the tyrannical rule of Abdul-Hamid. In Geneva, Paris, and other emigre centers, reformists and revolutionaries of all the Ottoman nationalities conceived programs of change and envisaged a new, progressive government for their common homeland. In 1902 the first congress of Ottoman liberals, attended by Turkish, Armenian, Arab, Greek, Kurdish, Albanian, Circassian, and Jewish intellectuals, convened in Paris and joined in demands for equal rights for all Ottoman subjects, local self-determination, and restoration of the constitution, which had been suspended since 1877. A second congress in 1907 pledged its constituent groups to a united campaign to overthrow Abdul-Hamid's regime by the swiftest means possible and to introduce representative government.[14]

Within the Ottoman Empire itself, Turkish opposition elements, especially among the junior military officers and the faculty of the technical institutes, merged into the Committee of Union and Progress (Ittihat ve Terakki Teshkilati), popularly referred to as the Young Turks. Thereafter, events moved quickly toward confrontation. When Young Turk army officers in Macedonia were about to be exposed by the sultan's agents in 1908, they led their regiments toward Constantinople in a defensive maneuver and, as the mutiny spread, demanded the restoration of the constitution. Lacking loyal units to crush the rising, Abdul-Hamid bowed to the ultimatum in July and acquiesced in the formation of a constitutional monarchy. The Armenians hailed the victory of the army and its Young Turk commanders; at this historic moment manifestations of Ottoman Christian and Muslim brotherhood abounded.[15]

One of the most unexpected and, for the Armenians, most tragic metamorphoses in modern history was the process, from 1908 to 1914, that transformed the seemingly liberal, egalitarian Young Turks into extreme chauvinists, bent on creating a new order and eliminating the Armenian Question by eliminating the Armenian people. European exploitation of Turkish weaknesses contributed to this process. In the immediate aftermath of the Young Turk revolution, Austria-Hungary annexed Bosnia-Herzegovina, Bulgaria asserted full independence, Crete declared union with Greece, and Italy forcibly pursued claims to Tripoli and the Libyan hinterland. The impact of these troubles emboldened Turkish conservative elements to stage a countercoup to restore the sultan's authority. Although the movement was suppressed and Abdul-Hamid was deposed and exiled, the turmoil did not abate without renewed tragedy for the Armenians. Throughout Cilicia, Armenian villages and city quarters were looted and burned and some 20,000 Armenians were massacred. While there was evidence that Young Turk sympathizers, too, had been among those who incited the mobs, the party's leaders moved to placate the Armenians by ascribing the bloodshed to the Hamidian reaction and by conducting public memorial services for Muslim and Christian sons of a common fatherland who had fallen in defense of the revolution.[16]

The abortive countercoup prompted the Young Turk cabinet to declare a state of siege and to suspend normal constitutional rights for the next four years, until 1912. It was during this period that the concepts of Turkism and exclusive nationalism captivated several prominent Young Turks, who began to envisage a new, homogeneous Turkish state structure in place of the enervated and exploited multinational Ottoman Empire.[17] In a new coup in 1913 the ultranationalistic faction of the Young Turk party seized control, and thereafter, until the end of World War I in 1918, the government was dominated by a triumvirate composed of Enver, minister of war; Talaat, minister of internal affairs and subsequently grand vizier; and Jemal, military governor of Constantinople and later minister of the marine.[18]

The Young Turk revolution of 1908 allowed Armenian political parties to emerge from the underground and to operate clubs and newspapers and vie for the parliamentary seats allotted the Armenians. The most influential of those parties, the Dashnaktsutiun, was in fact linked in an alliance with the Young Turks. Despite increasing signs of Turkish extremism, the Dashnaktsutiun resolved to remain loyal during the troubled years preceding the outbreak of World War I. Yet the seeming gains in the post-revolutionary period did little to diminish the hardships of the rural population. Armed marauding bands in the eastern provinces became all the more audacious when the Armenian youth went off to fight for the Ottoman homeland during the Balkan wars of 1912-13. European consuls in the region filled their dispatches with descriptions of the deadly anarchy. In Constantinople the petitions of the patriarch were answered with promises of action, but effectual measures did not ensue.

As a result of renewed international interest in the Armenian Question following the Balkan wars, the European powers once again raised the issue of reforms. Great Britain, France, and Russia on the one hand, and Germany, Austria-Hungary, and Italy on the other, ultimately reached a compromise settlement. Trebizond and the six Turkish Armenian provinces—Erzurum, Sivas, Kharpert, Diyarbakir, Bitlis, and Van—would be combined into two administrative regions with broad local autonomy, under the guarantee of the European powers and the supervision of inspectors-general selected from citizens of the small European nations. Without detailing the extensive diplomatic correspondence and the final provisions of the compromise plan of February 1914, let it suffice to say that the reform measure was the most comprehensive and promising of all the proposals put forth since the internationalization of the Armenian Question in 1878.[19]

The outbreak of world war in the summer of 1914 jeopardized implementation of the reform program and deeply alarmed Armenian leaders. Should the Ottoman Empire enter the conflict on the side of Germany, the Armenian plateau would become the inevitable theater of another Russo-Turkish war. In view of the fact that the Armenian homelands lay on both sides of the frontier, the Armenians would suffer severely no matter who might eventually win the war. For these reasons, Armenian spokesmen implored their Young Turk associates to maintain neutrality and spare the empire from calamity. When pressured to organize an Armenian insurrection in the Caucasus against Russia, the leaders of the Dashnaktsutiun declined, again urging neutrality but making it known that, if war did engulf the region, the Armenians would dutifully serve the government under which they lived.[20]

Despite the advice and appeals of the Armenians, the Germano-phile Young Turk faction, led by Enver and Talaat, sealed a secret alliance with Germany in August 1914 and looked to the creation of a new Turkish realm extending into Russian Transcaucasia and Central Asia. Turkey's entrance into the war voided the possibility of solving the Armenian Question through administrative reform. Rather, the Young Turk leaders were drawn to the newly articulated idealogy of Turkism, which was to supplant the principle of egalitarian Ottomanism and give justification to violent means for transforming a heterogeneous empire into a homogeneous state based on the concept of one nation, one people. Any vacillation that still may have lingered after Turkey's entrance into the war was apparently put aside as a result of the tragic Caucasus campaign, in which Enver Pasha sacrificed an entire army to his militarily unsound obsession to break through to Baku and the Caspian Sea in the dead of winter, as well as the subsequent Allied landings on the Gallipoli peninsula in April 1915 in an abortive maneuver to capture Constantinople and knock Turkey out of the war.[21] The major Turkish military setback and parallel Allied threat to the capital allowed Young Turk extremists to make Armenians the scapegoats by accusing them of treachery and persuading reluctant comrades that the time had come to settle the Armenian Question once and for all. In *Accounting for Genocide*, Helen Fein has concluded: "The victims of twentieth-century premeditated genocide—the Jews, the Gypsies, the Armenians—were murdered in order to fulfill the state's design for a new order. ...War was used in both cases ... to transform the nation to correspond to the ruling elite's formula by eliminating the groups conceived of as alien, enemies by definition."[22]

On the night of April 23/24, 1915, scores of Armenian political, religious, educational, and intellectual leaders in Constantinople, many of them friends and acquaintances of the Young Turk rulers, were arrested, deported to Anatolia, and put to death. Then in May,

Minister of Internal Affairs Talaat Pasha, claiming that the Armenians were untrustworthy, that they could offer aid and comfort to the enemy, and that they were in a state of imminent nationwide rebellion, ordered their deportation from the war zones to relocation centers—actually the deserts of Syria and Mesopotamia. In fact the Armenians were driven out not only from the war zones but from the width and breadth of the empire, with the exception of Constantinople and Smyrna, where there were many foreign diplomats and merchants. The whole of Asia Minor was put in motion. Armenians serving in the Ottoman armies, who had already been segregated into unarmed labor battalions, were now taken out in batches and murdered. Of the remaining population, the adult and teenage males were, as a pattern, swiftly separated from the deportation caravans and killed outright under the direction of Young Turk officials and agents, the gendarmerie, and bandit and nomadic groups prepared for the operation. The greatest torment was reserved for the women and children, who were driven for weeks over mountains and deserts, often dehumanized by being stripped naked and repeatedly preyed upon and abused. Many took their own and their children's lives by flinging themselves from cliffs and into rivers rather than prolonging their humiliation and suffering. In this manner an entire nation melted away, and the Armenian people were effectively eliminated from the homeland of nearly three thousand years. Countless survivors and refugees scattered throughout the Arab provinces and Transcaucasia were to die of starvation, epidemic, and exposure. Even the memory of the Armenian nation was intended for obliteration; churches and monuments were desecrated, and small children, snatched from their parents, were renamed and farmed out to be raised as Turks.[23]

The Turkish wartime rationalizations for these deeds were roundly refuted by statesmen and humanitarians such as Henry Morgenthau, Arnold Toynbee, James Bryce, Henry Adams Gibbons, Rene Pinon, Anatole France, Albert Thomas, and Johannes Lepsius.[24] It was not Armenian treachery, Lepsius declared, but the exclusivist nationalism adopted by the Young Turk extremists that lay at the root of the tragedy. Elimination of the Armenians would avert continued European intervention in the name of a Christian minority and would remove the major racial barrier between the Ottoman Turks and the Turkic peoples of the Caucasus and Transcaspia, the envisaged new realm of pan-Turkish champions.[25] Gibbons described the Armenian massacres as "the blackest page in modern history," and Ambassador Morgenthau wrote: "I am confident that the whole history of the human race contains no such horrible episode as this. The great massacres and persecutions of the past seem almost insignificant when compared to the sufferings of the Armenian race in 1915."[26]

While the decimation of the Armenian people and the destruction of millions of persons in Central and Eastern Europe during the Nazi regime a quarter of a century later each had particular and unique features, historians and sociologists who have pioneered the field of victimology have drawn some startling parallels.[27] The similarities include the perpetration of genocide under cover of a major international conflict, thus minimizing the possibility of external intervention; conception of the plan by a monolithic and xenophobic clique; espousal of an ideology giving purpose and justification to chauvinism, racism, exclusivism, and intolerance toward elements resisting or deemed unworthy of assimilation; imposition of strict party discipline and secrecy during the period of preparation; formation of extralegal special armed forces to ensure the rigorous execution of the operation; provocation of public hostility toward the victim group and ascribing to it the very excesses to which it would be subjected; certainty of the vulnerability of the intended prey (demonstrated in the Armenian case by the previous general massacres of 1894-96 and 1909); exploitation of advances in mechanization and communication to achieve unprecedented means for control, coordination, and thoroughness; and use of sanctions such as promotions and the incentive to loot, plunder, and vent passions without restraint or, conversely, the dismissal and punishment of reluctant officials and the intimidation of persons who might consider harboring members of the victim group.

News of the deportations and massacres evoked expressions of sympathy and outrage in many countries. On May 24, 1915, when the first reports had reached the West, the Allied Powers declared: "In view of this new crime of Turkey against humanity and civilization, the Allied Governments make known publicly to the Sublime Porte that they will hold all members of the Turkish Government, as well as those officials who have participated in these massacres, personally responsible."[28] In December 1916 the *Manchester Guardian* summarized the sentiments of most British leaders: "Another word remains—Armenia—a word of ghastly horror, carrying the memory of deeds not done in the world since Christ was born—a country swept clear by the wholesale murder of its people. To Turkey that country must never and under no circumstances go back."[29] A year later

Prime Minister David Lloyd George declared that Mesopotamia would never be restored to Turkish tyranny, adding: "That same observation applies to Armenia, the land soaked with the blood of innocence, and massacred by the people who were bound to protect them."[30] In his war aims, delivered in January 1918, Lloyd George reiterated that "Arabia, Armenia, Mesopotamia, Syria, and Palestine are in our judgment entitled to a recognition of their separate national condition."[31] And in August, shortly before the end of the war, he told an Armenian delegation: "Britain will not forget its responsibilities toward your martyred race."[32]

Similar statements were issued in France, as Prime Minister and Foreign Minister Aristide Briand declared in November 1916: "When the hour for legitimate reparations shall have struck, France will not forget the terrible trials of the Armenians, and in accord with her Allies, she will take the necessary measures to ensure for Armenia a life of peace and progress."[33] His successor, Georges Clemenceau, wrote to an Armenian leader in July 1918: "I am happy to confirm to you that the Government of the Republic, like that of Great Britain, has not ceased to place the Armenian nation among the peoples whose fate the Allies intend to settle according to the supreme laws of Humanity and Justice."[34] The Italians, too, expressed determination that the Armenian people would have a secure collective future. Prime Minister Vittorio Orlando declared: "Say to the Armenian people that I make their cause my cause."[35]

In the United States, incredulity and indignation were the reactions to the Turkish atrocities. The country rallied to assist the "Starving Armenians" through an outpouring of private charity. Until the Ottoman government broke diplomatic relations with the United States in April 1917, U.S. officials tried to assist the Armenian survivors as best they could. In the wake of the massacres, leaders of both parties and of all branches of government pledged themselves to the goal of caring for the survivors and restoring them to their ancestral lands. One of President Wilson's Fourteen Points for peace read: "The Turkish portions of the present Ottoman Empire should be assured a secure sovereignty, but the other nationalities which are now under Turkish rule should be assured an undoubted security of life and an unmolested opportunity of autonomous development."[36] This statement reflected a recommendation by the United States Inquiry, a special commission charged with the formulation of a U.S. peace program: "It is necessary to free the subject races of the Turkish Empire from oppression and misrule. This implies at the very least autonomy for Armenia and the protection of Palestine, Syria, Mesopotamia and Arabia by the civilized nations."[37]

The chain of events caused by the world war, the deportations and massacres, and the revolutions in Russia disrupted the lives not only of the more than two million Turkish (Western) Armenians but also of the other half of the nation, the Russian (Eastern) Armenians. One and three-quarter million Armenians lived across the frontier from the Ottoman Empire in the Caucasus region, which had been under Russian dominion for a century. Several hundred thousand Turkish Armenian refugees had fled into this area during the war years. Refugees and native inhabitants alike were caught up in the Russian revolutions of 1917, which imperiled the Caucasus front and cut the region from central Russia because of the civil war that engulfed the country. At this seemingly opportune moment, Enver Pasha again pursued his plan to seize Baku. Ignoring the advice and admonition of his German allies, he launched an offensive into the Caucasus in the spring of 1918, now bringing death and destruction to the Russian Armenians. It was in the midst of this powerful Ottoman campaign that the three main peoples of the Caucasus, the Georgians, Azerbaijanis, and Armenians, gave up attempts at collaboration and looked to their own individual salvation. The Georgians, acquiring German protection, and the Azerbaijanis, welcoming Turkish assistance, declared their independence from Russia in May 1918, leaving Armenian leaders no choice but to try to save the small unoccupied portion of Russian Armenia by declaring independence of the territory around Yerevan. The Armenian republic was the smallest and weakest of the three Caucasian states and lacked the minimal requirements for a viable existence, yet it managed to hold out until the end of the world war opened whole new vistas before the Armenian people.[38]

The surrender of the Ottoman Empire and the flight of the Young Turk leaders in October 1918 evoked thanksgiving and hope among the Armenian survivors. The prospect of compatriots returning to the homeland from all over the world, some refugees and survivors of the genocide, and others longtime exiles from the days of Abdul-Hamid, excited imaginations. Every Allied Power was pledged to a separate autonomous or independent existence for the Armenians in their historic lands. A small republic had already taken form in the Caucasus and now gradually expanded as the Turkish armies withdrew from the area. There were, of course, major obstacles to its incorporation of Turkish Armenia because the population had been massacred or driven out and the Turkish army still controlled the region. In drawing up the Mudros Armistice, British negotiators had required Turkish evacuation of the Caucasus but gave up their initial intent to demand also the clearance of Turkish Armenia, although they reserved for the Allies the right to occupy any or all of the region in case of disorder, an option never exercised. Nonetheless, to the Armenians and to an international legion of supporters and sympathizers, it seemed that the crucifixion of the nation would be followed by a veritable resurrection.

When the Paris Peace Conference convened in January 1919, one of the first decisions taken was that "because of the historic misgovernment by the Turks of subject peoples and the terrible massacres of Armenians and others in recent years, the Allied and Associated Powers are agreed that Armenia, Syria, Mesopotamia, Palestine and Arabia must be completely severed from the Turkish Empire."[39] During this immediate postwar period, the new Ottoman government conceded that the Young Turk leaders, now fugitives, had perpetrated criminal acts against both the Christian and Muslim populations of the empire. Military courtmartial proceedings were brought against the principal organizers of the Armenian genocide, with verdicts of death in absentia handed down on Enver, Talaat, Jemal, and Dr. Nazim. The logical continuation of proceedings against the hundreds of officials who had participated in the Armenian annihilation did not occur, however, because of subsequent developments in Anatolia. Nonetheless, in pleading the case of the defeated empire at the peace conference in June 1919, the grand vizier and chief Turkish representative admitted that there had occurred "misdeeds which are such as to make the conscience of mankind shudder forever."[40] In reply, the Allied Powers drew attention to the fact that Turkey's willful and inhuman pursuit of the war "was accompanied by massacres whose calculated atrocity equals or exceeds anything in recorded history." Any attempt to escape punishment would be rejected, for "a nation must be judged by the Government which rules it, which directs its foreign policy, which controls its armies."[41]

Sent out from Paris in the summer of 1919 as the chief of a fact-finding mission to Anatolia and the Caucasus, U.S. Major General James G. Harbord collected a large corpus of evidence regarding the massacres and saw with his own eyes the desolation caused by the genocide. At the end of his investigation, Harbord reported:

> Massacres and deportations were organized in the spring of 1915 under definite system, the soldiers going from town to town. The official

reports of the Turkish Government show 1,100,000 as having been deported. Young men were first summoned to the government building in each village and then marched out and killed. The women, the old men, and children were, after a few days, deported to what Talaat Pasha called "agricultural colonies," from the high, cool, breeze-swept plateau of Armenia to the malarial flats of the Euphrates and the burning sands of Syria and Arabia. ...Mutilation, violation, torture and death have left their haunting memories in a hundred beautiful Armenian valleys, and the traveler in that region is seldom free from the evidence of this most colossal crime of all the ages.[42]

Throughout 1919 and 1920 the Western powers remained publicly committed to the establishment of a united Armenian state combining the Russian Armenian and Turkish Armenian provinces, with an outlet on the Black Sea. The Allied leaders hoped that the United States would accept a League of Nations mandate over the projected state, just as Britain and France were to assume supervisory control over several Arab provinces to be severed from the Ottoman Empire. Yet, wishes alone were not enough to organize an autonomous Armenian state, repatriate several hundred thousand refugees, and provide the resources for the defense and development of the state. While all the Allies advocated a free Armenia, none was willing to commit the requisite resources to make that goal a reality. The United States, under domestic pressure for rapid demobilization and recoiling into "splendid isolation," declined the Armenian mandate, while Great Britain and France, trying to preserve the rights acquired in their secret wartime pacts relating to the Near East, concentrated their energies on the Arab provinces, where they intended to impose a long-range presence. Rivalries flared repeatedly among the Allies over the spoils of war and zones of influence, thereby contributing to the long delay in drafting the Turkish peace settlement.[43]

While the victors in war negotiated the treaties with the defeated European powers and tried to outmaneuver one another in decisions affecting many parts of the world, a Turkish Nationalist movement took form, aimed at the preservation of the territorial integrity of Anatolia and the rejection of an imperialist and colonialist settlement. Directed by Mustafa Kemal, the Nationalists gained momentum at the end of 1919, winning over much of the remaining Turkish army, and created a countergovernment at Angora (Ankara) in the spring of 1920. To impress the Armenians and the Allies with the seriousness of their intent, the Nationalists attacked the French garrison at Marash in January and killed or drove out most of the Armenians who had repatriated to the city under French and British auspices.

Thereafter, the Nationalists besieged many other cities and towns in Cilicia, where approximately 150,000 Armenians had returned in 1919. At the same time, Turkish emissaries, including former Young Turk leaders, sought the assistance of Soviet Russia, offering to incite Islamic peoples against Great Britain and to join forces against the common enemies in the West. During the summer of 1920 the first shipment of Soviet gold reached Anatolia.[44]

Under these circumstances, the Allies began to retreat in Armenian matters. Arguing that the formation of a greater Armenia was impossible without the participation of the United States, the Allies early in 1920 cut the projected state nearly in half by planning the union of the Russian Armenian republic with parts of the provinces of Van, Bitlis, and Erzurum with an outlet to the sea through Trebizond. To soften the impact of the retreat, the Allies extended de facto recognition to the existing republic, which, despite its fluid borders, landlocked location, crush of refugees, and famine conditions, had made significant organic progress and had expanded to the former Russo-Turkish frontier. The Republic of Armenia increasingly became the focal point of hopes and aspirations for a united national homeland.[45]

At long last, in August 1920, nearly two years after the end of the war, the Treaty of Sèvres was imposed upon the Ottoman Empire and signed by the sultan's representatives.[46] Imperialistic in its financial and economic clauses, the treaty was regarded as a compromise in relation to the Armenian Question. Turkey recognized the freedom and independence of the Armenian republic and renounced all rights over those portions of Van, Bitlis, Erzurum, and Trebizond that were to be included in the new united state. All religious conversions since the beginning of the world war were nullified, and the family or religious community of kidnapped or lost persons could claim and search for such persons through a mixed commission. The Turkish government would assist in the recovery of women and children who had been sequestered in Muslim households, would cooperate in furnishing information and seeking the extradition of persons guilty of war crimes and massacres of Armenians, and would accept nullification of the notorious abandoned properties law, which had made the Ottoman state beneficiary of all Armenian goods and properties having no living owners or legal heirs. In view of the fact that thousands of Armenian families had perished in their entirety, the law had rewarded the Young Turk government with enormous wealth as a corollary of genocide.

The Treaty of Sèvres offered the Armenians a solution to a question that had cost the lives of half their nation and the devastation of their religious, political, cultural, economic, and social infrastructure. Execution of the treaty, however, would require direct Allied involvement. Every Allied leader knew that the Armenians had been decimated and would need a period of support to take possession of the lands awarded them and to restore and rehabilitate the survivors. As it happened, however, no power was willing to shoulder the moral and material responsibilities. Allied armies did occupy Egypt, Palestine, Syria, Mesopotamia, and parts of Anatolia, but no troops could be spared for the Armenians, who were to be left to their own devices.

In order to break the Treaty of Sèvres and obviate the menace of an independent Armenia, in September 1920 Mustafa Kemal ordered the Turkish armies to breach the frontier and crush the existing Armenian republic in the Caucasus. The Allied Powers looked on with a mixture of distress and resignation as the Turkish armies advanced into the heart of the republic and in December forced the Armenian government to repudiate the terms of the Sèvres settlement, renounce all claims to Turkish Armenia, and even to cede the former Russian Armenian districts of Kars, Ardahan, and Surmalu, including Mount Ararat, the symbolic Armenian mountain. One of the ironies of the postwar era was that, of all the defeated powers, Turkey alone expanded its boundary, and this only on the Caucasus front at the expense of the Armenians. Desperate and forlorn, the crippled Armenian government had no choice other than to save what little territory was left by opting for Soviet rule and seeking the protection of the Red Army.[47]

By the beginning of 1921, the prospect of a free and independent Armenia had vanished. All Turkish Armenia and a part of Russian Armenia had been lost, several hundred thousand refugees were barred from ever returning to their native districts, and Armenians who had repatriated to Cilicia and western Asia Minor were again driven into exile, this time permanently. When the Turkish armies pushed the Greek forces into the Aegean Sea and burned the city of Smyrna in 1922, the Armenian presence in Turkey, except for Istanbul, was virtually eliminated.[48] The Allied Powers looked on with some embarrassment, but already two of them had moved to win favor with the new rulers of Turkey, even engaging in the secret sale of arms. Military, commercial, and colonial circles in the West exerted strong pressure to attain a rapprochement with Turkey, expressing all the while their undisguised disdain for weak and dependent subject peoples.

The effective Turkish response to the Treaty of Sèvres motivated the Allied governments to seek a normalization of relations with Mustafa Kemal. The Turkish hero, too, was ready to make peace. Dispatching envoys both to Moscow and London to gain greater leverage in the negotiations, Mustafa Kemal pushed the Allies toward a drastic revision of the treaty. He was not disappointed. During the Lausanne conferences in 1923, the Western diplomats acceded to most of the Turkish Nationalist program, despite their sundry protests and face-saving gestures. The British delegates tried to salvage something for the Armenians by urging the Turks to provide them a national home or foyer within the confines and under the suzerainty of Turkey, but the Turkish representatives understood well that no one was prepared to use anything more than words on behalf of the Armenians and therefore adamantly refused to yield. The absolute Turkish triumph was reflected in the fact that in the final versions of the Lausanne treaties neither the word *Armenia* nor the word *Armenian* was to be found. It was as if an Armenian Question or the Armenian people themselves had never existed. The Allies recognized the new frontiers of Turkey, including the annexations in the East and a revised southern boundary that left a string of cities from Aintab to Urfa and Mardin within Turkey.[49]

The Lausanne treaties marked the international abandonment of the Armenian Question. When their case had first been internationalized in 1878, the Armenians had taken hope, but to no avail. If in 1878 they were deprived of fundamental rights and the security of life and property, in 1923 they no longer even existed in their ancestral lands. The intervening years had brought repeated bloodshed and flight, and culminated in a genocide representing the most irreversible tragedy in their turbulent three-thousand-year history. Genocide had become the solution to the Armenian Question. It cleared the country of its largest Christian minority and laid the basis for the Republic of Turkey, which continued on a course of achieving increased homogeneity despite resistance from Kurds and other non-Turkish Muslim peoples.

The Armenian survivors were condemned to a life of exile and dispersion, subjected to inevitable acculturation and assimilation on five continents and facing an indifferent and even hostile world that preferred not to remember. For many years it seemed as though the genocide had been forgotten by all except the Armenians themselves, as efforts to draw attention to unrequited wrongs failed to reach into high political places. In time, a number of foreign scholars and politicians began to rationalize the Armenian calamity as a sad but perhaps inevitable step toward the formation of modern Turkey. This naive and self-serving attitude was already manifest in the 1950s when a professor at Princeton University wrote: "Had turkification and Moslemization not been accelerated there [in Anatolia] by the use of force, there certainly would not today exist a Turkish Republic, a Republic owing its strength and stability in no measure to the homogeneity of its population, a state which is now a valued associate of the United States."[50]

Several more recent writers and the Turkish government itself have transformed rationalizations into denials, asserting that there was neither genocide nor even wholesale deportations and massacres.[51] Yet, the ferment created by the perpetration of genocide with impunity is not easily dissipated and, despite the passage of time and concerted efforts to make the Armenian Question a non-issue, new generations have been stirred to demand that the world community address the problem. They insist that without action to close and eventually heal the raw wounds of the Armenian holocaust, current deliberations and resolutions concerning the prevention and punishment of the crime of genocide may become only hollow words.

REFERENCES

1. See, for example, Roderic H. Davison, *Reform in the Ottoman Empire, 1856-1876* (Princeton: Princeton University Press, 1963); A. Schopoff, *Les Réformes et la protection des Chrétiens en Turquie, 1673-1904* (Paris: Plon-Nourrit, 1904); Edouard Engelhardt, *La Turquie et le tanzimat*, vol. 1 (Paris: Cotillon, 1882); Bernard Lewis, *The Emergence of Modern Turkey* (London: Oxford University Press, 1961).

2. Great Britain, Parliament, House of Commons, Sessional Papers, 1877, vol. 112, command 1739, Turkey no. 16, *Reports by Her Majesty's Diplomatic and Consular Agents in Turkey respecting Conditions of the Christian Subjects of the Porte, 1868-1875;* Sessional Papers, 1876-77, vol. 91, c. 1641, Turkey no. 2, *Correspondence respecting the Conference at Constantinople and the Affairs of Turkey, 1876-1877;* Sessional Papers, 1877, vol. 91, c. 1738, Turkey no. 15, *Further Correspondence respecting the Affairs of Turkey,* and vol. 92, c. 1806, Turkey no. 25, *Further Correspondence . . .* ; Great Britain, Foreign Office, *British and Foreign State Papers,* 1875-76, vol. 68, 683-98, "Constitution de l'Empire Ottoman, promulguée le Zilhidjé 1293 (11/23 Décembre 1876)," and vol. 68, 1114-1207, "Protocols of Conferences between Great Britain, Austria-Hungary, France, Germany, Italy, Russia, and Turkey..., Constantinople, December 1876-January 1877."

3. Leo [A. Babakhanian], *Hayots hartsi vaveragrere* [Documents on the Armenian question] (Tiflis, 1915), 56-58.

4. Great Britain, Sessional Papers, 1878, vol. 83, c. 1973, Turkey no. 22, *Preliminary Treaty of Peace between Russia and Turkey Signed at San Stefano 19th February/2nd March, 1878*, and c. 1975, Turkey no. 23, *Maps Showing the New Boundaries under the Preliminary Treaty between Russia and Turkey Signed at San Stefano*.

5. Leo, *Hayots hartsi vaveragrere*, 63-69' Gabriel Lazian, *Hayastan ev hai date (vaveragrer)* [Armenian and the Armenian question (documents)] (Cairo: Houssaper, 1946), 86-88.

6. Great Britain, Sessional Papers, 1878, vol. 83, c. 2083, Turkey no. 39, *Correspondence relating to the Congress of Berlin with Protocols of the Congress*, and c. 2108, Turkey no. 44, *Treaty between Great Britain, Germany, Austria, France, Italy, Russia, and Turkey for the Settlement of Affairs in the East, Signed at Berlin*. See also W.N. Medlicott, *The Congress of Berlin and After* (London: Methuen, 1938).

7. Duke of Argyll [George Douglas Campbell, 8th Duke], *Our Responsibilities for Turkey* (London: J. Murray, 1896), 74.

8. Leo, *Hayots hartsi vaveragrere*, 113-33; A. O. Sarkissian, *History of the Armenian Question to 1885* (Urbana: University of Illinois Press, 1938), 89-90.

9. For documents relating to conditions after the Treaty of Berlin and to the diplomatic notes and correspondence about the introduction of reforms in the Armenian provinces, see, for example, Great Britain, Sessional Papers, 1878, vol. 81, c. 1905, Turkey no. 1; 1878-79, vol. 79, c. 2204, Turkey no. 53, and c. 2205, Turkey no. 54, vol. 80, c. 2432, Turkey no. 10; 1880, vol. 80, c. 2537, Turkey no. 4, vol. 81, c. 2574, Turkey no. 7, and c. 2611, Turkey no. 9, vol. 82, c. 2712, Turkey no. 23; 1881, vol. 100, c. 2986, Turkey no. 6. See also *British and Foreign State Papers*, 1877-78, vol. 69. 1313-47, and 1880-81, vol. 72, 1196-1207.

10. See Louise Nalbandian, *The Armenian Revolutionary Movement* (Berkeley and Los Angeles: University of California Press, 1963); Mikayel Varandian, *H. H. Dashnaktsutian patmutiun* [History of the Armenian Revolutionary Federation], vol. 1 (Paris: Navarre, 1932).

11. France, Ministère des Affaires Etrangères, *Documents diplomatiques: Affaires arméniennes; Projets de réformes dans l'empire Ottoman, 1893-1897* (Paris: Imprimerie Nationale, 1897); Great Britain, Sessional Papers, 1895, vol. 109, c. 7894, Turkey no. 1, pt. 1, *Events at Sassoun and Commission of Inquiry at Moush*, and pt. 2, c. 7894-1, *Commission of Inquiry at Moush: Procès-verbaus and Separate Depositions*. See also E. M. Bliss, *Turkey and the Armenian Atrocities* (Boston: H. L. Hastings, 1896); Victor Bérard, "La Politique du Sultan," *La Revue de Paris* (December 15, 1896): 880-89.

12. Great Britain, Sessional Papers, 1896, vol. 95, c. 7923, Turkey no. 1, *Correspondence respecting the Introduction of Reforms in the Armenian Provinces of Asiatic Turkey*; France, *Affaires arméniennes*, nos. 43, 57; Germany, Auswärtiges Amt, *Die grosse Politik der europäischen Kabinette, 1871-1914* (40 vols.; Berlin: Deutsche Verlagsgesellschaft für Politik und Geschichte, 1922-27), vol. 9, nos. 2184-89, 2203-12, vol. 10, nos. 2394-2444; Schopoff, *Les Réformes et la protection des Chrétiens en Turquie*, 475-526.

13. For reports and diplomatic correspondence relating to the Armenian massacres of 1895-96, see, for example, Great Britain, Sessional Papers, 1896, vol. 95, c. 7927, Turkey no. 2, vol. 96, c. 8108, Turkey no. 6, and c. 8273, Turkey no. 8, and 1897, vol. 101, c. 8305, Turkey no. 3; France, Affaires arméniennes, nos. 116-235, and Supplément, 1895-1896 (Paris: Imprimerie National, 1897), no. 1-178; Germany, Grosse Politik, vol. 10, nos. 2410-76 passim, and vol. 12 nos. 2883-2910, 3065-3113 passim. Of the hundreds of books and eyewitness accounts relating to the massacres, see, for example, Johannes Lepsius, Armenia and Europe (London: Hodder & Stoughton, 1897); Georges Clemenceau, Les Massacres d'Arménie (Paris: n.p., 1896).

14. Ernest E. Ramsaur, Jr., The Young Turks (Princeton: Princeton University Press, 1957), 65-76, 124-29; Paul Fesch, Constantinople aux derniers jours d'Abdul-Hamid (Paris: M. Riviere, 1907), 366-76.

15. Ramsaur, The Young Turks, 130-39; Feroz Ahmad, The Young Turks (Oxford: Clarrendon Press, 1969), 1-13; Charles R. Buxton, Turkey in Revolution (London: T.F. Unwin, 1909), 55-73.

16. For findings of the Armenian member of the inquiry commission sent to Cilicia, see Hakob Papikian, Adanayi egherne [The Adana calamity] (Constantinople: Kilikia, 1919). See also Dickett Z. Ferriman, The Young Turks and the Truth about the Holocaust at Adana in Asia Minor, during April, 1909 (London: n.p., 1913); Georges Brèzol, Les Turcs ont passé là: Receuil de documents sur les massacres d'Adana en 1909 (Paris: L'Auteur, 1911); Rene Pinion, L'Europe et la Jeune Turquie (Paris: Perrin, 1911); M. Seropian, Les Vèpres ciliciennes (Alexandria: Della Roca, 1909).

17. See Uriel Heyd, Foundations of Turkish Nationalism: The Life and Teachings of Ziya Gökalp (London: Luzac, 1950), esp. 71-81, 104-48. See also Arnold J. Toynbee, Turkey: A Past and a Future (New York: George H. Doran, 1917), 15-40; Victor Bérard, La Mort de Stamboul (Paris: A. Coller, 1913), 259-398.

18. Ahmad, The Young Turks, 92-120; Wilhelm Feldmann, Kriegstage in Konstantinopel (Strassburg: K. J. Trubner, 1913), 106-71.

19. See Roderic H. Davison, "The Armenian Crisis, 1912-1914," American Historical Review 53 (April 1948): 482-504; Russia, Ministerstvo Inostrannykh Del, Sbornik diplomaticheskikh dokumentov: Reformy v Armenii (Petrograd: Gosudarstvennaia Tipografia, 1915); Germany, Grosse Politik, vol. 38, nos. 15283-15434 passim; British Documents on the Origins of the War, 1898-1914, ed. G.P. Gooch and Harold Temperley (11 vols.; London: H.M.S.O., 1926-38), vol. 10, pt. 1 passim; Leo, Hayots hartsi vaveragrere, 342-57.

20. V. Minakhorian, 1915 tvakane [The year 1915] (Venice: St. Lazarus, 1949), 66-71. See also Johannes Lepsius, Der Todesgang des armenischen Volkes (Potsdam: Tempelverlag, 1930), 178-79.

21. W.E.D. Allen and Paul Muratoff, Caucasian Battlefields (Cambridge: Cambridge University Press, 1953), 240-84; N. Korsun, Sarykamishskaia operatsiia na kavkazskom fronte mirovoi voiny v 1914-1915 godu (Moscow: Gosudvarstvennoe Voennoe Izdatel'stvo, 1937). See also Winston Churchill, The World Crisis (2 vols.; New York: Scribner's, 1929), vol. 2 1915; Trumbull Higgins, Winston Churchill and the Dardanelles (New York: Macmillan, 1963).

22. Helen Fein, Accounting for Genocide (New York: Free Press, 1979), 29-30.

23. For archival sources and published studies on the Armenian genocide, see Richard G. Hovannisian, *The Armenian Holocaust: A Bibliography Relating to the Deportations, Massacres, and Dispersion of the Armenian People, 1915-1923* (Cambridge, Mass.: Armenian Heritage Press, 1980).

24. For Turkish rationalizations, see, for example, Ahmed Rustem Bey, *La Guerre mondiale et la question turco-arménienne* (Berne: Staemplfi, 1918); Turkey, *Aspirations et agissements révolutionnaires des comités arméniens avant et après la proclamation de la constitution ottomane* (Constantinople: n.p., 1916).

25. Lepsius, *Todesgang*, 215-29. See also Toynbee, *Turkey*, 20-27, 30-31.

26. Henry Morgenthau, *Ambassador Morgenthau's Story* (Garden City, N.Y.: Doubleday, Page, 1918), 321-22.

27. See especially Vahakn N. Dadrian, "The Structural-Functional Components of Genocide," in *Victimology*, vol. 3, ed. I. Drapkin and E. Viano (Lexington, Mass.: D. C. Heath, 1974), and "The Common Features of the Armenian and Jewish Cases of Genocide," in *Victimology*, vol. 4, ed. I. Drapkin and E. Viano (Lexington, Mass.: D. C. Heath, 1975).

28. Richard G. Hovannisian, "The Allies and Armenia, 1915-18," *Journal of Contemporary History* 3, no. 1 (1968): 147.

29. *Manchester Guardian* (29 December 1916), 4.

30. Great Britain, Parliament, House of Commons, *The Parliamentary Debates*, 5th series, 1916, vol. 100, col. 2220.

31. Carnegie Endowment for International Peace, Division of International Law, *Official Statements of War Aims and Peace Proposals, December 1916 to November 1918* (Washington, D.C.: Carnegie Endowment, 1921), 231.

32. *Armenia's Charter* (London: Spottiswoode, Ballantyne, 1918), 9.

33. *Le Temps*, 7 November 1918.

34. *Armenia's Charter*, 14-15.

35. Archives of Republic of Armenia Delegation to the Paris Peace Conference (now housed in Boston, Mass.), File 344/1, *H. H. Hromi Nerkayatsutschutiun ev Italakan Karavarutiune, 1918* [Republic of Armenia Rome Mission and the Italian Government, 1918].

36. U.S. Department of State, *Papers Relating to the Foreign Relations of the United States*, 1918, Supplement 1: *The World War*, 2 vols. (Washington, D.C.: G.P.O., 1933), vol. 1, 16.

37. Ibid., 1919: *The Paris Peace Conference*, 13 vols. (Washington, D.C.: G.P.O., 1942-47), vol. 1, 52.

38. See Richard G. Hovannisian, *Armenia on the Road to Independence, 1918* (Berkeley and Los Angeles: University of California Press, 1967).

39. U.S. Department of State, *Paris Peace Conference*, vol. 3, 795.

40. Ibid., vol. 4, 509.

41. Ibid., Vol. 6, 688-89; Great Britain, Foreign Office, *Documents on British Foreign Policy*, 1st series, ed. W. L. Woodward et al., 23 vols. to date (London: H.M.S.O., 1947-81), vol. 4, 645-46.

42. U.S. Congress, Senate, 66th Cong., 2d sess., Senate Document no. 266, Major General James G. Harbord, *Conditions in the Near East: Report of the American Military Mission to Armenia* (Washington, D.C.: G.P.O., 1920), 7.

43. See Richard G. Hovannisian, *The Republic of Armenia*, vol. 1 (Berkeley, Los Angeles, London: University of California Press, 1971).

44. See Richard G. Hovannisian, "Armenia and the Caucasus in the Genesis of the Soviet-Turkish Entente," *International Journal of Middle East Studies* 4 (April 1973): 129-47

45. See Richard G. Hovannisian, *The Republic of Armenia*, vol. 2 (Berkeley, Los Angeles, London: University of California Press, 1982); Levon Marashlian, "The London and San Remo Conferences and the Armenian Settlement," *Armenian Review"* 30, nos. 3-4 (1977): 227-55, 398-414.

46. The Treaty of Sèvres is included in Great Britain, Foreign Office, *British and Foreign State Papers*, 1920, vol. 113, 652-776.

47. Richard G. Hovannisian, "Caucasian Armenia between Imperial and Soviet Rule: The Interlude of National Independence," in *Transcaucasia: Nationalism and Socialism*, ed. Ronald G. Suny (Ann Arbor: University of Michigan Press, 1983), 277-92.

48. See Marjorie Housepian, *The Smyrna Affair* (New York: Harcourt Brace Jovanovich, 1966).

49. See France, Ministère des Affairs Etrangères, *Recueil des actes de la Conférence de Lausanne* (6 vols.: Paris: Imprimerie Nationale, 1923); Great Britain, Foreign Office, *British and Foreign State Papers*, 1923, vol. 117, 543-639.

50. Lewis V. Thomas and Richard N. Frye, *The United States and Turkey and Iran* (Cambridge: Harvard University Press, 1951), 61.

51. See, for example, Stanford J. Shaw and Ezel Kural Shaw, *History of the Ottoman Empire and Modern Turkey*, vol. 2 (Cambridge: Cambridge University Press, 1977), esp. 311-17, 322-24; *Setting the Record Straight on Armenian Propaganda against Turkey* (Washington, D.C., 1982); Turkey, Prime Ministry, Directorate General of Press and Information, *Documents on Ottoman Armenians* (2 vols.; Ankara, 1982-83).

Sources of Alienation and Identity Crisis in Ottoman Intellectual History

James J. Reid

My paper emphasizes the European influences in the development of the Ottoman autocratic mentality, militarism, and concepts of progress and social purity. From the outset it must be noted that there were many other culprits to blame for the explosive situation that came into being at the beginning of this century in the Ottoman Empire. First among the culpable ones was alienation: the identity crises of those caught between the ideals of a past civilization and the reform concepts of a perceived future affected both the reformers and the reformed. Forms of government, such as personalized household administration, were now seen as nepotism. Social customs, such as arranged marriage, now became strategies for social and economic advancement. Personal comportment as defined in the traditional virtue literature now adopted a double significance. Almost all psychological and social elements transformed into new images molded into composites of old and new.

The old religious government or *millet* system likewise came into question and occupied an ambivalent position. But, like the millets themselves, the diversity of peoples now came into question as a social principle underlying a multicultural empire. At first Ottoman-ism attempted to create a common "Ottoman" culture, whatever that may have been. Then, from the late 1890s on, Turkish nationalism attempted to create a common Turkish culture for the Empire. The elite and most of the Turkish-speaking intelligentsia saw such cultural reform as the best way to compete with European colonial powers based, as it was thought, upon unified nations. The Armenians and the other peoples of the Ottoman Empire were increasingly being placed into the ambiguous position between the old, multi-

cultural ideal and the newer reform ideals. Like many social customs and older governmental reforms, Armenian society encountered the identity crisis of the Ottoman Empire and became part of the alienation processes at hand. The most severe alienation occurred among the Ottoman elite and certain sectors of bourgeois society. Contact with European ideals created a nihilistic stance among them regarding the various forms and expressions of Ottoman society and past cultures. Their inability to find value in the cultures of the Ottoman Empire and in what was considered decadence in traditional circles contributed to the genocidal attitude that rationalized the extermination of cultures and populations in the empire.

INTELLECTUAL CHANGES

The Ottoman intelligentsia, Europeanized bourgeoisie, and reform military underwent social, cultural, and intellectual metamorphoses in the nineteenth century which affected all the populations of the Empire drastically and irreversibly. The most profound alteration came with the acceptance of Realism and Bourgeois Materialism as defined in Europe. Many governmental reforms proceeded out of rationalist presumptions encouraged by Realism and neoclassical roots of Realist philosophy.[1] "Realism" first appeared in the 1850s as a neologism in French and English. As a literary and philosophical concept, Realism (and related orientations) contrasted with idealist metaphysics in its emphasis upon materialism or (scientifically) determinable phenomena. Realist philosophy conflicted with Middle Eastern religious values, which historically had maintained a dominant metaphysical ideology of state and society.

During the nineteenth century adherence to the French cultural achievement as epitomized in the Enlightenment became a widely held ideal in Ottoman urban society. Translations of French authors appeared in newspaper serials published by Ibrahim Shinasi, Refik Bey, Namik Kemal, and others associated with "liberalism" in the Empire. Aristocratic authors of the Enlightenment period, such as Montesquieu, Fénelon, and of course Voltaire, appeared in the original French and in Turkish translation. The popularity of such authors as Victor Hugo, Honoré de Balzac, Emile Zola, and others demonstrated the growing attraction for Realism in Ottoman cultures interested in the west, when Ottoman translations of these authors appeared in the 1880s and 1890s. A brief flirtation with the Romantics such as Chateaubriand also spoke of an attachment to Romanticism in Ottoman intellectual culture of the nineteenth century.[2]

Bourgeois culture in general became attracted to the bric-a-brac of Paris and Parisian *haute couture*. Much of the Parisian fad was a mindless imitation of everything Parisian, even ending in the translation of books by Eugène Sue and Paul de Kock as early as the 1870s. The attraction for the mundane detailing of Realism proved predominant and created a new social climate, especially in Istanbul. An Ottoman "philistinism" similar to that found in European upper and middle classes developed out of the new, westernized lifestyle that emerged, particularly with those aspects connected to certain forms of Realism. This so-called "philistinism" may be seen as one source of a nihilistic alienation from Ottoman cultures and peoples.[3]

Even this Realism or neoclassical Realism was not the pure, unadulterated adoption of a European philosophy or art form that it might seem on the surface. Realism fitted into Ottoman intellectual culture in an Ottoman way. A very interesting passage from Namik Kemal's *Intibah* ("*Renaissance*") demonstrates the point by showing Realism as an allegorical personification. The passage reads:

> It is a story that has come to the West from India: Reality was a girl who used to go about naked. Wherever she went, she was turned away. Finally, she had to hide herself in a well. Story, on the other hand, was a lame and crippled old hag, bent in two, with a wrinkled face and no teeth left in her mouth, having bad breath and a runny nose. However, because she could adorn herself in embellished garments, she would be welcome everywhere. Finally, one day she met Reality at the well and gave her all the adornments she had, after which Reality came to be accepted wherever she went.[4]

The dualism of the literary change demonstrates that Realism or Romanticism were not in themselves independent trends, but that they could be joined together to fit into an Ottoman literary culture. The identity ambivalence is clear from this example and shows that even the very westernized intellectual could not accept western forms entirely in their original form.

Realism, or any other European influence, did not become the chief source of Ottoman problems, but simply the means by which the elite and bourgeois personality moved increasingly toward a collective identity crisis. Even those who rejected Europe as the world leader and refused to consider French, German, or English intellectual advancements now needed to define their "traditional" culture or religion within the context of the European-nativist debate. While nearly everyone faced a value conflict during their lifetimes in the nineteenth century, it is clear that the elite and bourgeoisie (western-ized middle class) experienced the most severe identity change during their individual lifetimes. It is this crisis of the elite personality more than anything else which served as the source of the increasing militarism and the genocidal stance assumed by the Ottoman state and military from the 1870s through World War I. The Ottoman elites, in borrowing many of the same European ideals, were undergoing many of the same identity conflicts as their European counterparts.[5]

The Ottoman search to establish the dying empire as a neocolonial power comparable to and competing with the European empires constituted a tremendous distraction in the whole reform process during the nineteenth century. The identity conflicts within many elite personalities argued for the combination of radically different intellectual strains, the clash of which produced a nihilistic framework. Ibrahim Shinasi (d. September, 1871) became so attracted to French culture and intellectual life that he gradually rejected his friendships with most of the Young Ottomans, but the siege of Paris in 1870 forced him to return to Istanbul, where he lived in bitter circumstances, rejecting almost all personal contacts, until he died of a brain tumor in impoverished surroundings. Namik Kemal (d. December, 1888), a former protégé of Shinasi, lived a dazzling intellectual and artistic life in Istanbul, London, and Paris. He combined Islamic tradition with European philosophy and history. This alone illustrates a bipolar orientation which was difficult for Namik to resolve.[6] Ziya Pasha (d. May, 1880), a sometime ally of Namik Kemal and a thoroughgoing Realist in orientation, was so cautious that he could not establish his own clear-cut philosophy of reform. Ahmed Jevdet Pasha was both a "traditional" Muslim scholar and an Ottoman legal reformer who borrowed extensively from European law codes to formulate the new Tanzimat-era law code. Ali Pasha, the reforming minister of the Tanzimat and enemy of many Young Ottomans, wished to glorify the golden age of Ottoman power and to build a new Ottoman state and army patterned on European models.[7]

The Young Turk generation simply inherited these problems and intensified them. Like their predecessors, the Young Turks—and those whom they opposed in the Ottoman government—were affected by the disastrous combination of intellectual and cultural streams which normally did not recognize one another's existence. Ahmed Riza, a Young Turk exile living in Paris, devoted himself to Positivist philosophy and befriended such figures as Ernst Renan (Jamal al-Din al-Afghani's erstwhile philosophical nemesis). Among the earliest

Young Turk exiles living in Paris, he alone refused to surrender to Sultan Abdul-Hamid II's bribery with promises of high office. Yet even he, as dogmatic as he was, could not entirely resolve his Positivism and his Turkish nationalist leanings. He engaged in debates with the other Positivist philosophers on this score. They saw his nationalist inclinations as a metaphysical tendency, not as a humanistic one. The other Young Turks perceived his ideas with doubt, and as a result Ahmed found himself constantly in struggles with one group or the other.[8] Murad Bey, another Young Turk of the early period, had more interest in wealthy Istanbul sinecures than in his ideal or cause. As a result, when the Sultan offered him a post, he abandoned the Young Turk cause immediately without hesitating for even a moment. His actions started a stampede among the Young Turk exiles in Paris, who left Ahmed Riza to carry on the struggle alone. Murad's personal conflicts proved stronger than his understanding of causes or ideals, and as it turned out most of the early Young Turks agreed with him.[9]

The Turkish nationalist sociologist and philosopher Ziya Gokalp gives a clear vision of one tormented in his early life by the conflicts raging within him. He was Kurdish by origin, but became not only a Turk, but the premier philosopher of Turkish nationalism. He was trained as a traditional Muslim in his childhood schooling, but very early sought out a secular education at a bigger university. The extreme conflict of value systems overpowered the young man, who almost committed suicide.[10] Enver Pasha, the Young Turk officer and general most often credited with the wholesale massacres of Armenians and others, developed an autocratic militarism which betrayed the democratic ideals he had once espoused as a young officer opposed to Abdul-Hamid's "despotism" (istibdat). More than many others, he was the romantic militarist who felt it necessary to preserve the integrity of the Ottoman state and army officer corps at all costs, even over the bodies of many innocent victims.[11] Mustafa Kemal (Ataturk) was a devotee of westernism who wished to emphasize the power and originality of Turkish culture. He was a democrat who pursued autocratic and militaristic policies. Here again, the identity crisis is clearly apparent. Such internal contradictions produced a search for a way out of the quandary and created a wide variety of solutions. Various ideals of reform and progress contributed most of all to beliefs that religious government, various subject populations, or certain local communities were obstacles to progress. The inability to resolve conflicts over the way to go led to the genocidal policies that exploded under the military direction of Enver Pasha.[12]

Many ideals and intellectual problems are involved here; only two of the most significant can be emphasized.

SOCIAL DARWINISM AND OTHER IDEALS OF PROGRESS

Social Darwinism is a label given to a wide variety of ideas concerned with social evolution. Since most labels prove to be unsatisfactory in the end, it is used here simply to refer to theories of social evolution.

Social Darwinism is an intellectual, cultural, political, and social orientation which seeks to apply a theory of evolution perceived to be originated by Charles Darwin to societal development. As an approach, it sought to explain the apparent advancement of some communities, civilizations, or "races" over others. In an age when European colonial powers dominated about ninety percent of the earth's surface, Darwinism assumed a special significance which explained the "superiority" of European civilization.[13] The Ottoman elite's search to reestablish a "superior" status for Ottoman culture (in the narrow sense of the word) gradually turned toward Social Darwinist theories as a means of explaining the need for reform of the Ottoman elite and the creation of a "super-westernized" mentality perceiving itself as superior to the old Ottoman identity.[14]

The foundations of Darwinist theoretical developments as exemplified by Ziya Gokalp and other Turkish intellectuals of the early twentieth century can be traced to the Young Ottoman attachment to European values. Ahmed Midhat, the publisher of the journal *Dagarjik*, allowed an article on Darwin to appear in an issue of 1873. Ibrahim Shinasi accepted articles about the "Great Chain of Being" for his *Tasvir-i Efkar*. The "Great Chain of Being" notion of the universe and the world contributed much to Darwin's own thought about evolution, especially in its deistic Enlightenment form which removed most of the mystery from the process of creation and the emergence of animal species in the world. Shinasi also accepted a number of other articles on the historical development of Turkish societies which demonstrated at least a latent interest in the changes of the past. Namik Kemal postulated a theory of progress (*terakki*) in an article for *Ibret* published in November of 1872. His notions here were based in part upon his observations of English society.[15] The Young Ottomans and other liberals of the Tanzimat and post-Tanzimat era voiced the desire to create a new and superior Ottoman society which could equal that of Europe. A specifically-voiced notion of Social Darwinism did not appear until the late 1890s and eventually received its strongest expression in Ziya Gokalp's sociology.

Two distinct strains of sociological argument emerged out of Darwinist philosophy in the late nineteenth century. Both forms attempted to postulate the typologies of human society and the evolutionary pattern followed by humanity from the earliest times. One group, dominated by Herbert Spencer, argued that human evolution moved from the simple society with the greatest social solidarity to the compounded societies where solidarity gradually disintegrated under the pressures of industrialization and/or militarization. Thinkers such as William Graham Sumner, E. T. Hobhouse, and many others adapted Spencerian reasoning into their thought and assumed a very significant role in bringing Spencerian Darwinism into the twentieth century.[16] The other Darwinist approach was characterized by Emile Durkheim, who held much in common with Spencer but disagreed with him on a number of crucial points. Durkheim felt that the simplest social form did not exist except as an ideal notion. He saw evolution of society taking a reverse direction than that established by Spencer; that is, that society evolved from the more complex primitive condition to the more unified and simpler community where division of labor created a broader social dependency. Both agreed, however, that evolution involved a progression toward a more perfect society; and that during the process of change, the older, less efficient societies would necessarily die out to make way for the new. Spencer even went so far as to say that the newer society must go out of its way to destroy and kill the older, and that such an act was more merciful in the long run.[17] Other forms of Social Darwinism developed in anthropology, psychology, and history during this period as well.[18]

Ziya Gokalp tapped both of these forms of Darwinism in his own sociological and historical writings. He consciously borrowed the Social Darwinists' desire to create a science of society and the equation of societies with biological organisms. While his theories were closer to Durkheim, it is evident that he at least paralleled some of Spencer's ideas as well. In any case both formulas in the wrong hands could encourage much cruder applications and could be used to explain the extermination of groups targeted as obstructive or "backward" as a natural process in which no guilt existed. Herbert Spencer argued the crass aspect well. He stated:

> Pervading all nature we may see at work a stern discipline, which is a little cruel that it may be very kind. That state of universal warfare maintained throughout the lower creation, to the great

perplexity of many worthy people, is at bottom the most merciful provision which the circumstances admit of. It is much better that the ruminant animal, when deprived by age of the vigor which made its existence a pleasure, should be killed by some beast of prey, than that it should linger out a life made painful by infirmities and eventually die of starvation. By the destruction of all such, not only is existence ended before it becomes burdensome, but room is made for a younger generation capable of the fullest enjoyment; and, moreover, out of the very act of substitution happiness is derived for a tribe of predatory creatures.[19]

When applied to the processes of societal evolution, Spencer's perception worked out as follows:

Meanwhile, the well-being of existing humanity, and the unfolding of it into this ultimate perfection, are both secured by that same beneficent, though severe discipline, to which the animate creation at large is subject: a discipline which is pitiless in the working out of good: a felicity-pursuing law which never swerves for the avoidance of partial and temporary suffering. The poverty of the incapable, the distresses that come upon the imprudent, the starvation of the idle, and those shoulderings aside of the weak by the strong, which leave so many in shallows and miseries, are the decrees of a large, far-seeing benevolence. . . . Nevertheless, when regarded not separately, but in connection with the interests of universal humanity, these harsh fatalities are seen to be full of the highest beneficence—the same beneficence which brings to early graves the children of diseased parents.[20]

The desire to create a superior Turkish society within the Ottoman Empire seems to have approximated this Spencerian approach. Aspects of Ziya Gokalp's thought could easily be converted into such an explanation. Gokalp's theory of social evolution argued that humanity would move from undifferentiated primitive communities with a clan basis at the lowest rung to the culture-nation at the highest peak of evolution.[21] His typology was rigid and total, and in fact he equated societies with species (neviler) in true Darwinist fashion. When society passed from one phase to the next in its evolution, the individual needed to adjust through struggle or die along with the dying societies. In his view of social evolution, he stipulated that the tribe was a "simple" social form which died out with the development of the theocratic and legislative nation (which were two phases in his evolutionary typology as he was applying it to the Ottoman Empire). He felt that his own society was moving in the direction of a culture-nation in which a total solidarity would be achieved, echoing here the influence of Durkheim. All people must surrender their original cultural backgrounds in order to become citizens in the newly-evolved utopian nation. This action explains his disavowal of a Kurdish ancestry and his personal association with a greater, "non-racist" Turkism. Even though Gokalp despised the racism of the more passionate or more violent Turkists and pan-Turkists, his theory of evolution and his own psychological attitudes appear close to those of Spencer. "Weak cultures," so to speak, such as his own Kurdish one, must die or be killed in order to make way for the new "culture-nation" of Turkey.[22]

The more emotional and less "scientific" Turkist and pan-Turkist writing before and during World War I assigned a powerful meaning to the development of a Turkish nation which, it was felt, must now displace the multi-cultural polyglot of the Ottoman Empire. Arabs, Kurds, Armenians, Greeks, and Jews must surrender their specific identities in order to assume a new cultural identification—one which was Turkish. The approaches of these Turkish nationalist groups came closer to the Spencerian ideal than did Gokalp's sociology.

Mehmed Emin Yurdakul, a Turkish nationalist poet of the early twentieth century, creates in his poem "*Irkimin Turkusu*" ("Turkish is My Race")[23] an allegory of the perfect Turk. He opens his poem with the following lines:

We are Oghuz Turks, We are Turks of pure blood
　　First fire blazing[24]
First wooden plow, throwing grain seed on the rough earth
First hearth placing its foundations, we are all of them.

The blowing winds tear out every corner leaving a desolate
　　wilderness
Setting up tents at Issik Kul, we are at hand[25]
Roan bears wandering about in the Urals (are we)
We are the first Uighurs[26] striking out in a caravan.

Yurdakul goes on in his long poem to create impressions of a far-flung people. His aim is to create the genie of a pure Turkish spirit by using the allegorical method of calling up images of past peoples or referring to symbols associated with Turkish culture. Out of many disparate parts he creates a single being. He converts the origins of the Turkish race into a mystery divorced from science, and thus represents the opposition to Gokalp's positivism. In attempting to create an ideal, pure-blooded Turk, a pure Turkish soul, Yurdakul attempts to degrade by inference any person or group who did not consciously identify with the model. He wanted to deprive the Armenian, Greek, Arab, or Persian of a soul. Turkish racist national-ism approximated Aryan racism developing in Europe from the time of Count Gobineau on. In commenting on the phenomenon, George Mosse has said: "The equation of Aryan with the life force meant that those who opposed Aryanism were indeed people without a soul, cut off from nature and universe."[27] In the end Yurdakul's ideal of progress—the pure Turk and pure Turkish civilization—was a distortion of Spencerian Darwinism. It created a caricature or exaggerated stereotype of the Turk as a superior being by highlighting a few prominent features of Turkish civilization to envision a consciously-distorted Image viewed, unlike comic caricatures, as a romantic ideal type. The inferior beings in his own mind were those who interrupted the vision. These included crudely-fashioned Turks, as well as other Ottoman subject peoples who needed refinement, conversion, or extermination.

OTHER INTELLECTUAL CHANGES

The broad spectrum of intellectual and cultural changes in the nineteenth century does not allow a complete analysis in this short paper. Most intellectual developments, literary transformations, and cultural trends of the nineteenth century were only peripherally related to the Armenian massacres at the end of the nineteenth and the beginning of the twentieth centuries. Love, marriage, friendship, adventure, personal animosity, ambition, slavery, *intisāb*, individualism, and other problems or issues had little or nothing to do with the "nationalities" of the Ottoman Empire and their fates in a disintegrating state. On the other hand, a few issues do and these will be discussed briefly.

The worship of force and the idealization of the powerful man led to the creation of a hero cult in the nineteenth century which is still potent to the present in some circles. Just as the source of Thomas Carlyle's hero-worship was a Calvinism which he converted into a more secular egoism and the worship of unrestrained individualism, the Ottoman hero-cult of the nineteenth century possessed its own sources in the Ottoman past. The traditional annals of Ottoman history divided the Ottoman imperial past into sultan's reigns. By the mid-nineteenth century, however, writers such as Namik Kemal looked increasingly to the heroic sultans such as Mehmed II or Selim I who extended the boundaries of empire. In his *Evrāq-i Perīshān* Namik Kemal glorified the heroes of Islam who were able to resist the incursions of Christian armies successfully or who defended Islam against the Mongol onslaught.[28] The idealization of powerful leaders led to a wide spectrum of results ranging all the way from the comic to the tragic. The cult of the powerful Turkish commander created a distance between the sixteenth and the nineteenth century and contrasted the power of earlier leaders over the ineptness and perceived cowardliness of the more recent ones. Military officers and government officials raised with a consciousness of inferiority about recent inheritors of the Ottoman tradition attempted to reverse the trend by creating new heroes.

The hero cult created an immense and undying sense of guilt among loyal officers, who sought to relieve this sense of guilt by punishing those they assumed to be at fault for the empire's disintegration. As the disintegration worsened, and the betrayal of the Ottoman past became more apparent, the officers sought to increase their efforts and destroy all opponents with ever-more extraordinary means. The genocidal stance taken by the Ottoman state in the early twentieth century in particular was due in part to the desire of the army to defend what it considered to be its legacy and to establish a sense of the heroic and the forceful which could inspire the defense of the homeland. Some, like Enver Pasha and other officers, felt that extraordinary forcefulness was the means of achieving the heroic end, and their intentions were scoffed by some and lauded by others. Yet the intense desire to defend empire through heroic and powerful means, developed through the medium of an undying guilt and shame at the lack of heroism and force in later Ottoman society, rested at the root of the genocidal position of the Young Turk government, and even at the heart of Abdul-Hamid's "despotism." This syndrome mixed European ideals with the strong identification entertained for certain Middle Eastern or Ottoman figures of the Middle Ages. This "medievalism" was a Napoleonization of Ottoman figures in a way that earlier Ottoman chroniclers had never done. The new history created a new sense of the heroic past.[29]

Another intellectual problem related to westernization was the increased attraction to Realism, whose impact on Ottoman society in the late nineteenth century is far too complex a subject to analyze here. Literary, historical, and philosophical Realism, combined with positivism, materialism, and other Realist correlates (like Social Darwinism), assaulted Ottoman intellectual culture, but succeeded only in making the identity crisis deeper. Certain elements in the Middle Class became like the philistines in Europe, certain Ottoman officers and politicians became impressed with Bismarck's *Realpolitik*, while novelists and the reading public found the French Realists enticing. Scientific materialism appealed to many scholars such as

Ziya Gokalp, historians like Mehmed Fuad Koprulu, educators and economic reformers, and, of course, the technocrats in the army and bureaucracy.[30] Realism and its correlates destroyed the cosmogonic concept of society which had predominated so long in the Ottoman Empire. The belief that earthly society was alchemically created by the imprint of divine ideas upon physical matter was challenged in certain important sectors, most particularly in the army, bureaucracy, and westernized middle classes, where a "scientific" education deemphasized a cultural training. The old *millet* hierarchy, conceived out of the cosmogonic principle, could no longer be understood or accepted. Although Realism was not accepted everywhere in Ottoman society, it did dissolve the social bonds that emanated from the center and created a cultural condition in which the subject groupings, "traditional" or otherwise, would cease to relate to one another and to the central government. Civil war, rebellion, and genocide were not far removed from the reforms of the Ottoman state inspired by "Realism."

Other factors to be discussed in future works include anarchism and its influence upon terrorism in the Ottoman Empire, Napoleon III's military dictatorship in France (1852-1870) and its relationship with the Tanzimat from 1856, and the influence of Total War (*Machtpolitik*) on late Ottoman development, including the Armenian Genocide.

To assume that the Armenians were slaughtered only by "wild" tribesmen coming out of the hills, or that the Kurds and rural Turks of eastern Anatolia committed the massacres is to recede into a Social Darwinism of one's own as long as their roles alone are emphasized. To say that the Kurds or Turks committed the genocide because they were barbarians living in a savage, eastern Anatolian climate or culture is to forget that the Armenians also came from and belong to eastern Anatolia. Indeed the greatest culprit in the genocidal attacks on the Armenians was the dissolution of the old social bonds at all levels of Ottoman society. This dissolution began with the policies of the reform elites and their opponents. Dissolution was a fate met by several other empires at the time in one degree or other; however, the Ottoman state collapsed in a most violent paroxysm which resulted from a most profound inner conflict of being.

REFERENCES

1. Robert C. Binkley, *Realism and Nationalism, 1852-1871* (New York: Harper and Row, 1935), 27-33, 122-23. The bibliography on 327-31 provides a survey of the sources on intellectual history in this period. Note especially the works of Jacques Barzun, *Darwin, Marx, Wagner: Critique of a Heritage* (Boston: Little, Brown, and Company, 1941); Roger Soltau, *French Political Thought in the Nineteenth Century* (New Haven: Yale University Press, 1931), 15-31, 203-250; Walter E. Houghton, *The Victorian Frame of Mind: 1830-1870* (New Haven: Yale University Press, 1957), 93-109, 137-217, 305-40.

2. Ahmet O. Evin, *Origins and Development of the Turkish Novel* (Minneapolis: Bibliotheca Islamica, 1983), 41-64, 173-220. Both Realism and Naturalism sought to apply in varying degrees the scientific method to literature, with a chilling result. See Emile Zola's statement in *La Fortune des Rougon* (Paris: Brodard et Taupin, 7-8), where he notes: "Physiologiquement, ils sont la lente succession des accidents nerveux et sanguins qui se déclarent dans une race, à la suite d'une première lésion organique, et qui déterminent, selon les milieux, chez chacun des individus de cette race, les sentiments, les désirs, les passions, toutes les manifestations humaines, naturelles et instinctives dont les produits prennent les noms convenus de vertus et de vices." For an English translation of this passage see George J. Becker (ed.), *Documents of Modern Literary Realism*, (Princeton: Princeton University Press, 1963), where Zola's discussion of the experimental novel appears (161, 162-96). The above quote, referring to a prototypical family, seems strongly laced with Darwinism, though, in the end, the metaphorical nature of Zola's "scientific" approach becomes apparent. He is attempting to use his characters as symbols of virtues or vices, and the family of Rougon as the symbol of all families. Science has become an allegory here. While many Turkish novelists rejected Zola's choice of "immoral" or "crude" subjects, they did follow his techniques of observation and his emphasis upon observing the material environment. Other Realists and Naturalists were also helpful in this regard. Realism also found its way into the intellectual milieu of the Young Ottomans and the Young Turks, as well as into the educated elite and urban society in general.

3. Ernest K. Bramsted, *Aristocracy and the Middle Classes in Germany, Social Types in German Literature, 1830-1900* (Chicago: University of Chicago Press, Phoenix Books, 1964), 217-22; W. H. Riehl, *Die bürgerliche Gesellschaft* (Stuttgart, 1858), 220ff.; J. A. Hess, *Heine's Views on German Traits of Character* (New York, 1929), 60. Soren Kierkegaard also dealt extensively with the issue of philistinism, as did Marx and Engels, Matthew Arnold, and others. Anarchism, which appeared all over Europe and America in the late nineteenth century, was a response to bourgeois culture and perceived oppressions such as autocratic monarchy and militarism.

4. Evin, *Turkish Novel*, 39; Namik Kemal, *Intibah (Renaissance)*, Mustafa Nihat Ozon (ed.) (Istanbul, 1971), 25-26.

5. The Nazi genocidal policies of the 1930s and 1940s so outdistanced other genocidal attitudes or policies of all previous states, elites, or societies that it has blinded commentators to the fact that it was the product of nineteenth century foundations in Realism, Nationalism (and Racism), and Colonial policies. At the very least the Ottoman state and its "conservative" reformers aimed at becoming "like" a European colonial power toward its subjects. The greatest problem for the European officer corps (and their Ottoman reform counterparts) from 1789 on was the defense of the military tradition. This

identity crisis in the military involved the transformation of the old chivalric code of the aristocracy, who dominated European armies even in the middle of the nineteenth century, and nationalist concepts of militarism. A varied assortment of writings about militarism, militarism and colonialism, and soldiers in the nineteenth and early twentieth century include: Nancy L. Rosenblum, "Romantic Militarism," *Journal of the History of Ideas*, 43-2 (1982), 249-68; Michael Lalumia, "Realism and Antiaristocratic Sentiment in Victorian Depictions of the Crimean War," *Victorian Studies*, 27-1 (1983), 25-51; and Michael Howard, *The Franco-Prussian War: The German Invasion of France, 1870-1871* (London: Methuen, 1961), esp. 18-29. Theodore Zeldin, *France, 1848-1945, Anxiety and Hypocrisy* (Oxford: Oxford University Press, 1981), 159-78, has an insightful discussion of French militarism and its role in the colonies; the problems of the French military are criticized by Emile Zola, whose novel *La Débâcle* (first published in 1892) and whose work in the Dreyfus case pointed out the inadequacies of the army.

6.   Sherif Mardin, *The Genesis of Young Ottoman Thought: A Study in the Modernization of Turkish Political Ideas* (Princeton: Princeton University Press, 1962), 340.

7.   Ziya Pasha, "Shiir ve Insha," *Hurriyet* (September 7, 1868: 4-7) opposed the classical style of Ottoman poetry and opted for a different, more modern style, but in his anthology entitled *Kharabat* (see E. J. W. Gibb, *A History of Ottoman Poetry*, London: Luzac and Co. 1908: v. 78) he seems to argue in favor of traditional Ottoman poetry. Such apparent indecisiveness is really due to a dual identification resulting in an ambiguity. Ziya Pasha's analysis of societal origins shows the influence of Rousseau at least, and in many ways appears close to the evolutionary theories of the contemporary Social Darwinists (see his article "Hatira," in *Hurriyet*, December 14, 1868: 5-8, where he recognizes the political decline of the Ottoman state). Ahmed Jevdet Pasha felt very strongly about the legacy of the Ottoman imperial tradition and he believed that many reforms symbolized a concession of defeat (Ahmed Jevdet Pasha, *Tezakir 1-12*, in Cavit Baysun, ed., *Turk Tarih Kurumu Basimevi*, Ankara, 1953: 68). While recognizing the repugnance of reform, Ahmed Jevdet Pasha participated in the modernization of the Ottoman law code and even used the Swiss law code as a model. Ali Pasha, one of the Tanzimat reformers and a minister of state, showed the dualism which existed within the Ottoman state and Ottoman society in his memorandum entitled *Réponse à son Altesse Moustafa Fazil Pacha au sujet de sa Lettre au Sultan* (Paris, 1867). He was concerned with the influences of European secular education on (Muslim) Ottomans of high standing and the resulting conflicts as well as the divisions growing up amongst the various "nationalities" in the empire.

8.   Ahmed Riza, "L'inaction des Jeunes-Turcs," in *Revue Occidentale*, 2nd series, 27 (1903), 91-98; "Our Program," in *Mechveret*, 27 Frederic, 107 (December, 1895). *Revue Occidentale*, 2nd series, 12 (1896), 128 also carries the text. On Ahmed Riza's debates with the Positivists over Islam's susceptibility to Comtian Positivism, see: Ernest E. Ramsaur, Jr., *The Young Turks: Prelude to the Revolution of 1908*, (Princeton: Princeton University Press, 1957), 90-91.

9.   Murad Bey did not originate from the Ottoman Empire, but came as a refugee to Istanbul from Daghestan. His own insecurity about his cultural origins, and his desire for stability may have contributed to his lack of spine. Some of his writings demonstrate the conflict in his nature originated in the duality of weakness and strength. Mourad-bey, *La Force et la Faiblesse de la Turquie: Les Coupables et les Innocents* (Geneve: J. Mouille, 1897). A touch of philistinism

may have also affected his surrender to Abdul-Hamid II.

10. The conflicts in Ziya Gokalp's life were most powerful. Given a traditional Islamic education as a child, he craved a secular university education. When at university he nearly committed suicide, as a result, it seems, of both personal and cultural conflicts. He began life as a Kurd (apparently) but became an ardent (non-racist) Turkish nationalist. Like many European intellectuals of the late nineteenth century and later, he was a believer in the powers of science as the basis of social, cultural, and literary studies. Also like his European counterparts, he had to deal with the conflicts that arose when applying scientific formulas to the humanities and social studies. A vast bibliography of Ziya Gokalp exists; a few of the most important works are: Niyazi Berkes, "Gokalp, Ziya," in *Encyclopedia of Islam*, 2nd edition, II, 1117-18; Niyazi Berkes, "Ziya Gokalp: His Contribution to Turkish Nationalism," in *Middle Eastern Journal*, 8 (1954), 375-90; Ziyaeddin Fahri, *Ziya Gokalp, sa vie et sa sociologie* (Paris, 1935); Uriel Heyd, *Foundations of Turkish Nationalism, The Life and Teachings of Ziya Gokalp* (London, 1950); Ali Nuzhet Goksel, *Ziya Gokalp, Hayati ve eserleri* (Istanbul, 1949).

11. Enver Pasha, more than most, represents the extreme of the conflicts between western and Turkish influences, aggravated by an intensive militarism. As the son of a railway official, he belonged to a partly westernized group. He admired Prussian militarism and military values and sought to implement German military tactics in his World War I campaigns, even to the point of employing German commanding officers for some of his armies. Bibliography on Enver Pasha is meager, but see the comments on his personality by Dankwart A. Rustow in "Enver Pasha," *Encyclopedia of Islam*, second edition, II: 701: Enver "had great personal courage, boundless energy, and a keen sense of drama—at times melodrama." Comments on Enver Pasha's career and military activities can be found in the memoirs of Ataturk, Jemal Pasha, and others.

12. For quotes accessible in English, see Lord Kinross, *Ataturk* (New York: William Morrow and Co., 1965), 74, 93.

13. Raymond F. Betts, *The False Dawn: European Imperialism in the Nineteenth Century* (Minneapolis: University of Minnesota Press, 1975), 156-83; Carlton J. H. Hayes, *A Generation of Materialism, 1871-1900* (New York: Harper and Row, 1941), 9-13; Jacques Barzun, *Darwin, Marx, Wagner: Critique of a Heritage* (Boston: Little, Brown, and Company, 1941), 100-109.

14. Sherif Mardin, "Super Westernization in Urban Life in the Ottoman Empire in the Last Quarter of the Nineteenth Century," *Turkey: Geographical and Social Perspectives*, P. Benedict, E. Tumertekin, F. Mansur, eds., (Leiden: E. J. Brill, 1974), 403-46; Evin, *Turkish Novel*, 79-128. This trend of seeking a superior status (in something resembling Social Darwinist terms) is evident in numerous early instances. 'Umar Pasha, commander of the Ottoman army in the Crimean War, spoke with Dr. Thomas Buzzard during the Caucasian campaign. Buzzard recalled: "I had a few words of conversation with Omer Pasha in the course of our ride, and he told me that he thought the political condition of the [Caucasian] tribes somewhat resembled that of the states of Greece in ancient times, between which internecine feuds constantly existed." Thomas Buzzard, With the Turkish Army in the Crimea and Asia Minor: A Personal Narrative (London: John Murray, 1915), 212.

15. Darwin, Darwinism, and the complex ideas, notions, and militaristic beliefs called Social Darwinism have not been well studied within the context of the Ottoman empire. While many could not accept Darwin's theory of evolution,

many did accept the ideas of Social Darwinism, which they saw as the means of achieving or regaining imperial superiority. On the "popular materialism" which was associated with Darwinism in Europe, and its "confusion" with science, see Jacques Barzun, *Darwin, Marx, Wagner: Critique of a Heritage* (Boston: Little Brown, 1941), 96-97. An article on Darwin did appear in the gazette *Dagarjik* published by Ahmed Midhat in the late 1860s. More important than a direct connection with Darwin, however, was the predominance of a "popular materialism" among the reformers and certain groups of entrepreneurs (Mardin, *Young Ottoman Thought*, 66). By the time of Ziya Gokalp, Social Darwinist intellectual analyses had found an important place in some segments of Ottoman society.

16. Herbert Spencer, *Social Statics* (London, 1851) and *Principles of Sociology* (London: D. Appleton and Co., 1897), vol. I. The influence of Spencer or any other figure was usually indirect, since the more popular understanding of material advancement, and the identity crises caused by reforms, acted as screens through which ideas were filtered.

17. Emile Durkheim, *De la division du travail social* (Paris: Librairie Felix Alcan, 1932), 245-59, especially. The connection between ideas of survival of the fittest and *anomie* are major. That Durkheim involved himself in a Darwinist orientation is evident in his discussion of society in evolutionary terms, even if he disavowed the organicist approach of Spencer and others. Linda Clark, in *Social Darwinism in France* (University, Ala.: University of Alabama Press, 1984), 126-34, identifies the Darwinist elements in Durkheim's sociology. Note also the distinction between reform and conservative Social Darwinists. Spencer belonged to the latter, while Durkheim would have been more inclined toward reformism. See Burt James Loewenberg, *Darwinism: Reaction or Reform?* (New York: Holt, Rinehart and Winston, 1957), 1-8.

18. L. T. Hobhouse, G. C. Wheeler, M. Ginsberg, *The Material Culture of the Simpler Peoples, An Essay in Correlation* (London: Routledge and Kegan Paul, 1915), 1-45. Edward B. Tylor, *Primitive Culture, Researches into the Development of Mythology, Philosophy, Religion, Language, Art, and Custom* (London: John Murray, 1920), 2 vols.; William Graham Sumner, *The Science of Society*, vol. I (New Haven: Yale University Press, 1927); and John Lubbock, *The Origin of Civilization and the Primitive Condition of Man*, Peter Riviere, ed. (Chicago: University of Chicago Press, 1978). Good discussions of Social Darwinism can be found in Walter Houghton, *The Victorian Frame of Mind* (New Haven: Yale University Press, 1957), 209-13; Richard Hofstadter, *Social Darwinism in American Thought* (Boston: Beacon Press, 1955), which is especially good for Herbert Spencer and William Graham Sumner; Carlton J. H. Hayes, *A Generation of Materialism* (New York: Harper and Row, 1941), 9-13; George Mosse, *Toward the Final Solution* (New York: Harper and Row, 1980); and in any of Stephen Gould's works, especially the *Mismeasurement of Man*.

19. Spencer, *Social Statics*, 322.

20. Spencer, *Social Statics*, 323. Ziya Gokalp, *Turk Medeniyeti Tarihi*, in Birinci Kisim, *Islamiyetten Evvel Turk Medeniyeti* (Istanbul: Gunesh Matbaacilik, 1976), demonstrates the benefit to material advances which wars of annihilation gave to the early Turks and their ancestors. The victors obtained great wealth. Gokalp demonstrates how ceremonial plunder-taking became a ritualized institution in the society of the so-called Oghuz Turks (201-3).

21. Ziya Gokalp, "Bir Kavmin Tetkikinde Takibolunajak Usul," in *Milli Tetebbular Mejmuasi*, I, no. 2, Istanbul, 1915.

22. Ziya Gokalp, *Turk Medeniyeti Tarihi,* 49-50. Gokalp indicates that each tribe (*il*) was its own species (*nev*) and each possessed its own power of existence and spirit of being ("*mana,*" which he translates into the Old Turkish word *kut*). Gokalp relied on European methodology to the degree that he even discusses a *Potlach* culture (73ff.). He cited such writers as Charles Gide (1862-1940, French economist), Rudolph Steinmetz (1847-1932, sociologist), Wilhelm Thomsen (1843-1927, Turcologist), Emile Durkheim 1858-1917, sociologist), Marcel Mauss (1872-1950), Lucien Levy-Bruhl (1857-1939), and Léon Cahun, Wilhelm Radloff, and other Turcologists. Gokalp was heavily influenced by Cahun, whose book, *L'histoire d'Asie: Turcs et Mongols* (Paris: Armand Colin et Cie, 1896), is an inspired Darwinist defense of the Turkish and Mongolian "races." Gokalp's studies are very important for explaining the impact of evolutionary perceptions—especially relating to struggle and superiority of groups—upon the reform-minded leaders of the Ottoman state and certain popular groups. The aims of Ottoman reformers eventually came to a rough equivalent of Darwinist notions, anyway.

23. Mehmed Emin Yurdakul, *Turk Sazi, Yaralar ve Sargilar* (Istanbul: Atlas Kitabevi, 1969), 134.

24. This line and the following two lines use allegorical symbols to portray the pristine condition in which Yurdakul imagined the early Turks to live. He traces the history of early Turkish humanity through synecdochic and metonymic symbols and at the same time implies that Turks were the first people to do such things as invent fire, develop the plow, invent dwellings, and so on. On allegorical usage of metonymy and synecdoche, see: Angus Fletcher, *Allegory: The Theory of a Symbolic Mode* (Ithaca, N.Y.: Cornell University Press, 1964), 85-87. The metonymy at work here creates a special national mystique and sense of superiority by connecting the modern Turk with his fabled and "superior" (it is implied) ancestor. Allegorical perception has here taken the place of Realist perception.

25. Issik Kul is a lake in Central Asia which had been the basis of Qarluq power before the Mongol conquest.

26. The Uighurs were a Turkish people living on the borders of the Chinese empire astride the old silk route. Uighur state and culture were once a monument to syncretic tendencies. Uighurs still exist today inside China, and less so, in the Soviet Union.

27. George Mosse, *Toward the Final Solution: A History of European Racism* (New York: Harper and Row, 1980), 99.

28. Namik Kemal, *Evraq-i Perishan* (Istanbul, 1288/ 1871-1305/ 1887) deals with the lives of Mehmed II, Selim I, Salah al-Din Ayyubi, and Amir Nauruz. On page 2 of the section discussing Selim I, Namik Kemal gives one of the sultan's most important characteristics as his power (*iqtidar*), and this sentiment is echoed throughout. The same sentiment can be found in Namik Kemal's other works. The hero cult even extended to European military men: Napoleon Bonaparte, *Tarikh-i Bonaparte,* Bulaq (1247/ 1831) was an abridged translation taken from his memoirs through an Arabic intermediary and intended for use in military academies.

29. The sense of guilt and defense of one's actions against critics can be seen as early as the edition of Ahmed Mukhtar Pasha's memoirs: *Serguzesht-i Hayatimin jild-i sanisi* (Istanbul, 1328). The memoirs of this general were a defense of his activities in the Russo-Turkish war (1877-1878). The disastrous outcome of this war for Ottoman forces created a defensive mentality in the Ottoman army

and indeed created the tone by which Abdulhamid II ruled. Defensiveness coupled with a paranoid fear of revolution can be claimed as another source of the Ottoman state's genocidal stance from the late 1870s on. In fact a useful comparison might be drawn with the paranoia experienced by the French military after their defeat in the Franco-Prussian war—a climate of paranoia which led to the Dreyfus case. The generation of Young Turk officers exhibit many attitudes derived from fears and anxieties over the Empire's disintegration and perpetual warfare.

30. Realism has an immense bibliography. Only a few titles will be noted here: Emile Bréhier, *The History of Philosophy*, VII, *Contemporary Philosophy Since 1850*, Wade Baskin, tr., (Chicago: University of Chicago Press, 1969), 197-222; Erich Auerbach, *Mimesis: The Representation of Reality in Western Literature*, (Princeton: Princeton University Press, 1953), especially 493-524; Hayden White, *Metahistory: The Historical Imagination in Nineteenth Century Europe* (Baltimore: The Johns Hopkins University Press, 1973), especially 45-48; Jacques-Henri Bornecque, "L'influence des écrivains réalistes et naturalistes sur l'évolution des classes sociales au XIXe siécle," in *Philologica Pragensia*, I (1966), 38-56. One of the few efforts to study Realism's influence in the Ottoman Empire is Evin, *Turkish Novel*, 173-220.

The American Response to the Armenian Massacres of 1895: A Foreign Policy Dilemma

Barbara J. Merguerian

On November 30, 1894, Sultan Abdul-Hamid II invited President Grover Cleveland to appoint an American representative to the Turkish government's commission charged with investigating the reported massacre of Armenians living in Sassun, a remote mountainous district in the eastern part of Turkey. For several weeks the government of Ottoman Turkey had been insisting publicly that persistent reports of fighting in Sassun had been grossly exaggerated, that a minor revolt by Armenians living in the area had been efficiently put down by Turkish armed forces, and that the incident was closed. Information gradually reaching Western capitals from Sassun, however, indicated that major atrocities against the Armenian population of the area had been committed by Turkish regular troops acting in conjunction with Kurdish irregular forces.

The invitation by the Turkish sultan was totally unexpected in Washington. According to the terms of the Treaty of Berlin, signed in 1878, the six Great Powers of Europe (England, Russia, France, Germany, Italy, and Austria-Hungary) were charged with the responsibility for supervising the "ameliorations and reforms" to be carried out by the Ottoman government in the provinces of Turkey inhabited by the Armenians. The United States had not been a signatory to the Treaty, nor had it played any role in the subsequent sporadic efforts by the Powers to secure reforms in the Armenian provinces. It was the Great Powers (England and Russia in particular) who, over the years, with varying degrees of vigor, had called for reforms; it was England who, following the reports of fighting in Sassun, had pressed for a full and impartial investigation.

Most likely it was the hope of keeping the Great Powers from further intervention in the administration of the Armenian provinces and specifically from taking part in the Sassun investigation that had prompted the Sultan's appeal to the United States. But President Cleveland, imperfectly informed of the facts and anxious to avoid participation in the political manoeuvering that marked Great Power policies toward Turkey in this period, declined the invitation. "While appreciating Sultan's confidence, President unwilling American be sent with Turkish commissioner to investigate alleged atrocities," Secretary of State Walter Q. Gresham cabled the U.S. Minister in Istanbul on December 2, 1894. Justifying the decision to the British Ambassador in Washington, Gresham indicated that the President believed that interference in the matter "might lead the U.S. Government into complications which it was their policy to avoid."

Three days later, on December 5, 1894, President Cleveland changed his mind. A report from Alexander W. Terrell, the U.S. Minister in Istanbul, indicated a far greater loss of life and more widespread atrocities in Sassun than earlier reports had suggested; moreover, the British government had strongly urged the United States to participate in the investigation. Gresham now cabled Istanbul instructing that Dr. Milo Jewett, the U.S. Consul in the interior city of Sivas (Sebastia), accompany the Turkish investigative commission, "not, however, as a member of it," and "after full and impartial investigation report the facts for the information of this Government." The independent nature of the proposed mission was stressed; Jewett "will not join the Turkish or other commissioners in any report," the Secretary of State directed.

In those three days, however, the Sultan in turn had changed his mind. Upon learning of the President's initial refusal to take part in the investigation, Abdul-Hamid had bowed to Great Power pressure and had agreed to accept representatives of England, Russia, and France in the Sassun commission; evidently he now no longer wished to complicate matters by bringing the United States into the picture, a development which in turn was expected to bring demands for participation from Italy and Austria as well. Acutely aware that the resolve of the Great Powers to partition the Ottoman Empire among themselves had been held in check only by their inability to agree on a division of the spoils, the Sultan did not hesitate to include the United States in his complex strategy of playing one power off against the other, but he was anxious to avoid if possible the involvement of yet another outside nation into what he considered to be an internal matter. Perhaps, too, he was troubled by the American insistence on the independence of its representative; the Sultan initially may have foreseen U.S. involvement as a means of finding a sympathetic ally less knowledgeable about conditions in the area and more likely to be swayed by the Turkish point of view. In any event, in a three-hour interview with the U.S. Minister in Istanbul, the Sultan made the "earnest request. . .that the United States will appreciate the present great embarrassment of the Turkish Government and that the President will withdraw his demand for Jewett's appointment." Although the United States initially pressed for Jewett to proceed with the investigative commission, Gresham finally, on December 24, quietly advised Terrell to drop the matter; the United States played no role in the subsequent Sassun investigation.[1]

This incident marked the first of several instances during the second Cleveland administration (1893-1897) when the United States came to the brink of major involvement in the political affairs of the Ottoman Empire, particularly as those affairs affected the empire's Armenian population, who became increasingly victims of Turkish violence. The reluctance of the United States to act, even in response to such a minor request as to name a representative to a Turkish investigative commission, reflected the continuing strong American aversion to involvement in European politics (and by extension to the Ottoman Empire and the Near East). Subsequent events in the Ottoman Empire gave rise to increasing pressures upon the United States to take some kind of decisive action. But in order to intervene, President Cleveland would have had to change the traditional basis of U.S. foreign policy.

Both Cleveland and the two Secretaries of State in his second term (Walter Q. Gresham and Richard Olney) held traditional and un-sophisticated views about America's role in world affairs. Cleveland was unalterably opposed to foreign policy adventures, having once declared bluntly that, if the American people "did not stay at home and attend to their own business, they would go to hell as fast as possible."[2] In the great foreign policy debates that took place in the United States in the last decade of the nineteenth century between, on the one hand, the "imperialists" who cited America's "manifest destiny" and called for an expansion of the navy and an increase in American possessions and influence in the world, and on the other hand the non-interventionists who believed the country should avoid foreign policy entanglements, Cleveland was clearly on the side of the latter. A firm advocate of the Monroe Doctrine, he strongly opposed European interference in the affairs of the Western Hemisphere (his administration is best known, in foreign policy, for the strong stand taken against Great Britain in the Venezuela boundary dispute). At the same time Cleveland steadfastly refused to put into effect the treaty negotiated by his predecessor to annex Hawaii and he resisted pressure from Congress to intervene in Cuba. Preoccupied for most of his second term with the domestic problems arising from the economic depression (or "panic") of 1893, Cleveland showed only cursory interest in issues lying outside the traditional areas of American concern in the Western Hemisphere; his foreign policy has been summarized as "on the whole, conservative, and strikingly unimaginative."[3]

The massacres of the Armenian population in Turkey, which spread from Sassun in 1894 throughout the Armenian provinces in 1895 and 1896, severely tested the non-interventionist policies of the Cleveland administration and posed a troublesome dilemma for the United States. The massacres represented a serious threat to the survival of the vast network of American religious, educational and benevolent institutions that had been carefully built up during the previous seventy-five years of missionary activity in the Ottoman Empire. That work had been essentially private and did not directly involve the United States government. Yet the missionaries were American citizens whose life, property, and rights it was the duty of the United States government to protect. Besides, there were moral issues to consider; Americans could not but feel some responsibility for the fate of the Armenian people who were the chief clients for the American missionary institutions and whose main offense as far as the Turkish government was concerned was their Christian religion and their desire to enjoy basic political and economic rights. The pressures on the government of the United States to intervene, the question of what form any intervention should take, and the opposing pressures that limited the American response set a pattern for subsequent decades and had a significant bearing on future of the Armenian question.

Relations between the United States and Turkey during the nineteenth century may be described as basically friendly, but not particularly close. In 1880, for example, in an effort to reduce his expenditures, the Sultan temporarily closed his diplomatic mission in four countries considered relatively unimportant, including the United States.[4] While the commercial relations between the two nations developed rapidly in the first three-quarters of the nineteenth century (in 1876 the United States ranked third in the value of merchandise imported into and fifth in the value of goods exported by the Ottoman Empire), by 1892 the United States had been displaced by several European nations in its trade with Turkey (ranking that year thirteenth in the value of exports and tenth in the value of imports).[5]

In the absence of important commercial ties, the relations between the United States and Turkey revolved mainly around the activities of the American Protestant missionaries, most of whom operated under the auspices of the American Board of Commissioners for Foreign Missions (ABCFM), headquartered in Boston. In 1895 the ABCFM operated in Turkey eighteen stations and 326 outstations, which included 178 American missionaries, 124 churches, 5 theological schools, 54 college, high and boarding schools, and 393 common schools.   In addition to the projects of the ABCFM, which were supported in the main by the Congregational Church, programs were operated by the Presbyterian Mission Board as well as several independent institutions (Robert College in Istanbul and Saint Paul's Institute in Tarsus, for example). The total value of the American Protestant investment in the Ottoman Empire at the time has been estimated at $6 million.[6] The missionaries were well connected politically; they had relatives or associates in politics, the press, the professions, and particularly in higher educational institutions. A member of the U.S. Legation in Istanbul in the late 1890s wrote in his memoirs: "The missionaries had been among the first to learn how to exert pressure in politics—even the head of our State Department used to quake when the head of a Bible Society walked in."[7]

Thus, the efforts of the American diplomatic mission in Istanbul were directed largely to protecting the interests of U.S. missionary preachers, educators and professionals. In giving instructions to his newly appointed Minister to the Ottoman Empire, President Cleveland specified the dual tasks of protecting the American missionaries stationed in Turkey and of preserving friendly relations with the Turkish government.[8] But these two instructions became increasingly contradictory in the 1890s as the Turkish government began to view the American missionary establishments with suspicion because they served Christian, and mainly Armenian, subjects. This was a direct result of Ottoman government policy, which discouraged proselytizing among the Muslims and strongly disapproved of participation by Muslims in the American schools and institutions. The Western ideas represented by the missionary enterprises were perceived as a serious threat to traditional Ottoman society. And although the missionaries strictly eschewed any involvement in

Turkish politics and discouraged participation by their students in revolutionary activities, the emphasis in their education on individualism and rationalism, coupled with their Yankee determination and pragmatism in overcoming obstacles, had obvious political implications. As a British observer in Istanbul noted of the missionaries: "As these gentlemen are the representatives of a Republican country, where free institutions and liberal ideas prevail, their teaching doubtless spreads among the Armenians subversive ideas and discontent with the narrow and backward Turkish administration."[9]

Given the weak state of Turkey in this period, the virtual collapse of her economy, her defeats in the wars, and her losses of territory, it is not surprising that the Westernism of the missionaries became a target for the frustrations of the Turkish government and population. The unfortunate result of this situation was that, instead of finding ways to benefit from the willingness of the missionaries to educate the people and to introduce modern improvements into the country—a process that may have helped Turkey withstand pressures from the European Powers—the Turkish government responded largely by distrusting and harassing the missionaries.

No discussion of American foreign policy toward Turkey during the second Cleveland administration would be complete without some discussion of the controversial man who represented Washington in Istanbul during this period, Alexander W. Terrell. Born in Virginia, educated in Missouri, and engaged in the practice of law in Texas for many years, he preferred to be called "Judge" Terrell because he had been elected to the court, in Texas, shortly before the outbreak of the Civil War. At the expiration of his term, Terrell had joined the Confederate Army, reaching the rank of Brigadier-General during the Civil War. After the War, he resumed his law practice, and served in the Texas House and Senate. When he was appointed Minister to the Ottoman Empire, he had no experience in foreign policy or diplomacy, nor did he possess any special knowledge about Turkey.[10]

From the very beginning of his service in Istanbul, however, Terrell made a great effort to establish a rapport with the Turkish officials with whom he came into contact, including the Grand Vizier Jevad Pasha and the Foreign Minister Said Pasha. Terrell's direct approach to diplomacy, though it often disturbed the conservative bureaucracy at the State Department, appears to have been welcome among the officials at the Porte as a contrast to the sophistication and polish of European diplomats. The Sultan frequently invited the U.S. Minister to social events, especially during the first two years of Terrell's service in Turkey. The following story was told by the dragoman at the American legation, Alessandro Gargiulo, about Terrell:

> At his first audience he had told Abdul Hamid that all Turkey needed was a representative constitutional government on the American plan; the Sultan had taken a fancy to him and invited him to the opera. There Mr. Terrell had leaned back, his jaws working steadily on his plug of tobacco; every now and then he bent forward to spit, frequently striking the superb gold brocade which hung over the front of the royal box. Each time Gargiulo had noticed the Sultan shudder.[11]

During their conversations, Terrell and the Sultan covered a wide range of topics: Abdul-Hamid exhibited a tremendous curiosity about the United States, about the native Indians, about the Blacks, about agriculture and industry. Terrell gave the Sultan advice about the type of crops that might do well in the climate of the Ottoman Empire; he later proudly boasted of having introduced the cultivation of the sweet potato into Turkey. The Sultan showed interest in information about the U.S. army, for example about the use of bicycles, and the latest models of guns. Particularly during his first two years in Turkey Terrell did all he could to encourage contacts. He pressed the State Department to cooperate in the Sultan's requests for American professionals to come to Turkey to fill several posts.[12]

During this period, the U.S. minister constantly advocated an increase in American commerce and shipping with Turkey. The fact that no American merchant ship had been seen at the Turkish capital for the past seven years was cited as a dismal sign of the decline in commerce. Terrell noted that items manufactured in the United States were in great demand in Turkey, but were simply not available. "Daily it becomes more painfully apparent that our many manufacturers are neglecting this splendid field for marketing our factory products to nearly 50,000,000 people," he wrote in 1894. "Merely to send our factory products here with a commercial agent to sell would be folly. To succeed, our agricultural implements must be accompanied by a man always accessible to instruct in their use."[13]

Because of his eagerness to establish and preserve contacts, Terrell was sometimes accused by his critics of being "pro-Turkish" or "pro-Sultan." In fact Terrell's efforts to understand the character of Ottoman officials and the reasons for their actions sometimes made him appear sympathetic to Turkey. But Terrell's analysis of the Turkish character led him to advocate a strong, firm, and consistent policy in dealing with the Ottoman Empire. He called upon his superiors in the State Department to clearly assert American rights

in the empire vigorously, by force if necessary. In many instances he
advocated a stronger stand than that taken by the State Department,
in the question of protecting native employees of missionary institutions or of preserving the rights of U.S. citizens, for example. He
constantly pressed for a greater U.S. presence in Turkey, especially
by the posting of U.S. warships in nearby waters. More than once, in
the face of intransigent responses from the Porte to U.S. demands, he
urged Washington to sever relations between the two nations.
Frustrated by the fact that he was often held responsible by the
public for the policies set forth by the State Department against his
own recommendations, he pleaded with the Department repeatedly to
clarify the situation and to take responsibility for its policies.[14]

Terrell advocated a strong U.S. stand in protecting the rights of
American citizens and American institutions in the Ottoman Empire.
The proper U.S. response to persecution by the Ottoman government
of its Armenian subjects, however, was a much more complex issue.
Protecting the rights of Armenian subjects who had acquired U.S.
citizenship was a duty Terrell pursued with his customary vigor and
energy. A large portion of his time and effort was consumed in the
affairs of these naturalized Armenians, whose American citizenship
was not recognized by the Ottoman government.   For the large
majority of the Armenians in Turkey who did not enjoy U.S. citizenship, however, Terrell found little scope for U.S. action. Terrell did
believe that his Southern background gave him a unique insight into
the question, however. He compared the position of the Armenians
in Turkey to that of the Blacks in the United States prior to the Civil
War—both were oppressed minorities. He watched as, in response to
the growing unrest and terror in Turkey, Great Power pressure on the
Turkish government to introduce reforms into the Armenian provinces
increased—but not enough to actually bring about meaningful
progress. In October 1895, when the Sultan at last accepted a reform
plan for the Armenian provinces proposed by the Powers, Terrell
expressed a strong foreboding. Amelioration of the lot of oppressed
minorities through outside pressure, as in the case of northern
pressure in the United States to improve the lot of the Blacks in the
South, was bound to have disastrous effects, he wrote.[15] He argued
that the Armenian Question was being used as a pretext for the
intervention by the Great Powers into the internal affairs of the
Ottoman Empire.[16]

Early in his service in Istanbul, Terrell had persistently but
unsuccessfully urged Washington to cooperate with other powers in

developing a united policy to deal with the growing Ottoman restrictions on its Christian populations, arguing that he "could so manage things so as to neither violate our traditional policy, nor become isolated in attempts to secure observance of treaty rights."[17] The refusal of Washington to sanction such a policy left Terrell with no justification for attempting to intervene in favor of the Armenian subjects of the Sultan. While lamenting the sad fate of a people whose only crime was their strong adherence to the Christian religion, Terrell characterized the Armenian question as an internal affair of the Ottoman Empire and declared at one point that "the United States would avoid the Armenian Question in Turkey as readily as it would the Irish Question in England."[18] Later, when missionary pressure for a more active U.S. foreign policy escalated, Terrell wrote the following explanation:

> Whether, in view of the long-established foreign policy of the United States, which has avoided complications with the internal administration of foreign governments, our government should interpose to stop inhumanities in Turkey you will not expect from me an opinion. That established policy has promoted our marvelous growth. It is worthy of consideration, whether a departure from it now might not in the end result in more misery to the human race than that which now affects Asiatic Turkey.
>
> As a man I deeply sympathize with the unfortunate race now perishing; as a representative of the United States my duties are restricted to the protection of the lives and interests of our own citizens.[19]

Terrell clearly perceived the ambiguities implicit in the missionary presence in Turkey and he never developed a close relationship with the missionary establishment. It was no coincidence, Terrell contended, that the growth of the American missionary programs in Turkey had been accompanied by the rise in the Armenian national movement.[20] While one could hardly blame the missionaries if their instruction led their pupils to seek better government, or if the Turkish population refused to attend their schools, the enlightenment of one sector of the population of the Ottoman Empire, without any corresponding education to benefit the ruling and majority portion of the society, was bound to lead to trouble. What then was the responsibility of the missionaries, and their leaders and supporters in America, when the fury of the Turks was unleashed against the Armenian students of missionary ideals? Terrell argued that it was not and should not be the policy of the United States to intervene in such situations; reading between the lines, one finds an implicit criticism of a policy that enlightens a people who have no recourse against the power of their government other than from cynical European powers bent on their own aggrandizement. At the end of 1895, after the brunt of the massacres had struck the centers of Armenian population, Terrell penned a pessimistic letter to missionary Henry O. Dwight, in which he observed:

> Impatience under despotism is the natural result of enlightenment. The education of the Armenian race has naturally engendered a desire for larger freedom. Though our missionaries have discouraged sedition and are now in danger from an undeserved popular prejudice which has been fostered by calumnies, a present remedy, in this era of suspicion and massacre, is not apparent.[21]

There were other reasons why Terrell was never able to gain the support or respect of the missionary establishment whose interests he spent so much of his time protecting. Despite his lack of knowledge about the Ottoman Empire, Terrell seems to have neither solicited nor to have followed the advice of the missionaries, many of whom had lived in Turkey for decades; on the contrary, he questioned how a group of people who had no direct contacts with the Turkish government could form such definite opinions.[22] Then there are the intangibles of class and geography. Most of the missionaries were from New England and the midwest, the very areas that had formed the backbone of the abolitionist movement in America; despite the passage of years some of them may have harbored a trace of antipathy to one who, like Terrell, had been a Confederate officer. Then there was the fact that Terrell, though not a practicing member of any faith, had a Quaker background and retained an element of Quaker skepticism of the militant Christianity practiced by the missionaries. Although he was wont to describe the missionaries as "good men," Terrell on occasion was given to wondering why they did not use their reforming efforts in the "slums of Christian cities," rather than in remote Muslim villages in Turkey.[23] Finally, his personality was in direct contrast to the traits stressed by the missionaries (as well as to those generally attributed to Quakers): Terrell was self-confident, even self-centered, outspoken, frank, and rather flamboyant—a contrast also to the conventional, soft-spoken, reticent officials of the Cleveland administration.

As the threat to the American missionary establishment in Turkey and the people it served grew, Americans both in and out of the government looked for a suitable response. A greater American official presence in Turkey was one obvious step, and demands were made for an increase in the number of American consulates, then numbering in the Ottoman Empire, in addition to the Legation in Istanbul, two consuls general, five consulates, and twenty-three consular agencies, most of them in the coastal cities. The only consul in the interior of Turkey, where most of the missionaries (and the Armenian population) were located, was Dr. Jewett, in Sivas.[24] Although there was not much that a single diplomat could do, isolated in a village in the interior of Turkey, it was generally believed that such Western eyewitnesses exercised a restraining influence on the excesses of local officials.[25]

Working through their friends, the missionaries saw to the appropriation in March 1895 of funds to support two additional consulates in the Ottoman Empire: in the interior cities of Kharpert and Erzurum. The administration cooperated with these efforts and in June 1895 appointed Robert S. Chilton, Jr., as consul in Erzurum and William Dulany Hunter as vice consul in Kharpert. The two new consuls were immediately sent to Istanbul, on the way to their new posts, but requests to the Turkish government to recognize them by issuing a diplomatic exequatur were unavailing. The Porte argued that neither Kharpert nor Erzurum was of sufficient commercial importance to warrant a consul. The United States countered by pointing out that the 1830 Treaty regulating relations between the two countries gave the United States the right to establish consulates wherever it deemed them appropriate. On August 24, Terrell proposed ordering the two new consuls to proceed to their posts without the exequatur, and demanded from the Turkish government proper escort and protection. Although the Ministry for Foreign Affairs promised the awaited exequatur and urged Terrell to delay the departure of the consuls, the State Department finally, on September 11, authorized Terrell to send the consuls to their posts without official recognition by the Ottoman government. But the delay undermined their mission. On the way to their posts, the new consuls arrived in Trebizond just as the wave of violence against the Armenians was sweeping through Asia Minor; fearful for their safety, Terrell ordered them to return to Istanbul.[26] In the violence unleashed in the fall of 1895 by the Sultan's government, leaving an estimated 200,000 Armenians killed and countless others reduced to homelessness and abject poverty, the American consuls (except for Jewett) were absent. The violence directed at the Armenian population naturally affected the American missionary institutions, stationed as they were in the Christian quarters of the villages; in the major missionary centers of Kharpert and Marash, the American institutions were specific targets of attack.[27]

A stronger response by the American government was the posting of warships in Turkish waters. Even before the Sassun incident, in September 1893, Terrell began badgering the State Department to arrange for the presence of U.S. warships in Turkish waters, arguing that the Turkish government would listen to his demands only if those demands were backed up by force.[28] In early 1894 Terrell was informed that two ships in the American Mediterranean fleet—Rear Admiral Henry Erben's flagship, the cruiser *Chicago*, and the gunboat *Bennington*—would visit Smyrna (Izmir). When the ships did not appear, Terrell grew increasingly impatient. Have not the officers of the ship spent enough time "dancing at Nice with the nobility of Europe?" he crossly wrote to the State Department on February 4, 1894, when he was in the midst of negotiations with the Porte over the arrest of Armenians who were naturalized U.S. citizens. The ships eventually did visit Smyrna, but a proposal to make that major Turkish port a naval rendezvous station for the U.S. Mediterranean squadron met no success.[29]

In 1895 the growing tensions resulting from the massacres led Terrell once again to ask for ships, and the USS *San Francisco* and the *Marblehead* were sent to Turkish waters in April of that year. According to Secretary of the Navy H. A. Herbert, the ships had been sent for the purpose of "ascertaining the grounds existing for the circulation of reports regarding the massacre of Christians in that portion of Asia Minor."[30] The *San Francisco*, under the new commander of the U.S. Mediterranean fleet, Rear Admiral W. A. Kirkland, made stops at Smyrna, Alexandretta, and Mersin, while the *Marblehead* visited Beirut, Alexandretta, Mersin, and Smyrna. In the fall of 1895, news of the wave of massacres of Armenians in the Turkish interior brought the two ships back to the Turkish coast, and in December they were soon joined by a third ship, the *Minneapolis*. In recognition of the growing seriousness of the violence in Turkey, the new commander of the U.S. naval forces in Europe, Rear Admiral Thomas O. Selfridge, was instructed not only to take missionaries and other Americans on board, if necessary, but he was given broad latitude: "Act promptly if in your judgment advisable to land force," Secretary of the Navy Herbert cabled. At the same time Selfridge was instructed to keep at least one vessel in the area. Indeed, during the following year, at least one U.S. warship, and often more than one, remained off the coast of Alexandretta and Mersin.[31]

The Ottoman government expressed displeasure over the presence of the ships and delivered protests to the U.S. government through the Turkish Minister in Washington and through the U.S. Minister in Istanbul. When the Porte made inquiries of Terrell concerning the visit of the USS *San Francisco* to Smyrna in April 1895, the U.S. Minister replied that the visit was a friendly one, but that "such vessels are designed to protect U.S. interests."[32] When the Turkish Minister, Mavroyeni Bey, in Washington, protested the visit, Secretary of State Gresham replied blandly that the *San Francisco*, joined by her consort, the *Marblehead*, was "about to cruise in the Levant, a part of the Mediterranean which I trust may be more frequently the scene of these friendly visits than has heretofore been practicable." When Mavroyeni Bey continued to transmit protests of his government to the presence of the ships, the Acting Secretary of State Edwin F. Uhl adopted a firmer tone. "This Government employs its naval agencies abroad...for the protection of American citizens and American interests in other countries," he informed the Turkish representative: "I cannot suppose you . . . intended to question the right of this Government to use its several agencies in its own discretion for the purpose of gaining information or carrying out its determined policies."[33]

The effectiveness of the American warships in the eastern Mediterranean is difficult to judge. Missionaries and consular officials were convinced that the presence of U.S. ships near Mersin and Alexandretta saved Adana from the massacres that swept the eastern provinces in the fall of 1895. Terrell repeatedly argued that the presence of the U.S. naval vessels made Turkish officials listen more carefully to his persistent demands throughout 1895 and 1896 for the protection of the American missionaries. On the other hand the effectiveness of the naval presence was limited by the general ignorance of the U.S. commanders concerning conditions in the Ottoman Empire and by an appalling lack of coordination between the diplomatic and naval officials of the U.S. government. Stopping in the various seaports of the Ottoman Empire, the American officers were invited to ceremonial visits with the local Ottoman officials during which they were assured that all was well within the empire. The fact that the U.S. commanders refused to meet with anyone who might have provided an alternate point of view further confirmed their one-sided view of the empire; for example Commander O'Neil of the *Marblehead* declined a request to meet with the Armenian Bishop during his visit to Mersin in October 1895.[34] The succession of three different Admirals commanding the Mediterranean fleet in this period, Erban, Kirkland, and Selfridge, meant that none of them had the opportunity to become familiar with the situation. With a superficial contact with conditions in Turkey, the naval officers would assure their superiors in Washington that there was no need for concern.

Reporting from Alexandretta on April 21, 1895, Rear Admiral Kirkland wrote that he could find "no foundation for apprehension of a massacre of Christians" and on April 30 he indicated that no U.S. officers on either the *San Francisco* or the *Marblehead* found "any reliable information of any contemplated or feared massacre of the Christians." Indeed, after a visit to Smyrna, where he informed the local governor of U.S. concerns about rumors of a planned massacre of Christians, Admiral Kirkland concluded: "I believe that the governor of Massachusetts is as much liable for the murder of settlers by the Apaches as is the governor of Smyrna for the murder of the Armenians by the Koords." His assessment of the situation upon his return to Naples was conveyed in a report to Secretary of the Navy Herbert on May 1, 1895. "I find no outrages against American citizens in Turkey and heard of none," Rear Admiral Kirkland wrote, adding that "there is no need to keep a vessel on that coast.[35] Such superficial reports infuriated the missionaries, who were themselves to be caught in the middle of the most severe massacres less than six months later; it was observed in the *Missionary Herald* that American admirals had submitted comforting reports from the Ottoman Empire even though they managed to get no closer to the missionary stations in the interior of the country than San Francisco is to Boston.[36]

The lack of communication between the U.S. State Department, the Navy, and the diplomatic legation in Istanbul hindered the development of an effective policy. In the fall of 1895, at the same time that Terrell was in constant contact with Ottoman officials in Istanbul in order to insure the protection of the American missionaries during the wave of massacres, Admiral Selfridge was in contact with local Turkish officials in Alexandretta without providing any information about the nature of his conversations either to the U.S. consulates in the area or to the Legation in Istanbul.[37] In a later incident, on November 21, 1895, Terrell informed the State Department that the Porte had turned down a request for the U.S. Frigate *Marblehead* to pass the Dardanelles and come to Istanbul. Caught completely unawares, the State Department cabled back to ask what had impelled Terrell to make such a request. Terrell replied that he had been so instructed in a letter from Admiral Selfridge. It thus appears that the U.S. Navy was making plans to send a warship through the Dardanelles, a passage strictly regulated by international treaties, without informing Washington of its intention.[38]

Whatever the problems of coordination, it was clear that there was little that U.S. warships could accomplish directly to help the bulk of the missionaries living in the interior of Turkey. As news of the worst of the massacres in the fall of 1895 reached the United States, the administration ordered a concentration of vessels in Turkish waters. While the fleet commanders had been authorized to protect missionaries and other Americans by taking them on board ship, if necessary, the missionaries refused to abandon their posts. As to the authorization to Admiral Selfridge to land forces if needed,[39] there is no evidence that this was ever a serious consideration. The missionaries sometimes informally and unofficially suggested that a bombardment of a major coastal city, Smyrna for example, or seizure of valuable Turkish property, such as the island of Rhodes,[40] might have a beneficial effect; others warned that such a course might result in more harm than good. The missionaries, in common with the Armenian population they served, were in effect the hostages of the Turkish government. If American warships were to bombard a coastal city of Turkey, what was to stop the Turkish government from annihilating the missionaries in the interior? Government files hold a memorandum of an interview that Navy Secretary Herbert conducted with a Christian missionary doctor who had just come out of Turkey—Dr. Thom—on January 23, 1896. One suspects that Secretary Herbert took the unusual step of having a stenographer present to record the conversation in order to preserve on file a justification for naval inaction in the midst of public criticism of the ineffective U.S. response to the crisis in the Ottoman Empire.

> *The Secretary.* Suppose this country should send a fleet there to demand indemnity from Turkey for the loss of property that has been suffered in these riots and should find it necessary to bombard any Turkish city in order to enforce the demand, what, in your opinion, would be the effect upon the American missionaries who are in the interior and beyond the reach of our fleet?
> *Dr. Thom.* To be honest, in stating my opinion it would be hazardous.
> *The Secretary.* You do not think having in view a proper regard for the lives of these people, it would be safe for the Government to venture to do anything of that kind?
> *Dr. Thom.* I do not think so at present, although we feel that strong pressure ought to be brought upon them to pay the indemnity. At Harpoot alone they lost over $100,000.

The Secretary. The Government means to insist upon the indemnity, but in doing this it might be necessary to bombard a Turkish port which would jeopardize the lives of missionaries in the interior.

Dr. Thom. They say openly that if war is declared they will simply kill the Christians around them first.

The Secretary. Why is it Doctor that your missionaries have all refused to come to the shore and take refuge in American ships and leave the country? . . .

Dr. Thom. They feel that they must protect those who are there under their charge. If they leave they feel that they could not return.

The Secretary. It is then a sense of duty that keeps them there.

Dr. Thom. Yes sir and they think the Government will protect them in remaining there.[41]

Washington was under increasing public pressure to take decisive action in Turkey. Rev. John P. Peters, of the St. Michael's Church in New York City, a man who had lived in Turkey and had close ties with the missionaries, met with Secretary of State Olney in February 1896 on the subject. The Rev. Peters was surprised to hear Olney state that a display of force by the United States in Turkish waters might result in a massacre of the missionaries in the interior. In a letter written subsequently to Olney, Peters argued that the opposite was true; that the danger to the missionaries in the interior stations was due to "the lack of vigor in the action of our Government, but no danger from excess of vigor." As to what the government could do in the situation, Rev. Peters offered the following:

The head of our Government by message addressed to Congress can state the abhorrence of the Executive Branch of our Government toward the perpetrators of the outrages upon the Armenians. . . .

I think that by enforcing to the very utmost the full observance of our treaty rights, and exacting instant and exemplary reparation where Turkish officials attack, or connive at attacks upon the persons or property of our citizens in Turkey, we can exert pressure upon the Turkish Government to cease its barbarous murders of its own Armenian subjects; that is, such determined and vigorous action of our Government toward Turkey in regard to our own subjects, will make the Turkish Government hesitate to order massacres of Armenians, at least where there are Armenian subjects in the vicinity, for fear lest it may infringe upon American rights, and bring about a conflict with our Government.[42]

While the administration was clearly limiting U.S. action in the Ottoman Empire to those areas in which interests narrowly defined as American were involved, the missionaries and their many friends—in Congress, in the press, in higher educational institutions, to say nothing of the churches—were making much larger claims. To be sure these critics of administration policies stressed the importance of U.S. interests in Turkey. But they used a broader definition of U.S. interests, one that applied not only to U.S. missions and schools in Turkey but to the Armenian people who were served by these institutions. The annihilation of the Armenian population of Turkey that was threatened by the government of Abdul-Hamid endangered the entire American missionary presence in the Ottoman Empire. Some Americans took an even more comprehensive view of U.S. foreign policy interests, asserting that America had a moral obligation to come to the aid of a people persecuted because of their tenacious faith in the Christian religion.

If one looks at the debates about the Armenian massacres that took place in Congress in 1894, 1895, and 1896 as these debates were printed in the Congressional Record and other publications, one can find any number of powerful and eloquent statements by Senators and Representatives from all parts of the United States calling for decisive action to save Armenians. Mass meetings were held in cities and towns all over the country to discuss the fate of the Armenian population in Turkey, reports of these meetings and of the atrocities in Turkey that prompted them were printed prominently in the press, and the Resolutions (or Memorials) of these meetings were forwarded to Senators and Representatives for insertion into the Congressional Record. At the time there were only about 10,000 Armenians in the United States, so that most of this political activity was carried on by non-Armenians. During the Second Session of the 54th Congress, for example, which met in late 1896 and early 1897, Memorials were submitted calling for the protection of citizens in Turkey from groups in Virginia, Pennsylvania, New York, Illinois, Pennsylvania, Ohio, Maine, Wisconsin, Vermont, Wyoming, and Kansas, and several other states.[43]

Resolutions had been introduced in Congress beginning in December 1894, as news of the Sassun massacre became known. And while several of the strong resolutions failed passage, others were successful. A Joint Resolution introduced by Senator Newton C. Blanchard of Louisiana in December 1894 failed: it stated "that the people of the United States view with horror and detestation the atrocities" committed on the Christian inhabitants of Armenia under the domination of Sultan and "do hereby protest, in the name of common humanity, against the same." However, a substitute resolution was approved by the Senate requesting the President to communicate to the Congress any information in his possession "in regard to alleged cruelties committed upon the Armenians in Turkey" and to inform the Senate "whether any expostulations have been addressed by this Government to the Government of Turkey in regard to such matters" or "any proposals made by or to this Government to act in concert with other Christian powers regarding the same.[44] The President replied to this Resolution on December 11, 1894, that no expostulations had been made to Turkey "in the absence of such authentic detailed knowledge on the subject as would justify our interference."[45]

The next year the 54th Congress, convening in its first session in December 1895, once more passed a resolution asking the President to communicate all information available on the condition of affairs "in reference to the oppression or cruelties practiced upon the Armenian subjects of the Turkish Government." In reply, the President, on December 19, submitted a report prepared by Secretary of State Olney summarizing all the information in the hands of the State Department on the situation there.[46] Dissatisfied with the response of the administration, the Senate and House, in January 1896, after lengthy debate, passed a Resolution that had been reported favorably out of the Foreign Relations Committees of both Houses. Recognizing the responsibility of the European Powers to secure reforms in the Armenian provinces of Turkey, according to the provisions of the Treaty of Berlin, this Resolution requested that the President communicate to the Great Powers the importance of taking "such decisive measures as shall stay the hand of fanaticism and lawless violence, and as shall secure to the unoffending Christians of the Turkish Empire all the rights belonging to them both as men and Christians."[47] In the lengthy debate that took place in both Houses the major issue was not whether the Resolution should be passed or not, but whether it was strong enough. Despite its overwhelming approval by Congress, the Resolution was ignored by the President and no communication about the Christians in the Ottoman Empire was made by President Cleveland to any of the Great Powers. The popular feeling on the issue became so strong, however, that a section about the Armenian massacres appeared in the Republican Party platform as the election of 1896 approached:

> The massacres in Armenia have aroused the deep sympathy and just indignation of the American people, and we believe that the United States should exercise all the influence it can properly exert to bring these atrocities to an end. In Turkey, American residents have been exposed to gravest dangers and American property destroyed. There, and everywhere, American citizens and American property must be absolutely protected at all hazards and at any cost.[48]

As the pressures on the Cleveland administration mounted to take more decisive action in Turkey, the popular discontent became focused on the U.S. Minister in Istanbul, Alexander W. Terrell. Never popular with the missionaries, Terrell in 1896 became the target of a missionary campaign to remove him from office. The campaign, with its accompanying acrimony, was particularly unfortunate because, according to all accounts, Terrell's active on behalf of the missionaries at the Porte was at least partly responsible for the fact that, despite their exposed position in the midst of the violence that swept through the Armenian provinces, not a single American missionary was killed or seriously wounded in the fall of 1895. Terrell visited the Porte constantly in this period, demanding that telegraphic orders be sent to the provincial leaders to provide armed protection to the missionaries (he no longer was given the direct access to the sultan he had enjoyed earlier in his service in the Turkish capital). The protection of the Americans sometimes arrived late, it was often lackadaisical, it was in some areas accompanied by demands for bribes which the missionaries considered intolerable, but it was effective.[49]

The final break came late in 1895 when, in the wake of the violence in the provinces, Terrell suggested that the missionary women and children be evacuated from the interior of Turkey and taken to the port cities, where they could be more easily protected or sent home to America. Terrell's position is understandable; he held the responsibility for the lives of these Americans. The missionaries were incensed at the suggestion. They saw it as an abdication by the government of U.S. responsibility to protect them and as an attempt on the part of a U.S. official to dictate to them their course of action in the Ottoman Empire; they also believed that such a policy would be viewed as a retreat, as the beginning of a missionary withdrawal from Turkey. They considered it most important at this time to remain at their stations and to show their solidarity with the Armenian people. From the missionaries' point of view, their people had every right to be in the Ottoman Empire, and it was up to the government to devise a means to secure their safety. In a personal letter to Secretary of State Olney written in late December 1895 just after learning of a decision issued by the American Board of Commissioners for Foreign Missions, in Boston, requiring that missionaries remain at their posts in Turkey and guard the property there, "for reasons which I cannot appreciate," Terrell speculated: "Can it be that there is a hope that the United States may be forced by the sacrifice of our missionaries to resort to armed intervention?" In a letter to missionary Dwight enclosed in the same dispatch, Terrell asked: "If inspired by that lofty zeal which incites to martyrdom—our grown missionaries prefer to risk destruction rather than withdraw—I have nothing to say, but the little children (and there are many among those 170 missionaries) should be saved. They are not missionaries." Some may escape harm but "the risk in remaining is too great, for if these massacres continue the Central Government may soon be unable to restrain the fanaticism of the very soldiers I have secured as guards."[50]

With that pragmatism that accompanied their idealism, the missionaries gradually (but quietly) withdrew their children and sent them home to the United States.[51] But they never forgave Terrell for what they considered to be his hostility to their interests, and they began to campaign in earnest for his removal. For his part, Terrell was convinced that the missionaries were engaged in clandestine negotiations with the British to force the United States into open intervention in the Eastern Question. He believed that the missionaries pressed for his removal because they considered him an obstacle to their designs. "They will not see that even armed intervention could not give state autonomy to the Armenians unless the Turks ...are first destroyed," he wrote.[52] Nonetheless, the Judge had offered on more than one occasion to resign if the President lost confidence in him. The uneasy relations between Terrell and the missionaries continued until the end of the Cleveland administration.

In response to the loud criticism of its inaction in Turkey, the Cleveland administration during its final months formulated a dramatic plan to assert the American presence in a visible way, in the country's capital, Istanbul. The Treaty of Paris (1856) and a Protocol of 1871 barred warships from the Dardanelles except that each of the Powers was permitted a dispatch boat in the service of its legation at Istanbul. In the wake of increasing violence throughout the country, and particularly after unrest in Istanbul in the fall of 1895, the missionaries pressed for a U.S. vessel in the capital. In late 1895 and early 1896 the matter was under active discussion within the U.S. government. On January 6, 1896, Under Secretary of State Uhl directed Terrell to seek permission from the Porte for the United States to station the *Bancroft* at Istanbul; despite its designation as a despatch boat it was a good-sized ship, with an 839-ton displacement, a main battery of four four-inch guns, and a crew of about 70, including officers. The Turkish Minister of Foreign Affairs, objecting that the treaties limited despatch boats to the signatories of the

Treaty of Paris, turned down the request. On February 1, 1896, Terrell reported to Washington that the Porte had informed him that the Great Powers had objected to the despatch boat. Upon the advice of the French Ambassador, and after obtaining instructions from Washington, Terrell then asked permission for a visit from the *Bancroft* to Istanbul for a short period only. It then became known that the Russian government was opposed to such a visit. In an interview with Terrell the Russian Ambassador, A.I. Nedilov, said that his country would not permit an American boat to pass the Dardanelles, insisting that "the admission of an American war ship now would excite the Armenian people here to imprudent action again, which in the present unsettled state of affairs would seriously threaten the peace of Europe"; the Ambassador promised, however, that when the situation quieted down, his government would remove its objection.[53]

Terrell continued to press the matter with the Russian Ambassador, and by August 25 he was able to report: "Russian Ambassador will cooperate to secure entry of *Bancroft*. We both think no application should be made to the Porte until boat is at Smyrna and then he will join me in asking her admission. I would apply by telegram when on boat and come up on her. Let boat come quick with destination concealed from the Press."[54] The next day he provided additional details of his plan, saying that he personally would enter the Dardanelles on board the ship even if the Turkish government refused permission,[55] thus relying on the fact that the Turkish government would not fire on a U.S. ship, especially if the U.S. Minister was on board. On October 7, Terrell learned that the *Bancroft* was at Gibraltar, and went to tell the Russian Ambassador. Mr. Nedilov pointed out that the situation had changed as a result of the massacre of the Armenians in Istanbul that had followed the Ottoman Bank seizure. Nedilov finally agreed to inform Turkey that Russia would not object to the *Bancroft* entering the harbor en route to the Black Sea to convey Terrell and to remain a short time.[56]

On October 14, however, the situation changed when the news of the plan became public. The *New York Sun*, in its issue of that date, reported that on the previous day the Cleveland Cabinet had decided to direct Mr. Terrell to board the *Bancroft* at Smyrna and proceed with the vessel to Istanbul. If obstacles were raised by the Turks, Admiral Selfridge was ordered to take his fleet to assist passage of the Dardanelles. Soon the U.S. plan to force the Dardanelles was featured in newspapers throughout the United States and Europe. A

Reuters correspondent in New York reported that the rumor was received with "incredulity mixed with ridicule." Experts were quoted as saying that the idea was absurd, for even if the vessel reached Istanbul she would be helpless after she arrived. Olney and Herbert refused to discuss the matter. Naval officials would say only that the *Bancroft* was ordered to Gibraltar, and then to Smyrna. The story was sensational enough to attract attention above the election din. On October 22, Terrell telegraphed the State Department to inquire if he should press for the Bancroft matter. Two days later, before he received a reply, Terrell was approached by the Sultan, who directly informed the American diplomat of his objection. Abdul-Hamid said that the boat was not necessary, because "he assures the safety of all foreigners," and observed that the presence of the boat has a "disquieting tendency." The Sultan offered Terrell the use of one of his Imperial boats to convey him wherever he wanted to go.[57]

In the face of this personal intervention by the Sultan, Terrell advised the State Department to postpone the matter, expressing his opinion that Russia in the final analysis would side with the Sultan. In reply, Olney advised Terrell not to rush the matter and to avoid making a direct request for the boat unless certain of a positive response.[58] Although Terrell continued to talk about bringing the *Bancroft* to Istanbul, the plan was quietly dropped. Such decisions appeared to be better left to the new McKinley administration about to take office. The premature publication of the plan in the press dampened enthusiasm for it, because a critical ingredient in its success would have been the element of surprise.

The possibility of a new approach to the Armenian Question arose toward the end of the Cleveland administration, when Great Britain suggested the possibility that the two nations might develop a coordinated approach to the problem. In a letter of September 19, 1896 to Secretary of State Olney, the British diplomat Joseph Chamberlain, who was in the United States to work out the details of an agreement over the Venezuela boundary dispute, ended by asking whether Olney "would care to express a confidential opinion as to the reception which would be given by the American government to any proposition from our side tending to cooperation in regard to Turkey."[59]

In discussing the response to this British proposal, Cleveland wrote to Olney:

> It is hard to restrain one's self on this cursed Turkish question, but we must do so I suppose. Of course you will not repel the idea he advances

any more decidedly than necessary and will speak of protection to our people very distinctly indeed.

We don't want *him* to have any excuse for saying that we are in the least unmindful of the duty that rests upon us—even if his country is backward in doing hers.[60]

Here as in all his statements on the subject, Cleveland obviously considered the Armenian Question to be the responsibility of the Great Powers, especially England, and he was critical of the failure of the Powers to fulfill their duty. Thus while Cleveland did not wish to rebuff the British offer and appear to sanction British inaction in the Armenian Question, he intended to make it very clear that, however much the United States might be willing to cooperate with Great Britain, she would limit her actions to protection of U.S. interests. Accordingly Olney wrote to Chamberlain that

> ...nothing would more gratify the mass of the American people than to stand side by side and shoulder to shoulder with England in support of a great cause—in a necessary struggle for the defense of human rights and the advancement of Christian civilization.
>
> That a great cause of this sort is now presented by unhappy Armenia I cannot doubt—not more can I doubt that the English people and the American people are as one in their sentiments in regard to it.[61]

Olney went on to make it clear, however, that the United States would not move from its traditional foreign policy, and that any intervention into the Turkish situation by the United States would be limited to the protection of American interests there. Nonetheless, an action by the United States in defense of the missionaries might be planned in conjunction with a British action for the Armenians.

> Now, American interests in Turkey are not pecuniarily enormous, but are nevertheless most warmly regarded and highly valued by the American people. ...If, therefore, England should now seriously set about putting the Armenian charnel-house in order, there can be little doubt that the United States would consider the moment opportune for vigorous exertion on behalf of American citizens and interests in Turkey. It would feel itself entitled to demand full indemnity for past injuries to them, as well as adequate security against the like injuries in the future. It would support such demands by all the physical force at its disposal—with the necessary result, I think, that its attitude would both morally and materially strengthen the hands of England. How valuable such incidental assistance might prove it is not, of course, easy to predict, but that it would be real and appreciable cannot, I think, fairly be doubted.[62]

Following the exchange of these noble sentiments, the proposal for joint American and British action in Armenia was quietly dropped.

President Cleveland may well have felt a basic affinity with the programs of the missionaries. His father had been a Presbyterian minister, and his brother had followed in their father's footsteps. Yet there is evidence that the President and his Secretary of State shared some skepticism about the claims coming from the missionaries in Turkey; at one point Secretary of State Gresham, describing a conversation he had had with Cleveland about U.S. policy in Turkey, indicated to the British minister in Washington that "it was quite hopeless...to expect any degree of impartiality from missionaries or the Professors of Robert College." In the summer of 1896, however, at the recommendation of Secretary of State Olney, Cleveland read the book by the Duke of Argyle entitled *Our Responsibilities in Turkey*, which vividly described the Armenian massacres.[63] It was probably this book that occasioned Cleveland's remark about "this cursed Turkish question" and his more outspoken statements about the issue at the end of his administration.

In his final message to Congress, delivered in December 1896, Cleveland finally responded to persistent public demands that he publicly recognize the tragedy that had struck the Armenian people in Turkey. In the message he tried both to express the aspirations of the American people for an end to the violence in Turkey while at the same time justifying the administration's inaction. The importance of the issue is clear from the fact that Cleveland mentioned Turkey first in his address. Referring to the "continued and not infrequent reports of the wanton destruction of homes and the bloody butchery of men, women, and children, made martyrs to their profession of Christian faith," the President went on to express relief that no United States citizens had been either killed or wounded in the events there. He then suggested that:

> the deep feeling and sympathy that have been aroused among our people ought not to so far blind their reason and judgement as to lead them to demand impossible things. The outbreaks of blind fury which lead to murder and pillage in Turkey occur suddenly and without notice, and an attempt on our part to force such a hostile presence there as might be effective for prevention or protection would not only be resisted by the Ottoman Government, but would be regarded as an interruption of their plans by the great nations who assert their exclusive right to intervene in their own time and method for the security of life and property in Turkey.[64]

The President went on to note the presence of several naval vessels in the Mediterranean "as a measure of caution and to furnish all possible relief and refuge in case of emergency." He closed with an expression of optimism characteristic of the times, but showing him to have been a poor prophet:

> I do not believe that the present somber prospect in Turkey will be long permitted to offend the sight of Christendom. It so mars the humane and enlightened civilization that belongs to the close of the nineteenth century that it seems hardly possible that the earnest demand of good people throughout the Christian world for its corrective treatment will remain unanswered.[65]

The events of the 1890s indicate that the United States government believed its vital interests in Turkey were limited and that it did not wish to intervene in a foreign quarrel already complicated by the designs of the European powers. The more thoughtful American statesmen attempted to address the gulf between the desire of the citizens of the United States to help the downtrodden people of the world and the practical difficulties standing in the way of decisive action. Secretary of State Olney, who had limited U.S. actions in the face of the Armenian crisis to moving battleships about in Turkish waters when he was in office, argued once he was out of power that the United States should act more decisively in such instances. In a major foreign policy address delivered at Harvard College in March 1898, the former Secretary of State asserted that the United States had joined the ranks of the great powers and scorned a policy that did not go beyond "moral support."

> Do we want the Armenian butcheries stopped? To any power that will send its fleet through the Dardanelles and knock the Sultan's palace about his ears, we boldly tender our "moral support." We come to the rescue ourselves with not a gun, nor a man, nor a ship, with nothing but our "moral support."[66]

Two years later, arguing against intervention in the Philippines, Olney asserted that a policy of non-interference in the internal affairs of other nations should not prevent the United States from positive actions to relieve human suffering and to advance civilization. Clearly the U.S. failure to act more decisively in the Armenian case is on his mind:

> Should there, for example, be a recurrence of the Turkish massacres of Armenian Christians, not to stop them alone or in concert with others, could we do so without imperiling our own substantial interests, would be unworthy of us and inconsistent with our claims and aspirations as a great Power.[67]

Another American statesman of the period, Theodore Roosevelt, was particularly critical of the failure of the United States to act more forcefully during the Armenian crisis. In a speech made in 1897, when he was Assistant Secretary of the Navy, Roosevelt asserted:

> It is not only true that a peace may be so ignoble and degrading as to be worse than any war; it is also true that it may be fraught with more bloodshed than most wars. Of this there has been melancholy proof during the last two years...The peace of Europe has been preserved, while the Turk has been allowed to butcher the Armenians with hideous and unmentionable barbarity . . . No war of recent years, no matter how wanton, has been so productive of horrible misery as the peace which the powers have maintained during the continuance of the Armenian butcheries.[68]

Yet once President, Roosevelt was hardly more sympathetic to the Armenians than his predecessors had been, and not at all inclined to use force to support reform efforts in Turkey. His Secretaries of State, John Hay and Elihu Root, both dismissed petitions on behalf of the Armenians with arguments that the United States neither could nor should act in such cases.[69] Then, as now, it proved much easier for political leaders out of office to demand a foreign policy based on justice and humanity; once in power the same individuals tend to find pragmatic justifications for doing nothing.

Once the wave of violence against the Armenians had come to a halt in 1896, the entire issue was forgotten, for all practical purposes. That is to say, American missionaries continued their programs with the Armenians in Turkey as if nothing had happened; United States diplomats went on trying to preserve friendly relations with the Sultan; and events moved inexorably to the much greater catastrophe that struck the Armenian people in 1915, a catastrophe that found the American government once again unable or unwilling to intervene.

It is true that the traditional non-interventionist policy of the United States had been strongly tested by the threat to American institutions represented by the Turkish massacres of the Armenians during 1895. Beyond the immediate and obvious need to protect American citizens and their institutions, there was the moral question of saving the Armenian population of Turkey from destruction. The natural desire of an idealistic growing country to improve the human condition elsewhere on earth became overruled by the practical realization of the limits of power and the sovereign rights of nations.

The power of the United States has grown tremendously since the Cleveland administration, and foreign policy is no longer viewed in terms of the Monroe Doctrine. A vast body of international law and international institutions to enforce the law have developed. In a very basic sense, however, the dichotomy between the impulse to assist human beings in need anywhere in the world and the practical realization of the limitations in the foreign policy of even the most powerful nations continues to pose a moral dilemma for Americans seeking the establishment of a just and humane world order.

REFERENCES

1. The negotiations over U.S. participation in the Sassun investigation are described in the National Archives, Record Group 59, General Records of the Department of State, *Diplomatic Instructions*, Turkey 6, Microfilm 77, Roll 167, and *Diplomatic Despatches*, Turkey, Microfilm 46, Roll 57. Supplementary material can be found in Great Britain, *Further Correspondence Respecting Asiatic Turkey, 1894*, Confidential 6583, S830, F.O. 424, Vol. 178 (Microfilm).

2. Quoted in Gerald G. Eggert, *Richard Olney: Evolution of a Statesman* (Pennsylvania, 1974), 177.

3. Ernest R. May, *Imperial Democracy: The Emergence of America as a Great Power* (New York, 1961), 3. Among the many works on U.S. foreign policy in the 1890s are: David Healy, *U.S. Expansionism: The Imperialist Urge in the 1890s* (Madison, 1970); Richard Hofstadter, *Social Darwinism in American Thought* (New York, 1959); Harold U. Faulkner, *Politics, Reform, and Expansion, 1890-1900* (New York, 1959); and Robert L. Beisner, *Twelve Against Empire: The Anti-Imperialists, 1898-1900* (New York, 1968).

4. The other countries were Sweden, Belgium, and the Netherlands. May, *Imperial Democracy*, 3.

5. Leland James Gordon, *American Relations With Turkey, 1830-1930: An Economic Interpretation* (Philadelphia, 1932), 52-53.

6. Statistics are taken from "Tabular View of the Missions of the A.B.C.F.M. for the Year 1894-95" in *Missionary Herald*, 1896, 14. A basic history of the Protestant missions to Turkey can be found in Joseph L. Grabill, *Protestant Diplomacy and the Near East: Missionary Influence on American Policy, 1810-1927* (Minneapolis, 1971). The $6 million estimate of the value of the American Protestant investment in the Ottoman Empire is given in a letter written by Missionary H. O. Dwight, Enclosure #2, in *Diplomatic Despatches*, No. 742 (Dec. 29, 1895), M. 46, Roll 60.

7. Lloyd C. Griscom, *Diplomatically Speaking* (Boston, 1940), 134. Griscom was the Secretary to the U.S. Legation in Constantinople in the late 1890s and early 1900s.

8. The difficulties inherent in the policy of protecting the American missionary interests in the Ottoman Empire without jeopardizing friendly relations with the Sultan's Government are mentioned many times in the despatches of the U.S. Minister to the Ottoman Empire, Alexander W. Terrell. See for example the letter from Terrell to Assistant Secretary of State Alvin A. Adee in the U.S. National Archives, Record Group 59, General Records of the Department of State, *Diplomatic Despatches*, Turkey, Microfilm 46, Roll 60, Constantinople, December 1, 1895.

9. Adam Block, letter dated Feb. 28, 1895, in Great Britain, *Further Correspondence Respecting Asiatic Turkey, 1894*, Confidential, 6654, S830, F.O. 424, Vol 181, enclosure 5 in #227, 178-79.

10. "Alexander Watkins Terrell" in *The National Cyclopaedia of American Biography*, vol. 5 (New York, 1907), 555, and in *Who Was Who in America*, Vol 1, 1897-1942 (Chicago, 1966), 1223.

11. Griscom, *Diplomatically Speaking* (Boston, 1940), 168-9.

12. In 1894 the Sultan asked Terrell for three men from the United States: a professor of agriculture, a "practical man" to oversee an experimental farm, and a "first class man" to take charge of his School of Arts; later, the Sultan asked for an American to head a commercial college. The State Department did not pursue these requests energetically, much to Terrell's disappointment. Terrell reported in detail on the substance of his conversations with the Sultan in his despatches to the Secretary of State: see for example the Memoranda contained in Despatch No. 214 (Mar. 14, 1894). M. 46, Roll 56; Despatch No. 326 (Oct. 20, 1894), M. 46, Roll 56; Despatch No. 366 (Dec. 12, 1894), M. 46, Roll 57.

13. *Diplomatic Despatches*, No. 326 (Oct. 20, 1894), M. 46, Roll 56.

14. A candid assessment by Terrell of the need for a firm policy toward Turkey is in a letter dated Dec. 5, 1893; because of its unusual nature it was not given a number, but is included in *Diplomatic Despatches*, following No. 120, M. 46, Roll 55.

15. *Ibid.*, No. 680 (Nov. 18, 1895), M. 46, Roll 59; and No. 742 (Dec. 29, 1895), M. 46, Roll 60.

16. *Ibid.*, No. 280 (Aug. 2, 1894), M. 46, Roll 56.

17. *Diplomatic Despatches*, No. 452 (Mar. 4, 1895), M. 46, Roll 57. In August 1894, Terrell had suggested that the United States cooperate with other embassies in Constantinople to develop policies to protect the native Protestants (Despatch No. 280, Aug. 2, 1894, M. 46, Roll 56); in February 1895 he observed that the dragomen of the other powers met periodically to compare notes on the treatment of Christians (No. 439, Feb. 21, 1895, M. 46, Roll 57); in March he suggested that the United States participate in these sessions (No. 452, Mar. 4, 1895, M. 46, Roll 57); upon the negative reaction of the State Department he wrote in November 1895 that he would not participate in conferences of representatives of the Great Powers on means to stop the massacres unless so instructed by Washington (Telegram, Terrell to Olney, Nov. 16, 1895, in *Diplomatic Despatches*, M. 46, Roll 57).

18. *Ibid.*, No. 167 (Jan. 24, 1894), M. 46, Roll 55.

19. Letter from Terrell to Rev. Eli Corwin of Chicago, President of the Congregational Ministerial Union, enclosed in a personal letter, Terrell to Adee, Feb. 1, 1896, in *Diplomatic Despatches*, M. 46, Roll 61.

20. See, for example, *Diplomatic Despatches*, No. 645 (Oct. 15, 1895), M. 46, Roll 59.

21. Letter, Terrell to Dwight, Enclosure 2, No. 742 (Dec. 29, 1895), *Diplomatic Despatches*, M. 46, Roll 60.

22. In accordance with their policy of separation of church and state, the missionaries avoided Turkish officials as much as possible. Terrell was proud of the fact that he had taken Dr. Edward Riggs, an American missionary serving in Marsovan, to visit the Grand Vizier: "I took him to the Porte that they might see the manner of men they were suspecting," he wrote of the Turkish officials (*Diplomatic Despatches*, No. 60, Sept. 18, 1893, M. 46, Roll 55).

23. *Diplomatic Despatches*, No. 639 (Oct. 8, 1895), M. 46, Roll 59.

24. "Report of the Secretary of State," Dec. 19, 1985, in *Foreign Relations 1895*, 1262. In the same report, Secretary Olney estimated that there were 172 American missionaries in Asia Minor and, taking into account U.S. business and professional persons and their families, a total of no less than five or six hundred U.S. citizens residing in the Turkish Empire.

25. Missionary Henry O. Dwight wrote in 1895: "In Turkey, one consul can hold in check, without lifting a finger, a horde of ruffians. He is like a policeman in a mob." *Foreign Relations, 1895*, 1457.

26. "Report of the Secretary of State," *Foreign Relations, 1895*, 1262-63; Despatches No. 567 (Jul. 8, 1895), M. 46, Roll 58.

27. There is a voluminous literature on the massacres of 1894-96. Several eyewitness accounts by the missionaries are in *Foreign Relations, 1895* and *1896*; these are particularly valuable for the accounts of the destruction of missionary property. The best estimates of the losses in the massacres are probably those made by Clara Barton's relief team, who reported soon after distributing relief supplies in Asia Minor that 120,000 people had been killed in the massacres (mostly men) and another 80,000 died as a result of starvation and disease that followed the massacres (reported by Terrell in No. 924, July 21, 1896, *Diplomatic Despatches*, M. 46, Roll 61). An assessment of the sources is in Robert Melson "A Theoretical Inquiry into the Armenian Massacres of 1894-96" in *Comparative Studies in Society and History* 24: 3 (July 1982), 481-509.

28. The United States at this time was pressuring the Turkish government to keep its promise to issue a permit for the American missionary college located in Marsovan. *Ibid.*, No. 62 (Sep. 19, 1893), M. 46, Roll 55.

29. Terrell's requests for the presence of ships in Turkish waters continued his initial reference in Sept. 1893 (see Note 17 above). The recommendation that Smyrna be made a naval station is in *Foreign Relations, 1895*, 1248.

30. *Foreign Relations, 1895*, Herbert to Gresham, 1245.

31. *Ibid.*, 1245-51, 1420.

32. *Diplomatic Despatches*, No. 511 (Apr. 21, 1895), M. 46, Roll 58.

33. *Foreign Relations, 1895*, Gresham to Mavroyeni Bey, 1248 and Uhl to Mavroyeni Bey, 1251.

34. *Ibid.*, 1354.

35. Selections from the naval reports are in *Foreign Relations, 1895*, 1244-49.

36. *Missionary Herald*, in July 1895, 265.

37. *Diplomatic Despatches*, No. 716 (Dec. 10, 1895) and no. 767 (Jan. 11, 1896), M. 46, Roll 60.

38. *Ibid.*, No. 685 (Nov. 21, 1895), M. 46, Roll 60; *Diplomatic Instructions*, Telegram, Olney to Terrell, Dec. 5, 1895, M. 77 Roll 167; *Diplomatic Despatches*, Telegram, Terrell to Olney, Dec. 6, 1895, M. 46, Roll 60.

39. McAdoo to Terrell, *Foreign Relations, 1895*, 1422.

40. In a letter to the Rev. John P. Peters of St. Michael's Church in New York City, missionary Henry O. Dwight said that he personally opposed the plan to bombard Smyrna "because it will harm more Christians than Turks" and suggested that the U.S. Navy should seize one of the Turkish islands, preferably Rhodes (Enclosure in letter from Peters to Olney, Mar. 21, 1896, Olney Papers, Library of Congress, #8568-69).

41. Olney Papers, Library of Congress, #7819-21.

42. *Ibid.*, #8256-57.

43. U.S., *Congressional Record*, 55th Congress, 2nd Session, Dec. 7, 1896 to Mar. 10, 1897. The movement in the United States protesting Turkish atrocities directed at the Armenians is described in Robert Mirak, *Between Two Lands: Armenians in America, 1890 to World War I* (Cambridge, Mass., 1983), 211-27.

44. *Congressional Record*, Senate, Dec. 3, 1894.

45. *Foreign Relations, 1894*, 714-15.

46. *Foreign Relations, 1895*, 1255-1266.

47. The Resolution and Senate debate is in *Congressional Record*, 54th Congress, 1st Session, 959-964, Jan. 24, 1896; the House Debate is in *Ibid.*, 1000-1016, Jan. 27, 1896.

48. The Republican Platform of 1896 is in *National Party Platforms*, vol. 1, 1840-1956, compiled by David Bruce Johnson (Revised edition, Urbana, 1978), 108.

49. The lack of missionary fatalities was due partly to luck; at Kharpert after part of the mission had been destroyed and the missionaries were left completely defenseless, a crazed Muslim appeared and fired a gun point blank at two of the missionaries. Either because of his frenzied state or because of his lack of marksmanship, the Turk missed, and the missionaries miraculously escaped harm. The incident is described in a letter dated Nov. 19, 1895 from missionary Caleb F. Gates to Terrell, enclosure 1 in No. 705 (Dec. 4, 1895), Terrell to Olney, *Foreign Relations, 1896*, 1373.

50. Letters, Terrell to Olney, Terrell to Dwight, both enclosed in No. 742 (Dec. 29, 1895), *Diplomatic Despatches*, M. 46, Roll 60.

51. As early as the summer of 1895, Edwin M. Bliss, a former missionary and author, wrote to Cleveland suggesting that the Minister to the Ottoman Empire in the first Cleveland Administration, Oscar S. Straus, replace Terrell in Constantinople: "It would be, we all feel, not only unjust but unwise to replace him [i.e. Terrell] except by someone who by reason of experience and peculiar adaptation would be sure to fill the place better." (A copy of Bliss's letter, dated Aug. 21, 1895, is in the Olney Papers, Library of Congress, #5761-62.) In the spring of 1896 the campaign opened in earnest; a delegation including missionary H. O. Dwight and prominent missionary supporter William E. Dodge met with the President on May 15 to ask for "a different order of diplomatic ability at Constantinople." (Dwight's letter to Terrell describing the interview is in the Olney Papers, Library of Congress, #9350-53.) There is no evidence that Cleveland ever considered replacing Terrell.

52. *Diplomatic Despatches*, No. 933 (July 20, 1896), M. 46, Roll 61.

53. *Diplomatic Despatches*, Telegram, Terrell to Olney (Dec. 4, 1895), M. 46, Roll 60; *Diplomatic Instructions*, Telegram (Jan. 6, 1895), M. 77, Roll 167; *Diplomatic Despatches*, No. 770 (Jan. 14, 1895), M. 46, Roll 60; Telegram, Terrell to Olney (Feb. 1, 1896), M. 46, Roll 61; No. 804 (Feb. 7, 1896) and No. 830 (Feb. 27, 1896), M. 46, Roll 61.

54. *Diplomatic Despatches*, Telegram, Terrell to Olney (Aug. 25, 1896), M. 46, Roll 61.

55. *Ibid.*, No. 964 (Aug. 26, 1896), M. 46, Roll 61.

56. *Ibid.*, Telegram, Terrell to Olney (Oct. 8, 1896); Despatch 1016 (Oct. 9, 1896), M. 46, Roll 61.

57. *Ibid.*, No. 1030 (Oct. 23, 1896); No. 1031 (Oct. 24, 1896), confidential, M. 46, Roll 61.

58. *Ibid.*, No. 1031 (Oct. 24, 1896), confidential, M. 46, Roll 61.

59. The exchange of correspondence between Chamberlain and Olney on the Armenian Question is printed in Chapter II, Appendix E of Alfred L. P. Dennis, *Adventures in American Diplomacy, 1896-1906* (New York, 1928), 58-62.

60. Olney Papers, Library of Congress, Container 153, Reel #59, Cleveland to Olney, Sept. 24, 1896.

61. Dennis, *Adventures*, 60.

62. *Ibid.*, 60-61.

63. Olney Papers, Library of Congress, Olney to Cleveland, July 11, 1896. The report of the British Ambassador is in Great Britain, *Further Correspondence*, Confidential 6583, S830, F.O. 424, Vol. 178, Goschen to Kimberly, Dec. 3, 1894.

64. *Foreign Relations, 1896*, xviii "Message of the President," Dec. 7, 1896.

65. *Ibid.*, xix.

66. "International Isolation of the United States," *Atlantic Monthly*, Vol. LXXXI, No. 487 (May 1898), 577-88.

67. "Growth of Our Foreign Policy," *Ibid.*, Vol. LXXXV, No. 509 (Mar. 1900), 289-301.

68. *The Works of Theodore Roosevelt*, Vol. XIII (New York, 1926), 184-85.

69. Dennis, *Adventures*, 465.

Britain as World Policeman: The Armenian Case And the Failure of Moral Imperatives

Christopher J. Walker

The moral force of British imperialism in the last quarter of the nineteenth century was undeniable. Across the world thousands of public servants were loyally and impartially administering peoples of an astonishing diversity, settling disputes in accordance with the typical British principles of justice and fair play, bringing the benefits of European civilization, and above all bringing peace. The presence of missionaries and Anglican clergymen attested to the moral basis of the far-flung imperial rule of Britain; and by her forthright actions, courage, and strength she proved that she, of all nations, had that indefinable quality—leadership. The vast respect paid to her, expressed in the homage paid to the sovereign person of Queen Victoria at her two jubilees, demonstrated this. By the turn of the century, there was something almost inevitable, and seemingly effortless, about British rule; it hardly seems surprising that a number of non-Britons, and many of the British people themselves, believed that British rule was God-given.

Yet, as so often, the picture which seems reassuring is less clearly in focus under examination. The will, expressed from many quarters, to believe that British rule was somehow ideal should not disguise its true nature. Certainly, by 1875, there was a moral element in the British Empire. But it was only one of the elements of British rule; it often ranked low in foreign policy priorities, and therefore, it is important to weigh the others beside it.

Initially the British Empire had a moral content of nil. In the sixteenth century England undertook imperial adventures for the sake only of trade and plunder. She did not even claim the dubious morality of seeking to impose a "true faith" on unbelievers. In the following century English imperial activities took on largely the aspect of colonization and settlement, sometimes, as here in Massachusetts, with a high moral tone. During the eighteenth century the nature of Britain's ventures was almost wholly commercial: the expansion of the sugar plantations, and the secure establishment of rule in India, were commercial enterprises, the former underpinned by extensive use of slave labor. The city of Bristol, in the west of England, was built almost wholly through profits created by slaves on sugar plantations.

However, when land has become British, it demanded defense, and could not be relinquished without loss of face. The consequent strategic considerations changed the complexion of the operation from a freebooter's adventure to a situation replete with aggressive and competitive considerations.

Despite the enormous profits made by the British Empire in the eighteenth century though slavery, and the acceptance and justification of slavery by all types of moral thinkers, Britain staged a remarkable moral about-face, and she (or rather sections of her society) led the campaign to abolish slavery. The names of the individuals are well known; but we should recall that Prime Ministers Pitt, Castlereagh, and Palmerston were personally opposed to slavery. Castlereagh was the prime mover of the declaration at the Congress of Vienna (1815) which formally condemned the slave trade, and his attitude was reinforced in succeeding decades by Palmerston. In a remarkable speech in July 1844 Palmerston spoke of his horror of the slave trade—of the night-time raids on peaceful villages, the seizure of the inhabitants, compelling the slaves "to barter their liberty for a few drops of water." He went on to describe the horrors of the starved march to the coast, in words curiously prophetic of those used in eyewitness accounts of what occurred in Turkish Armenia in 1915.

Palmerston's morality—some would dispute that it was such—was an aesthetic morality; he found the idea of suffering unattractive, not wrong it itself. Yet it almost certainly laid the foundation for the notion of Britain as a moral participant in international affairs. Sterner morality, which spread itself widely and deeply through almost all classes of British society, emerged principally with the rise of the Nonconformists; the influence of the Christian Socialists and the Tractarians was considerable, too. All these groups sought a higher standard of public morality, and many found a political home in the ranks of the Liberal Party.

The moral climate at home became more clearly defined; at the same time there was a tendency for British officials overseas to assume more responsibility than they actually had. As an end result of this process, perhaps we could think of Consul Graves's account of his time in the Erzurum Consulate in 1892 to 1898, or of the exertions of Major C.H.M. Doughty Wylie during the Adana massacre of April 1909. In both cases these British representatives showed an attention to the public good beyond their duty. Perhaps they, and others like them, encouraged the populations around them to believe that the whole British nation was as impartial, morally upright, and dedicated to justice as they as individuals were. Britain unquestionably had some fine public servants at this time; and their principles can probably be traced, at source, to the British educational system, which stressed discipline, self-reliance, and leadership—virtues similar to those of the Roman republic.

These then were some of the roots of Britain's moral stance in world affairs. Now, ranged against such tendencies were formidable elements, principally that by the late nineteenth century Britain's empire had at the same time within it constituents of desire for commercial gain, and to maintain national pride and prestige, to a commensurate level with any other. Of course at various times there were doubting voices from men of all parties, who saw the acquisition of colonies an encumbrance and a handicap; but where such tendencies had appeared among the Tories, these were swept away by Disraeli's election victory of 1874, which signalled the adoption of a forward and expansive foreign policy. Within the ranks of the Liberals, there were obviously far more doubters about Empire; but these lost their voice after the British had effectively seized control of Egypt in 1882, and more so after the 1885 debacle of General Gordon in the Sudan. Thereafter, the new breed of Liberals—men such as Lord Rosebery, Joseph Chamberlain, and Edward Grey—enthusiastically embraced the expansion of Empire. With the expansion of Empire, strategic and commercial considerations almost always overrode moral issues such as misrule of remote people. Keeping intact and strengthening the existing defenses—a factor often beyond the bland phrase "maintaining the balance of power"—became paramount, and international morality was reduced in importance.

For those who had little time for morality in international affairs, the new mood was congenial. And let us remember that throughout the allegedly moral epoch of the nineteenth century, there were many who believed that moral issues had little or no place in international affairs, where there was a clash with what they saw as the vital interests of England. Such men had always clustered around support for Ottoman Turkey. The Duke of Wellington "hated Navarino," the sea battle that resulted in the destruction of the Ottoman fleet through the joint efforts of Britain, France and Russia. Palmerston, despite his worthy support for the abolition of slavery, allowed himself to be drawn into blind support for Turkey through the basest of political motives, rivalry and jealousy of other powers. Disraeli threw all his diplomatic support behind Turkey, believing her backing to be vital for his prospect of Empire, and driven by a florid vision of Britain's imperial grandeur, in which considerations of the oppressed and misruled had no part. In the background were supporters of Turkey and the Turks like David Urquhart, whose personal devotion to all things Turkish bordered on the obsessional. Support for Turkey ran wide and deep through certain sections of British public life. To such men Ottoman Turkey was seen as a barrier to Russian expansion and was also an excellent market for British goods. After 1854 investment in Ottoman bonds provided a highly competitive rate of interest. The Ottoman Empire was seen as a high risk investment. These attitudes have to be understood before Britain's proclaimed and often self-proclaimed quality of "fair play" is accepted at face value.

Now what of Gladstone, the arch-moralist of the period? There is no denying the loftiness, even splendor, of his moral principles and commitment, derived from a dedicated High Anglicanism. He viewed Eastern Christians with fellow feeling, as separated brethren. Conversely, at least from 1876 onwards, he viewed the Ottoman Empire with a kind of demonic hatred, as though it were an earthly manifestation of the power of evil—a sentiment which was cordially returned to him by Sultan Abdul-Hamid. Gladstone's attitude derived partly from his contempt for the tyranny that the Ottoman Empire represented, and partly, too, because it was a Muslim power oppressing Christians. In a medieval manner, dangerous because it was unrealistic, he believed in "Christendom." It was not until after the Ottoman Bank Incident in 1896 that Gladstone spoke in terms of universal principles; and the mixture of Liberal and theological sentiments with which, prior to 1896, he viewed the Eastern Question seems to have weakened his ability to get to grips with it, either in attacking the pro-Turkish policies of the Conservatives, or later in dealing with the Sublime Porte itself when he was prime minister. Theology can be a good background guide to political questions—one thinks of the practical compassion of Bishop Harold Buxton—but it is of little practical benefit if a politician believes that he is actually wrestling with Satan.

That Gladstone's opponents, the Conservatives, were unmoved by moral considerations is not a matter for surprise; they were at this time straightforward expansionist imperialists. The change of Article 16 of the San Stefano Treaty into Article 61 of the Berlin Treaty is entirely consistent with their posture, as is the breaking of the Concert of Europe over the Berlin Memorandum and the Cyprus Convention, both of which were done so that Britain could gain a preeminent position in Near Eastern affairs. All this is the business of imperialism. They did not even bother to dress it up in lofty statements, as more recent imperialists have gilded their actions to extend their power. A more interesting question is: why did the Gladstone administration, which succeeded in 1880, do nothing to improve the Armenian situation—indeed, leave it worse off when it left office in 1885?

In the conduct of foreign affairs, Gladstone believed passionately in the Concert of Europe; there would be international disorder unless the powers worked together. This was his first principle. Thus he hated Disraeli's rejection of the Berlin Memorandum (by which all the powers had unitedly urged reforms on the Porte); and he castigated the Cyprus Convention as an "insane covenant." However, at first glance the Convention had a lot to recommend it; in its second paragraph the sultan "promises to England to introduce necessary reforms . . . for the protection of the Christian and other subjects of the Porte in these territories." ("These territories" meant Turkish Armenia.) However, Gladstone saw only the theoretical structure of the Convention, not its provisions; he saw it as the breaking of the Concert of Europe, and provoking the jealousy of other powers. Britain was stepping out of line, and no good would result from this. Gladstone recalled that the kingdom of Greece had been created by the agreement of the powers, and that only thus could there be effective action.

> There is this to be said—that some good has been done in the East of Europe and that, as far as any good has been done in the East of Europe by the Western Powers, it has been done entirely by European concert. The existence of the Kingdom of Greece is before us a monument of what could be obtained by European concert; for, although it was not unanimous action, yet it was action in which three of the greatest Powers of Europe were active and were united, and in which no Power of Europe was opposed. If that is so, is it not fair and reasonable to say that this principle of concert, which has, at least, produced one great triumph of humanity—freedom and justice in the East, and opened a great door of hope for the whole of one race in the East, is an instrument that ought to be tried, at least, until you can point to some other instrument which

has achieved results equally memorable and equally good. That is the mode in which we view the principle of the European concert without at all pretending to set it up as one of certain and infallible result, but, at the same time, saying that it is one which undoubtedly, so long as it can be maintained, carries with it by far the greatest amount of moral authority—which gives the fairest promise of excluding jealousy and ill-will, and which has something at least to point to on the page of history better than we can hope to achieve by sole and separate action. We shall, undoubtedly, endeavor to act on that principle—to work along with that combination which we feel to represent the moral authority of Christendom, the greatest moral authority in the world.

Consequently Gladstone did what he could to weaken and diminish the Convention when he was in power—such as removing the military consuls from Anatolia and Turkish Armenia in 1882. But this was not a way back to the united Concert of Europe, for if there is one general lesson to be learned from politics, it is that there is no way back to a former situation, there is only a way forward to a new set of international alignments; and all that the removal of the consuls meant was that the Armenians were more unprotected than before and the divisions between the sections of the population were greater. Britain had raised the hopes of the Armenians, dangerously so in view of the theological nation of Gladstone's utterances, and could now do little or nothing for them. Sometimes, in political life, it seems that theoretical objections have to be abandoned in favor of working with the actual situation on the ground. This Gladstone did not do.

The situation which was developing in the 1880s was not conducive to any concerted action. All the powers were engaged in scrambling for territory in Africa. Bismarck's Germany ostentatiously and deliberately refused to join the Concert of Europe on the matter of Armenian reforms. The matter rested, until Sultan Abdul-Hamid's creation of the Hamidieh cavalry, together with the Sassun rebellion, forced the issue into the open again. Yet if the spirit of Navarino had been dead when Gladstone had earnestly sought to revive it in the 1880s, how much more so was it in the 1890s. Lord Salisbury, who was in some ways a greater moralist than Gladstone, since he did not indulge in exaggerated rhetoric, or make statements which raised people's hopes unrealistically, was perplexed by the same problem: how to bring about action in the Ottoman Empire, a region in which were found so many rivalries and jealousies of the powers. Salisbury wanted action (and action, not words, is the hallmark of morality); even the German Kaiser was prepared to see a partition of Turkey after the Constantinople massacre that succeeded the Ottoman Bank incident in 1896. But—and here we should cast our minds back sadly to Navarino, seventy years earlier—Russia and France, the two powers which in 1827 had collaborated with Britain in destroying the Turkish fleet, were opposed to action. In Russia, intervention was opposed by two successive arch-reactionary Foreign Ministers, Lobanov-Rostovskii and Shishkin, who saw the Armenians as dangerously permeated with revolutionary sentiments; France was bound by a treaty relationship with Russia, and furthermore held sixty-one percent of the Ottoman Public Debt, and the continuation of high rates of interest for her bourgeoisie was placed above support for the life-or-death struggle of the Armenians. So Salisbury, unwilling to act alone, even though the Ottoman Empire was no longer seen, as it had been two decades earlier, as the key to Britain's Indian possessions, did nothing. And Gladstone? In his famous last speech given in Liverpool at the age of 87, he cast aside the idol that he had worshipped in foreign affairs for fifty years and urged Salisbury to break with the Concert of Europe and act alone. Here indeed was a reversal, and an acknowledgement that this policy was bankrupt so long as the other parties, for various reasons, none of them creditable, were content to avoid action and let things stay the way they were. The Concert of Europe, so admirable at Navarino, so full of potential after the Crimean War, had in fact been a dead duck these last twenty years. Why? Because the powers themselves were not animated by any spirit of cooperation or compromise, and without those two qualities no solution was possible. Starting with Disraeli's grandiose visions of Empire, from which there derived his strong support for Turkey, and leading on to the rush of all the powers for territory and commercial privileges, turning Africa and Asia into a gigantic thieves' kitchen, the Concert of Europe had become a sham. It worked only when imperial ambitions were restrained, and when there was a consensus among the powers that the general good, or indeed the specific good—in this context, the protection of the Armenians—was more desirable than satisfaction of exclusively national goals.

The Armenians too, it must be said, continued to believe in the ultimate benevolence of the European powers, despite all the evidence to the contrary, and Article 61 of the Berlin Treaty was invoked right up to the First World War. And while it was clear that Russia was, despite reactionaries like Lobanov-Rostovskii, von Plehve, and Prince Golitsyn, the best prospect for the secure advancement of Armenians, many influential Armenians continued to look for support from western Europe, especially from Britain and France, and expressed surprise when it was not forthcoming—despite Britain's long-standing strategic support of Turkey and France's enthusiasm for dividends from the empty coffers of Constantinople. A number of Armenians, too, seem to have accepted the propaganda of Britain and France and the rest that these powers were bringing what they called "civilization" to the world, when they were carving it up for themselves, as territory and minerals, creating rivalries and jealousies and fostering an aggressive spirit of competitiveness, which effectively prevented the Concert of Europe from functioning.

Nothing happened to benefit Armenians during the High Noon of imperialism; but with the Young Turk revolution there was a chance for a new start. A more conciliatory spirit had created the Triple Entente. There was a chance that the Turkish Revolution of 1908, if guided along the pathways of constitutionalism and democracy, might have fulfilled the high hopes which were raised by the revolt in Macedonia. True democracy in the Ottoman Empire, such as animated the country in the first month or so after the revolution, would have solved the Armenian question better than any amount of foreign interference, which was deeply insulting to Turkish sensibilities. The revolution needed guidance and support if it was to succeed. The populace instinctively looked to Britain, as if subliminally recognizing that, whatever her shortcomings, the British system of constitutional government was the best guarantee of internal freedoms. The cheering which greeted the arrival of the somewhat bemused new British ambassador, Sir Gerard Lowther, after the revolution, betokened a trust and a hope in Britain. Yet Britain turned away from this chance to make up for her inaction, despite an astonishing fund of goodwill shown to her in July/August 1908. In a confidential despatch of more than usually harsh cynicism, Foreign Secretary Sir Edward Grey spelt out to the British ambassador why Britain should distance herself from the Turkish revolution. He wrote:

> If Turkey really establishes a constitution and keeps it on its feet, and becomes strong herself, the consequences will reach further than any of us can yet foresee. The effect in Egypt will be tremendous, and will make itself felt in India. Hitherto, wherever we have had Mohammedan subjects, we have been able to tell them that the subjects in the countries ruled by the head of their religion were under a despotism which was benevolent. Those Mohammedans who have had any opportunity of comparing the conditions of those ruled by us, have generally been ready to admit the difference in our favor. But if Turkey now establishes a Parliament and improves her government, the demand for a constitution in Egypt will gain great force, and our power of resisting the demand will be very much diminished. If, when there is a

Turkish constitution, in good working order, we are engaged in suppression by force and shooting a rising in Egypt of people who demand a constitution, the position will be very awkward. It would never do for us to get into conflict on the subject of Egypt, not with the Turkish government, but with the feeling of the Turkish people.

Thus Britain, fearful for the mood of her imperial subjects, turned away yet again from a chance to assist, indirectly, the Armenians. And the result? The Prussianization of the Committee of Union and Progress, which Ambassador Morgenthau describes so clearly in his memoirs. Germany was all too happy to step in where Britain feared to tread—and would treat the constitution as she wished. As we know, within two years the constitution was seen by all parties to be a sham. A mood quickly grew among Turks which changed from seeing Armenians as colleagues who had helped overthrow the sultan's tyranny to viewing them virtually as sub-human objects who stood in the way of a grand imperial design known as pan-Turkism.

During World War I Britain, cut off from the Armenians physically by the war, was nevertheless close to them in their time of tragedy diplomatically and politically. The publication of the Blue Book, *The Treatment of Armenians in the Ottoman Empire*, testifies to that, a work which is of continuing relevance in the Armenian debate, since it provides some of the clearest and most irrefutable evidence of what happened in 1915 and early 1916. Perhaps Britain would have shown her concern for Armenians more if she had forced a landing at Alexandretta in 1915; but there were sound strategic reasons for her not doing so, and these, in war, are always paramount.

During the war, leaders in Britain and other allied countries made powerful statements in favor of the Armenians. Prime Minister Asquith promised "an era of liberty and redemption for this ancient people." A fine promise; but already the word "redemption" should give us a warning signal. Where does one usually find the word "redemption"? In this sense, in church, not in the context of international affairs, and not in the day-to-day business of peasants and traders in their towns and villages. No person looking at the hard realities of life for Armenians would use that word. Asquith, in fact, was speaking theologically, to appear to himself and to his audience to be solemnly and incontrovertibly good—for there are few things that a politician appears to like more, stuck deep in a morally unclear world full of compromise and grey areas, than to show evidence, widely acknowledged, of moral uprightness. The trouble is that for most of them the mere saying of it, with the attendant ten-feet-tall feeling as the crowds cheer, is sufficient; and they do not bother to undertake any course of action that will transform words into deeds. Words uttered spiritually by politicians almost always remain in the world of the spirit; it is noticeable in the Armenian context that the men who were real believers, like Bishop Buxton and Reverend Harcourt, eschewed the language of saving souls (least of all their own) for a stark and simple portrayal of the harsh world around them. English clergymen after 1921 were able with remarkable facility to cooperate with the Soviet regime in Yerevan, whereas the show-Christian politicians of Western Europe were uttering anathemas against Bolshevik barbarism, and by implication praising their own civilized selves. And what were their actions at this time, at least as far as Britain was concerned? Withholding money from practical schemes to resettle Armenian refugees in the Ararat region. Of all the British politicians who showed a gap between words and deeds, who spoke highly and acted (or failed to act) basely, none exceeded David Lloyd George. On all kinds of domestic and foreign issues Lloyd George's reputation has been steadily slipping during the past twenty years. On Britain's moral failure in previous years with regard to the Armenians, he himself wrote:

> The treaty of San Stefano provided that Russian troops should remain in occupation of the Armenian provinces until satisfactory reforms were carried out. By the treaty of Berlin (1878)—which was entirely due to our minatory pressure and which was acclaimed by us as a great British triumph which brought "Peace with honor"—that article was superseded. Armenia was sacrificed on the triumphal altar we had erected. The Russians were forced to withdraw; the wretched Armenians were once more placed under the heel of their old masters, subject to a pledge to "introduce ameliorations and reforms into the provinces inhabited by Armenians." We all know how these pledges were broken for forty years, in spite of repeated protests from the country that was primarily responsible for restoring Armenia to Turkish rule. The action of the British government led inevitably to the terrible massacres of 1895-1897, 1909, and worst of all to the holocaust of 1915. ... regard to the part we had taken in making these outrages possible, we were morally bound to take the first opportunity that came our way to redress the wrong we had perpetrated, and in so far as it was in our power, to make it impossible to repeat the horrors for which history will always hold us culpable.

It almost convinces us. But convinced we must not be, for despite its rhetoric, the postwar period was as somber as ever for Armenians, perhaps more so; and in Britain the administration was that of Lloyd George, offering half-promise of support, yet still unwilling to act for them though with the power to do so. Action would have meant providing troops and giving diplomatic support, yet none was forthcoming. Innumerable were the excuses found for not giving real assistance to Armenians; and the new version of the breakdown of the Concert of Europe—rivalry between Britain and France in the Near East beginning in earnest in late 1919 and developing with rancor on both sides—killed off any chance of positive action. In the end British and French influence was ousted from the Caucasus, and the world of Soviet Armenia and Kemalist Turkey supervened. Nothing at all had been done by the western powers to bring any real support to Armenia apart from the generosity of individual citizens of those powers in providing relief, after the terrible losses of 1915-1916. The international morality of the Europeans, which was already low down on their list of priorities, turned out to be, by 1923, no more than a form of words.

Can any general principles be extrapolated from looking at the moral issues of Britain's involvement with the Armenian case? I think they can. In the first place moral considerations, though they may exist in a nation's outlook, come a long way down the list of diplomatic priorities. A government will always secure its perceived strategic and economic necessities before righting wrongs, however terrible and widely acknowledged these wrongs will be. Most governments will tend to disregard lobbies which are neutral or opposed to their central policies, unless the lobby itself is astute, strong, and clear-headed enough to compel its policy on to the government. Support for Armenians ran widely among sections of the British establishment and people at the time when Britain was a powerful nation, but never widely enough. Turkey and the Turks always had plenty of supporters, especially among Conservatives and military men. Their arguments were never examined or refuted with vigor, nor was their sentiment understood. And the supporters of the Armenians do not seem to have emphasized the right things, nor to have been on occasion confrontational enough to gain the necessary support for their cause.

In the second place, when in an imperial nation with international responsibilities a leader of genuine moral convictions emerges, who is or may be prepared to put into practice what he believes, he will gain nothing if the spirit of the times is one of aggressive competitive anarchy. No one listened to the rights and wrongs of the Armenian situation when the national policies of the great powers were those of self-aggrandizement through imperial adventure. A different spirit had prevailed in the 1820s, when the powers were able to achieve a measure of harmony over Greece, and set her free. Without this spirit of global harmony, the consensus which was a necessary concomitant of any attempt to do right on the international scale was missing.

Nevertheless, none of this lessens the fact that there was a moral failure, indeed several moral failures, across the forty-five years from 1878. Because of her power, and because of her primacy in international affairs, Britain must bear much of the responsibility; but at the same time we should never ignore the actions and policies of the other powers, which often either were directly hostile to Armenian interests or created an international climate that frustrated the legitimate settlement of Armenian claims.

BIBLIOGRAPHICAL NOTE

On the growth of the British Empire, see the relevant volumes of *The Cambridge History of British Foreign Policy*. Palmerston's speech of July 1844 is partially quoted in Jasper Ridley, *Lord Palmerston* (London, 1972), 403. A.J.P. Taylor's *The Trouble Makers* (London, 1957) is the best guide to the Nonconformists and the Christian Socialists. Consul Graves's account of the Erzurum Consulate appears in *Storm Centres of the Near East: Personal Memories 1879-1929* (London, 1933), chapters 6-9. Doughty Wylie's reports from Adana are to be found in Great Britain, Public Record Office (FO 424/219), 80-92. On the growth of Liberal Imperialism, see C.J.H. Hayes, *A Generation of Materialism* (London, 1963), 216 ff. G.D. Clayton, *Britain and the Eastern Question* (London, 1971) has material on the Near Eastern policies of Wellington and Palmerston (pages 54, 61-79).

On Disraeli, see George Earle Buckle, *Life of Disraeli* (London, 1920), vol. VI, 1-368. On Gladstone, see R.T. Shannon, *Gladstone and the Bulgarian Agitation, 1876* (London, 1963) and the same author's biography of Gladstone, in progress; also the relevant volumes of *The Gladstone Diaries*, edited by H.C.G. Matthew, in progress. Gladstone's views on the Eastern Question can be found in his *Political Speeches in Scotland*, 2 vols. (Edinburgh, 1880). His speech in the House of Commons of July 23, 1880, is in *Hansard*, 3rd series, vol. 254, cols. 1289-90. On the ineffectiveness of concert diplomacy in the 1895-96 crisis, see M.S. Anderson, *The Eastern Question, 1774-1923* (London, 1966), 255-59. Gladstone's Liverpool speech can be found in full in the *Liverpool Daily Post*, September 25, 1896. The reception accorded to Sir Gerard Lowther as British ambassador in Constantinople is described in Sir Edwin Pears, *Forty Years in Constantinople* (London, 1916), 238, 241. Sir Edward Grey's seminal dispatch to Lowther appears in Great Britain, Foreign Office, *British Documents on the Origins of the War, 1898-1914*, eds. G.P. Gooch and Harold Temperley (London, 1928), vol. V, 263.

Ambassador Henry Morgenthau's account of the growth of German influence among the Young Turks is in chapters 1-4 of his memoirs, published in London with the title *Secrets of the Bosphorus* and in Garden City, N.Y., entitled *Ambassador Morgenthau's Story* (1919). The quotation from Asquith's Guildhall speech appears in Akaby Nassibian, *Britain and the Armenian Question, 1915-1923* (London, 1984), 110. Harold Buxton's relations with the Bolsheviks are touched on in his *Trans-Caucasia* (London, 1926). Lloyd George's deceptive words on the Armenians appear in his *The Truth about the Peace Treaties* (London, 1938), vol. 2, 1256-57.

The State's Crime: On the Subject of the Armenian and Jewish Genocides

Yves Ternon[*]

Genocide is a particular type of mass murder which cannot be perpetrated without the approval, and the direct intervention, of the State. To eliminate a national minority, the support of the political party in power and the participation of all state institutions, their complicity, their submission, and their discretion is required at every stage, from the conception of the crime up to the execution. Genocide unites the "criminal" and the "political," amalgamating a marginality and a deviance. It is only in modern times that states have had the means to realize the desire to annihilate entire populations. The primary element of genocide is a monolithic political party which, in complete control of the state apparatus, transforms the illegal into the legal. The State, in the role of the criminal, possessor of an exorbitant power, is a monstrous beast, a behemoth. It bears no resemblance at all to the individual criminal who satisfies his personal needs in a haphazard fashion. War provides the opportunity to perpetrate this heinous crime by freeing the State from the monitorial watch of other nations. The two world wars that have bloodstained our century gave two sovereign states—the Ottoman Empire ruled by the Ittihat and Germany under the heel of the Nazi Party—the chance to exterminate those Armenians and those Jews who found themselves subjected to their power. Theirs was a crime designated since 1944 by the name "genocide," a crime judicially defined in 1948 by the United Nations and one that has been since 1948 outlawed.

Several jurists have protested the use of the word genocide and have replaced it with the phrase "crime against humanity." In fact,

---

[*]Translated by Julie Korostoff

the word genocide does not account for all the aspects of the crime. In spite of this opposition, the use of the word has been consecrated by historians. The ultimate expression of genocide was found in the annihilation of European Judaism. To emphasize the singularity of this event,[1] survivors made a point of calling it the "Holocaust." This word, of Greek origin, describes total destruction caused by fire. It is used in the Old Testament to refer to a sacrificial victim who is to be burned alive. However there seems to be a contradiction between the religious fervor understood in "Holocaust" and the criminal wrath of Nazism. In any case, the historian must accept the designation of the genocide of the Jews by the word Holocaust, for here as well the word has prevailed.

The isolation of the Holocaust as a singular event that cannot be shared and that cannot be repeated risks impairing the preventive measures provided by a global analysis of the genocidal phenomenon. To claim exclusive rights in such a case would have dangerous implications and would go against the objective, that "never again" cried out as a sign of distress by the Holocaust survivors. "It becomes imperative" writes Irving Horowitz, "to understand the unified character of genocide, the common characteristics of its victims, and ultimately the need for alliances of victims and potential victims to resist all kinds of genocide."[2]

The two genocides, that of the Armenians and that of the Jews, bearing several common traits, can serve as models of twentieth century genocides. The same sickness, the same deviance, is present in both cases. The only real differences concern the personality of the sufferers from the sickness, the severity of the attack, and the environment. The number of Jewish victims totals many more than that of the Armenians: six million compared to 1,200,000. But the proportion of the entire nation subjected to amputation is almost equal: approximately one-half of each of these two populations was murdered. To try to go one better than someone else when the issue concerns death and suffering and to claim what is the most painful for oneself is a shameless indulgence. In the same way, to assume that the extermination of the Armenians and of the Jews was only one step further in the long history of their persecution would be admitting their nature as victims, assuming their behavior to be deviant, and implying their responsibility in the tragedy they suffered. No guilt can be attributed to the victims. The two populations were in no way predisposed to be massacred. The state was entirely responsible for its criminal acts. The victim's identity can in no way be seen as an extenuating circumstance.

Before studying the similarities and the differences between the two genocides, it is fitting to pose a certain question: Did the fact that the first criminal went unpunished facilitate the action of the second? In other words: would international legislation against the crime of genocide have dissuaded the Nazis from annihilating the European Jews?

THE WORLD'S SILENCE AND HITLER'S COMMENT

After the First World War neither the signers of the peace treaty nor the members of the League of Nations showed an interest in developing the concept of "violation of laws and of customs of war," as formulated in 1907 by the Hague Convention. It was only with the treaty of Sèvres that the punishment of the organizers of the massacres in Turkey during the war was recognized as necessary, and a tribunal in charge of judging those accused was established. But Sèvres was never ratified, and the Treaty of Lausanne put an end to any toying with the idea of Human Rights. The powerlessness of the League of Nations left the Fascist states to do whatever they wanted to their citizens. Permissiveness incited excess.

Nazi leaders, at the time their party was created, were somewhat aware of the treatment of the Armenians under the Ottoman Empire. A part of the Wilhelmstrasse archives had been published, and these documents are sufficient to establish the responsibility of the Young Turk government in the Armenian tragedy.[3] Some members of the future Nazi Party were stationed in Turkey during the war and had at that time encountered the passiveness of the Berlin Foreign Office and of the German embassy in Constantinople. One of Hitler's closest collaborators, Max Erwin von Scheubner-Richter, considered before 1923 to be ideologist of the party (and one of the few victims of the unsuccessful Munich putsch), had been vice-consul at Erzurum and one of the first to reveal Ittihat's criminal intentions.[4] The Prime Minister of Foreign Affairs of the Reich, Konstantin von Neurath, former advisor at the embassy in Constantinople, was a determined opponent of the Young Turks' policy of extermination. The publicist Paul Rohrbach, one of the directors of the German-Armenian Society, introduced Karl Haushofer to the "Thulé Society," the founder of which, Baron Rudolf von Sebottendorf, a Turk, had been the first owner of the "Volkischer Beobachter."[5] The Baron is known to have bragged about having sown the seeds that the Führer had made grow.

Of course these are only suppositions, but it is clear that Hitler had been, before 1923, in close contact with diplomats and soldiers who had not hidden their pro-Armenian feelings. However he is known to have mentioned the fate of the Armenians only once, on the twenty-second of August 1939, when he said, "Who, after all, speaks today of the extermination of the Armenians?"[6] This small comment, branded as proof of a connection between the two genocides, must be considered in context. It was part of a discourse delivered to the German army generals just before the invasion of Poland. In his speech Hitler first alluded to Genghis Khan, pointing out that history remembered him only as the great founder of a state; he then added that the conquest of "living space"—that being his objective in the war he was about to undertake—imposed the physical annihilation of the enemy. Although some doubts exist concerning the authenticity of this quotation, the evidence supports its truthfulness.[7] Yet, this small comment alone indicates that the Führer realized that the massacre of civil populations—and he was speaking about the Poles, and not only about the Jews in Poland—would be made easier in wartime, an obvious fact. If the massacre of 1915 had not taken place, Hitler would have without a doubt assumed the same right to kill. But how, counting on this fragile proof alone, can one establish a casual connection between the two genocides? Certainly in 1939 the world did not imagine that the outbreak of a war would be exploited by a totalitarian state in order to destroy its national minority. Hitler took advantage of this loss of memory.

THE CRIME OF WHICH THE STATE IS GUILTY

Genocide is by nature a crime against humanity. As it violates those "basic obligations essential to the international community,"[8] it can be defined as an international crime and other states can demand the punishment of the guilty state. Regarded in this light, the two genocides represent the same phenomenon. One certainly preceded the other, but one did not engender the other. In the same way neither one facilitated those that occurred subsequently. It was the totalitarian structures of the states and the technological resources at their disposal that made such crimes possible. The state had the exorbitant power to take the life of its internal enemies, who in fact posed no real threat but possessed only that fictional force ascribed to them by the state. A collective ailment was the primary cause of the two genocides. It overtook the state's leaders, feeding on itself and expanding, until finally exploding in a frenzied crisis. The germ was a doctrine cooked too long in the melting pot of surrounding

nationalist ideologies and eventually declared as a set of unquestionable certitudes, a political credo. Nationalism possesses, by nature,
an emotional density harder to contain than to let explode. If the
nation is weakened, if territory is reduced, nationalism compensates
for the resulting frustrations with its myths. The people take to
finding their roots, here the Turks, there the Aryans, and nationalism
strays in the direction of "tribalism."[9]

This nationalist zealotry is radically different from nineteenth
century nationalism which, within a multi-national empire, sought to
give each nation back its liberty. Tribalism is irredentist. It identifies
a fictional group whose members share an identity and are engaged
in an exclusive universe of obligations. They belong to a superior race
that has a messianic mission to accomplish: that of reuniting on
their own soil all members of the chosen people. Tribalism defines in
this way who belongs and who is excluded. Outside, the others, the
strangers, are, at the same time, excluded from this universe and
responsible for the troubles within it. When the tribal chiefs gain
control of the state, they transform it into a totalitarian instrument
devoted to their political credo, disposing of any "consensus juris," of
law applicable to all. The totalitarian state legitimizes the domination
and the free expression of the tribal nation, claiming certain privileges
and breaking down moral barriers that might have posed obstacles to
the realization of their messianic ideal. The two genocides were the
consequence of an obsessional neurosis, born in the time of a
national identity crisis, which expressed itself in an ideological
delirium and attacked the vital organs of the state. The neurotic
nation expelled its obsession by projecting it onto the alien body that
was charged with threatening the national whole and whose destruction was seen as necessary to assure survival. A scapegoat is
indispensable. It must be kept alive, otherwise another has to be
found. On the other hand, the alien body, like a tumor, must be
completely extirpated. A state struck by this obsessional neurosis
transcends the law and authorizes itself to dispose freely of all human
lives. For such a state, murder is not only permitted, but becomes an
obligation.

Passionate at the outset, the nationalistic frenzy develops from
then on in a logical fashion. The Young Turk State, like the Nazi
State, premeditated its crime and elaborated a plot with several points
in common. The best moment to carry out the project was during a
war, a time when a screen of smoke rose between the State and its
neighbors, and an event which permitted the State to provide ulterior

justifications. In both cases the perpetrators knew that they did not have to fear immediate sanctions, for they had been testing out the territory for a long time with calculated measures of oppression and violence against their victims. The execution of the project was entrusted to a small number of police or paramilitary units with discretionary power: the Special Organization or the SS organization. The conviction that the Jews or the Armenians were solely responsible for the nation's troubles had been firmly implanted in the minds of the population by programs of propaganda and political molding. The general plan of extermination was kept a secret. It was disclosed to only a small number of initiates. In spite of the demands placed on the nation by the war, the execution was not deferred. The annihilation of the internal enemy was considered a top priority. The process was even accelerated at times when the war scenes drew near the zones of massacre.

In short, be it the Young Turk State or the Nazi State, in both instances the eruption of a fanatic ideology distracted and perverted political discourse. It was the leaders of the State, the heads of the party, who were the first to be convinced of the necessity of destroying the people they had defined as the target. They imparted their fervor to their militants, assembled the undecided and the timorous, and terrorized their opponents. Having presented the choice as nothing less than an obligation, the final solution became easy. The victims had no power whatsoever. The State, making use of all available means, led a total war of annihilation against them. In both cases the obsession was fatal for the accused. By alleviating its anguish with a process of self-mutilation, one which was meant to be only the beginning of a series of amputations—Arabs, Greeks, and Kurds were next on the Young Turk's list; Poles, Russians, and other Slavic populations on that of the Nazis—the State achieved its own destruction.

DIFFERENCES BETWEEN THE TWO GENOCIDES

If the pathological process, the development of a neurosis, was identical in both cases, the personality of the criminal and the nature of his obsession were different. The Turanian myth in Turkey had hardly anything in common with the Aryan myth in Germany. A departure from Pan-Islamism and Pan-Turkism, Turanism gave special importance to a religion, a language, and the lands where they were practiced and spoken.[10] It was without doubt a racist doctrine, exalting the virtues of the Turk, but it did have a historic notion at its base: the gathering of the sons of Oghuz, Turks and Turkmen, born to a new entity—Turan.[11] The myth begot excessiveness; and the Turanian ideals, the dreams of philosophers and poets, took priority. The Armenians stood in the way of the future conquests of Turanianism: they had to be destroyed. The explication is simple, primary, and straightforward.

Explained as such, the Genocide of the Armenians was more comprehensible than that of the Jews: claim to a national territory obliged this criminal to kill. The Genocide of the Armenians was the prototype of the twentieth century genocides, an exemplary case in which all aspects of the State's crime—national, religious, and cultural—are found together.

The Holocaust, on the contrary, was the excessive, high-pitched manifestation of the sickness, a mystic exaltation of the myth. The Turanian myth asserted its authority; it was not looking to prove itself. The Aryan myth tried to prove scientifically the irrational. It was a paranoia based exclusively on racism. The Aryan theory was directly in line with the stream of scientific progress of the nineteenth century. It was part of "those baby steps taken by the social sciences, who looking to model themselves after the exact sciences, turned into the dead end of mechanical and determinist theories where they have been stuck for a century."[12] When doubts began to be raised, these theories passed from the hands of the scholars to those of the demagogues, to become the official doctrine of the Third Reich.

The Nazi discourse retained this scientific color, but the science itself was corrupted and used to form a structure of truth for racist ideas. Anthropology became the racial science. Medicine researched racial hygiene and extolled the identification of persons in terms of race. Social Darwinism, sprinkled with Nietzschean ideals, supported the cult of the superman, the final product of the selection of the strongest, and leading into "human breeding utopias."[13] The budding science of genetics demonstrated the dominance of nature over nurture, and its limited sphere was abusively stretched to apply to mental characteristics as well as physical. Eugenics was used positively to improve the race, and negatively to eliminate the "lives not worth being lived" (lebensun werten Leben).[14] The German people, the Volk, were supreme beings, their bodies made of cells, blood, and genes that were identical and superior. The one who was not of the Volk was definitely to be excluded. Among these strangers, some were considered as humans and destined to become slaves. Others were seen as nonhuman and destined to be destroyed. The messianic mission of the Volk encompassed not only the necessity to expand their living space but also, in order to assure cohesion and to affirm their election, the elimination of the only adversary that possessed that cohesion and that election: the Jews.   Ancient, thousand-year-old myths resurfaced, and anti-Semitism took on metaphysical dimensions: the struggle of the Pure against the Impure, the Good against the Evil, the human against the nonhuman.   The Holocaust was the tragic consequence of this fantastic perversion.

The Young Turks desired to annihilate the Armenians, but they allowed their executioners to rape and take away Armenian women, to shut Armenian children up in Turkish orphanages, and even to accept conversions to Islam. The Nazis tried to protect their race from any stain. All Jews, identified as such back to the third generation, were carriers of genes dangerous to the German race, and were therefore excluded and condemned. The Young Turks wanted only to rid themselves of the Armenians in order to procure the Armenians' possessions and land. They had a simple motive: theft. The Nazis were looking desperately for an image of themselves, wiping out that of the other from their reflection. One committed a heinous crime; the other, a passionate crime. One, to reach their objectives, excluded neither ruse nor compromise; the other participated in the mystic celebration of a holocaust, beginning with an auto-da-fé and finishing with crematoriums.

Paradoxically the more delirious of the two conceived the most efficient means of extermination. The quality of the annihilation was in proportion to the myth. The Young Turks were clumsy artisans, the Nazis were criminal geniuses. Ittihat's plan was improvised. Known by public officials, by tax collectors, and by their neighbors, the Armenians were easy to identify. To render useless any individual resistance, the Ottoman government ordered the assembly of all men, whether soldiers or not, and arrested or killed them on the spot. Subsequently the elderly, the women, and the children were deported, and their convoys regularly decimated. There were very few concentration camps and most of the resettlement centers were destroyed. The Armenian provinces were transformed into a wasteland and the site of an open grave; around the rest of the country, strewn along the rivers and the roads, were corpses of the deportees, offering a free exhibition for both the civil population and foreign witnesses.

The Nazis, on the contrary, aimed at constructing an industry of death with sophisticated technology. They proceeded in stages, spread out along a period of ten years. They began by identifying their victims; then, bit by bit, they deprived their victims of their social status and their means of existence by passing a series of laws. The Nazis did as much as possible to dehumanize the victims; then they resettled them in camps or in ghettos. At that moment the German State perfected its system of concentration camps and integrated them into the channels of production. On the scale of horror, Auschwitz ranks a bit higher than Treblinka, Sobibor, Belzec, or Chelmno, which were simply extermination camps. Its selection ramps and its gas chambers ensured Birkenau's place as the anus of the world, the home of the most abominable perversion that man has ever imagined. The Young Turks had nothing resembling the technical resources placed at the disposal of the Nazi executioners. The only hint of modernity was the utilization of the internal part of the railroad to deport the Armenians. The Turks declined to exploit the servile manpower and had the deportees who were working on Arab farms or on the construction of the Amanus or Taurus tunnels executed. They killed the strongest first, while the Nazis began by gassing the weakest and kept the able-bodied prisoners to support the industrial war effort. The Armenian corpses were strewn about the land of the Empire. Those of the Jews departed in smoke, and the Nazis retained clothing, hair, gold teeth, and even human fat. The Turkish executioners were free to choose their method of elimination. The Nazi program was strict and did not authorize improvisation. The Young Turks and the Nazis were possessed by the same destructive frenzy. They held the same power. The means of destruction were concentrated in the hands of a totalitarian party which did not burden itself with moral considerations. But one acts in disorder, the other acts with method. They shared neither the same criminal mentality nor the same cultural heritage; most significantly they did not have the same reasons to kill.

DIFFERENT CONSEQUENCES OF THE TWO GENOCIDES

The two genocides apparently had the same result. European Judaism was almost completely destroyed and Yiddish culture was wrenched from the center of Europe. The Armenians disappeared from the Ottoman Empire. The two populations demonstrated a remarkable resistance to the extermination and, within a few decades, they had to a certain extent reconstituted the human and cultural resources destroyed by the genocide.

But, in fact, the consequences were quite different. The genocide of the Armenians deprived a people of their land and condemned them to exile. The genocide of the Jews destroyed a people living in exile. Afterwards the United Nations recognized the right of the Jewish survivors to establish an independent nation on the land historically belonging to them, whereas thirty years earlier the League of Nations refused to grant permission to the Armenians to keep their already existing, although not internationally recognized, independent republic. Armenia did not survive the genocide. The creation of the state of Israel was precipitated by the genocide. Worldwide, the human conscience was horribly shocked by the Holocaust; and after the Nazis downfall, the German people totally abandoned the ideology that gave it rise. Turkish nationalism rose again from the ashes of the Ittihat. Touranianism was forgotten, but Turkism took its place and generated new ambitions, ambitions that were expressed fully in Kemalism. Not only was the genocide of the Armenians not acknowledged, but the Turkish State has continued to deny its reality, reducing the event to a passing incident, inevitable in wartime. Nor has the State stopped refuting the accusation of premeditation.

The genocide of the Jews was senseless murder which, at the most, soothed a pervert's obsession. Today it is accepted as an unquestionable historical truth. The murderers of the Armenians reaped their desired profit, the control of the land inhabited by the Armenians for twenty-seven consecutive centuries. However, while the Germans slowly free themselves from the weight of their horrible past, the reality of which they do not attempt to hide, the Turkish Government is caught in the trap of its negation. By refusing to admit the truth, in the same way that one might send back a body to a family, the life of a seventy-year-old crime is prolonged. It is obvious that for the victims the memory of the genocide is ineffaceable; but as for the criminal, the second crime, which was by far the most inconceivable, the most unforgettable, was achieved. The Nazis fell. Like an epileptic in the height of an attack, they destroyed everything on their way down. Historians have looked into their case. They have analyzed and interpreted it. With more or less vigilance, the world lies in wait, prepared to deal with any return of the vile beast with a revival of racism. Since the Holocaust, racists have become ashamed and they disguise their discourse to conceal their true nature. The first crime, on the contrary, remains unfinished, and every so often it reenters abruptly into the present. It did not serve as a model for the second. It played at the most a role of facilitation. The Holocaust however has permitted the historic consciousness of the 1915 event. It gave that event a name, genocide, and it shed a light on its totalitarian character. The other genocides of this century resembled the Young Turk model, the heinous crime, more than the Nazi model, shut in its metaphysical dimension. On the other hand, the Turkish denial has comforted neo-Nazis and encouraged the historic revisionism of the Jewish genocide, which, arising from Paul Rassinier's digressions,[15] have been made concrete in the book of Arthur Butz[16] and the articles of Robert Faurisson.

How is it possible not to see in this rocking movement a desire for dialogue between man and the Golem? It was the Maharad of Prague that molded the Golem to be used by the Jewish community. It was a creature made of clay, that had a human appearance but was deprived of a soul. To breath life into it the word "*Emeth*" (truth) was stuck on its forehead. To destroy the robot, the first letter had to be erased, changing "*Emeth*" to "*Meth*" (death). When the creature escapes from its master and sets out, roaming the ghetto, destroying everything in its path, it is the rabbi who manages to erase the first letter from its forehead, and it becomes once again a lump of clay.[17] Having foregone an amputation, Truth was renamed Death. The totalitarian state is a Golem, a mechanical and inhuman concept which easily transforms itself into a destructive machine. The truth that it claims to embody reveals itself as a source of death, but the well-intentioned sorcerer that conceived the robot no longer has the means to reduce it into a shapeless mass. The genocide is the Golem's masterpiece. May man save himself from his inventions and never forget history's lessons.

REFERENCES

1. Eugène Arenonanu, *Le Crime contre l'humanité* (Paris: Dalloz, 1961).

2. Irving L. Horowitz, *Taking Lives: Genocide and State Power* (New Brunswick: Transaction Books, 1982), 206.

3. Johannes Lepsius, *Deutschland und Armenien, 1914-1918: Sammlung diplomatischer Aktenstücke* (Postam, 1919).

4. Konrad Heiden, *Histoire du national-socialisme, 1919-1934* (Paris: Stock, 1934); Dr. F. Achille Delmas, *Adolf Hitler, Essai de biographie psycho-pathologique* (Paris: M. Rivière, 1946), 40.

5. Werner Gerson, *Le nazisme, société secrète* (Paris: Belfond, 1976), 170.

6. Louis Lochner, *What about Germany?* (New York: Dodd Mead, 1942), 2.

7. Yves Ternon, *La Cause Arménienne* (Paris: Seuil, 1977), 167-69.

8. Tribunal Permanent des Peuples, *Le crime de silence: Le génocide des Arméniens* (Paris: Flammarion, 1984), 346.

9. Hannah Arendt, *The Origins of Totalitarianism* (New York: Harcourt, Brace and World, 1966), 226-27, quoted by Helen Fein, *Accounting for Genocide* (New York: The Free Press, 1979), 8.

10. Serge A. Zenkovsky, *Pan Turkism and Islam in Russia* (Cambridge, Mass.: Harvard University Press, 1967).

11. Zarevand, *United and Independent Turania: Aims and Designs of the Turks* (Leiden: E. J. Brill, 1971).

12. Leon Poliakov, *Le mythe aryen* (Paris: Calman Levy, 1971), 349.

13. Hedwig Conrad-Martivs, *Utopien der Menschenzüchtung, der Socialdarwinismus und seine Folgen* (München: Kösel-Verlag, 1955).

14. According to the book of Karl Binding and Alfred Hoche, *Die Freigabe der Vernichtung lebensunwerten Lebens* (Leipzig, 1922). cf. Yves Ternon and Socrate Helman, *Le Massacre des Aliénés* (Tournai: Casterman, 1971), 33-40.

15. Paul Rassinier, *Le mensonge d'Ulysse* (Paris: Documents et témoignages, 1950).

16. Arthur R. Butz, *The Hoax of the Twentieth Century* (Torrance, Calif.: Noontide Press, 1976).

17. Saul Friedlander, *Quand vicot le souvenir...* (Paris: Seuil, 1978), 25.

Experiences During 1915-1916 and the Outlook

Richard Ashton

You see before you a member of a disappearing species that will be extinct by the year 2015—thirty years from now. Few, if any, will be left—unless some decide to live well over one hundred years.

I am a survivor of Talaat's order that was based on the assumption that when there are no more Armenians in Turkey, there will be no Armenian question!

Actually some two million Armenians were deported. Other than the 250 political, intellectual, and business leaders who were taken out of Constantinople, most of the Armenians in the capital were not involved, because of the risk of too many foreign people observing the brutal methods used in the deportations, which were intended for destruction, rather than resettlement.

I was born in Van in September 1908. The people of Van decided to resist Talaat's orders for their removal. A defense plan was agreed on. Boulders were placed in open areas so that men lying down had an advantage over exposed attacking infantry. Certain houses were evacuated and set up as lookout and defense posts.

The Armenians had only a few hundred rifles and no cannon. Turkish cannons were blowing up many homes and the only way the Armenians could offset the Turkish advantage was to dig underground and tunnel in darkness until they got under the barracks and blew them up. This panicked the Turkish soldiers. Eventually Armenians captured an old cannon—it was a morale booster. Finally the Turks retreated in the face of the advancing Russian army.

Before the battle for Van, when the Tsarist Russian army crossed into northeastern Turkish Armenia, the Turks decided to evacuate all Turkish families from the east shore of Lake Van to the west shore and safety.   My father, having been an experienced seaman and having an interest in the only steam vessel on Lake Van, was among hundreds conscripted to move the Turkish families to safety. Now you might think that, having served the Turkish families, these men would be held until war's end. Instead they were forced to dig mass graves for fifteen or twenty persons each and then the Turks lined them up at the edge and shot them. You might well ask, if they shot everyone—who would recount the event? One man, badly wounded, fell into the grave and, pretending death, lay there under a thin layer of dirt until dark. Traveling through sparse country by night and hiding by day, months later he turned up in Yerevan, Armenia, and described the brutal event.

The heroic struggle of another group of villagers—over 5,000 in number—who fled Musa Dagh, the Mount of Moses, has been made famous by author Franz Werfel in his *Forty Days of Musa Dagh*. Actually their ordeal lasted a total of 53 days and, when rescued by French warships, only 4,058 were still alive: 427 babies under four, 1,136 children 4 to 14, 1,441 women, and 1,054 men. This means that battle deaths and illness claimed over 1,000 lives. At least they did better than the government deportees, 75 percent of whom died: one and a half million out of the two million deported.

The epic struggle of Van in self-defense was doomed for two reasons:

1. Failure of Winston Churchill's great adventure, the attempt to capture Gallipoli, on the European side north of Constantinople. Churchill hoped to command the Dardanelles Straits and open passage to the Black Sea, making it possible for a pincers movement against the Turks. The blunder of that strategy was that it was based on the assumption that, after weeks of bombardment and heavy losses, the Turks would give up. They did not. The ships withdrew until land forces were brought in to occupy Gallipoli, but the first three attempts by the British failed to gain their objective. Moreover, the delay between the first bombardments and the arrival of British troops that eventually reached 95,000 in number allowed the Turks time to replace men and munitions; with the guidance of expert German officers it finally caused a decisive defeat and withdrawal for the British.

2. When Tsarist Russian troops arrived in Van, all Armenian defense plans there were abandoned with, "The Russians will be in Constantinople in two weeks." An impossibility! Can you imagine in your wildest dreams troops walking more than 800 miles in two

without resistance?

The Russians also had a turnabout.   Orders came from their leaders, "All units are to return to Mother Russia immediately." While the Bolshevik Revolution did not overthrow the Tsar until 1917, already the impact of the war on production and loyalty, plus the losses on the German front, with shortage of supplies and replacements, led to the abandonment of the Turkish front in July 1915. The Russian Command ordered all Armenians to leave Van, as they burned all barracks, public buildings, and food and military supplies before withdrawing. At the end of July 1915 we left Van. My father, who was an amateur Luther Burbank, toyed with cross pollination. As we left the house, I asked my mother if I could taste one of the seven new apples, which, as I recall, looked like a golden delicious. She replied, "No son, your father needs all the seeds. We should be back in three or four days. When dad gets the seeds, you can taste the apple." It has been a long three or four days! We found out months later that dad was already dead the day that Turkish families were moved to safety on the west shore of Lake Van.

We walked for five weeks from Van to Tiflis, Georgia, then down to Yerevan. The shorter direct route was extremely dangerous, being under frequent Turkish and Kurdish attacks. For eight days of the five weeks we had no food and for the three days in the desert there was no water.

Early one morning a young lady approached my brother and said, "I see that you have a tea kettle. I know a place nearby where there is a spring. If you let me borrow your kettle, I'll bring you and my grandmother some good drinking water." People schemed to get things they needed, so my brother hesitated. "Don't worry," she said, "I'll be back. I'll leave my grandmother with you." That tea kettle, worth about $3.98, is one reason I am here. Toward evening my brother said, "We can't stay here any longer—it is dangerous." He asked the girl's grandmother to go with us. She refused, saying, "I won't move from this spot until my granddaughter returns." Was it a trick, or did the young lady meet with foul play? We moved on. The next day at noon we came upon an awful sight. The Turks had attacked the column and about seventy persons and animals had been brutally cut up and killed. Many of these were faces in the column from which we had dropped out to get good drinking water, and lost a tea kettle instead.

When we finally arrived in the Yerevan area, we were settled in a Near East Relief Camp of about 30,000 refugees, about three miles from Echmiadzin. We thought we were safe at last...*wrong!* Cholera broke out in the camp. Deaths reached 150 to 300 every day. Our family tents, about four by six feet, were skimpy, and food consisted of one bowl of soup a day—and was not prepared by Oscar of the Waldorf.

In eight days, five of our family died of cholera. The last to go was my mother. Weak and suffering, she motioned to me, her youngest, to come near. "My son, I am sorry I cannot fulfill all my motherly obligations to you. I am going to leave you now, and all I have to give you is this: Always live as though I were with you and approved." It took several years to understand what a rich inheritance she had given me!

With mother, grandmother, and brother's wife and two children gone, my brother Yervant said, "If we don't leave this camp, we too will be dead from cholera." We spent six months in Baku, and six more in Yerevan, when my brother Hagop returned from America, expecting peace by Christmas 1916. Finding only the two of us alive, and the war intensified, he married in Yerevan and returned to America with his new bride, taking me with him. Yervant refused to come with us, saying, "Five of our family are dead here. I will not leave. I'll live and die here." We heard from him until 1929, then silence. Efforts to locate him failed. All Russian ports were closed to commercial shipping, so we travelled by way of Christiana (now Oslo), Norway. From there we arrived in Ellis Island on December 19, 1916.

II

In 1915 the Turkish outlook for the future appeared to be based on the assumption that, once the Armenians were eliminated from Turkey, and their wealth and property confiscated, the Turks would enjoy all the commerce and prosperity of the Armenians.

They have eliminated almost all the Armenians from Turkey—but has Turkey prospered? Let us look beyond the 1915 to 1922 years. How has Turkey fared since the Armenians were driven to death or out of the country? After all, the Turks confiscated the property of the Armenians. Is there one city in Eastern Turkey of 100,000, let alone a million? Even with billions of American aid, Turkey is on the border of bankruptcy. Over two million Turks have left Turkey to find jobs elsewhere in Europe.

The Turkish-American Newsletter of April 1980, published in Chicago, states: "There are 60,000 Armenians living free, prosperous lives in Turkey." Archbishop Shnork Kaloustian, Patriarch of the Armenians in Turkey, said in 1984, "There are 50,000 Armenians living in Turkey." Now what happened to another 10,000 Armenians in the four year interval? Names changed to Turkish to assure acceptance and survival—or a gradual exodus?

Speaking of figures, according to a 1913 census, as published in *Hairenik Monthly* of some years back, there were 2,300,000 Armenians living in Turkey out of a total population of 14,000,000. Turkish Armenians who survived the genocide can be divided into three groups:

A. Some Armenians who went, or were sent, abroad to escape the dark clouds of war, as well as memories of the 1909 and 1912 massacres of Adana and Zeitun.

B. Some 200,000 Armenians who defied or resisted the deportation orders and fled to Russian Armenia, Syria, Palestine, Egypt, and other parts of the world.

C. Altogether an estimated 500,000 who escaped from Turkey.

After the massacres the world Armenian population declined to a low point well under four million. We need to point out that the most capable people in industry, commerce, and the arts were deliberately taken out of towns and cities and murdered. One can imagine what might have happened if:

1. The harsh terms, economically, had not been imposed on Germany at Versailles.

2. If the Allies had kept their promise for an independent Armenia in Eastern Turkey.

3. If there had been a firm world stand against the first genocide of the twentieth century, which Turkey still denies. Do you know the latest *gimmick* Turkey uses? That there were only 600,000 Armenians living in Turkey in 1915, so there were not 1,500,000 Armenians in Turkey to begin with.

The first may have avoided the downfall of the Weimar Republic in Germany and the seizure of power by Adolph Hitler and the Nazis.

The second and third actions might have avoided Hitler's course of action. In Obersalzberg, in 1939, he said, "Our strength is in our quickness and our brutality. For the time being I have sent to the east only my Death's Head Units, with orders to kill without pity or mercy, all men, women, and children!!" He concluded with, "Who talks nowadays of the extermination of the Armenians?" Is it possible that World War II and the terrible Holocaust of the 6,000,000 Jews of Europe might never have taken place?

Why does the present Turkish government deny the intended destruction of all the Armenians in Turkey, when it was not the government in power at the time?

1. Possibly fear that admission of guilt would open the entire case to evaluation and review, even causing justification for land claims, as well as property and damage claims?

2. Or shame that authentication would portray the Turks as a ruthless, plundering, parasitic people? Right here I want to point out that any Armenian who indicts all Turks as guilty, also becomes guilty of indicting the innocent!

During the recording of an Oral History taping now in the collection of the Armenian Assembly, a survivor told me about two Turkish men whose families were friends with Armenian neighbors and tried to hide them in their homes. Both Turkish men were dragged out of their homes and hanged right in town, as an example to those who defied government orders. We also have the case of some provincial governors being replaced for lack of enthusiasm in carrying out these inhumane acts.

In an effort to whitewash the harsh treatment of the Armenians in 1915, the Turkish government in Ankara issued a document in 1978, in English, French, and Turkish, titled, "Displacement of the Armenians: Documents," by a Dr. Salahi R. Sonyel. The preface starts out with the assertion that Armenian citizens have co-existed on good terms for centuries within the boundaries of the Ottoman Empire, etc., etc.

Pursuing it further, I was tempted to find out what deportations they were talking about. Document #172, signed by Minister of the Interior, Talaat, on July 20, 1915, states in part:

Item 6: Information was received that the moveable goods of the Armenians, who are to be transported to other areas, have been sold at very low prices, and thus the owners of the said goods suffered losses on a large scale.

Item 6C: If there are any persons who have purchased Armenian goods at ridiculous prices, necessary measures should be taken in order to cancel the purchase, to raise the prices to normal levels, and to prevent the obtaining of illegal profits.

Item 6D: The Armenians are to be allowed to take with them all kinds of goods they desire.

Documents #190, 191, and 192 show only one date: 28 August, 1915.

#190, Item 9: The Armenians to be displaced are to be provided with food, and the expenses of food for the poor Armenians will be met from the Immigration Funds.

Document #190, Item 10: The districts where the displaced Armenians are gathered, should be constantly inspected and watched. Necessary measures should be taken to ensure their security and rest. Food should be provided for the poor and disabled. A physician should be assigned every day for controlling the health conditions. All the necessary material should be provided for the treatment of the sick as well as the protection of the health of pregnant women and children. ... etc.

Reading this document, I truly find myself *Alice in Wonderland.*

Unfortunately for the Turks, the whitewash is of such poor quality that I find the black dirt underneath coming through. It is difficult to determine if this document is a figment of Dr. Sonyel's imagination, a propaganda ministry bungle, or an actual record. Giving the benefit of the doubt, if it is actual record, even that proves the hypocrisy of the document. None of these noble edicts carried a date until about *three months after* April 24, 1915!

It was in the *first three months* that the brutal savagery of the Turkish government and many Turks—please note that I did not say *all*—were made manifest!

Terrorism is certainly not the answer to the world's problems, especially when it punishes the *innocent*—but one can certainly understand the frustration of the children and grandchildren of the victims of genocide when falsification cloaks the *truth* and denies *justice!*

In spite of claims of democracy for all, the non-Islamic ethnics—the Kurds, the Greeks, and the Armenians—are still second and third class citizens in Turkey.

Prof. Stanford Shaw, at UCLA, who is a strong advocate of Turkish claims, has stated in his lectures and writings, "There are no archives to support Armenian allegations of genocide." Let me ask him and you:

What officials would admit and report that they rounded up 5,000 Armenians, stripped them of their clothing and belongings—in winter—and, taking them out to an open field, told them that if they accepted Islam, they would be spared? The mother of our narrator, in the Oral History interviews I spoke of, told her small 13-year-old daughter, "*Aghchiges, pakhir, pakhir*"—daughter run, run! The daughter's response, "The soldiers will kill me." "Better to die that way, *run!*" Evidently the two soldiers between whom she ran may have thought this naked little girl wouldn't get very far and wasn't worth a wasted bullet.   Terrified, she ran some distance and hid under a low lying tree branch. She told this story:

Some twenty or thirty Armenians accepted the Islamic faith and were taken away—never to be heard from again. Throwing coal oil, which we know as kerosine, over the straw strewn around them, the Turks set fire to the remaining group, including her mother. Petrified with terror, she remained under the tree branch and saw the soldiers rifle butt mouths for gold teeth, and slashed stomachs for swallowed gold and jewelry.

In a separate incident, some thirty or forty refugees were huddled naked under a bridge embankment. Cavalry passing over the bridge could not shoot them from above so they tossed bread and cheese over the river bank. As the hungry ones dashed for the food away from the bridge, they were shot, and in panic jumped into the river, and the survivor says: you saw the red blood of the dying as the current carried them away.

Beneath the claims of democracy in Turkey, there still exists the spots of the leopard that have not changed.

The western mind has trouble understanding the ways and customs of the east. The Turks had regarded the authority of the Sultan as absolute; popular tradition among the Turks was that the Sultan had the right to execute seven men or more every day, without any other reason save that it was his prerogative to do so.

As for truth being a stranger: Raphael De Nogales, a soldier of fortune from Venezuela, serving in Van, was told that Armenians were attacking Van. Arriving on the scene, he found that Kurds and rabble rousers were led by civil authorities and that this was actually a Turkish attack on innocent women and children. Objecting, he was told he had no authority to stop it, since orders came from Jevdet Bey, Governor General of Van, to kill all Armenian males twelve years and over.

Some of my American friends have asked me this question: How can you Armenians, who refused to give up your faith in Turkey, now live in a Godless Society in the Soviet Armenian Republic? A good question. But in spite of government policy, churches still function in Moscow and in Armenia. Contrary to government policy, a great deal of faith exists, and religion refuses to die. People everywhere still seek an anchor of faith and hope beyond themselves.

A few years ago, a young lady of nine, living in Leningrad, in a school exam, was asked this question: "What is written at the base of Lenin's statue in Leningrad Square?" She confidently replied, "It is written, 'Religion is the opiate of the people.'" As the day wore on, her confidence in her reply sagged. When school let out she went to the square and read the inscription, "Religion is the opiate of the people." Crossing herself, she said, "Thank God I got it right!"

Visiting Moscow, Tiflis, Georgia, and Armenia in 1978, I discovered that, despite government efforts, the churches were functioning. In fact the day after we had visited Echmiadzin, the seat of the Armenian Mother Church, and the residence of Vasken 1, the Catholicos, I was introduced to an Armenian official who, knowing we were from America, asked how we liked what we saw in the fatherland. In the conversation I mentioned we had visited Echmiadzin the day before. Hearing this he said, "*Pan meh me asser* (don't mention this), but both of my children were baptized in Echmiadzin!" Now I ask you, was this an act of faith—or insurance, *just in case?*

Yerevan, a starving, ragged city of 30,000 to 35,000 in 1915 and 1916, when I first was there, passed the million mark in April 1978.

While the Armenians endured untold suffering and death, the Turks, in driving the Armenians out, also drove out the best creative and productive resource of the country. It is in Turkey's interest to recognize the facts of the 1915 tragedy, even as West Germany has admitted Germany's black page in history. As for the 500,000 Armenians who survived, I can almost hear the words of Martin Luther King, ringing out over the diaspora, "Free at last, free at last, Thank God, we are *free at last!*

There is an old Armenian song that goes: "*Ani kaghak nuster goolar, chiga asogh, me lahr, me lahr.*" Loosely translated, it says, "The city of Ani sits and weeps, there are none to say, don't cry, don't cry!"

Whether it be Sydney or Melbourne, Montreal or Toronto, Buenos Aires, San Francisco, Fresno, or Los Angeles, Detroit, Chicago, or Philadelphia, New York, Boston, or many other places where Armenians have been free to contribute to their adopted countries, the response comes to the once proud Armenian capital of one thousand and one churches, now totally destroyed: To the city of Ani, a resounding, *me lahr, me lahr,* don't cry, don't cry!

The 1915 Massacres of the Armenians in the State of Angora, Turkey

Alice Odian Kasparian

I was born in Angora, the present capital of Turkey, named Ankara since the 1920s. I am a survivor of the 1915 Genocide. I was very young then, but I remember many details of terrible happenings I witnessed or heard about. However, the details given in this paper are not based on my memory alone, but on documented facts and on reliable information obtained from eyewitnesses, from Turkish prison guards, drivers who transported the prisoners, and from friendly Turks who gave reliable reports about the tragedy of the Armenians.

According to our family traditions, my father's ancestors had migrated from Armenia after the fall of fortress of Ani in the fifth century A.D. The descendants of Prince Oda Amaduni, from whose name (Oda) derives family name Odian, had preferred to move westward and live in territories not under Persian rule. After spending some time in the district of Van, they had come all the way to Angora, then a Roman province. They traveled in forty carriages, bringing with them many goats and sheep from Van, and settled in Angora and in the nearby town of Istanos, where for centuries they produced wool, which was used for industry and export.

The Odian family owned thousands of acres of farmland, where wheat, rye, barley, and other crops were planted. The family also owned vast lands for grazing sheep and goats. Both of my parents had inherited ancestral vineyards and orchards from their parents.

Father was an industrialist and manufacturer like his forefathers. He operated an exporting and importing establishment in Angora while his brother supervised the manufacture of carpets, rugs, and especially a very fine textile made from hand-spun, hand-woven Angora wool, obtained from goats' hair. This silk-like fabric, known as Angora mohair or Angora soff, was exported by father's firm to Europe and within the Empire. Our ancestors had exported large quantities of this washed and combed Angora wool to England for the manufacture of the silky white periwigs of the British lords and barristers. The sheep's wool was exported to England for the manufacture of woolen fabrics. Father's most important order for the woven fabric came from the Turkish sultans. Since the occupation of Constantinople (Istanbul) by the Turks in 1453, when the sultans moved into the Byzantine Emperor's palaces, they continued to order the Angora mohair from father's family not only for their own use, but for the favorite officers of the court. Every year a gold medal was received from the sultan as a citation for the excellence of the product.

Angora was the ancient Ancyra, known also as Galatia. It was the habitat of a large Armenian community living in this territory since early centuries. The native Armenians considered themselves descendants of the first Christians to whom St. Paul the Apostle addressed his famous Epistles to the Galatians. The territory had been inhabited since Paleolithic and Neolithic times. By the sixteenth century B.C. it was a part of the powerful Hittite Empire. Beginning in the thirteenth century B.C., the Armeno-Phrygians began to penetrate and occupy the area. The Phrygians ruled over this area for nearly 1,000 years. They were excellent builders and constructed many bridges, baths, canals, circular buildings, and roads for communication and commerce. They were expert craftsmen, artisans, and tradesmen. In 760 B.C. King Midas I, son of Gordius, built the castle-fortress city, named it Ancyra, and made it the capital of the kingdom of Phrygia.

Phrygia was invaded by Persia; Alexander the Great held the city for a short period. In 276-277 B.C. Gauls invaded and occupied the land. They changed the capital city's name from Ancyra to Galatia and the name of the kingdom from Phrygia to Galatia. In 25 B.C. Rome incorporated Galatia into Roman Empire. Rome changed the city's name to Angora but retained the name of Galatia for the state.

In 51 A.D. St. Paul the Apostle visited Galatia. He converted some of the natives to Christianity. He also converted and consecrated an ancient pagan temple of the mother goddess Maya of the natives. The name of the temple was changed to Surb Astvatsadin (Holy Mother of God), or Garmir Vank. Its vast lands, fertile fields, orchards, and vineyards belonged to the Armenians. The converted temple, since the adoption of the new faith, had been the seat of Armenian prelates who resided in this monastery until the 1915 Genocide. Not far from the temple, in the nearby vast fields, King Mithradates had fought the Romans, and his Armenian son-in-law, King Tigranes the Great, had come to his assistance.

Byzantines inherited Angora from the Romans. The Armenian adoptionist, religious rebels, the Tondraki or Paulicians, held the fortress-castle for some years in retaliation for Byzantine cruelties. Arabs overran the city. Seljuks occupied it. The Crusaders held it for eighteen years. The Tatars, Mongols, and others invaded the territory, and finally it passed to the Ottoman Turks in 1433.

Despite all these territorial invasions and occupations, the natives retained their ethnicity. They remained and constituted the majority in the rural areas and almost the sole inhabitants of the towns and villages. The natives preserved their racial characteristics, customs, culture, arts and crafts, and their language which, according to the Encyclopedia Britannica, Heronimus, and others, was neither Gallic nor Greek. The natives were called Galatians but they were not Gauls. Neither were the natives Hellenized or Latinized.

Joseph Pitton Tournefort, the French Royal Botanist, traveled in Asia Minor in 1700-1702 and wrote a book in French which has been translated into English under the title *A Voyage into the Levant*. In this book the author states that the Armenians outnumbered the Turks in most major cities in Asia Minor. From Tournefort's date of 1700 to the 1915 Genocide, there is a span of 215 years. Since the Christians in Turkey, before the New Constitution, were exempted from Turkish military service and were required instead to pay a head tax, the Armenian males were not exposed to wars to be killed on the battleground. Why, then, did their numbers, instead of multiplying to several millions of souls during 215 years, diminish to a mere three million in 1914? Armenians migrated to Europe and elsewhere, true, but the numbers of migrated Armenians during this period could not have reached many millions of souls. What happened to the generations of this prolific people?

For the study of Armenian Genocide, the extermination of the Armenians in the state of Angora provides all the necessary historical facts to refute the fabricated lies, misstatements, arguments, and denials by the modern Turks.

1. The province of Angora was not near the eastern frontier of Turkey and thus did not endanger the security of the borders.

2. All the able-bodied Armenian males of ages 18 to 50 years were inducted into the Turkish army in 1914 and were sent to work as

laborers on the Baghdad Railway.

3. The rest of the population in the state was totally unarmed.

4. The natives were artisans, tradesmen, industrialists, professional men, and merchants. They had lost the use of their language under severe punishment and spoke Turkish. They were not involved in nationalistic movements. Indeed, they were peaceful, useful, and loyal citizens.

5. If their extermination was not pre-planned, why then following their so called "temporary displacements," a year after the Genocide, in the summer of 1916, did the Turkish authorities in Angora begin a systematic operation of vacating the Armenian homes, shops, schools, and churches from their material contents?

6. If the extermination of the Armenians was not planned, why then after emptying every construction in Angora of their contents did the Turkish authorities deliberately set fire to the entire Armenian quarter? If the extermination of the Armenians of Angora was not planned, why did the Turks destroy thousands of homes when there was such a shortage of housing facilities for the Turkish refugees from the war zones?

7. If the systematic, preplanned extermination of the Armenians was not committed by the leaders of the Ottoman Turks, why then were not only churches and cathedrals dynamited and destroyed by fire, but in addition, methodically, one by one, all of the Armenian inscribed monuments and gravestones were removed from three national cemeteries, belonging to the Apostolic, Catholic and Congregational communities of Angora? The Turks completely destroyed not only the physical, but the religious, cultural, and the historical presence of an ancient people who had been the inhabitants of these territories since centuries before the Turks set foot in Asia Minor.

The Armenians of Angora were considered to be one of the most Westernized people of Asia Minor. They dressed in European style and socialized in Western manner. They were wealthy, hospitable, refined, and industrious people. Angora had been the center of commerce since the pre-Roman period. All the major caravans headed for the Balkans and Europe started passed through Angora. The ancient Persian-Roman trade roads crossed here.

The governor, or *vali*, of the province of Angora was a good Turk. The Armenians respected him. In 1915 many educated Armenians were employed in the government in various administrative positions. According to one source quoted in the Blue Book of Lord Bryce:

The Vali of Angora, a really good man, refused to carry out orders from Constantinople to deport the Armenians of Angora, so the Commander of the Military Forces of the Vilayet and the Chief of Police agreed with the Vali and supported him. The leading Turks of Angora including the religious leaders, were all of the same mind. They knew that the Christians of the place were all loyal and useful subjects of the Empire. The Armenians here were chiefly Roman Catholics and were all truly loyal to the Turkish Government. They had no sympathy with any national aspirations. There were some 15,000 to 20,000 of them and they were the leaders in commerce and trade. They had more outward polish than other Armenians. They spoke Turkish and wrote in Armenian characters. The Armenians' houses and shops were searched in July 1915 and neither arms nor incriminating documents were found. But the Central Authorities had decreed their extermination, and as the Vali refused to obey them, both he and the Chief of Police were dismissed. Their successors made themselves ready tools to carry out any orders given from above. They succeeded in deporting all the Armenians in Angora.[1]

Weeks before the massacres and deportations of the Angora Armenians, a very important historical event took place which was the prelude to the Armenian Genocide of 1915.

On April 24, 1915, in Istanbul and its suburbs, throughout all the afternoon, several police and Turkish gendarmes rounded up some 300 Armenian leaders, clergy, statesmen, lawyers, doctors, writers, poets, and educators and took them to the police headquarters. They were held there without questioning, incommunicado, until midnight. Then by special express train, they were sent to Angora. They traveled all night non-stop, except at Sinjan Keuy, the last station before Angora. Here half of the arrested Istanbul Armenians were one by one escorted out of the wagons by the supervising gendarmes, and after being robbed of all their money and valuables, gold watches, rings, diamond pins, and such, they were all chained and bound in fours, then pushed into animal carts to be taken to the prisons of Ayash, Changiri, Asi-Yozgat, and elsewhere. Their comrades in the train headed for Angora.

The Chef-de-Train, or Station Master of Sinjan Keuy, Mr. Avakian, was an Armenian, a native of Angora. He was an indispensable officer of the Ottoman Railroad Company. This officer, as well as other Armenians located in different stations (such as Mr. Afkerian on Konya Railroad), knew fluent Turkish and Armenian, in addition to the French, German, and English languages. They were experts in telegraphic communications, coded and uncoded. At Sinjan Keuy station he had wished to talk with his compatriots from Istanbul, but he was instructed not to communicate with them. Thus he sadly had witnessed what was going on, and later personally related these episodes to my father, to whom he was related.

Meanwhile the train had arrived at Angora. The prisoners were escorted out, robbed of their money and valuables, chained, and thrown into the city's prisons without hygienic facilities. The Armenians had not been fed since their arrests. When a few of them made requests for food or something else, they were brutally beaten. A few friendly Turks confidentially had informed the local Armenians (who were not as yet arrested and slaughtered) about the plight of their compatriots from Istanbul. Soon, several families rushed food and drink, soap and water, towels and linen to be given to these men. The guards took these items with the promise to give them to the prisoners, but it was later disclosed that none of these items were given to the Armenians from Istanbul; instead they were given each a piece of stale moldy bread as their daily nutrition.

After a short confinement, some of the Istanbul Armenians were separated from the rest of the imprisoned leaders and sent away to undisclosed destinations; among these were the writers Siamanto, Daniel Varoujan, Krikor Zohrab, and others. A few of them were released and sent home through the mediation of foreign diplomats, representatives of the Vatican, other Christians, missionaries, or American and European friends to whom the families and friends of the arrested men had desperately appealed for help. Among these released men were Theotig, composer Komitas Vardapet, and others.

In early June 1915 we heard that a second convoy of some 300 Istanbul leaders were arrested in Istanbul and in similar manner they, too, were brought to Angora, where they were thrown into the already crowded filthy prison cells where their comrades had been held for about seven weeks, under the most unsanitary conditions and almost without food.

In June the arrival of the second convoy of arrested Armenians from Istanbul, as planned, coincided with the sudden arrest and imprisonment of several hundred noted Armenian dignitaries from the city and the province of Angora. On June 15, 1915, these distinguished natives of Angora, including many lawyers, doctors, professional men, bankers, industrialists, wealthy merchants, educators, clergy, etc., were all brought to the same prisons where their compatriots from Istanbul were confined. These men were also robbed of their money, gold watches, and jewelry, and were chained and bound in fours, and then thrown into prison cells to be annihilated together with the rest of the Istanbul Armenians. Under strict supervision of specifically assigned police and gendarmes, they were all packed into dozens of animal carts and driven towards isolated valleys of Ayash, Changiri, Zenjirly Kouyou, and Asi Yozgat.

And what took place in these isolated valleys?

The following details were provided by reliable Turkish friends of the local Armenians:

On June 15, 1915, as planned by the authorities, hundreds of sentenced Turkish criminals were released from various prisons and in return for their freedom and pardon of their death sentence, they were brought to these notorious valleys and assigned to perform an act they knew too well how to perform. To assist them, the new Governor of the State had hired several expert butchers who, according to Ambassador Morgenthau's report, "brought to these valleys their clubs, hammers, axes, scythes, spades, saws and daggers to slaughter their hapless, chained and bound victims."[2]

A Turkish carriage driver, an acquaintance of ours, told my father that before his brother and cousins were killed, the prisoners were led by a few clergy, among them Reverend Hayrabed Odian, to say their final prayers. After being stripped of their clothing, the victims were clubbed; those who resisted or screamed were tortured and axed first. Each prisoner was tormented before being killed. Their legs and arms were amputated, their eyes were bored, their ears cut off. Their abdomens were split, axes and daggers were raised, and one by one each head was severed. One by one these human beings became heaps of crushed, smashed skulls, dissected limbs, mutilated bodies, their blood flowing like a red stream. When all was over and the performers had left the stage, the echo of the victims' cries of agony lingered in the valleys, and then there was a gruesome silence.

In June 1915, many English soldiers, captured in the Dardanelles Campaign, were brought to Angora as prisoners of war. According to information in the Blue Book of Lord Bryce:

> Some of these men had been carried in the night from Angora eastward. When they started out from Angora, they could not understand why they were taken at night, but when in the utter darkness they passed the bridge over the river beyond Asi-Yozgat, and for an hour were nearly suffocated with the odor that came to them from decaying flesh, then they knew why they were not allowed to pass in daylight.[3]

Several months before the general deportations and massacres of the Armenians had begun in Turkey, an order was issued from Istanbul to have the census of all the Armenians in the province of Angora. It was stated that the census was for wartime information.

A proclamation commanded every Armenian to register at the police headquarters. There was a punishment for those who failed to do so. Father felt that there was something ominous about the order and he did not register. His suspicion about the census proved to have been well founded.

Father was spared the terrible fate of his compatriots on June 15, 1915, his name not being on the list. Similarly on August 15, 1915, when every Armenian resident of the city—men, women, children, Apostolic, Catholic, Protestant—all were hastily rounded by hundreds of Turkish police and gendarmes and hurried to the railroad station, either to be pushed into the freight wagons headed for Eskishehir, Konya, and to the Mesopotamian deserts, or earmarked for extermination in the nearby valleys. Our family was not touched, apparently because our names were not on their list.

On August 15, 1915, just as father was about to lock his office building, a woman relative rushed in to tell him that all the Armenian males were being arrested in the streets. Father rushed home through the back alleys. Fortunately we were all there, my sister, mother, the maid, and myself. Father immediately locked the iron door and secured the iron bars behind it. The window shutters were closed, windows locked, and blinds pulled down. Father then turned off the lights and led us downstairs to the basement.

There was a thorough search in every street. The police and the gendarmes knocked on every door, house by house, name by name. We could hear their calling of our neighbors' names. A few of them knocked at our door to find out if anyone was in the house. Our house was located in the Armenian section where most of the foreign consuls and diplomatic representatives resided. Due to the war, many had left Turkey temporarily. Others had gone away for summer vacation. The arresting officers eventually decided that the house was vacant and left the premises. We remained in our house hiding, without ever making a noise, without ever lighting even a candle. Our house was a six-story, thick-walled brick building. Viewed from the street it looked like a four-story building. Having been build on a slope, it had two stories below the street level. These two basements, which received their sunlight from an inner court, served as our refuge. We used our bedrooms after dark, climbing the stairs in total darkness without making the least bit of noise. Our water, what there was of it, came from the well in our court. As for food, we had provisions stored in our sub-basement.

Mother insisted that we girls make laces to keep our minds

occupied. Sister preferred to crochet, and I made Armenian needle-laces. Sometimes in desperation I would stop and mother would say, "Please practice and become expert at it. Remember, whatever you create may be taken away from you, but whatever you learn, that knowledge is yours and no one can take it away. Knowledge is like gold bracelets on your wrist, it will support you and save you from begging."

Our court was long and extended to the back street. At the far end was another house that father rented to an elderly Armenian couple who were exempted from deportation by reason of their son's enlistment in the Turkish army. The woman occasionally dressed in Turkish *feredje* (costume) and went to the Turkish market to buy what she needed. A few times our maid, similarly dressed, accompanied her, but they were frightened to walk through isolated streets, afraid that their disguise would be detected. One day during their shopping, they heard that Catholics and Protestants had been exempted from deportation, due to the mediation of the Pope and other European dignitaries and the protests of the missionaries and the United States Ambassador Henry Morgenthau.

At first father did not pay attention to this rumor, but he did ask our tenant to get factual information from a Greek Protestant friend. The Greek confirmed the news. Thereupon father took a chance one morning, disregarding our tearful pleading not to go, and left the house for his office. Father was expected to come home at noon; he did not. We waited all afternoon, and still he didn't appear. Then the door bell rang. A Greek friend of father's had come to let us know that father was in prison. He had witnessed the police taking him off. Mother asked him to accompany her to the prison. She took some food with her. The guards took the food but refused to let mother see her husband. She came home crushed in sorrow. The Greeks, Jews, and other minorities had not been affected by the order for deportations. The reason the Armenians were singled out was that half of the territory then known as Turkey had at one time or another during 3,000 years been settled and owned by Armenians. By displacing and killing them, the Turkish government would acquire the great wealth and vast lands they owned. That was the reason why even little children were not spared. The Turks did not want any heirs to live.

The next morning our door bell startled us. Mother opened the door and faced a policeman with a telegram in his hand. "Is this Garabed Effendi Odian's residence?" he asked. Mother nodded. He handed her the telegram, written in Arabic script. "Would you kindly read it?" mother requested. He obliged and explained that it was an order from the palace of the sultan for a large quantity of Angora soff. Then mother and the policeman took the telegram to father at the prison. Father asked for pen and ink and stationery. He addressed a petition to the sultan, with copies to the Chief Justice and the Chief of Police, asking for his release so that he could produce the textile for the sultan as soon as possible. He wrote that since the fifteenth century his family had supplied this fabric to the sultans, and if he were given his freedom, he would continue to produce the internationally known fabric for the glory of Turkey. He also invited the government to assign young Turkish workers to his factory to learn the trade. He said that since skilled Armenians artisans had been deported, unless he was allowed to perpetuate this centuries-old craft, it would be lost forever to Turkey.

The Chief Justice knew father very well. He received mother with much courtesy, promising to send father's petition as a telegram to the sultan. A copy went to the Chief of Police.

Despite mother's daily visits to the prison and inquiries, no order for his release came. Finally on the fourth day another visit by mother to the Chief Justice's office revealed the fact that the sultan's order for father's release had indeed arrived, but the Chief of Police had shelved it. The Chief Justice angrily intervened and that very afternoon father arrived home with mother carrying the sultan's order for his freedom. An Armenian craft had saved us from deportation, torture, and death!

We had hardly finished supper when the door bell rang again. It was the Chief of Police demanding to see Father. The two spent more than an hour alone in our parlor. At length we heard father hurry down to the basement. Within five minutes he was back upstairs, closing the parlor door behind him. Shortly thereafter the Chief of Police left. Father refused to tell us why he had come. "It doesn't concern you," he said, smiling sadly. Months later, after the Armistice, we learned that the Chief of Police had demanded a large sum of ransom money, threatening otherwise to deport our entire family immediately on the pretext that the sultan's order for father's release had arrived too late. He also had warned father not to tell anyone about his demand.

As soon as father was released from prison, he began very diligently to work for the establishment of a large plant in the Turkish business quarters. The released Armenian artisans were put to work. Father had offered the authorities to work without any monetary compensation in lieu of his and his family's freedom, but he made sure that the Armenian workers were each paid for their labor. Soon the goats were sheared. Their wool was washed and dyed in required colors. Dozens of women combed and spun the wool into hair like fine threads. Expert weavers set the looms and began weaving. Within a few weeks several rolls of fine, silky Angora fabric were ready for shipment to the palace of the sultan in Istanbul. The authorities were extremely pleased and highly complimented father's achievement.

Days passed. The Armenians being successfully eliminated, further arrests, killings, and deportations had all stopped. We were free to go out; but except for father, we remained in our house. New Year and Armenian Christmas arrived, but there were no celebrations. We were mourning the death of our relatives and of our nation. Mother was an intelligent and courageous woman. She kept sister and me busy and occupied. She taught me how to make laces, embroideries, and other needle-art. Father supplied books from our family library. I read numerous adult books. As there was no recreation, schools, or playmates, father would take me sometimes to the textile plant. There I watched with fascination the process of weaving the Armenian fabric, commercially exported as Angora soff. In early spring father took us—mother, sister, and our maid—to his washing and dyeing plant, located at the base of the ancient fortress not very far from Sangarious River. Years earlier father had bought this ruined six-acre estate because it had facilities for his needs. This estate had two spacious courts, surrounded with thick, high stone walls. During the pre-Roman period it had served as a palace, with formal gardens and three large swimming pools with sculptured lion-headed fountains. During these visits we usually had our lunch, seated on an Armenian-made rug, under the huge walnut tree beside the marble swimming pools, watching the Armenian men wash the dyed wools in the pools. Elsewhere other men were busy dyeing the wools in huge copper vats containing the required dyes. Of this once ancient palatial complex there remained only a small stone construction which father used as his storage, for utensils and dyes he himself prepared from vegetable and insect sources. I loved this place; it was so removed from our experienced tragedies. Its splendor, though buried in remote past, yet could be felt. Our pleasant visits to this ancient estate suddenly were interrupted in the spring of 1916.

Despite the assurance of the Ottoman authorities that the deportations of the Armenians were only temporary and that every resident would return home at the conclusion of the war, suddenly a hectic activity broke the tragic silence within the lifeless Armenian streets. Hundreds of horse carts invaded the Armenian quarter. They stopped in front of every house, shop, church, and business building, while specially assigned police and officers systematically emptied the contents of each building until there was nothing left behind. More than 2,000 shops, sixteen schools, three ancient stone cathedrals, nine churches, trade and needlework schools, kindergartens, and thousands of homes were emptied. This activity lasted from morning to evening for more than six months, until every Armenian building had been stripped of its last article. Thousands of wealthy Armenians were forced to leave behind all their jewelry, money, and valuables when they were hastily taken away from their residences. Millions of dollars worth of wealth was expropriated by the Ottoman government and sent to Istanbul, loaded in thousands of freight wagons. Only rummage-type articles, considered not suitable to send to the capital, were given to the local Turks, to be sold in the Turkish open bazaar to benefit the province.

When all the movable wealth of the Armenians of Angora had been removed from every building, on one late October night in 1916 a huge conflagration burst throughout the entire Armenian quarter. The fire was not confined to a particular area, but several separate fires were simultaneously spreading all over the streets. The artificially set fire was so intense that within a few hours the whole area was alighted with rapidly engulfing flames.

Our family owned in the city three beautiful houses, two of which father had let to Armenian widows whose sons were in the service of Turkish army and who were not deported. From our burning house quite a few necessary articles were salvaged and carried to our second house, but soon the flames reached it. Then, from the second house, we fled to the third house with fewer salvaged items. But soon that section too was in flames; at the end every Armenian who had survived the Genocide was left homeless and destitute. Everyone had to flee to the open fields, leaving behind all their personal effects to be burned. Everyone ran away from the smoldering flames and smoke.

For three nights and two whole days the entire Armenian section burned. After spending a few days in the open fields, without beds and blankets, father had finally been lucky in his search to find, in the Turkish quarter, a three-room residence which he had rented instantly. The bare rooms needed furnishing. All our expensive furniture, rugs, drapes, curtains, silverware, china, household items, clothing, books, pictures, and souvenirs—everything had become ashes. Except for a handful of gold coins father had removed from his personal safe, kept in the basement, all other valuables were destined to perish.

Mother had not allowed us to weep for our material loss, either during or after the fire. She even reprimanded me when I cried bitterly for my beautiful Lenox china doll that was left behind in our burning house. She reminded me that many Armenian children not only lost their homes, toys, and dolls, but they also lost their parents and were left orphans.

Gradually father bought necessary furnishings and household articles from the Turkish shops. One day he bought from the open bazaar used kitchen wear, once belonging to Armenians. As mother cleaned and washed them, I noticed that there were tears in her eyes.

We adjusted to our life in this small apartment. Father had to walk to his supervising work every day, crossing the ruined and burned Armenian residential area, until he reached the manufacturing plant which was not burned, being in the Turkish business district. It was emotionally very hard for father to pass each day once familiar streets and roads, now cluttered with heaps of charred bricks, stones, and debris that smelled of smoke.

Time passed. We spent two winters in our small apartment, living day by day, waiting for the war to end. One day during the summer of 1918, father received a letter from the Minister of Education in Istanbul, requesting him to find an Armenian woman to teach spinning, weaving, and needle-art to young Turkish girls in a newly organized trade school in the capital. Father informed him that he knew no one to recommend. The local Turkish authorities insisted that father send mother as a teacher. Mother refused. She did not wish to leave her family and her young daughter behind. But the Turkish authorities decided otherwise. They arranged for me to accompany mother. Thus on an early September morning, in 1918, mother and I parted from my dear father and sister and boarded the train headed for Istanbul.

It was a painful parting at the station. The train was so long you couldn't see to the end of it, and it was packed with Turkish soldiers. We traveled twenty-four hours and on our arrival we found the Turkish Minister of Education and Trade, Kemal Pasha, waiting for us. He took us to a building in the district of Shishly. It had an impressive entrance, leading into an elegantly furnished hall. From there we were taken to the second-floor reception room sumptuously decorated in European style. We were introduced to the mistress of the house, the wife of the Minister, addressed as Hanum Effendi. She informed us that we would have our breakfast in our rooms but dinner and supper would be served in the dining room. Finally we were taken to our private quarters on the third floor. Our apartment consisted of a tastefully furnished bedroom with two beds, a living room, and a luxuriously tiled bath.

We rested until a maid came to take us to the dining room. Though there were only three women and a child my age (men ate separately), the table was banquet size. The child was the daughter of the Hanum Effendi, we were told. Two of the women had been members of the sultan's harem, and the third at table was the maid who had come for us.

The dinner, consisting of boiled cracked wheat and pieces of lamb's meat, was served on large platter which went round and round while each person helped herself with her fingers and spoon. Following half an hour of socializing with the Hanums, we retired to our rooms. For supper we had a thick soup with some cheese and olives and so-called Turkish coffee (actually Arabic).

There were no books or magazines around, and I was bored in our room. Mother asked the maid to supply us with some thread and needles for lace work. She also gave her money to buy wool thread to make a sweater for me.

On the third day mother asked the Pasha about the trade school. She was told that the school would be adjacent to our building but that we had to wait a few weeks until it was organized. Every day I made Armenian laces until I wearied. We wanted to go out walking or shopping but were not allowed. Although mother was given a very generous salary in gold, she told the Pasha she did not like to be paid for services not rendered. She suggested that we might go to stay with friends until the school had been organized. Kemal Pasha would have none of it. "You are our guests, you are going to live here until the school is opened," said he.

One day we were surprised to be told that a lieutenant had come to visit us. He was my mother's elder sister's son, who was in the Turkish military. We had not known that he was stationed in Istanbul, nor that he was even alive. Cousin Garbis looked very handsome in his uniform. He had learned of our whereabouts from father and requested permission to take us out. He took us, in his hired landau, to the park, where we had ice cream and pastries. We listened to the band and then he brought us back. After that he came once a week.

One day when mother and I were out with cousin Garbis, we were riding on an electric trolley car when suddenly we heard aerial bombing. The glass windows of the car were shattered but no one was hurt. The bombing was by the British, someone said. Cousin Garbis returned us promptly to our apartment and promised to keep in touch

Two weeks later, on the morning of November 12, 1918, we heard an unusual commotion: thousands of horns blowing and church bells ringing. We saw the maid going up to the roof garden and followed her. From the top we could see a spectacular panorama of the port. It seemed the entire fleet of the Allied forces had entered the harbor. Through binoculars we could identify the British, Italian, French, Greek, Russian, and American flags. Hanum Effendi lost her temper and began cursing. She retreated downstairs muttering to herself, "Finally they came." We never saw her again.

When everybody had left and we were alone with the young Serayli Hanum, she told us she was not Turkish but Circassian. When a very young girl she had been taken by force into the sultan's harem. After she had become seriously ill, she was let go with a small pension. "I came to live with my cousin," she said, referring to the maid. "You see, my cousin is not a maid, but she takes care of the little girl because she is her mother. Pasha is the girl's father."

After a pause she continued, "I knew that there was not going to be a school in this building. The Turks were losing the war, and they did not dare to establish a school next door because this building does not belong to them. It is the former Italian Embassy. They knew the Italians would come some day to take it back."

We stayed in our rooms and that evening we packed our things, wondering what we were going to do next.

Throughout the night we heard the noise of carriages coming and going, people moving about. By daybreak everything was quiet. We went down to the second floor and found that all the rooms and halls had been stripped bare. The young Serayli Hanum, who was taking her belongings to the elevator, explained that the Pasha and his family had fled during the night, taking all the Italian furnishings with them.

A servant came to tell us that we were going to the Turkish girls' trade school in the city. Two policemen placed us and our two valises in a landau and took us to the Turkish quarter.

The girls' school turned out to be a huge barrack in which hundreds of mattresses were lined upon the floor. The woman guard directed us to two mattresses and blankets. Mother took one look at the dirty beds, crawling with lice, and warned me not to sit on them. She suggested to the guard that we could stay with friends, but she refused to allow us to leave.

Mother placed our two suitcases one on top of the other and we sat on them, watching the women sleep. They were middle-aged women and did not look like students. Presently we saw a lieutenant in Turkish uniform and heard him ask the guard for us. "I have come to take them to Pera," he said. Without suspecting that he was mother's nephew, the guard let us go and we were rushed into a landau. On the way to the office of my father's best friend, Cousin Garbis told us about all the inquiries he had had to make in order to find us.

Father's friend and business associate received us warmly and gave mother the keys to his house in Pera. We were invited to stay as long as we wanted. "Now that the Armistice is signed," he said, "I am going to ask your husband to come to Istanbul as soon as he can. So, you have a place to stay. Please feel at home."

We were very comfortable in our new residence. Meanwhile father had been able to secure places for my sister and himself on a troop train that was transporting former British prisoners of war. After they joined us, we lived in Pera for a year until we were able to obtain visas from the Allied Forces to enable us to leave for the United States.

We arrived at Ellis Island on the November 19, 1919. My three older brothers, who had immigrated to the United States prior to World War I, came to Ellis Island to meet us. We were not detained. After spending a night in a New York City hotel, we arrived in Boston the next day. Five days later we celebrated our first Thanksgiving and our freedom.

Seventy years have passed since the 1915 Genocide. Turkey's transformation into a Democratic Republic was welcomed by the surviving Armenians. We had hoped that modern Turkish leaders, for the sake of the honor and prestige of their Republic, would have the honesty and the integrity to face the historical events of 1915 to 1922 as they happened, without resorting to lies to cover up the atrocious crimes committed by the Ottoman leaders.

Alas! It is very disturbing to read in the American news media articles by Turkish statesmen full of distortions and misstatements. I quote the following statement of the Ambassador of Turkey to the United States.

In response to the open Armenian uprising, as well as threat of further revolts, the Ottoman Authorities concluded they had no alternative but to relocate the Armenians from the eastern front regions to Syria and Palestine (at that time Southern Provinces of the Empire). Armenians in other parts of the Empire, including the capital Istanbul, were untouched by this wartime decision.[4]

How does the Honorable Ambassador of Turkey reconcile his statement with the arrest on April 24, 1915, in Istanbul, of several hundred Armenian dignitaries and their subsequent murder in Angora valleys, if "the Armenians in other parts of the Empire, including the capital, Istanbul, were untouched"? Were the native Armenians of Angora insurgents? Why were the good Vali and Chief of Police of Angora dismissed from their positions and punished? Did they not testify that the native Armenians of the area were loyal, useful citizens of Turkey and they could not deport or massacre them? Was the Province of Angora within the eastern war zone? Had the loyal citizens of Angora ever revolted against their government? Were their massacres temporary relocations? If their deportations were temporary, why were their personal properties and wealth confiscated and expropriated by the Ottoman authorities? If the Armenians were returning to their homes after the war, why were their homes, shops, churches, schools, and business establishments deliberately destroyed, burned to ashes?

Why were thousands of beautiful summer resorts and vineyards expropriated by the Ottoman authorities, not to mention the hundreds of cities, villages, and towns of the Armenian provinces and Cilicia which were destroyed? Were the following cities, towns, and villages located in the Eastern front regions? Where are the Armenian residents of Adapazar, Akhissar, Akseray, Akshehir, Ak-Dagh-Maden, Amasia, Armash, Aslanbeg, Al-shehir, Alaja, Baghcheji, Balukesir, Bandurma, Baybazar, Bilejik, Bolu, Bursa, Chakmak, Chavoushlar, Chorlu, Chiftlik, Chorum, Denekmaden, Efkereh, Eskishehir, Ereyli, Everek, Gemerek, Geyveh, Gurin, Gurindos, Haimanah, Herek, Ismid, Kalayjik, Karaman, Kassaba, Kavak, Kayseri, Kershehir, Kesab, Kiliseh, Killis, Konya, Kotchisar, Kunjular, Kushla, Kutahia, Kuzulja, Ladik, Lefkeh, Maden, Manisa, Merzifon, Moujour, Mounjousoon, Nallukhan, Nevshehir, Nigdeh, Nigsar, Nirseh, Ovajuck, Oushak, Severek, Sivas, Sivrihissar, Songourlu, Stanos, Talas, Tokat, Uluja, Yenijeh, Yozgat, and numerous other towns and villages not mentioned? Is it not a fact that the native Armenians of these towns and villages were all displaced, deported and massacred and their lands and ancestral wealth expropriated by the Ottoman Turks?

The present leaders of Turkey are deceiving only themselves by their lies, distortions of truth, and denial of facts. The Armenians know, and the nations of the entire world know, that the Turkish leaders' denial of the Armenian Genocide stems from two major reasons. The first is that the Turkish diplomatic leaders do not wish to face reparation payments of billions of dollars for the expropriated wealth of the murdered, displaced, and annihilated Armenian people. The second reason is that the present-day leaders are aware of President Woodrow Wilson's map of Armenia and the historic rights of ownership to these occupied lands by the Armenians, wherever they may be.

If Turkey's leaders consider themselves civilized individuals, then they should follow the example of Germany, where crimes of the Nazis were admitted and full reparation was made to those who were victims of the Nazi crimes.

The present Turkish leaders make themselves laughing stocks by their ridiculous comparisons of their war casualties on equal terms with the victims of the Armenian Genocide. By propagandizing the fact that Turkey also lost many souls during this period, they suggest that the Turks were not victims of war but were killed by the Armenians. What a flagrant lie! How could the murdered Armenian males and the 400,000 Armenian soldiers inducted into the Turkish Army and deliberately, one by one, killed by the order of Enver Pasha have been responsible for Turkish war casualties? How could the hungry, starved, deported Armenian women and children in the deserts, without arms, kill Turkish soldiers or civilians?

The shameless lies and distortions of the leaders of the Turkish Republic are a mockery and insult to the intelligence of the nations of the world who had in all the major cities in Turkey consular representatives and correspondents during the First World War. In their archives are abundant references to the Armenian Genocide committed by the Ottoman Turkish leaders during World War I.

Denial of truth cannot succeed in the long run. Sooner or later the truth will prevail.

REFERENCES

1. *The Treatment of Armenians in the Ottoman Empire, 1915-16: Documents presented to the Secretary of State for Foreign Affairs by Viscount Bryce* (London, 1916), Document #95, 382.

2. Henry Morgenthau, *Ambassador Morgenthau's Story* (New York, 1918).

3. *Treatment of Armenians*, Document #96, 385.

4. Sukru Elekdag, Letter to the Editor, *Wall Street Journal*, Sept. 21, 1983.

Young People Caught Up in a Catastrophe: Survivors of the Armenian Genocide of 1915

Frank A. Stone

The year 1985 has the distinction of being both the seventieth anniversary of the beginning of the Armenian Genocide in the Ottoman Empire, and also the United Nations International Year of Youth. It therefore seems appropriate to examine the tragedy of the Armenian Genocide of 1915-1922 from the perspective of individuals who were its victims when they were, themselves, experiencing childhood and adolescence. The purpose of the inquiry is not only to recognize what happened to some young survivors during a harrowing time in their lives, but also to engage the attention of today's youth. Young people who reflect on the impact that a genocide has on people their age should be especially committed to preventing the occurrence of future genocides.

THE GENOCIDE CONCEPT

Officially sanctioned mass violence has existed throughout history, but only recently has the process been described and a term coined to designate it. Selected as the counterpart to homicide (the intentional murder of an individual), genocide means the destruction of a group as the outcome of governmental policy. The word and concept did not exist in 1915, and therefore it was not part of the thinking and perceptions of the children and young people who have written accounts of their experiences as victims of the widespread massacres and deportations in the Ottoman Empire.

After years of effort by Raphael Lemkin, global attention was drawn to the problem of recurring genocides when in 1946 the General Assembly of the United Nations declared such acts to be "a crime under international law, contrary to the spirit and aims of the

United Nations and condemned by the civilized world."[1] On December 9, 1948 the U.N. General Assembly unanimously adopted a Convention against genocide. It went into effect in 1950, after being ratified by twenty nations. Sadly, however, the United States Senate failed to ratify this vital international Convention until 1986.

According to Article II of the document, genocide is defined in these words.

> In the present Convention, genocide means any of the following acts committed with intent to destroy, in whole or in part, a national, ethnic, racial or religious group, such as:
> a. Killing members of the group;
> b. Causing serious bodily or mental harm to members of the group;
> c. Deliberately inflicting on the group conditions of life calculated to bring about its physical destruction in whole or in part;
> d. Imposing measures intended to prevent births within the group;
> e. Forcibly transferring children of the group to another group.[2]

These specifications make it clear that the term "genocide" represents an inclusive concept covering a spectrum of acts and policies. The process of deculturation is the least physically violent option. A group is being deculturized when its language, values, patriotism, personal security, health, dignity, and economic survival are threatened. Next in their degrees of violence come acts such as lynching, terrorism, massacres, and pogroms. The most violent forms of genocide include deliberate starvation, defoliation, biological and chemical warfare, mass bombing of civilian populations, and the holocaust.

The authors of the six memoirs that are the data base for this inquiry certainly did not know about the detailed theoretical aspects of genocide when they wrote their survivor accounts of the events that took place between 1915 and 1922. As will be ascertained by examining the documents they wrote, however, each individual was the victim of genocidal procedures. Through their eyes and ears we can learn what it is like to undergo such a catastrophe in childhood or adolescence.

LITERARY SOCIOLOGY

The inquiry methodology of literary sociology usually involves using works of fiction, such as novels and short stories, written by recognized authors as the sources of social insights. The present study, however, is an investigation of six survivor's accounts of the Armenian Genocide of 1915 to 1922. Only one of the writers of these memoirs, Leon Surmelian, has achieved fame as an author. The others are not professional writers, but rather individuals who were eyewitnesses to traumatic events. Their motives in writing were to preserve their recollections for posterity and to reflect on the impact that these experiences had had on them and their fellow Armenians.

The literary sociologist[3] examines the relevant documents from a number of interrelated perspectives. First, the hermeneutics of the rhetoric must be studied. How is the writer's message communicated to the reading audience? Which views are explicitly stated, and which can only be inferred? What is the thought world and presuppositions from which the author writes? Is the writer presenting contemporary events, or recalling incidents that occurred earlier? Was the writer actually a participant in the events that are reported, or is the testimony based on other people's experiences?   Second, it is standard to the approach of literary sociology to consider the semiotics of the document. By semiotics is meant its distinguishing characteristics of diction, morphology, and syntax. Does the writer employ any unusual vocabulary? If English is their second or third language, is their mother tongue reflected in their distinctive grammar or word usage?

The third dimension that a literary investigator analyzes is the imagery of the work. Are there recurring images, and, if there are, what do they picture? What metaphors does the writer employ? The fourth aspect, one that is particularly germane to studying the memoirs of genocide survivors, is to identify the normative side of their narrative. What values do they advocate? What appears to be the basis of the judgments that they make? What moral and ethical principles are stated or reflected?

It would also be desirable to undertake a sociology of literature concerning the same items used for this literary sociology. This second, complementary process, however, is more complex and requires additional time and data. It would be helpful to know the exact circumstances under which each account was penned.   In which language was it originally written? Has much editing taken place, or is the published memoir essentially as originally written? Who was the intended audience at the time of writing?

Additionally, for a sociology of literature we would have to know the types of publishers and the sizes of the editions of these books. How were they publicized and disseminated? Who actually bought and read copies? Were any of them adapted for use with other media such as radio, films or television? Did the writers of the more recently published memoirs know about the earlier accounts of genocide

survivors? Are the incidents recounted in the memoirs verified by any
other corroborating sources, such as contemporary reporting by
newspaper correspondents and journalists, the accounts written by
foreign observers, or the contents of archives? Is there photographic
evidence that supports the assertions made in the eye witness
accounts? And do the hundreds of oral histories that have now been
compiled from informants who were also genocide survivors substantiate the claims of the writers of published memoirs?

Using the six published reminiscences of the Armenian Genocide
we can obtain an immediate and phenomenological awareness of what
happened. The accounts are subjective—after all it was the writers
and their families who were the victims. On the other hand, we
should not expect many profound explanations of what caused the
massacres and deportations. Most of our writers were quite young at
the time these events happened to them, and they were in no position
to know very much about the motives of the Young Turk leaders in
Istanbul, or the international intrigues of the European Powers in the
Middle East. They were not politically active, and too young or of the
wrong gender to be involved in military action.

Our six informants are: Kerop Bedoukian, *The Urchin: An
Armenian's Escape* (London: John Murray, 1978); Abraham H.
Hartunian, *Neither To Laugh nor To Weep. A Memoir of the Armenian
Genocide* (Boston: Beacon Press, 1968); Alice Muggerditchian Shipley,
We Walked, Then Ran (Phoenix, Ariz.: 1983); Leon Surmelian, *I Ask
You, Ladies and Gentlemen* (New York: E.P. Dutton, 1945); Elise
Hagopian Taft, *Rebirth: The Story of an Armenian Girl Who Survived
the Genocide and Found Rebirth in America* (Plandome, N.Y.: New Age
Publishers, 1981); and Serpouhi Tavoukdjian, *Exiled. Story of an
Armenian Girl* (Takoma Park, Washington, D.C.: Review and Herald
Publishing, 1933).

The informants are three girls and three boys whose ages in 1915
were: Alice, nine; Elise, nine; Serpouhi, ten; Abraham, twenty-three
in 1895 when he survived the Hamidian massacre; Kerop, nine; and
Leon, about eleven. Two, Elise and Serpouhi, lived in western
Anatolia not too far from Istanbul (Constantinople) at Bandirma (the
seaport for Bursa) and Ovaljik (Ovacik), a town not far from Izmit.
Two were residents of central Anatolia: Abraham in Marash in 1915
(originally he came from Severek in the province of Diyarbakir), and
Kerop in Sivas (ancient Sebastia). Two were inhabitants of eastern
Anatolia; Alice in Diyarbakir (ancient Dikranagerd), but she was in
Harput (Kharpert) with her mother and siblings attending school at

the time of the Genocide, and Leon in Trabzon (Trebizond).

The present writer has visited all of these locations at one time or another in the 1950s and 1960s and is therefore familiar with the original settings of the memoirs as they were in the mid-twentieth century. Classified according to their Christian persuasion (that of their families), three of the informants belonged to the Armenian Apostolic Church and three were Protestants—two members of the Armenian Evangelical Church and one a Seventh Day Adventist.

The earliest of the six memoirs was written in 1933. The next came out in 1945, followed by another in 1968. The other three were published in 1978, 1981, and 1983. Three were issued by well known major publishers, and three were either privately published or put out by a very small publisher.

We can surmise, therefore, that achieving publication was not easy. Apparently it required a period of adjustment and adaptation to the new society before writing activities could be undertaken. Thus, although the authors reminisce about experiences from their childhood and adolescent years, on the whole, they are doing so after periods of time ranging from eleven to more than forty years. We have no way of knowing whether or not they used diaries or other informal notations made at the earlier time for their memoirs—but the circumstances that they were in make this doubtful. On the other hand, oral tradition is still strong among Middle Eastern peoples and many of the incidents being recalled were so climactic that they must have been etched in the memory. It is not difficult to believe that they can be vividly and accurately remembered even after the passage of long time intervals.

Let us now turn to sketching a literary sociology of genocide experiences based on the written accounts of six young survivors.

CONDITIONS BEFORE THE CALAMITY

All six memoir writers describe their homes and local communities prior to the start of the Genocide in the spring of 1915. Two recount their lives as the children of socially prominent families that were among the Armenian notables of the area. Two belonged to less prominent shopkeeper and merchant class families that apparently were part of the middle class in the contemporary society. One was the son of a tanner of hides and shoemaker who had had little or no formal schooling. As a skilled craftsman, however, although the father certainly wasn't well off, it seems that he was able to adequately feed and support his family. The last informant was the son of a small landowner and merchant of food staples who earned his living by a combination of farming and selling household commodities in a small shop in the local market. It is evident, therefore, that our six informants came from various socioeconomic strata in the Armenian communities located in the Ottoman Empire.

Their original homes are recalled as having been relatively happy places, although they were not immune to natural tragedies. It seems that infant mortality was commonplace in early twentieth century Armenia as several of the informants mention having lost brothers and sisters. In one case the writer was raised by a step-mother when his natural mother lost her life as the result of a faulty folk cure for arthritis. Another account opens with the death of a young uncle from disease. So we know that even before the war years, life was not always easy for the Armenian subjects of the Ottoman Empire.

As they are remembered in these accounts, all of the local towns were ethnically segregated. Each residential block or neighborhood, called a *mahalle*, was inhabited by one or another religious and linguistic group known as a *millet*. In western Turkey these were Christian Armenians and Greeks, and Muslim Turks. In the eastern parts of the country, besides these three groups, Christian Assyrians, and Muslim Arabs and Kurds are mentioned. Jews are referred to infrequently as a very tiny minority of the local population.

Although in the marketplace of the town the craftsmen's shops and the merchants' stores were again segregated so that Christian areas were separate from Muslim, yet here there was some inter-ethnic mixing. The local government officials were almost entirely Muslims, with the higher ranked civil servants being appointed from Istanbul, the capital city. The military forces were also almost entirely staffed by Muslims, with units of the regular army regarded as being of better quality than the gendarmerie, the internal security organization. The local police were almost completely drawn from the Muslim Turkish population. Each of the Christian millets, or *azinlik* (minority), represented itself to the Ottoman authorities through its community leaders, usually prominent clergy, professionals, or affluent merchants.

Sometimes there were other types of inter-communal contacts. For example, our informants recall that Muslim itinerant peddlers or beggars might come to their homes. They usually passed by in the narrow streets and alleys, hawking their wares or calling out for charity. They might then be invited into the walled garden or compound that invariably surrounded Anatolian homes to make the transaction or receive the assistance in the form of food or clothing. Also, if the Armenian family owned farmland, often it was cultivated by Turkish villagers, usually with a form of sharecropping. Then there were contacts between the Christian landowner and the Muslim Turkish or Kurdish villagers. In at least one case there seems to have been another form of inter-ethnic relationship through the Masonic orders to which some Europeanized Armenians and Turks both belonged.

On the whole, however, ethnic separation was much more visible than was ethnic integration. For example, personal bathing was usually done in the public baths that invariably were located near mosques, but usually where they were accessible to people from the various millets. As Leon recalls, his family bathed at the Bathhouse of the Infidels—the Gâvur Hamami, so named because it was originally a Byzantine Church.

> Both Christians and Turks bathed in the Giaour [Gâvur] Hamami, but never together. There were separate days for each. Women and children bathed during the day, men at night. It was situated in a maze of medieval lanes, with white and red roses climbing garden walls. A small gate led into the wood yard where you could see the huge furnace in the basement—a fearful sight. It made me think of the fires of hell.
>
> (Surmelian, p. 24)

This passage illustrates the segregated way of life, and also gives an example of the imagery of foreboding that is frequently encountered in the memoirs. Yet, outwardly, the inter-ethnic relations seemed to be cordial. At the bathhouse, for instance:

> The manager, a handsome, passionate-looking Turkish woman with a milk-white face, sat cross-legged in a railed dias at the door furnished with rugs and cushions, smoking a cigarette. She might have been a reigning queen of a sultan's harem. She welcomed us with all the polite, poetic phrases of the ceremonious East, inquiring after our health and showering compliments on us, which Mother duly returned.   (ibid.)

Like most of the other aspects of everyday life, schooling in Ottoman Turkey was also segregated. According to our informants, most Armenian families placed a great value on providing their children with educational opportunities. Serpouhi recalls,

> Father and mother were strong believers in education, and so we went regularly to school. This was a school for Armenian children only, and some of our neighbors and friends could not afford the tuition for their boys and girls, so father often paid for them.   (Tavoukdjian, p. 19)

In Bandirma, Elise gives us this picture:

> Every Armenian child, dressed in a clean uniform, went to our national school in the church compound. The kindergarten girls wore bright red pinafores, and the boys wore white shirts and navy blue shorts. Unlike the Moslems, who were segregated by sex, Armenian boys and girls attended the same classes (as did Greek children) until the age of puberty, after which they went their separate ways—"to avoid temptation" was the way elderly folk put it.   (Taft, p. 4f.)

Apparently, however, there were some cases where Armenian educators taught Turkish children. After the start of the genocide, for instance, Kerop had this reminiscence.

> All of a sudden I paid attention to the conversation. My mother was saying that we had had an offer from the Mayor via my aunt, a teacher who had established six Turkish kindergartens, the first in the city. The offer was that my aunt and forty-two of her relatives could be saved from deportation if they turned Mohammedan.   (Bedoukian, p. 8)

Although it was rejected, this offer suggests that the services of Armenian educators were at least sometimes valued by their Turkish rulers.

Another important dimension of the picture that we are given of pre-genocide Armenian life in Anatolia is its extended family and patriarchal characteristics. Usually, one's relatives lived nearby in the same section of the town, or at least in the same region of the country. Celebrations involved one's entire clan of relatives. The extended family was also present in times of sorrow. The honor and reputation of the family involved everyone connected with it, not just the few members of a nuclear family.

In most cases three generations lived together. If still living, it was the grandfather and his brothers who received the greatest degree of deference. Often, however, because the grooms were usually quite a bit older than their brides at marriage, the family patriarch was deceased at the time when our informant was writing. Then his widow might reign in his stead, as it were. Also, the grandmother had complete charge of the female part of the household, as well as the child-rearing.

Kerop describes a central Anatolia situation, saying,

> The household was ruled by a matriarch, Mariam Marig, the grand-mother, paralyzed on one side, chain-smoking with occasional hashish thrown in. She was especially harsh on the daughters-in-law, who, according to custom, were not allowed to speak at all, let alone talk back. The girls over fourteen were not handled with kid gloves either, but her orders and requests to the men had a tone of respect. It was the children, especially me, nine years old and a boy, who were the objects of her affections. Every time my mother slapped me, and this was a

daily occurrence, my grandmother would curse her until she got out of ear-shot.   (Bedoukian, p. 1)

As is made evident in this passage, boys had greater prestige than girls. In the Armenian Apostolic households boys were likely to receive more formal schooling, but one of the Protestant Armenian emphases was on the education of women. Thus, several of the mothers described in the memoirs had had high-school level training.

As we will see, the massacres and deportations associated with the Armenian Genocide disrupted at its roots the previous family life. Often the fathers and older brothers lost their lives, so women had to accept responsibilities in domains that had previously been strictly male ones. Also, the rigors of deportation quickly killed off many of the elderly, so the tradition of matriarchal rule in the home life had to cease. Finally, the Armenian adolescent girls and young women, who previously had been reared in very protected environments, found themselves completely uprooted when being deported. Plucked from the protection of their male family members, they became the targets of rape and other forms of exploitation.

DEPORTATION AND MASSACRE

Only one of our six informants had experienced massacres prior to the genocide of 1915. In 1895 Abraham was teaching in an Armenian school located in the eastern Anatolian town of Severek. He recalls how rumors of terrible massacres and plunders began to spread among the Armenian community beginning on October 27. In Severek lived about seven thousand "unarmed, unprotected, innocent" Armenians among more than thirty thousand Muslims. There were more than four hundred surrounding villages inhabited by more Muslims—Arabs, Circassians, Chechens, Kurds, Turks and Zazas. Thus, the Armenians were a small minority here.

This is Abraham's beginning account of what happened in Severek.

> It was Saturday, November 2, 1895. The Armenian men, according to their custom, had gone to their shops and were busy at their trades. The women and children were in their houses or, worse, in the public Turkish baths. All at once the city was surging with mobs, tumultuously alive with human wildness and desolation. The butchers were eagerly sharpening their knives and axes, and those to be slaughtered, wringing their hands, were groveling and bewailing the inevitable.
>
> (Hartunian, p. 11)

The account makes it clear that the Hamidian massacre wasn't merely a local event, nor did it occur by happenstance. The pogrom started on orders from the Ottoman authorities in Istanbul, and was garbed in the form of religious fanaticism. The Christian Armenians were commanded to accept the Prophet, "*Muhammed'e salavat!*" The alternative was to be slaughtered.

As the Armenian Protestant pastor was decapitated by a blow with an axe before his eyes, Abraham was stabbed in his left arm with the dagger of one of the assailants. He fell down and lost consciousness.

> When I squatted on the floor, three blows fell on my head. My blood began to flow like a fountain, and I rolled over like a slaughtered lamb. The attackers, sure that I was dead and seeing no need to bother further, left me in that condition. Then they slaughtered the other men in the room, took the prettier women with them for rape, and left the other women and children there, conforming to the command that in this massacre only men were to be exterminated.   (Hartunian, p. 14)

Seven hours later, Abraham, only twenty-three years old at the time, regained consciousness when he felt himself being stripped of this clothing by a Kurdish scavenger. He concludes this part of the episode saying,

> I was naked, bloody, weak, lashed by the wind, my eyes blinded with blood, my breath faltering.   (Hartunian, p. 15)

Abraham survived being beaten up and left for dead in 1895, but most of his community were not so fortunate.

> On Sunday morning, November 3, 1895, the church bells were silent. The churches and schools, desecrated and plundered, lay in ruins. Pastors, priests, choristers, teachers, leaders, all were no more. The Armenian houses, robbed and empty, were as caves. Fifteen hundred men had been slaughtered, and those left alive were wounded and paralyzed. Girls were in the shame of their rape, mothers in the tears of their widowhood, orphaned children in wild bewilderment.
>   (Hartunian, p. 17)

Abraham lived to observe another massacre in 1909, which he escaped only because illness had prevented him from travelling to a church meeting. It was with these previous experiences in mind that he confronted the Armenian Genocide of 1915 as one of the leaders of the Armenian community in Marash. Among our six informants, Abraham was the only one who was a middle-aged adult in 1915.

There are ways in which the previous massacres indicated the process of the 1915 genocide. However, as described by our six eyewitnesses, the dynamics of this series of events was different both in intensity and sequence.

Usually the series of episodes in 1915 began with a public announcement. Serpouhi states:

> The first we knew of trouble was when a proclamation was made by the town crier in the streets of Ovajik, calling all the chief men of the town to meet in the schoolhouse. When they arrived there, they were received by Turkish officers, who told them of the declaration of war, and announced that all able-bodied men between the ages of twenty and forty-five years were to be mustered into the Turkish army for immediate service. They were also told that their families would have four days—and only four—to prepare clothes and food for a long journey. The soldiers made them understand that this would be a final leave-taking of home—a final parting of loved ones. Then the men were beaten by the Turks. (Tavoukdjian, p. 23)

Elise reports that parallel events took place in Bandirma. Here there had been good relations among Armenians, Greeks and Turks in the past. The local Armenians considered themselves to be the *istikametli millet*—the loyal people—a designation reserved for the Armenians of Istanbul by their Turkish rulers. The outcome was the same. All the able-bodied Armenian men were separated from their families and sent into the interior. Allegedly they were to have been in military service, but they actually were placed in *amele taburu*—work squads. They served as virtual slave laborers on the Turkish section of the Berlin to Baghdad railway then being constructed by the Germans, as also recounted by Abraham. A few survived, but almost all were eventually massacred.

House to house searches were instituted in order to discover any arms that the Armenians might possess, or bring traitorous books to light. Elise remembers that

> Armenian homes continued to be searched for arms and "revolutionary" literature. Nothing was ever found. But even an innocent book on ancient Armenian history or music was deemed dangerous and there had been a frantic cleanup of all such books. My brother, Garo, belonged to a youth organization and its small library was in our home. At father's insistence Garo buried the books in a corner of our garden, lest their discovery endanger the entire family. Since the Turks could not read Armenian, any printed book would be construed as "revolutionary" and the entire family jeopardized. It could even mean death. (Taft, p. 34)

Another stage of the genocidal process was the requisition of Armenian churches and schools for use as barracks by the Ottoman army. The military officers also occupied the better Armenian houses, such as the Terlemezian mansion in Bandirma.

In Sivas the genocide began with the rounding up of the Armenian men by soldiers. Kerop recalls:

It had become public knowledge that the men were taken to the
government building which combined city hall, the courthouse and jail.
Also the rumor was that some visitors were allowed if the guards were
bribed.   (Bedoukian, p. 6)

The men were being taken out to unknown destinations in groups
every night. Soon Kerop's father's turn came, and he was never seen
again.

I still feel his goodbye kiss on both my cheeks. We parted. No one
shed any tears.   (Bedoukian, p. 8)

Leon and his family happened to be spending a summer holiday
in an Armenian village near Trabzon when the genocide began.

A Turkish soldier with fixed bayonet stood at our door.
A Turkish soldier was stationed before every Armenian house in the
village and we saw numbers of them guarding the roads, their bayonets
flashing in the early morning sun. The sparrows were chirruping under
the eaves of our cottage as usual, my beans were opening their fuzzy
leaves, the blackbirds whistled, and in the blue bays of Lazistan lateen-
rigged sailing boats floated like graceful white swans in painted lagoons.
But the Turkish soldiers kept watch on us like grim sentinels of death.
                                                     (Surmelian, p. 77)

Alice's father was employed as a *dragoman* or native interpreter at
the British Consulate in the eastern Anatolian town of Diyarbakir.
After nineteen years of service, he had been granted British citizenship, but in the spring of 1915 Great Britain and the Ottoman Empire
were at war. The rest of the Muggerditchian family was living in the
town of Kharpert so that the children could attend the schools there,
but in 1915 their father was evacuated to Egypt, which was then
under British control. Thus, the mother and children found themselves regarded as hostile aliens in the midst of wartime.

In Kharpert, as elsewhere, the genocide began with the rounding
up of the Armenian men. As Alice tells it:

When the *djenderms* [gendarmes] began entering the nearby houses
our hearts sank within us....
Presently the *djenderms* appeared again, dragging unarmed professors, teachers, doctors, and all leading businessmen, half clad, out into
the street. Professor Lulajian, who lived across the square to our left,
made himself available to the *djenderms* in order to give a chance for his
brothers, who lived under his roof, to disappear in the cave through their
basement. His wife, two sons, and two daughters followed him out and
shouted in a loud voice, "What has he done? Let him go! Let him go!"
                                                     (Shipley, p. 52)

Of the men who were rounded up, only one who could prove that he was Assyrian rather than Armenian survived.   One other man was also released after he lost his mind due to torture and the horrible prison conditions.

According to our informants, the next phase of the genocide soon started.   The deportation or *sürgün* decree had been publicly announced and posted.   The able-bodied men had already been sent away.   Now the remaining Armenian families had to get ready as best they could for a lengthy journey, largely on foot, from which they knew few if any would ever be able to return.   Serpouhi relates her experience.

> I was only a little girl ten years old, but how vividly I remember those four sad days of preparation.   My mother was ill from grief and sorrow, and my sisters sewed frantically on garments which we would wear on our long journey.   Into the seams of the wide bloomers we were to wear they sewed money and our few precious pieces of jewelry, which might be bartered along the wayside for food when the little supply we could carry was gone. . . .
>
> Then came the last hour!   The last moment!   The Turkish soldiers on horses, with their guns and long knives ready for business, told us that we must start, and saw that we started!   Where?   We did not know, and we dared not question.   There was hardly time for a farewell look at the dearly beloved home.   Frightened, sorrowful, bewildered, we were driven out and joined hundreds, thousands of our countrymen who were as frightened, as sorrowful, as bewildered as ourselves.
>
> (Tavoukdjian, pp. 24-26)

Elise recalls similar events taking place in Bandirma.

> Then one day late in August the dread news came: the order for the deportation of the entire Armenian population of Bandirma to the wild, arid, uninhabitable, bandit-ridden interior regions of Turkey....
>
> Early one morning soldiers barked out orders that our time had come. We were to leave immediately.   Block by block the homes and shops were emptied of people, the doors locked and sealed, and the keys given to the police, who with their confederates and riff-raff later looted everything, the remains left to the gypsies to carry off.   The poor of Bandirma were driven out, together with the well-to-do.   (Taft, p. 36)

The deportees from the western towns began their journey by being herded into box cars and hauled east on the railroad, provided they could pay for their transportation.   The survivors recount the rigors of this part of their travel, because no sanitary facilities had been provided, nor had any provisions been made to house and feed the people being sent into exile at way points on the various stages of their movement.

In central Anatolia rail transportation wasn't involved, and the deportation columns usually started out with some animals to help carry the people and their moveable possessions. Kerop remembers that his mother sent an appeal to the Turkish villagers who share-cropped land that belonged to his father. On the day before their departure, two ox-drawn wagons came to their house in Sivas to help them move. They were accompanied by drivers, Turks from the villages, who went out on the deportation route for several days with the family.

As Kerop tells about it,

> Early next morning (July 3, 1915) the wagons were loaded with food and clothing of which we had plenty. At the hour of departure two donkeys also were loaded with saddlebags. We were intentionally dressed poorly in order not to attract attention and I looked like a scruffy village boy. At last the moment to see the Great World had arrived; I made up my mind not to miss a thing.

At the end of the first day on the road, Kerop recalls,

> I looked around me. About fifty wagons and hundreds of animals were parking helter-skelter. The voices of women and the cries of babies and children reached such a high pitch that to carry on a conversation was impossible. Then the problem arose as to where to go to the lavatory. A blanket was drawn around the wagon and many took turns to go underneath though some did not even bother to get behind a cover; they just performed in public. (Bedoukian, p. 10)

The process of depriving the exiles of their human dignity had begun. Within a few days, the wagons had to be abandoned. Soon the elderly and infirm could no longer keep up the pace and dropped in their tracks. The girls were molested and sometimes turned over by their families to Arab or Turkish villagers in order to save them from being raped. Adolescent boys were also attacked and killed along the route of march. Drinking water became scarce and food unavailable after the supplies brought from home ran out. Any coins or jewelry were stolen.

Before long many of the *muhajir* (deportees or refugees) were suffering from dysentery and diarrhea. They became the victims of other diseases such as smallpox, typhoid, and typhus. Their bedding was infested with lice and other vermin. Malaria was common and trachoma epidemic. Thus, thousands lost their lives to the illnesses caused by the primitive conditions in which they were forced to live.

The deportations from Marash, the other central Anatolian town from which we have a memoir, took place similarly. In this case, however, the local Ottoman *mütessarif* (sub-governor) intervened to some extent, and was able to slow down and in some cases to prevent the Armenian population from being sent out as refugees to die on the

roads and in the fields.   Eventually the convoys marched out of
Marash, too, and the loss of life there was equally large.

The deportation process in an eastern Anatolian town is described
by Leon.

> A proclamation by the governor-general was posted in the streets of
> the city and announced by town criers. Copies of it reached Zefanoz and
> Mr. Ohanian, our instructor of Turkish, read and translated it to the
> anxious people who gathered around him. ... It went like this:
> "Our Armenian fellow-countrymen, having allied themselves with the
> enemies of the state and religion, and being in revolt against the
> government, are to be deported to special districts in the interior and
> shall remain there for the duration of the war.
> "We hereby order every Armenian in the province of Trebizond to be
> ready to leave in one week, June 24 to July 1. Every Armenian without
> a single exception is subject to this decree. Only those who are too ill or
> too old to walk will be temporarily exempted from deportation and taken
> care of in government hospitals.   Armenians from this day on are
> forbidden to sell anything and are allowed to take with them on their
> journey only what they can carry with them.   No carriages can be
> supplied."   (Surmelian, pp. 80-81)

Along with all the other Armenians in Trabzon, Leon was rounded
up to begin the long march.   He remembers his last view of his
grandmother.

> At sundown we saw our paternal grandmother seated at a window on
> the third story of the hospital, which was close by our orphanage.   I
> cried, 'Neneh! Neneh!' and waved my fez but she did not hear me. What
> was she thinking of, we wondered? She did not move, but sat there as
> if she were not our dear Neneh but her ghost. . . . We never saw her
> again.   (Surmelian, p. 98)

Leon's previously secure world of childhood was collapsing. His
final contact with his parents was a letter and a blanket. Reflecting
on how he felt when he received these last tokens, Leon wrote:

> It was Father's handwriting, there could be no doubt about it. We
> learned he had given himself and Mother up to the police after hiding
> three weeks. He had lost his mind. As gendarmes led them through the
> streets like two captured criminals Mother sobbed aloud, "Give my
> children back to me! Where are my children? Where have you taken
> them?" Greeks who heard her hysterical cries closed their windows and
> wept.
> But we did not cry on reading Father's letter, and said nothing. There
> are sorrows too deep for words or tears.   (Surmelian, p. 99)

Within a few days the orphans were collected by the gendarmes. Leon
speaks up.

> "Where are you taking us?" I asked him.   I wanted to show my

companions that I was not afraid of a gendarme and could talk to him. "*Sürgün,*" he said. "Deportation."   (Surmelian, p. 100)

After the march started, Leon recalls what happened.

> They (the gendarmes) lined us up along the road and robbed us one by one. Aunt Azniv had to give them all the money she had, ten or fifteen gold pounds and six piasters in silver and coppers. They took the gold and let her keep the small change. Fearing they might later take even those six piasters—thirty cents—she gave them to me. ...
>
> Those who could not walk for any reason were killed on the spot. The gendarme stood by her (a much perspiring heavy woman who shuffled along in house slippers) while the rest of us trudged on. When the road made a turn and we could not see them any more the valley resounded with a rifle shot. A few minutes later the gendarme rejoined our convoy, a killer's glitter in his beady eyes.   (Surmelian, p. 103)

Eventually the trials of the deportees become so bad that the remnant of the Surmelian clan who were marching together attempt to commit suicide using a small amount of poison obtained from the pharmacist before they left Trabzon. Alas, it is too little to put them all out of their misery, and merely gives them upset stomachs.

At Kharpert Alice and her family were able to escape deportation by becoming workers in the local hospital that was run by American missionaries. Due to their father's post with the British Consulate in Diyarbakir, they were wanted by the authorities. But they succeeded in eluding capture because the military needed the services of the hospital to nurse the sick and wounded troops. Although overworked, underfed, and constantly moving their quarters to avoid detection, the Muggerditchian mother and her children succeeded in escaping from deportation until they were able to find an escape route out of Ottoman Turkey and become refugees from their homeland.

LIVING AS EXILES

The experience of being deported culminated in the survivors becoming refugees living in exile. According to the accounts written by our informants, this phase of the genocide sequence made an important impact on them.

Serpouhi remembers that she and her mother were on the verge of starvation. They had reached a place where most of the population was Arab, and the little girl pleaded with her mother to sell her to one of the Arabs so that they would be fed.

> And so several of the Arabs came and looked at me. They examined my teeth and felt of me. There was really nothing left but skin and bones, and I had every sign of starvation. All the men who came spoke

kindly. But finally the kindest one of all, an Arab of middle age, offered to give my mother a little gold money for me.   (Tavoukdjian, p. 46)

The little girl had not realized that if she was sold she would be separated from her mother and brother. When she was led away by her purchaser, she saw them for the last time. Serpouhi now belonged to her master, Allel Moose, who brought her to his village on the bank of the Euphrates River in Syria. Her new owner was personally kind to Serpouhi, but his wives cruelly mistreated her whenever he was away from the home. Seriously ill, she was abandoned on the riverbank to die, when Allel Moose rescued her and saved her life. Eventually Serpouhi, now named Helema, was accepted into the Arab household and given facial tattoos, considered beauty marks by the local Arabs. Thus she lived for more than three years, until she was rescued and returned to the Armenian community living in Aleppo, Syria.

Elise summarizes the exile phase of her genocide experience saying:

> I had lost my entire family within the span of a week or two and now at the age of ten I was left an orphan in the middle of the Syrian desert, utterly alone but miraculously still half-alive. In despair, I lay down my head on a pile of tattered bundles—my inheritance—and lost consciousness.   (Taft, p. 65)

Elise lived with other Armenian refugees in this oasis village in the desert for almost a year. From there she was able to move into other temporary quarters in the city of Damascus. Eventually Elise was able to return, briefly, to her old hometown of Bandirma. With an aunt she visited her former home, now occupied by a Turkish family. This is how she narrates the encounter:

> You could see from the expression on their faces and their conversation that they were compassionate toward the Armenian people and felt genuinely sorry for what had been done to us. After all they were human beings—parents too, and their only son was still in the army. Turks were not all bad.
>
> It was obvious that this Turkish family had meager means. The father, a retired Turkish army officer, was living on a very small government pension. Our once gay, well-furnished and comfortable reception room was now without rugs, curtains, draperies and decorations which had made it so cheerfully homey. It was now bare and cold, unpainted and inhospitable, like a grave!   (Taft, p. 77)

After Elise and her aunt had sipped Turkish coffee with their hosts, they left.

> As the door closed my childhood memories rushed upon me all at

once: my parents, sisters, dear brother Garo, friends, relatives, playmates with whom we frolicked and laughed all day long. They were no
more. The sorrow in my heart was too deep and bitter for tears. I could
not cry. It was all pent up. My anger, fury, and frustration were
emotions which had frozen, and I walked away numb and unfeeling.
Inside I felt alone and empty.   (Taft, p. 77)

The first place of exile for Kerop and the survivors in his family
was the town of Birejik on the Euphrates River. Here a sister and the
mother could help support the family by working as weavers in the
local textile manufacturing. They spent long hours hunched over the
looms, and Kerop learned to thread the bobbins so that he, too, could
help his family.

Later they moved to the city of Aleppo, Syria where the mother
worked in a refugee camp and Kerop was placed in an Armenian
orphanage. The British army now occupied the city, and many of the
soldiers were Sikhs from India. French forces also patrolled the area.
However, there was little security, and Kerop relates an incident in
which Arabs and Turks attacked the orphanage. The Armenian
director and one of the women who had been a substitute mother to
the boys there were killed. It was a new massacre perpetrated right
in front of the children.

Realizing that the orphanage was no longer a safe haven, Kerop
left it and went back to the remnants of his family. Later, he reflected
on their situation:

As time went by I began to realize that our existence was an unsatisfactory one. We were still refugees, living in one corner of a room, in an
inconspicuous khan, off a narrow street. We were not short of food but
the quality was only what we could afford. Our clothes were those we
had brought from the keshla (refugee barracks) and my suit was made
from a blanket which my sisters had somehow managed to put together.
My mother, Aghavni and Barouyr did their best to earn enough money
for bare necessities while Rebecca, Zareh, and myself attended school.
    We were thirteen people in one room, four under one blanket, and
tension and resentment in the family were never far away.
                                                    (Bedoukian, p. 154)

After many trials in the deportation column, Leon succeeded in
getting to the town of Batum, in Russian territory. Here, as a young
Armenian refugee, he encounters a friend of his mother's who asks
about his parents.

"The Turks killed them," I said. "They were deported and killed. I was
deported too; they gave me a Turkish name and tried to make me a
Moslem, but I ran away."
. . . Then I went to the orphanage on an excursion train—my first train

ride. It was located in the village of Kobuleti, the second station on the
railway to Tiflis, and like a fashionable suburb of Batum. The orphans
lived in a handsome villa fronting the beach. They were deeply tanned,
barefoot boys with their hair sheared off. Here, I learned to swim and
gained weight, after months of hunger.   (Surmelian, p. 159)

Several months later distant relatives came to take Leon from the
orphanage, and he then lived with them in Batum.

The phase of exile for Alice involved an incredible journey in
which, with the assistance of Kurdish chieftains the Muggerditchians
were able to escape from Ottoman Turkey and get to Tiflis, Georgia.
From there they proceeded to Baku, then by steamer on the Caspian
Sea to Astrakhan, by river boat up the Volga River, and by train first
to Archangel on the frozen White Sea, and finally to the port of
Murmansk on the Artic Ocean. This saga took more than a year of
time, during which the refugees found themselves caught in the Civil
War in the Russian Revolution. Finally they reached England by ship.

We arrived in London during the night and were taken to the War
Refugees' Camp through pitch-dark streets. Our bus passed through a
very large gate and unloaded us. Some women led us through a gigantic
hallway, wide enough, it seemed, to let fifty people walk side by side. We
went up ten wide steps, more hallways, down ten steps and into an
enormous dining room with black curtains on all windows. More hot
tea, this time with bread and butter, then to a huge dormitory with fifty
beds on either side of the room. . . .
Mother and we girls were given four cots between sleeping women. I
slept on the end cot and wondered who was on the cot next to me. A
deep sleep without the rocking of the bed put an end to my question.
                                                        (Shipley, p. 229)

IMMIGRATION

Each of our genocide survivor informants had a final phase of that
traumatic experience—immigration.   All had become homeless
refugees. Many of the Armenians who were exiled from Turkey settled
permanently in countries adjoining Turkey: Syria and Lebanon,
Greece and Bulgaria, and Armenia or Georgia in the Soviet Union.
The individuals whose memoirs we have been examining, however, all
immigrated to North America. One went to Canada and the rest to
the United States.

By this time Serpouhi, briefly reunited with her father, had
reached Salonika (Thessaloniki), Greece and therefore she sailed for
America from the port of Piraeus. She traveled alone, seeing her
father—the last other survivor in her family—for the final time on the
dock. Serpouhi landed in New York, passing through Ellis Island, and

then went by train to Washington, D.C. where she had a distant relative. Here she worked in a brush factory to earn her living while attending college and completing nurses' training. Finally, in 1933, Serpouhi had undergone three plastic surgery operations that removed the hated tattoo marks that she felt disfigured her face. She wanted to assist at a mission hospital in Morocco, but the United States Immigration and Naturalization Service was threatening to deport her.

> At last I received final word from the immigration office that I must stay in the United States. I am not a citizen of any country, but a refugee; therefore, I cannot have a passport to leave, neither will any country receive me without a passport. But now I may work for wages—if I am fortunate enough to find work—for the first time since I finished my nurses' course.   (Tavoukdjian, p. 125)

Elise had gone from Bandirma, where she was now an outcast, to the city of Smyrna, in order to live in an orphanage there, and later to attend the American Collegiate Girls' Institute. At this time Smyrna was occupied by the Greeks, and Elise was there when the Turkish army under Mustafa Kemal recaptured it. She saw the city go up in flames. With the help of an American missionary teacher, King Birge, Elise was able to escape to an American merchant ship in the harbor, the *Winona.* On this she and her fellow students were transported to Piraeus, where their school was reopened in exile.

Through the intervention of one of her Armenian teachers who later settled in New York, Elise was sponsored to come for her college education to Syracuse University by a Mr. and Mrs. Robert Dey. These wealthy philanthropists—he owned the Dey Brothers Department Store—helped Elise get through college. She was graduated in June 1931, and married another Armenian who had survived the Genocide too, Zarmain Taft (Tohafjian).

Now, as a grandmother, Elise reflects on her life.

> If I grieve in a nostalgic sense at the loss of Armenianism in my grandchildren, I do so because I survived by remaining Armenian in a world which had sought to devour me. *I would not let it destroy me.* And it was only my "Armenianism"—and all that it implies in terms of survival—that saved me as a human being.   (Taft, p. 141)

Abraham and his family had also moved to Smyrna as refugees, and they too found themselves standing with thousands of people on the harbor quay as the city burned. Through the intervention of an American the Hartunian family was rescued and rowed out to the battleship *Simpson.* From there they were transferred to the *Winona,* which took them to Piraeus, Greece. Abraham remembered his last night on the deck of the ship in Smyrna harbor.

> I did not sleep at all. I was happy that my wife and children were resting on deck, but all night long I viewed the awful scene of Smyrna's destruction. It was now my brain that was photographing the pictures of this hell.
>
> The quay was jammed with terror-stricken, abandoned people. The sea, as a mighty wall, stood with its silent waters to prevent escape. The roaring fire was eating its way toward the quay. ... There was no means or hope of saving the people.   (Hartunian, p. 200.f)

The Hartunians also came to the United States by ship from Greece. They too passed through Ellis Island, after a quarantine of twelve days, during which the family was separated and feared that they might never be reunited. At last room was found for them on the immigrant quota and they arrived at the house of Abraham's brother-in-law in Buffalo, New York, to start new lives.

Kerop had gotten to Liverpool, England, ready to sail on the White Star Line to Canada, when he was turned back because of the trachoma in his eyes. The steamship line authorities knew that he would never be admitted to Canada until that condition was cleared up. So he stayed with a local Armenian family as a companion for their son, while undergoing a series of painful treatments for his eyes. His mother, who had gone on ahead to Canada, was now a house mother at the Georgetown Armenian Boys' Farm there.

Finally, Kerop was able to sail on the S.S. *Doric* in 1926. The ship brought him to a wharf in Quebec City, where he was soon separated out for special treatment. He tells what happened to him.

> Five hours after being locked up, four people entered the building; they talked to the immigration men and they all looked my way. One immigration officer came and unlocked the door and guided me to an adjoining office where three of the newly arrived men were already waiting. One of them introduced himself as a representative of the White Star Line, and the others as a physician and eye-specialist from Quebec City. I was asked to strip. While undressing, such a feeling of despair and hopelessness swept over me that I did not care what happened. To expose my chest and back which were full of pimples was degrading to say the least, but since I was in their hands, I stripped naked. They poked me here, they poked me there, and went thoroughly over me. The physician said something about my pimples, the eye-doctor said something about my eyes, the agent told me to get dressed, and they all walked out and went to the immigration supervisor's office. I was getting angry, the humiliation of being handled like a nobody hurt my feelings.
>   (Bedoukian, p. 181)

Fully expecting to be rejected and deported back to England, Kerop was overjoyed to receive his *laissez-passer* back bearing an immigration stamp for Canada in it.

> Suddenly I realized that the unbelievable had happened and that I, Kerop Bedoukian, was the possessor of a valid immigrant visa.   (Ibid.)

Next, Kerop receives the gift of a bilingual Bible. One column was in Armenian, the other in English. Suddenly he realizes his freedom. A Bible or anything else printed in Armenian in Turkey could be the cause of persecution. Yet in Canada he can receive such a book freely.

Leon had come to Istanbul from Batum, after a series of adventures. It was from there that he set sail for the United States, travelling fourth class, with exactly $29 in American money, $4 more than the absolute minimum required by the immigration laws. After twenty-four days at sea, America appeared on the horizon. The anchor was let down and the immigrants transferred to Ellis Island.

> The guards ordered us into a launch. We were a motley crowd of Greeks, Albanians, Jews, Hungarians, Rumanians, Yugoslavs, Czechoslovaks, Russians, Armenians, and there was even a Turk among us. All of us were bewildered and worried as we were taken to Ellis Island, where I had to declare again that I did not believe in polygamy, anarchy, in overthrowing organized government by force; that I had never been an inmate in an insane asylum, imprisoned for a crime, and nobody in America had promised me employment.   (Surmelian, p. 286f.)

Surmelian was headed for an American college in Kansas where he was to study agriculture. He was detained on Ellis Island for a month, however, because the steamship company had misspelled his name. After his release and admittance to the United States, Leon made his way to Manhattan, Kansas. He had learned that the Armenian rug merchant who had been supposed to finance his education, now had withdrawn the offer. With a work-study position, Leon began his career as a penniless student in an American institution. He wrote:

> Now, for the first time, I felt really homeless. I sighed to myself when I saw American children playing before their homes and witnessed scenes of happy family life behind lighted windows at night, as I walked alone through the streets, sick with loneliness and memories.
> (Surmelian, p. 295)

Alice and the other members of the Muggerditchian family also were able to immigrate to the United States with the help of their relatives who had come before them. After visiting the various members of their clan, they settled in Fresno, California, which reminded them of Diyarbakir. At first the new arrivals had to do manual labor on the local farms, working as hired hands. Later they found other types of employment as factory workers and tailors. Although their father was eventually reunited with the family, he had been retired from the British Consular Service with a tiny amount of severance pay and no pension. Broken in spirit, he was never able to adjust to the new conditions of their life in America.

The reception the immigrant children received from their American peers was often less than cordial. Alice remembers that on the first day in sixth-grade her American desk-mate, Annie Johnson,

> made a face at me, stuck her tongue out, and moved to the far end of the double desk.

Later, when Alice couldn't form the English words fast enough to answer a query from the teacher,

> Annie leaned over and said, "Ha, you're just as dumb as the rest of the damned Armenians, why don't you go back to where you came from?"
> (Shipley, p. 280 f.)

Instead of discouraging Alice, however, this outburst made her determined to master the English language as spoken in America in order to show Annie and the rest of her classmates that "a damned, dumb Armenian" she was not.

SUMMARY AND CONCLUSIONS

All of the evidence presented from the six memoirs has been confined to immediate eyewitness accounts. It is not possible, however, to introduce all of the firsthand narratives in an inquiry of this size, so the investigator has had to select the passages to be quoted word-for-word and the sections of the reminiscences to be briefly summarized. The perspectives are those of the six informants, and the sequence of events conforms to their accounts.

Even though our informants were communicating in English, their second or third language, on the whole (one memoir was translated from the Armenian), they still found it necessary to employ some specialized indigenous vocabulary in order to talk about their experiences. This diction is all Turkish, the official Ottoman tongue, and includes terms such as these.

amele taburu	a forced labor work detail
azinlik	a minority group
dragoman	a native foreign consulate interpreter
istikametli millet	"the loyal nation"

jandarma (gendarme or *djenderm)*	the rag-tag security forces
keshla	barracks, in this case those of a refugee camp
khan	an old inn with an enclosed area for animals where travellers stop for the night
laissez-passer (French)	the temporary travel document used by stateless persons in lieu of a passport
millet	a recognized ethno-religious community within an Islamic society, in this case the Ottoman Empire
muhajir (muhacir)	a fugitive or refugee
nine (neneh)	grandmother
sürgün	political exile by decree as a form of punishment

The imagery and metaphors employed by our writers are striking. The flames of a bathhouse furnace symbolize the impending destruction of the Armenian people. Conventional polite conversation among members of different ethnic groups masks their mutual distrust and friction. Examples of inter-religious bigotry and rivalry abound. The high-handed rule of an elderly matriarch of an Armenian extended family is vividly described. Incidents of death and near-death are likened to the slaughter of animals. We encounter the hostility of the Turkish authorities to anything written in the minority alphabet, which they can't decode. The rampant bribery and corruption of the Ottoman officials is communicated. Readers learn about the brutality of the *jandarma*. Attempts of threatened Armenians to hide, preserve a little jewelry or money, or maintain their dignity are portrayed. Soldiers bark out orders. The riff-raff loots Armenian homes. Village boys are supposed to look "scruffy."

The accounts that we have examined make it clear that the victims of a genocide experience many forms of violence. They are subject to verbal abuse and accusations. The security of their goods and property is removed and they are quickly impoverished. They encounter religious bigotry and prejudice. Their personal relationships are destroyed as grandparents, parents, siblings, relatives, and neighbors lose their lives. They have a well founded, constant fear of physical abuse, molestation, and rape. Infectious diseases are rampant. Starvation becomes commonplace. There is a lack of sanitation and means of maintaining personal hygiene. In the end, some of the victims must seek shelter from the violence all around them by becoming attached to the households of their enemies.

According to the perceptions of our six informants, a predictable sequence of events is associated with this genocide. The nation is plunged into a time of crisis by the decisions of its rulers, and soon the government authorities begin to charge a minority with the culpability for the disastrous situation. Rumors of official policy changes and types of intervention begin to circulate. The minority is vilified in the official media.

Next, many of the private resources of the minority group members are confiscated by the government. Then the intellectuals and community leaders of the group are rounded up and exterminated. Orders are given that the remaining able-bodied males will be conscripted, and they are placed in forced labor battalions. Few survive the ordeal.

Then the deportation orders are issued for everyone of a particular ethnicity. A few exceptions are offered for individuals whose skills can contribute to the war effort, provided that they will abjure their identity and at least outwardly join the majority. Most of the target group are marched off and either perish along the way or become despised refugees living in exile. Eventually, these displaced persons either regroup and settle in their places of dispersion, or they immigrate to North America.

These immigrants are not necessarily received with open arms by their adopted country. Some of the previous immigrants from the same ethnic group now are ashamed of their poor refugee relations. The new immigrants also encounter nativism in the form of hostility from some of the native-born citizens, although other citizens of the adopted country assist them to adjust to the new society.

We can thus conclude that, although they adhere to a sequential framework, genocide experiences are highly personal in nature. It is not as statistics but as persons that human beings undergo a genocide. The people who survive a genocide carry its effects with them for the rest of their lives. In most cases the effects of a genocide include a sudden loss of one's socioeconomic class and relegation to a marginal position in society. It takes years of struggle to compensate for these conditions and again enter the social mainstream.

The psychology of genocide survivors includes nagging speculation about why one individual should have lived when so many other people died. Sometimes this is accompanied by a haunting sense of guilt and shame, thinking that perhaps the person could have done something more to resist the destructive process and preserve life. Having been officially charged by the regime of sedition, rebellion, and disloyalty certainly influences the feelings of individuals, even when they were children or youth at the time. Repeatedly our informants state that they preserved their human dignity and maintained a sense of identity by clinging to their Armenian heritage.

None of our informants wrote as a spokesperson for a political point of view. They do not advocate any contemporary policies to be followed in order to achieve official recognition that the genocide of which they were victims actually occurred in 1915—at least in these memoirs. They do not suggest how compensation and reparations should be obtained for the survivors and their heirs. They wrote prior to the start of the terrorist attacks on diplomatic representatives of the Republic of Turkey. None of them advocate employing violence in retaliation for the violence that they experienced.

It is evident that the motivation of these informants for writing their accounts of the genocide was to communicate what had happened to them to their children, grandchildren and the general public.   The younger generations of Armenian Americans were perceived to be becoming highly Americanized, and our informants were concerned that they might neither remember nor understand what happened to the Armenians of the Ottoman Empire between 1915 and 1922.

An implied second motive for writing was clearly to try to prevent future genocides. The informants believe that if new generations only know what happened, and why and how it took place, that they will be committed to countering any signs of impending genocides in the future. It may be difficult for us in the mid-1980s to share this sanguine view of human nature, but it seems to have been the perspective of our informants.

TEACHING SUGGESTIONS

Today genocide awareness is a recognized part of human rights and social justice education. It is necessary that genocide studies be included in programs teaching about intergroup conflict resolution and peace. Usually the curricula have limited themselves to the Jewish Holocaust, but they need to be broadened to include other instances, such as the Armenian Genocide.

Literary sociology is one good approach to this type of instruction in high schools and colleges. Perhaps this inquiry could serve as a model of that type of teaching. At least four other information sources can be used in units of genocide awareness education: contemporary newspaper accounts written by reporters and journalists who were at the scene; historical studies based on the documentary evidence; photographs and films—often pretty grim for younger viewers; and oral histories that have been taped by survivors and transcribed. Thus, there is an abundance of appropriate sources that can be used by educators who wish to encourage genocide awareness.

REFERENCES

1. *Yearbook of the United Nations*, 1947-1948 (New York: The United Nations, 1949), 595-99.

2. *Yearbook of the United Nations*, 1948-1949 (New York: The United Nations, 1950), 959 f.

3. Literary sociology has been described by Hugh Duncan in *Language and Literature in Society* (Chicago: University of Chicago Press, 1953), 3. See also Lewis A. Coser, ed., *Sociology Through Literature: An Introductory Reader* (Englewood Cliffs, N.J: Prentice-Hall, 1963) and H. L. Nostrand, "Literature in the Describing of a Literate Culture," *The French Review* 37:4 (December, 1963), 145.

Armin T. Wegner, Polemicist for Armenian and Jewish Human Rights[*]

Sybil Milton

The connection between the Armenian and Jewish Holocausts has been tenuous at best, although historians have made perfunctory reference to Hitler's observation made on the eve of the invasion of Poland in late August 1939: "Who today remembers the Armenian extermination?"[1] But many eyewitnesses to the deportations and murder of the Armenians during the First World War continued to write about the Armenian tragedy, including the German author Armin T. Wegner, who described his life "as a solemn pledge to do everything possible to maintain alive the memory of the Armenian fate."[2] The accidents of Wegner's career form a more tangible link between the Armenian and Jewish genocides; his impassioned personal advocacy of Armenian and Jewish rights were directly connected both to his central concerns as a writer and to the fate of his own immediate family. Yet today, Wegner's writings are consigned to oblivion, relatively unavailable in even major American and European research libraries, although he is still remembered by a few cognoscenti of expressionist poetry and German exile literature.[3] Who was Armin T. Wegner, what impact and influence did his writings on Armenians and Jews really have, and why has he been neglected since the Second World War?

In his own autobiographical sketches, Wegner expressed the conviction that his lifelong involvement with Armenians and Jews had been predestined from earliest childhood.[4] He was the second son of Gustav Wegner, a surveyor and civil servant employed by the German

---

[*]A slightly revised version of this paper appeared in the *Armenian Review*, Vol. 42, No. 4/168 (Winter 1989), 17-40.

Imperial Railroad. His father's career necessitated frequent moves during his childhood. His mother, Marie Wegner, née Witt, was a suffragette and pacifist, founder of the *Schlesischer Frauenverband* (Silesian Women's Association), and the feminist editor of the periodical *Die Frau der Gegenwart* (The Contemporary Woman).[5]

In autobiographical essays written during the last decade of his life (born 1886 - died 1978), Wegner repeatedly mentioned three formative childhood encounters that predetermined his later advocacy of Armenian and Jewish rights.[6] The first was the memory of reading a newspaper account of the Armenian massacres of 1895 at the age of nine. This childhood impression of Armenian suffering was reinforced by his later experiences in the Ottoman Empire during the First World War; moreover, the 1895 massacres became the starting point for many of his short stories and for his never completed novel "The Expulsion."[7] The second episode was Wegner's friendship with a Jewish classmate in 1896, when both children were outsiders in school. Wegner later married the Jewish poet Lola Landau, who fled Nazi racial persecution by emigrating to Palestine in the mid-1930s, and his second wife was the part-Jewish sculptor and ceramicist, Irene Kowaliska.[8] The third incident was Wegner's rescue of a girl drowning in the Rhine in 1900, for which he was subsequently awarded a medal for heroism.[9] His personal ethical code, molded in childhood, included civic courage, defense of individual freedom, and social justice; it was reinforced by his non-conformity as a poet and writer and his flight from paternal brutality and authoritarianism.

Wegner used historical and allegorical analogies associated with his first name and surname as a form of biographical self-revelation and identification. The surname Wegner literally means "wanderer" or "traveler." During the 1920s, Wegner was a best-selling travel writer who visited England, Scandinavia, Italy, Russia, Persia, Syria, Palestine, and Egypt.[10] The family name Wegner was translated into the word *Tarik* in the Turkish language. Tarik was also Wegner's pen name during the First World War. During an American lecture tour in 1972, Wegner discovered that several American libraries cataloged his publications under "Armin Tarik Wegner," ignoring his legal middle name Theophilus, usually abbreviated by the letter T. He was amused that his identification with Ottoman Turkey was so pervasive that few American libraries consulted his biographical entry in the *Reichshandbuch der deutschen Gesellschaft* of 1931.[11] Tarik was also a historical personality, the Berber leader who invaded Gibraltar and Spain in 711. Armin, Wegner's first name, was a cognate derived from the Latin name Arminius, a Germanic national hero who (according to Tacitus) defeated the Roman Legions in the Teutoberg Forest in 9 A.D. Wegner's own family heritage included this mixture of deep Germanic roots and affinity for the Near East; several of his ancestors had been soldiers and Templars during the Crusades.

Despite the military allusions in Wegner's pseudonym Tarik and his first name Armin, he was a pacifist and co-founder of the *Bund der Kriegsdienstgegner* (Association Against Military Service) and served as its director from June 1919 to early 1924.[12] Wegner placed great stock in the formative influence of names and he named his first child, a daughter born in 1923, Sibylle Anush. The middle name, *Anush*, was the Armenian word for "sweet," and it was Wegner's intention to thus honor the memory of Armenian children who had been killed during the First World War.[13] Wegner's concern with names reveals his deeper preoccupation with interpreting and uniting the Armenian and German heritages.

From 1903 to 1909, Wegner quit school and left home to work on a farm; this was partly a flight from paternal abuse and partly a teenage revolt against family and school, both perceived as authoritarian institutions. He travelled extensively, including a stint as a dockworker in Marseilles experiencing the "romanticism of poverty and dirt."[14] During the last years prior to the First World War, Wegner studied law and political science at the Universities of Zurich, Paris, and Berlin, receiving his doctorate in jurisprudence from the University of Breslau in 1914 with a dissertation titled "The Strike in Penal Law." Concurrently he attended Max Reinhardt's acting school in Berlin between 1910 and 1912. He also frequented Berlin's literary cafes, particularly the *Kaffeehaus des Westens*, where he joined such left-wing liberals as the journalist Kurt Hiller and the Jewish poet Else Lasker-Schüler.[15] His first two volumes of poetry from his years of *Wanderschaft* (literally "on the tramp") were published in 1909 and 1910.[16] In this auspicious milieu, Wegner began his career as a free-lance poet and journalist shortly before the First World War.

With the outbreak of war in 1914, Wegner volunteered as a male nurse, serving initially as a medic in Poland in the winter of 1914-15. He received an Iron Cross for assisting the wounded under fire. He described his encounters with *Ostjuden* (Jews from Eastern Europe) during his military service in Poland and considered their culture as "the only true, deep, and essential Judaism."[17] This somewhat sentimentalized perception of *Ostjuden* continued in his later writings about the Eastern Jewish immigrants forging a "new splendid nation" in Mandate Palestine.[18]

In the autumn of 1915, Wegner was transferred to Turkey, where he was reassigned to a German medical mission building a new hospital in Istanbul; he later served as a medical officer on the staff of German Field Marshal von der Goltz in Bagdad. In the course of his travels through wartime Turkey, he witnessed and recorded with both pen and camera the systematic annihilation and deportations of the Armenians. Although two of Wegner's letters to his mother about conditions in the Turkish Empire were published in his mother's anti-war magazine, *Die Frau der Gegenwart*, in 1915 and 1916, most of his correspondence and diaries could appear only with the cessation of military censorship after the war ended.[19] In late June 1916 Wegner was arrested by soldiers of the German military mission in Turkey because of censorship violations; and taken ill with typhus, he was sent back to Berlin in November 1916.[20]

Despite stringent Turkish prohibitions, Wegner visited Armenian refugee camps in Constantinople, Aleppo, and Bagdad. He wrote on October 19, 1916, from a relief center run by German missionary sisters in Aleppo:

> I have taken numerous photographs during the past few days. I was told that Jemal Pasha, the hangman of Syria, imposed the death penalty on anyone violating the prohibition on photography inside the [Armenian] refugee camps. I carried these images of horror and accusation rolled into a bundle against my stomach. I also collected many petitions in the camps at Meskene and Aleppo and delivered them to the American Embassy in Constantinople, since the mails would not forward such letters of entreaty. I have no doubt that I am committing high treason, but I am conscious that perhaps I have been able to assist these poor people even a little.[21]

Although there is no explicit record in the State Department files that mentions Wegner, it is probable that he was in touch with the American Chargé d'Affaires in Constantinople, Hoffman Philip, or one of his deputies in October or November 1916.[22] In late 1915 German missionary sisters had delivered similar information about the plight of the Armenians to the American Ambassador, Henry Morgenthau.[23]

During a brief period of home leave in early 1916, Wegner contacted a number of dissident German politicians, journalists, and opinion makers, hoping to make them aware of the Armenian tragedy and thus influence German policy towards its military and diplomatic ally, Ottoman Turkey. Wegner met with Hellmut von Gerlach, editor of *Die Welt am Montag* and founder of *Bund Neues Vaterland*; Maximilian Harden, editor of *Die Zukunft*; and Walter Rathenau, director of Germany's power and electricity company and later a controversial Foreign Minister during the early years of the Weimar Republic.[24] Wegner also provided data to Johannes Lepsius, head of the German Orient Mission and the German Armenian Society, whose exposé about the desperate situation of the Armenians was published in the summer of 1916.[25] Wegner learned both Turkish and Armenian in the course of his travels, although he never claimed total fluency.[26] Wegner's Berlin contacts were outsiders to the political and military hierarchy of Germany during the First World War, and only with the defeat of the Central Powers in 1918 was it possible to influence German public opinion about Turkey.

By early 1917, Wegner had already completed the manuscripts of his first two books about his experiences in Turkey, including travel sketches about Arab and Armenian life. The volumes were later published in 1920 and were titled *Weg ohne Heimkehr: Ein Martyrium in Briefen* (The Road Without Return: A Martyrdom in Letters) and *Im Hause der Glückseligkeit: Aufzeichnungen aus der Türkei* (In the House of Bliss: Notes from Turkey).[27] During 1917, after his transfer to Germany, Wegner was officially assigned to the Propaganda Office of the Sixth Army and was required to mobilize public support and contributions for war loans and to write and speak about a "victorious peace" for Germany. Although unable to write openly about his growing revulsion against the war, Wegner believed that he never betrayed his pacifist beliefs by following orders. His volume of "big city" expressionist poetry, *Das Antlitz der Städte* (The Face of Cities), was published in the spring of 1917, but was banned as erotic and salacious literature.[28]

Wegner evaded front-line military service because of his health. In 1918 he became editor of the bimonthly magazine of the German Foreign Office, *Der Neue Orient*. Only after the November 1918 revolution could Wegner openly publish stories about the Turkish murder and deportation of the Armenians and support the creation of a Zionist state in Palestine as a homeland and asylum for Jews fleeing anti-Semitic pogroms in eastern Europe.[29] From April 1918 to April 1919 Wegner founded and edited a new literary journal, *Der Osten*, which also published many of the manifestos of the *Politischer Rat Geistiger Arbeiter* (Political Council of Intellectual Workers) during the 1918-19 revolution. This body included many of the writers that Wegner knew in 1912-13, such as Kurt Hiller. Wegner also briefly belonged to the Spartacists, the German Communist party, between February and August 1919.[30]

In January 1919, with preparations for the Versailles Peace Conference a major subject of concern in Germany, Wegner published an open letter to President Woodrow Wilson, appealing for an independent Armenian nation. The text of Wegner's letter was first published in *Die Frau der Gegenwart* on February 1, 1919, and subsequently reprinted in the daily *Berliner Tageblatt* on February 23, 1919. It was widely circulated as brochures in German, English, and Armenian.[31] Wegner wrote:

Mr. President:

In your message to Congress of 8 January 1919, you made a demand for the liberation of all non-Turkish peoples in the Ottoman Empire. One of these peoples is the Armenian nation. It is on behalf of the Armenian nation that I am addressing you.

As one of the few Europeans who have been eyewitnesses of the dreadful destruction of the Armenian people, ... I venture to claim the right of setting before you these pictures of misery and terror which passed before my eyes during nearly two years, and which will never be obliterated from my mind. I appeal to you at the moment when the Governments allied to you are carrying on peace negotiations in Paris, which will determine the fate of the world for many decades. But the Armenian people is only a small one among several others. ... There is reason to fear that the significance of a small and extremely enfeebled nation may be obscured by the influential and selfish aims of the great European states, and that with regard to Armenia there will be a repetition of the old game of neglect and oblivion of which she has so often been the victim in the course of her history.

But this would be most lamentable, for no people in the world has suffered such wrongs as the Armenian nation. The Armenian Question is a question for Christendom, for the whole human race.

The Armenian people were victims of this war. When the Turkish government, in the spring of 1915, set about the implementation of its monstrous project of exterminating a million Armenians, all the nations of Europe were unhappily bleeding to exhaustion, owing to the tragic blindness of their mutual misunderstanding, and there was no one to hinder the lurid tyrants of Turkey from carrying on to the bitter end those revolting atrocities which can only be likened to the acts of a criminal lunatic. And so they drove the whole people—men, women, elders, children, expectant mothers, and suckling infants—into the Arabian desert, with no other object than to let them starve to death.[32]

After referring to his own experiences and to the published reports by Lord Bryce and Johannes Lepsius, Wegner continued:

By what right, then, do I make this appeal to you? I do it by the right of human fellowship, in dutiful fulfillment of a sacred promise. When in the desert I went through the deportees' camps, when I sat in their tents with the starving and the dying, I felt their supplicating hands in mine, and the voices of their priests, who had blessed many of the dead on their last journey to the grave, adjured me to plead for them, if I were ever in Europe again.

But the country to which I have returned is a poor country; Germany is a conquered nation. My own people are near starvation; the streets are full of the poor and the wretched. . . .

The voice of conscience and humanity will never be silenced in me, and therefore I address these words to you. This document is a request. It is the tongues of a thousand dead that speak in it. Mr. President, the wrong suffered by this people is immeasurable. . . . On behalf of the Armenian nation, I venture to intervene; for if, after this war, it is not given reparation for its fearful sufferings, it will be lost forever.[33]

These rhetorical pleas for an independent Armenia remained of course unfulfilled.

In October 1919 Wegner delivered several illustrated slide lectures about the Armenian massacres, and his short stories were serialized in German newspapers and periodicals throughout 1920 and 1921.[34] In 1921 he published four short stories about his Armenian experiences under the title *Der Knabe Hüssein: Türkische Novellen*.[35] In 1923 Wegner published a second manifesto for Armenian rights, entitled "The Cry from Ararat."[36] In 1924 he began to write a multi-volume novel about twentieth century Armenia to be entitled "The Expulsion," but the exigencies of earning a living through free-lance journalism impeded the completion of this book.[37] In 1930 Wegner received a subsidy from the Prussian Academy of the Arts to complete this novel. He described the projected first volume as a prologue. The main protagonist was to be a young Armenian boy, born in 1890, orphaned in the 1896 massacres, who grew up in a Syrian orphanage in Jerusalem. This first volume was to be entitled "In the Shadow of God." The second volume, "Eternal Hatred," was to be set in an Armenian mountain village and was to cover the first decade of the twentieth century until the victory of the Young Turks. The third volume, "The Cry from Ararat," was to deal with the First World War, the deportation of the Armenians, and the confrontation between Johannes Lepsius and Enver Pasha. The fourth and final volume, "The Desert," would have ended with the assassination of Talaat Pasha in Berlin.[38] In 1921 Wegner had published an edited version of the stenographic reports of the trial of the Armenian student Solomon Tehlirian for the murder of Talaat Pasha.[39] However Wegner never completed his ambitious multi-volume Armenian novel. He was apprehensive and envious about the advance publicity for Franz Werfel's *Forty Days of Musa Dagh*, and wrote two lengthy defensive letters in December 1932 and January 1933 in an attempt to dissuade Werfel from writing a book about Armenia because of his prior claims to the subject.[40] Wegner realistically feared that his short stories and editorials would be disregarded once Werfel's completed novel was available.

During the 1920s Wegner lectured actively on the pacifist circuit. He spoke about draft resistance and traveled widely to England, Holland, and Scandinavia, using his trips also as sources for numerous travel stories he published in the German press.[41] In 1921 he married the Jewish lyric poet Lola Landau, who brought two sons from a previous marriage into their relationship. Their first child was a daughter born in 1923. Wegner's first major commercial and financial success was the novel *Moni*, about one year in the life of a child; it sold 200,000 copies in 1928 and also appeared in Dutch and Japanese translations.[42] Together with Landau, he also scripted a Turkish puppet play, *Wassif und Akif*, that was performed on stage in Berlin in February 1926.[43]

During the winter of 1927-28, Wegner completed an extended trip to the Soviet Union. Upon his return, he briefly rejoined the Communist Party, but dropped this affiliation after several months. During the winter and spring of 1928-29, Wegner and Lola Landau travelled by motorcycle and sailboat to Teheran and Egypt. His experiences were published as *Jagd durch das tausendjährige Land* in 1932, which sold 30,000 copies before it was seized by the Nazis in 1933.[44] Wegner's motorcycle adventures through the desert of Samaria and the Galilee were also serialized as newspaper articles.[45] The book also openly supported Jewish settlement in Palestine, and Wegner clearly advocated the formation of a Jewish national state. The volume closed with a letter to his daughter in Germany:

> My little one: During the next days, you will be starting school for the first time. Sooner or later you will face malicious enmity and be treated as a stranger. Wear this hatred as though it were a medal! With your father's blue eyes and your mother's black hair, remember that you have a double honor to defend: the honor of Germans and the honor of Jews![46]

With the Nazi accession to power in 1933, Wegner's income declined precipitously and he never received the royalties owed to him for his last travel book, *Jagd durch das tausdendjährige Land*.[47] His works were banned, his books purged from the shelves of German libraries, and some were burned in the auto-da-fé of May 1933. In order to earn money to support his family, Wegner tried to publish under the pseudonym Klaus Uhlen. He submitted a five-part article about Persia to the *Berliner Tageblatt*. One segment was published as "The Bazaar of Dreams," but the series was canceled when the

Tageblatt discovered that Uhlen had plagiarized substantial sections of an earlier Wegner essay of the same title. The newspaper never realized that the ostensible plagiarist and the author they were protecting were one and the same person.[48] In November 1936 Wegner was expelled from the *Reichsschrifttumskammer* and his name was expunged from the lists of journalists and writers allowed to publish in Nazi Germany.[49] As a Jew, his wife Lola Landau also faced new publishing restrictions, and she took an office job with the Berlin branch of the Zionist organization Keren Hajessod.

Shortly after the April 1933 boycott, Wegner—unable to publish a manifesto praising Jewish contributions to German culture—addressed a letter of appeal to Adolf Hitler on Easter Monday, April 11, 1933. He headed his petition with the words "For Germany," although the letter is known today as "The Warning."[50] Wegner prophetically warned Hitler that

> it is not only a matter of the fate of our Jewish brethren, but also concerns the destiny of Germany. . . . The Jews have survived the Babylonian captivity, Egyptian slavery, the Spanish Inquisition, the Crusades, and sixteen hundred years of persecution in Russia. With the same tenacity that this ancient people has always shown, the Jews will also survive this danger. The shame and misfortune will however be allotted to Germany and will not be quickly forgotten, even in the future![51]

Wegner warned Hitler that he "had been badly advised," and implored him "to protect Germany by protecting the Jews."[52] The letter was mailed to Hitler at the Party Chancellery in Munich and was forwarded from there to Berlin in May 1933 over Martin Bormann's signature. Wegner was arrested and placed in protective custody on August 19, 1933. He was initially taken to Gestapo headquarters on Prinz Albrecht Strasse in Berlin for interrogation and subsequently moved to the basement of Columbia House concentration camp, where he was brutally beaten. He was then transferred to the prison in Leer for two months and then remanded to a further sentence of four months in three concentration camps: Oranienburg, Börgermoor, and Lichtenberg.[53] After the first week in solitary confinement and the initial brutality, Wegner was handled with relative leniency for the remainder of his incarceration. At Börgermoor he was permitted to set up a camp library for his fellow inmates and he was also allowed to lecture about his travels or to read from his poetry and fiction for an audience that often contained both prisoners and guards.[54]

Assisted by a Quaker British attorney, Wegner was released in the spring of 1934 and followed his wife, who had already fled to England.

Although he was able to publish a few travel sketches in the German press under the pseudonym Klaus Uhlen, Wegner felt alienated and isolated in London, unable to write or to secure an income for the support of his family. He returned to Germany in the autumn of 1934 and toyed with the idea of writing a book about his camp experiences. However, he was never able to overcome his inhibitions about describing the physical and psychological traumas of incarceration. Manuscript fragments entitled *Die Pferdepeitsche* (The Horsewhip), composed between 1936 and 1938, were found posthumously in Wegner's literary estate.[55]

In 1935 Wegner followed his wife and daughter when they emigrated to Palestine. Although Wegner visited his family twice, in May 1936 and February 1937, he felt alienated in Mandate Palestine and knew that, unable to secure permanent resident status there, he had few alternatives but returning to Germany. Wegner and Lola Landau drifted apart and were eventually divorced in 1938. Wegner later bemoaned the fact that "Germany took everything I had: my home, my fame, my freedom, my work, my friends, my child's home, and everything else I held dear. Last of all, it robbed me of my wife; and yet this is the country that I still love!"[56]

In 1937 Wegner moved to the small fishing village of Positano on the Gulf of Salerno in Italy. He was allowed to ship more than fifty crates of books, manuscripts, photographs, and research materials to his new home. In Positano he met the Galician-born but German-educated Jewish artist Irene Kowaliska, who later became his second wife.[57]

Despite superficial similarities between Italian fascism and German national socialism, Italy provided a comparatively lenient atmosphere for German political and racial refugees. Until late 1938 restrictive immigration legislation did not exist in Italy, since the Italian government feared reprisals against the numerous Italian citizens residing and working abroad. Visas were not required, religion did not have to be listed on passport or police registration forms, and work permits were relatively easy for foreigners to obtain. Italy was neither anti-Semitic nor xenophobic before 1938, and was generally more tolerant of cultural pluralism than Nazi Germany. Thus, Heinrich Mann's novel *Young Henry IV*, banned in Germany, could be published by Mondadori in 1936, and Alban Berg's modern opera *Woyzeck* could be performed in Rome in 1938.[58]

The number of German-Jewish refugees to Italy grew slowly, and by May 1936 the Alien Police reported to the Ministry of Interior that

1,515 German Jews could be identified among the 5,925 foreign Jewish residents in Italy. The German colony in Italy then consisted of approximately 20,000 people. Since religion was not listed on passports, it was often difficult to distinguish Jews from non-Jews. It is important to remember that Italy was the major transit stop for Jews en route to Palestine. In 1933 and 1934, nearly two-thirds of all emigrants to Palestine, approximately 38,500 people, embarked from the port of Trieste. Moreover, the ports of Genoa and Naples served emigrants leaving for destinations in North and South America.[59]

Between 1933 and 1938 cooperation grew between the governments of Italy and Germany. In September 1935 Colonel Mario Roatta, head of Italian military intelligence, signed an agreement with his German counterpart, Admiral Canaris, to coordinate the collection of information about communism. In April 1936 the Germans and Italians negotiated a secret police treaty that permitted Gestapo access to name lists of German and German-Jewish refugees in Italy. Italian-German police cooperation intensified after Mussolini's September 1937 visit to Germany with the formal exchange of police attachés. In March 1938 Heydrich went to Rome accompanied by twenty-two German detectives; their job was to register and screen suspicious German and Jewish refugees residing in Italy. At the end of April 1938 Heinrich Müller, chief of the Gestapo, arrived in Rome with thirty-seven additional Gestapo agents; and during Hitler's visit in May, a total of 200 Gestapo and SS officers were stationed on temporary assignment in Italy. These measures were part of the security precautions for Hitler's state visit to Rome. In a memorandum dated April 14, 1938, the Italian Ministry of Interior reported that 1,025 suspicious German and Austrian refugees, mostly Jewish, were arrested in Rome, Florence, Naples, and other Italian towns as part of the elaborate security measures required to protect Hitler. Armin T. Wegner was among those arrested; he was initially detained by the *carabinieri* in Positano and then transferred to prisons at Amalfi and Salerno for almost five weeks.[60]

In the summer of 1939 Wegner accidentally met his fellow German refugee Emil Stumpp, a portrait painter. Stumpp noted:

> I finally remembered his name; it was the writer Armin T. Wegner, whom I had sketched thirteen years before. I was shocked by the changes in his appearance. He looked like an old man of almost seventy, a direct result of his traumatic experiences in jail.[61]

Stumpp also described Wegner's home in Positano:

It was located atop 540 feet of steps. It was a small house with a lovely terrace overlooking the water. Wegner's work room was cluttered with books and mementos from his many trips. The house had been built with money provided by (Dutch) patrons who assisted and supported him.[62]

Wegner felt increasingly vulnerable and isolated in Italy after 1938. The dislocations of flight and the attendant loss of professional status and income reinforced the traumas of persecution and detention in German concentration camps and Italian jails. Nor was Italy a major center for refugee intellectuals, although a number of German exile writers resided there for brief periods before 1939, including Alfred Neumann, Walter Hasenclever, Elisabeth Castonier, and Kurt Wolff. None lived in geographical proximity to Positano, where Wegner and Irene Kowaliska made their home.[63]

In the spring of 1939 Wegner joined an ethnic association under Nazi auspices for German expatriates, which he rationalized in a letter to his ex-wife, dated July 24, 1939:

Don't draw false conclusions about my true beliefs. This membership was expected of all Germans living abroad and is without further significance; moreover, it imposes no obligations on me.[64]

With the promulgation of harsher anti-Semitic legislation in Italy in late 1938 and Italian entry into the war in June 1940, foreign Jews and other foreign residents were arrested and interned in hundreds of newly opened detention centers and internment camps.[65] In August 1940, Herbert Kappler, then Gestapo chief of Rome, ordered Wegner's arrest and confinement in the Potenza detention camp. Wegner fled to Rome, where he went into hiding; he contacted acquaintances at the German Embassy who canceled the warrant for his arrest. After the Gestapo checked Wegner's record with Berlin, he was surprisingly given a clean bill of health, since his divorce from Lola Landau and her emigration freed him from the onus of mixed marriage. Neither his 1933 arrest nor his expulsion from the Reich Chamber of Writers was mentioned.

Unable to publish or write for a living, Wegner worked as a stringer accredited to the Italian Ministry of Propaganda in 1940. From May 1941 until the summer of 1943, he taught German language and literature at the German Academy in Padua, where he was listed on the faculty roster as Dr. A. Theo Wegner.[66] It is unlikely that this slight modification of his name was enough to hide his identity from the German police, but it served as an excuse for accusations of collaboration after the war.[67]

With the Allied liberation of southern Italy and the Badoglio coup, the Germans assumed control over northern Italy in September 1943. Wegner was once again vulnerable to arrest and deportation. He thus fled to southern Italy, where his common-law wife Irene Kowaliska and his infant son, born in 1941, were already in hiding. Without a regular income, Wegner sold many of his possessions, including jewelry, tableware, books, and oriental Turkish carpets. He married Irene Kowaliska in 1945 and continued to reside in Positano until 1955.

Wegner never fully adjusted to his life in Italian exile. Despite his cosmopolitan veneer as a world traveler, Wegner was nevertheless rooted in a specifically German culture for both the language and subject matter of his writing. After 1945 he was suspended in a vacuum between his conscious and subconscious preoccupation with the past, including his memories of persecution and torture, and his plans for the future completion of his Armenian novel and an autobiographical novel about his experiences between 1933 and 1945. He found some solace and escape in the seductive beauty and climate of southern Italy, but his once prodigious literary productivity diminished after 1945 to a few essays on familiar themes.[68]

In the first decade after the end of the war, Wegner's income came from a few travel articles about Israel and Italy that appeared in the German and Swiss press under the pseudonym Johannes Selbdritt.[69] Wegner also prepared more than fifty radio programs for German and Swiss stations, including radio plays, travel reports, reviews of modern German and Jewish literature, and commemorative programs about Jews and Armenians.[70] Unable to complete any major new works, he prepared an anthology of his work and also published one major new essay to demolish the "irreconcilable wall between Germans and Jews after the Holocaust."[71] He returned to Germany for the first time in 1952, but concluded that "after a twenty-year hiatus, he could no longer return to his native land. It would mean a new emigration—this time back to [his] own country."[72]

His slim productivity decreased further after he moved to Rome in 1956. In 1965, on the fiftieth anniversary of the Armenian Genocide, the press discovered Wegner's historic photographs, praising their quality and poignancy.[73] He also published a commemorative essay entitled "*Para Lues: Das gute Licht*," about the Armenocide of 1915.[74] As an old man, Wegner began to receive international recognition. He was the recipient of the Eduard von der Heydt Prize of his home town, Wuppertal, in 1962; of Yad Vashem's award as "one of the Just" in

1968; and also accepted the Order of St. Gregory in Yerevan in the Soviet Republic of Armenia later that same year.[75] Wegner characterized his new role as witness in a poem entitled "The Old Man":

> Zum Zeugen bin ich aufgerufen von mir selbst
> Die Stimme der Vertriebenen bin ich in der Wüste.

This can be translated as:

> My own conscience calls me as a witness.
> I am the voice of the exiled, declaiming in the desert.[76]

In 1969 Wegner attended the first international symposium on German exile literature in Stockholm.[77] His two early volumes of city expressionist poetry, *Das Antlitz der Städte* and *Die Strasse mit den tausend Zielen*, were reprinted in the Library of Expressionism.[78] He made his first lecture tour of the United States at the age of 86 in 1972 and published a representative cross section of his writings in all genres in 1974.[79] Shortly before his death, he negotiated the posthumous transfer of his library and archives to the Deutsches Literaturarchiv in Marbach, West Germany. He died in Rome at the age of 92 in 1978.

Wegner's open letters to President Wilson in 1919 and to Adolf Hitler in 1933 are the basis of his reputation as a polemicist for Armenian and Jewish rights. The two documents cannot be compared in a facile manner, since the circumstances surrounding the two texts were not comparable. Wegner's 1919 letter was published openly in mass circulation dailies. It was also circulated simultaneously in pamphlet form in German, Armenian, and English. Like Lepsius, Wegner was one of the few German eyewitnesses to the Armenocide who knew Turkish and Armenian and spoke with the survivors. Wegner was unwilling to rationalize the Armenian Genocide to bolster the German-Turkish diplomatic and military alliance, nor would he suppress uncomfortable truth about German complicity during the postwar German preoccupation with defeat, revolution, and economic collapse. Although his passion influenced statesmen like Walter Rathenau, it probably never mobilized an indifferent public preoccupied with more immediate concerns. His plea for a separate Armenian state and compensation for Armenian survivors went unheeded at the Paris peace negotiations. In addition to the open letter of 1919, Wegner addressed another plea to the Allied powers in 1923. He also published nonfiction essays, poems, and short stories derived from his Turkish and Armenian experiences in the First World War. It is impossible to speculate about the impact of Wegner's unfinished multi-volume novel about the Armenian tragedy.

Wegner's photographs from 1915-16 are almost as important as his writings. He photographed Armenian families, refugee camps, columns of orphans, corpses, scenes in Istanbul, Aleppo, and Bagdad, and portraits of Talaat and Jemal Pasha. The high artistic quality of his photographs combine dignity and suffering. Although the subject of the photograph is clear, Wegner's lists identifying the numbered glass positives by name, location, and date have been lost.[80] Many of these photos have been used in books and newspaper stories about the Armenian Genocide, although Wegner's name as photographer is mentioned only sporadically.[81] The best of his images are comparable in quality to Margaret Bourke-White's Buchenwald photographs or the images of southern rural poverty gathered by the photographic teams of the Farm Service Administration in the United States.[82] The literature about photographs of the Armenian Genocide is unfortunately meager, and it is not clear whether current analyses of Holocaust photographs as historical evidence provide a viable research model for the Armenian Genocide.[83] Wegner also photographed his trip to Russia and Palestine, and the images appeared in his travel books published in the late 1920s. His empathy with his subjects and his ability to extract cogent details made him an above-average amateur photographer.

Wegner's open letter to Hitler in April 1933 was not published at the time and was known to only a limited number of individuals. It was first published after the war in the *Stuttgarter Zeitung* on April 1, 1953 and subsequently reprinted in other newspapers and periodicals in German, Hebrew, and Italian. His personal courage and integrity in defending German Jews is unquestioned. Yet there is a certain naiveté in his belief in the efficacy of open letters.

Wegner's overt advocacy of Armenian and Jewish rights was not matched by any coherent stand against Italian fascism. The trauma of maltreatment in Nazi concentration camps and Italian jails contributed to his failure of nerve and his evasive and ambivalent relationship to Italian fascism. Wegner's sins of omission were never those of apathy or prejudice. His reputation today as a writer manqué is partly deserved. He was not a political pragmatist but rather an idealist and rationalist confronting the two major twentieth century genocides. It is clear that his involvement in defending Armenians logically led to his later defense of Jews. Although his humanitarian protests went unheeded, his work nonetheless stands as an example of personal courage and moral commitment.

REFERENCES

1. For debate about Hitler's remarks on the Armenians, see "Letters to the Editor,"
    New York Times (June 8, 1985), 16; (June 18, 1985), 26. See also Winfried
    Baumgart, "Die Ansprache Hitlers vor dem Führern der Wehrmacht am 22.
    August 1939," *Vierteljahrshefte für Zeitgeschichte* 16, no. 2 (Apr. 1968), 120-49,
    and 19, no. 3 (July 1971), 294-304. See also Gerhard L. Weinberg, *The Foreign
    Policy of Hitler's Germany: Starting World War II, 1937-1939* (Chicago and
    London, 1980), 610-12.

2. Deutsches Literaturarchiv, Marbach am Neckar, Federal Republic of Germany,
    Armin T. Wegner Papers: subject file "Armenien Briefe, 1921-75." This quote
    comes from an undated carbon of Wegner's letter to J. Michael Hagopian,
    probably 1974.

3. Wegner's poetry *Das Antlitz der Städte* (Berlin, 1917) and *Die Strassen mit den
    tausend Zielen* (Dresden, 1924) were included in "The Library of Expressionism,"
    Paul Raabe, ed., reissued by Kraus Reprints in 1973. References to Wegner as
    an expressionist poet are found in Hermann Friedmann and Otto Mann, ed.,
    Expressionismus: Gestalten einer literarischen Bewegung (Heidelberg, 1956), 59,
    61, 64, and Deutsches Literaturarchiv, *Expressionismus: Literatur und Kunst,
    1910-1923* (Marbach a.N., 1960), 278-79. For Wegner's place in exile literature,
    see Jürgen Serke, *Die verbrannten Dichter* (Weinheim and Basel, 1979), 38-51;
    Wilhelm Sternfeld and Eva Tiedemann, *Deutsche Exil-Literatur 1933 bis 1945:
    Eine Bio-Bibliographie*, 2nd rev. exp. ed. (Heidelberg, 1970), 530-31. See also
    Reinhard M. G. Nickisch, "Vergessen oder verdrängt?" in *Göttinger Informationen*
    no. 8 (Nov. 25, 1976), 9-31; Johanna Wernicke-Rothmayer, *Armin T. Wegner:
    Gesellschaftserfahrung und literarisches Werk* (Frankfurt and Bern, 1982); and
    Armin T. Wegner, *Am Kreuzweg der Welten: Lyrik, Prosa, Briefe, Autobiogra-
    phisches*, Ruth Greuner, ed. (East Berlin, 1982).

4. Armin T. Wegner, "Die dreifache Wiederkehr: Ein Schriftsteller sieht sich
    selbst," and idem, "Wer war ich?" in the anthology Armin T. Wegner, *Fällst du,
    umarme auch die Erde oder der Mann, der an das Wort glaubt: Prosa, Lyrik
    Dokumente* (Wuppertal, 1974), 128-45.

5. Anna Fritze, "Die Gründerin des Schlesischen Frauenverbandes," *Die Frau der
    Gegenwart* 13, no. 17/18 (1919), 66. The papers of Marie Wegner are located
    in the Armin T. Wegner Papers at the Deutsches Literaturarchiv.

6. See note 4.

7. Wegner, *Fällst du, umarme auch die Erde*, 128-31.

8. Ibid., 143-45.

9. Wernicke-Rothmayer, *Wegner*, 18.

10. His travel books included *Im Haus der Glückseligkeit: Aufzeichnungen aus der
    Türkei* (Dresden, 1920); *Am Kreuzweg der Welten: Eine Reise vom Kaspischen
    Meer zum Nil* (Berlin, 1930); *Fünf Finger über Dir: Bekenntnis eines Menschen
    in dieser Zeit, Aufzeichnungen auf einer Reise durch Russland, den Kaukasus
    und Persien, Oktober bis Februar 1927/28* (Stuttgart, Berlin, and Leipzig, 1930);
    Maschinen in Märchenland: Tausend Kilometer durch die mesopotamische Wüste
    (Berlin, 1932); and *Jagd durch das tausendjährige Land* (Berlin, 1932), about
    Wegner's 1929 motorcycle trip through Jewish settlements in Palestine and the

Sinai. Many of Wegner's books included his travel photographs. He also wrote more than 120 newspaper travel articles; a comprehensive bibliography is in Hedwig Bieber, "Armin T. Wegner Bibliographie," in *Fällst du, umarme auch die Erde,* 245-54 (entries 284-430).

11. *Reichshandbuch der deutschen Gesellschaft: Das Handbuch der Persönlichkeiten in Wort und Bild* (2 v.; Berlin, 1931), 2: 1999-2000.

12. Wegner, *Fällst du, umarme auch die Erde,* 137-45. His manifesto against military service, including alternate medical service, appeared under the title *Die Verbrechen der Stunde, die Verbrechen der Ewigkeit* (Berlin, 1922; reprinted Hamburg, 1982).

13. Wernicke-Rothmayer, *Wegner,* 53.

14. Armin T. Wegner, "Als Arbeiter im Hafen von Marseile: Erlebnis einer Reise," *Der Osten* 39 (Oct. 1913): 188-97.

15. Armin T. Wegner, "Unser Kaffeehaus oder Die Arche," in *Else Lasker-Schüler: Ein Buch zum 100. Geburtstag der Dichterin,* Michael Schmid, ed. (Wuppertal, 1969), 87-99, 237; and Kurt Hiller, *Leben gegen die Zeit* (Reinbek bei Hamburg, 1969), 1: 107, 127, 134, 138, 152, 165, 231.

16. Armin T. Wegner, *Zwischen zwei Städten: Ein Buch Gedichte im Gang einer Entwicklung* (Berlin, 1909) and idem, *Gedichte in Prosa: Ein Skizzenbuch aus Heimat und Wanderschaft* (Berlin, 1910).

17. Wernicke-Rothmayer, *Wegner,* 31.

18. Armin T. Wegner, *Jagd durch das tausendjährige Land* (Berlin, 1932), 173-81.

19. Armin T. Wegner, "10. Juni 1915," *Die Frau der Gegenwart* 9, no. 20 (1915): 147-48; see also Wernicke-Rothmayer, *Wegner,* 31-35.

20. Armin T. Wegner, *Der Weg ohne Heimkehr: Ein Martyrium in Briefen* (2nd ed.; Dresden, 1920), unpaginated two-page preface dated January 1919.

21. Ibid, 169-80; translation by S. Milton.

22. National Archives, Washington, D.C., Microfilm Publication 353, Reels 43-48, containing Record Group 59, decimal files 867.4016, General Records of the Department of State, "Race problems in Turkey, 1911-1929." See also Record Group 84, Records of Foreign Service Posts of the Department of State, especially the dispatches and reports from Constantinople, Aleppo, and Bagdad.

23. Henry Morgenthau, *Ambassador Morgenthau's Story* (New York, 1919). See also Armen Hairapetian, "Race Problems and the Armenian Genocide: The State Department File," *Armenian Review* 37 (Spring 1984): 45-145.

24. Armin T. Wegner, "The Armenian Question and the German Pacifists," *Hayrenik* (Boston), Nov. 19, 1922, and idem, "Walter Rathenau," Dec. 14, 1922. Translations from these articles in Armenian provided by the National Association for Armenian Studies and Research.

25. Deutsches Literaturarchiv, Wegner Papers: Unlabelled file containing Wegner's correspondence with Franz Werfel, carbon copy of Wegner letter to Franz Werfel, December 14, 1932: 2. See also Johannes Lepsius, *Bericht über die Lage des armenischen Volkes in der Türkei* (Potsdam, 1916); idem, *Deutschland und Armenien, 1914-1918: Sammlung diplomatischer Aktenstücke* (Potsdam, 1919); and idem, *Der Todesgang des armenischen Volkes: Bericht über das Schicksal des armenischen Volkes in der Türkei während des Weltkrieges* (Potsdam, 1919). For Lepsius's position in the context of German-Turkish relations during the

First World War, see Ulrich Trumpener, *Germany and the Ottoman Empire, 1914-1918* (Princeton, NJ, 1968), 240-41.

26. Deutsches Literaturarchiv, Wegner Papers: Wegner letter to Franz Werfel, Dec. 14, 1932: 2.

27. See note 20 and Armin T. Wegner, *Im Hause der Glückseligkeit: Aufzeichnungen aus der Türkei* (Dresden, 1920).

28. Armin T. Wegner, *Das Antlitz der Städte* (Berlin, 1917), and Kraus Reprint, 1973. Wegner was defended against the charge of pornographic literature by such prominent German literary figures as Richard Dehmel, Heinrich and Thomas Mann, Hermann Stehr, and Carl Hauptmann.

29. *Der Neue Orient* 3, no. 3/4 (1918/19): 101-4.

30. The text of the 1918 manifesto of the *Politischer Rat Geistiger Arbeiter*, including Armin T. Wegner and Kurt Hiller among the signatories, appeared in "Die Mobilisierung der Menschheit: Ansprache im politischen Rat geistiger Arbeiter, Berlin" and "Program der Gegenwart," *Der Osten* 1, no. 9/11 (Apr.-June 1919), 118-28. Some of Wegner's texts are also found in Wegner, *Fällst du, umarme auch die Erde*, 70-87. See also Wernicke-Rothmayer, *Wegner*, 38-43.

31. Armin T. Wegner, "Armenien... Offener Brief an den Präsidenten der Vereinigten Staaten von Nordamerika, Herrn Woodrow Wilson, über die Austreibung des armenischen Volkes in der Wüste," also appeared as a separate brochure in Berlin-Schöneberg, 1919. The text, retitled as "Ein Vermächtnis in der Wüste, 1919," is printed in Wegner, *Fällst du, umarme auch die Erde*, 164-72.

32. Aram Andonian, ed., *The Memoirs of Naim Bey* (Cambridge, Mass., 1965), 72-84. The quote is taken from this English translation of Wegner's Open Letter to President Wilson.

33. Ibid. The volume includes eight of Wegner's Armenian photographs in an appendix.

34. Wegner's speeches are reported in the following articles: "Die Austreibung der Armenier in die Wüste: Vortrag mit Lichtbildern in der Urania in Berlin," *Deutsche Zeitung* (Berlin), Oct. 11, 1919, and "Bericht über Armin T. Wegners Vortrag 'Die Austreibung der Armenier in die Wüste,'" *Vaterländische Arbeit*, Oct. 25, 1919; see also "Armenien in der Dichtung: Bericht über einen Vortrag A.T. Wegners in der Deutsch-Armenischen Gesellschaft," *Vorwärts*, May 11, 1920. See also Deutsches Literaturarchiv, Wegner Papers: File "Briefe zu Armenien, 1916-1919," which contains correspondence about the Urania slide lecture and sixty photos from his glass positive images. Wegner's letter to Franz Werfel, Dec. 14, 1932, (page 2) mentions the Urania lecture and the photographs he provided for Lepsius's use in 1915.
    Wegner's stories included "Der Sturm auf das Frauenbad," *Berliner Tageblatt*, serialized in Sept. and Oct. 1921; "Der Knabe Hüssein: Erzählung," *Der neue Merkur* 4, no. 10 (1920/21): 669-84; and "Eine armenische Mutter: Erinnerung an den türkischen Feldzug," *Frankfurter Zeitung*, Feb. 23, 1919. Wegner's correspondence with Efraim Frisch, editor of *Der neue Merkur*, about publishing this short story and several poems between 1920 and 1924 is located in the Archives of the Leo Baeck Institute, New York, Der neue Merkur editorial archive: AR 2555/Box 4, 6, 9, 10, 13, 16, totalling fourteen letters and postcards.

35. Armin T. Wegner, *Der Knabe Hüssein: Türkische Novellen* (Dresden, 1921). The four short stories were also published separately in German newspapers and

two were translated in Russian in the Reklam Universitätsbibliothek in 1927.

36. Armin T. Wegner, "Der Schrei vom Ararat: An die Regierung der sieghaften Völker; Aufruf zum Schutze Armeniens," *Die Weltbühne* 19 (1923): 348-55.

37. "Franz Werfel und Armin T. Wegner," *Berliner Tageblatt*, Dec. 30, 1932.

38. Deutsches Literaturarchiv, Wegner Papers: Wegner letter to Franz Werfel, Dec. 14, 1932: 3.

39. Armin T. Wegner, ed., *Der Prozess Talaat Pascha: Stenographischer Bericht über die Verhandlung vor dem Schwurgericht des Landgerichts III zu Berlin* (Berlin, 1921).

40. Deutsches Literaturarchiv, Wegner Papers: Wegner letter to Werfel, Dec. 14, 1932, and Jan. 10, 1933; Franz Werfel, *The Forty Days of Musa Dagh* (New York, 1934).

41. See the report "Gruss an die englischen Quäker," *Frankfurter Volksstimme*, Dec. 20, 1924, and Armin T. Wegner, "Das neue England; Gentlemanideal und Puritanismus," *Dresdner Neueste Nachrichten*, Sept. 2, 1924. See also Armin T. Wegner, "England nach den Wahlen," *Berliner Volkszeitung*, 6 part article on March 5, March 9, March 16, March 23, March 30, and April 12, 1924.

42. Armin T. Wegner, *Moni oder die Welt von unten; Der Roman eines Kindes* (Stuttgart, Berlin, and Leipzig, 1929), initially published in thirty-seven serialized segments in *Berliner Tageblatt*, April 7 - May 14, 1928. Dutch and Japanese translations were published in 1930.

43. Armin T. Wegner and Lola Landau, *Wasif und Akif, oder die Frau mit zwei Ehemännern: Ein türkisches Puppenspiel* (Berlin, 1926); performed on Feb. 28, 1926, at the Komödie am Kurfürstendamm, Berlin.

44. For the trip to the Soviet Union, the Caucasus, and Persia from October 1927 to February 1928, see Armin T. Wegner, *Fünf Finger über Dir: Bekenntnis eines Menschen in dieser Zeit* (Stuttgart, 1930); see also Armin T. Wegner, *Am Kreuzweg der Welten: Eine Reise vom Kaspischen Meer zum Nil* (Berlin, 1930), and idem, *Jagd durch das tausendjährige Land* (Berlin, 1932). Wegner also published more than 50 articles about his Soviet and Middle East trips.

45. Armin T. Wegner, "Aug der Strasse der Ewigkeit: Auf dem Motorrad durch Samaria und Galiläa," *Vorwärts* (August 22, 1931) and *Berliner Tageblatt* (June 14, 1931).

46. Wegner, *Jagd durch das tausendjährige Land*, 209; translated by S. Milton.

47. Deutsches Literaturarchiv, Wegner Papers: Wegner's drafts requesting restitution, dated February 1954.

48. Wernicke-Rothmayer, *Wegner*, 78-82.

49. Deutsches Literaturarchiv, Wegner Papers: Letter of expulsion from the Reichsschrifttumskammer to Wegner, November 5, 1936, prohibiting Wegner from publishing under his own name or under pseudonyms.

50. Wegner, *Fällst du, umarme auch die Erde*, 186-98. See also, Armin T. Wegner, "Ich beschwöre Sie, wahren Sie die Würde des deutschen Volkes," *Zum Nachdenken* (Informationsdienst der hessischen Landeszentrale für politische Bildung, Wiesbaden), no. 23 (1967): 3-8.

51. Wegner, *Fällst du, umarme auch die Erde*, 190, 194-95; translated by S. Milton.

52. Ibid.

53. Armin T. Wegner, "Die Warnung, 1933; Sendschreiben an den deutschen Reichskanzler Adolf Hitler," *Freiheit und Recht* 14, no. 1 (1968): 14-17, with preface about Wegner's fate. See also Wernicke-Rothmayer, *Wegner*, 260-61.

54. Wolfgang Langhoff, *Die Moorsoldaten: Dreizehn Monate Konzentrationslager* (Frankfurt, 1981), 260-61. See also Willy Perk, *Hölle im Moor: Zur Geschichte der Emslandlager, 1933-1945* (Frankfurt, 1979), 79, and Elke Suhr, *Die Emslandlager: Die politische und wirtschaftliche Bedeutung der emsländischen Konzentrations-und Strafgefangenenlager, 1933-1945* (Bremen, 1985), 229, 259.

55. Using the pen name Klaus Uhlen, Wegner published three articles in the *Berliner Tageblatt*: "Der Weg nach Norden: Mit dem Motorrad auf Englands grösster Autostrasse" on Oct. 10, 1934; "Liebe zum Loch Lomond: Herbsttage am einem schottischen See" on Oct. 26, 1934; and "Wir zelten in England: Das grosse Herbsttreffen bei Polsden Lacy" on Nov. 18, 1934. See also Deutsches Literaturarchiv, Wegner Papers: Manuscript fragments of *Die Pferdepeitsche*.

56. Quoted from Wegner correspondence to Lola Landau, letter of October 24, 1936, in Wernicke-Rothmayer, *Wegner*, 78.

57. Ruth Greuner, "Deshalb sterbe ich im Exil," in Wegner, *Am Kreuzweg der Welten*, 456-60.

58. Klaus Voigt, "Gli emigranti in Italia dai paesi sotto la dominazione nazista: tollerati e perseguitati, 1933-1940," *Storia Contemporanea* 16, no. 1 (Feb. 1985), 45-87.

59. Meir Michaelis, *Mussolini and the Jews: German-Italian Relations and the Jewish Question in Italy, 1922-1945* (Oxford, 1978).

60. Voigt, *Storia Contemporanea*, 62-78; see note 58. See also Peter Hoffmann, *Hitler's Security* (Cambridge, Mass., and London, 1979), 126-30.

61. Ruth Greuner, "Deshalb sterbe ich im Exil," in Wegner, *Am Kreuzweg der Welten*, 457; translation by S. Milton.

62. Ibid.

63. Sybil Milton, "Exile and Hiding in Italy and Belgium," Paper presented at the Jewish Museum, New York, symposium *Artists and Intellectuals in Nazi-Occupied Europe*, April 28, 1985. See also Sybil Milton, "The Artist in Exile, Internment, and Hiding," in Emily Bilski, ed., *Art and Exile: Felix Nussbaum, 1904-1944* (New York, 1985), 70-71, 80.

64. Wegner letter to Lola Landau, July 24, 1939, quoted in Wernicke-Rothmayer, *Wegner*, 82.

65. Michaelis, *Mussolini and the Jews*, 292f.

66. "Una riunione dei partecipanti ai corsi di tedesco dell' Associazione Italo-Germanica," *Il Veneto* (Padua), Nov. 13, 1941.

67. Wernicke-Rothmayer, *Wegner*, 82f. When Wegner was briefly employed as a porter in an American Red Cross center in 1945, he had contact with both American-Jewish servicemen and the rabbi of the Naples Jewish community; they both reproached him for accepting the Padua job, since it implied cooptation by the Italian fascist regime.

68. For the problems of exile writers' "silence" and adaptation to new milieus, see Helene Maimann, "Sprachlosigkeit: Ein zentrales Phänomen der Exilerfahrung," in *Leben in Exil: Probleme der Integration der Flüchtlinge im Ausland, 1933-1945*, Wolfgang Frühwald and Wolfgang Schieder, eds. (Hamburg, 1981), 31-38.

See also Helmut F. Pfanner, *Exile in New York: German and Austrian Writers after 1933* (Detroit, 1983).

69. Johannes Selbdritt, "Die Stadt ohne Mitte, Tel Aviv," *Stuttgarter Zeitung*, July 14, 1953; "Spaniens Strasse," *Stuttgarter Zeitung*, July 11, 1953; and "Sonate im Blau: Mit dem Faltboot im Tyrrhenischen Meer," *Deutsche Zeitung und Wirtschaftszeitung*, Oct. 13, 1951.

70. Bieber, "Wegner Bibliographie," in Wegner, *Fällst du, umarme auch die Erde*, 256-59.

71. Armin T. Wegner, "Das jüdische und das preussische Ghetto," *Eckart* 25 (Oct.-Dec. 1955): 1-13.

72. Deutsches Literaturarchiv, Wegner Papers: "Fremdling in der Heimat," *Südwestfunk* (Stuttgart), Jan. 21, 1962, part 8 of the autobiographical transcript of *Der Weg ohne Heimkehr: Armin T. Wegner erzählt aus seinem Leben*, Oct. 15, 1961-Jan. 21, 1962.

73. The importance of Wegner's historic 1915/16 photos of the Armenocide are discussed in commemorative fiftieth anniversary stories in the Armenian newspapers *Zartonk* (Beirut), May 18, 1965, and *Burak* (France), May 19, 1985.

74. Armin T. Wegner, "Das gute Licht: Ein Gruss an das armenische Volk zur Erinnerung an seine Vertreibung in die Wüste im Jahre 1915," *Die Weltwoche* (April 7, 1966), 25-26. See also Armin T. Wegner, "Die Feuerkugel," *Frankfurter Allgemeine Zeitung*, Oct. 14, 1966.

75. For the Wuppertal prize, see "Wuppertal ehrte Wilhelm Hüsgen und Armin Wegner," *Neue Rhein-Zeitung*, May 14, 1962; "Medal of the Righteous," *AJR Information* (London), July 1968: 4; "Yad Waschem Medaille für einen deutschen 'Gerechten der Völker': Zum Grüss für Armin T. Wegner bei seinem Besuch in Israel," *Maariv* (in Hebrew), May 14, 1968; and for the St. Gregory Order "PEN-Zentrum deutschsprachigen Autoren im Ausland," *Publikationen* 19, no. 5 (1969), 6.

76. Wegner, *Am Kreuzweg der Welten*, 394-95; translated by S. Milton.

77. Ulrich Seelmann-Eggbert, "Die Literatur des deutschen Exils seit 1933: Zu einem Symposium im Deutschen Institut der Universität Stockholm," *Neue Zürcher Zeitung*, Oct. 15, 1969, and Arno Reinfrank, "Die Literatur der Flüchtlinge: 65 internationale Germanisten trafen in Stockholm zusammen," *Mannheimer Morgen*, Sept. 24, 1969.

78. Paul Raabe, ed., *Bibliothek des Expressionismus; Nachdrucke der Erstausgaben der wichtigsten Bücher und Schriftenreihen, 1910-1924* (Nendeln, Liechtenstein: Kraus Reprint, 1973).

79. Wegner, *Fällst du, umarme auch die Erde*.

80. Deutsches Literaturarchiv, Wegner Papers. There are no finding aids to Wegner's photograph albums and loose snapshots. Although the approximately eighty glass positives containing Armenian scenes are numbered and a few are still labelled, the photograph lists for the Urania slide lectures in 1919 were lost. If comparable Armenian photographs exist in other collections and are under better bibliographic control, it should be possible to reconstruct details about location and date of many of these images.

81. Wegner's photographs are found as an appendix to the *Memoirs of Naim Bey* and in Edmond Kowalewski, *Turk at Work: The most fearful genocide* (Venice, 1965) as well as in the *Frankfurter Allgemeine Zeitung*, Oct. 14, 1966.

82. See Sean Callahan, ed., *The Photographs of Margaret Bourke-White* (Boston, 1975) and Michael Lesy, *Bearing Witness: A Photographic Chronicle of American Life, 1860-1945* (New York, 1982).

83. Recent literature about using Holocaust photographs as historical evidence includes: Gerhard Schoenberner, *Der gelbe Stern: Die Judenverfolgung in Europa, 1933-1945* (rev. exp. ed.; Frankfurt, 1982); Sybil Milton, "The Camera as Weapon: Documentary Photography and the Holocaust," *Simon Wiesenthal Center Annual* 1 (1984), 45-68; and Sybil Milton, "Images of the Holocaust," *Holocaust and Genocide Studies* (Oxford) 1, no. 1 (1986), 27-61, and idem, no. 2, 193-216.

The Genocide and Armenian Political Violence: Attitudes of Armenian Militants to the Genocide[*]

Dickran Kouymjian

A decade of Armenian terrorism has passed (1975-1985). Militants, whether organized or acting alone, have profoundly and, perhaps, irrevocably changed the outlook and attitudes of Armenians about themselves and the world's perception of them.

What have been the consequences of Armenian political violence for Armenians, for Turks, and for other governments?

What has been the reaction of each of these to this violence?

By 1975 Armenians understood that six decades of struggle to present their case before national and international bodies had produced no tangible results. Even the establishment of university programs in Armenian studies to help present intelligently and convincingly Armenian history and the modern diasporan experience did not result in a palpably higher public awareness of the Armenian dilemma. The question of Paragraph 30, mentioning the tragedy of 1915 as the first genocide of the twentieth century and its eventual deletion from the United Nations Human Rights subcommission report on genocide, dramatically underlined the regression of world public opinion concerning the Armenian Genocide.[1]

Armenians were also forced to see that annual proclamations, especially in the United States and France, by local and national officials on April 24 usually amounted to nothing more than lip service from astute politicians appeasing a minority group whose history and problems they barely understood.[2]

---

[*] This paper is published in the form originally presented in April 1985. Armenian political violence stopped at about that time. Today, in 1992, it is a virtually forgotten episode, replaced in the popular imagination by the combined efforts of the December 1988 earthquake and the establishment of the new Armenian Republic.

A "frustration of patience" set in which engendered more radical, more violent methods. Some Armenians turned to a "terrorism of frustration" which eventually became "media terrorism." It fell upon the world totally unexpected, at first in 1973 through Kourken Yanikian's individual desperate act, a forewarning perhaps of what followed two years later in 1975 with assassinations by mysterious new organizations: the Armenian Secret Army for the Liberation of Armenia (ASALA) and the Justice Commandos of the Armenian Genocide.[3]

For Turkey so surprising was this violence committed against the symbols of the state which perpetrated genocide in 1915 that for years the government in Ankara—indeed even many Armenians— could not and would not accept that these deeds were actually carried out by Armenians. Even after it became clear to Turkish intelligence that Armenians were in fact responsible for the more than 100 incidents from 1975 to 1979, Turkish officials still preferred to ascribe blame elsewhere.

After a half century of total silence about the Armenian question, the Turkish press was suddenly talking daily about this ancient minority. Even after 1980, when individual Armenians were arrested, when the identity of the groups was undeniably exposed to the world, the Turkish government at first kept officially silent on the issue, not wishing to provoke an international debate. Later, however, in 1981- 1982, the Turkish government's strategy was carefully formulated in preparation for a major propaganda offensive: a process of historical revisionism to underpin an official position of denial of the Genocide. The "Big Lie" was launched with the aid of state apparatus, academic institutes, scholars, and sophisticated western public relations firms hired to package that lie in a media blitz which still continues.[4]

Western nations, especially those active during the Genocide in documenting and reporting it, and those states which harbored the miserable survivors of that atrocity, have, since the instrusion of radical militancy, dusted off the Armenian dossier.

*   *   *

Seventy years have passed and Armenians still cannot forget, because this first genocide of the twentieth century, that is of modern times, was committed against the Armenians on their own land, and because the genocide resulted in the loss of that very ancestral homeland; thus, there is an additional and insurmountable obstacle to forgetting. A trauma seems to have been genetically, or at least indelibly, programmed into the race. Someday it may be sublimated by Armenia forgiveness, but as yet the Turk has not been prepared to ask for it.

Today, governments are once again confronted by the Armenian problem. Their jails contain Armenian political prisoners. Their courts are crowded with trials which test the very validity of certain legal presumptions concerning political assassinations and the question of guilt. Their streets are the locus of protests against official inaction towards the Genocide. And their media, ever more sophisticated and nuanced about the Armenian past, are more demanding of rational explanations. France, the United States, and other countries are being asked to articulate their policy toward the Genocide clearly; their statesmen have understood that Armenians will not be satisfied until there is a firm and continuing reaffirmation of positions taken against this crime at the very moment it was committed, in 1915 and after.

Armenians refuse to tolerate any compromise with this historical truth. Though they understand that Turkey is a present-day partner of the western alliance led by America, they will no longer allow this to take precedence over their expectation of pressure from these governments on the Turkish state to work toward a resolution of the Armenian question by—in the first instance—accepting the fact of the Genocide.

If as a group Armenians are repelled by the use of violence, especially indiscriminate terror, they are also unanimous in their feeling that the cause of this abnormal, at least atypical, behavior is the national trauma caused by the mass murder and forced exile of their nation seventy years ago coupled with the psychosis resulting from the denial of the crime by its very perpetrator—the Turkish state.

It became clear sometime ago that the only way to stop Armenian political violence—short of Turkey's willingness to admit to its misbehavior—is to replace it by effective non-violent actions working toward the same goals as the militants. Steps in this direction have multiplied dramatically in the past few years. Seminars, conferences, such as this one, "hearings," lectures, university courses, have given way to the creation of institutes, especially in the United States, which are devoted in part to the collection and study of documents relating to the Genocide and its consequences. The 1984 verdict of the Permanent Tribunal of the People concerning the Armenian Genocide has provided not only the facts surrounding the events in detail, but has also clearly outlined the procedure for the peaceful, yet forceful, pursuit of Armenian claims.

The fear displayed until now by the complacent Armenian middle-class establishment, of having its image tarnished by acts of violence committed in the name of the nation, has been to a great extent overcome or banalized as the years have passed and the violent acts have multiplied.

A radicalization of the Armenian community has been forced upon it by its own youth—less patient, more sophisticated, totally secure in its Armenian self-identity, and, therefore, less fearful than their parents and grandparents before the authorities. They dare!

Armenians have also come to understand the paradoxes of their situation, and by understanding them, they have slowly learned to live with them. The most striking of these are: (1) continued Armenian militancy versus the traditional image of a peaceful, law-abiding people; (2) Armenian demands for recognition of the 1915 Genocide from a Turkish state which denies ever more categorically its very occurrence; (3) the official governmental outcry against Armenian terrorism versus the universal and habitual use of violence, overt and covert, by states and individuals alike; (4) remorse on the part of many Armenians over the death of Turkish diplomats versus the cynical Turkish remorselessness toward the brutal demise of at least 300,000 Armenians (this minimal number representing the lowest official Turkish admission of the Armenian deaths caused by their own government's action during World War I).

Due to this unwanted terrorism, Armenians have lost their naivete, in part because they have had their accepted illusions and dreams mercilessly ignored by universal indifference. They have been confronted with an intense discussion of their national problems in public, in non-Armenian media, and they have found a profound and at times shattering difference between the perception of these problems by the general public and that echoed in the consensus discussions of their own ghettoized, parochial press.

Because of the violence Armenians have been forced to confront their dilemma, to relive almost daily the pain of a genocide nearly forgotten by everyone else. They have also been forced to reexamine their quest for nationhood and the recovery of lands lost because of genocide. They have become engaged.

Though for a time Armenian political violence threatened the very unity of the Armenian community, causing an effect quite opposite to that hoped for by Armenian terrorists, its persistence eventually forced the Turkish state to escalate the verbal war and inflate the "Big

Lie" of denial to the point where unwittingly and ironically Turkey has provoked Armenians to reunite by attacking the one issue they all agree upon.

At this moment it is impossible to know if Armenian militancy will give way totally to a non-violent struggle.[5] If media terrorism has succeeded in bringing the Genocide and its victims back into the arena of international politics, it is hard to imagine what further use it can serve. Violent means are never acceptable, even when committed out of the desperation caused by the terror of a continuing genocide.

That a dispersed nation has succeeded in reasserting itself by itself against the powerful and well financed campaign of distortion of a large state (Turkey) enjoying the financial and material support of an even larger state (U.S.A.), says something eloquent about the Armenian struggle.

Let us consider for a moment the specific position of each of the major terrorist organization—the Justice Commandos of the Armenian Genocide, the Armenian Secret Army for the Liberation of Armenia, the Armenian Revolutionary Army—toward the Armenian question and the genocide.

The Justice Commandos appear from their communiques to seek to reclaim the lost Armenian homeland, as specified in the Treaty of Sevres, and to seek reparations and recognition of the crimes committed against their people by Turkey; they seek a solution similar to Germany's admission of guilt and reparations to Israel after World War II. In the earliest communiques after the October 1975 assassinations of Turkish ambassadors in Vienna and Paris, they addressed all people and governments as follows:

> Let the world realize that we will lay down our arms only when the Turkish government officially denounces the genocide perpetrated by Turkey in 1915 against the Armenian people and agrees to negotiate with Armenian representatives in order to reinstate justice.

After the October 1980 bombings in New York and Los Angeles, the Justice Commandos stated:

> We make clear that our struggle today against the Turkish government is not to be regarded as revenge for the 1915 Genocide in which 1.5 million Armenian men, women, and children were massacred. Our struggle today is directed to have the Turkish government admit to its responsibility for that murderous act, as well as to return to the Armenian people the lands taken forcibly and today occupied by the imperialist Turkish government since the genocide. We demand once again that the Turkish government admit its responsibility for the

Genocide of 1915 and make appropriate territorial and financial reparations to the long-suffering Armenian people.

And in 1982 after the killing of the Turkish consul in Boston a Paris communique said:

> The shooting was to reaffirm the permanence of our demands. The Turkish government must recognize the responsibility of its predecessors in 1915 in the execution and genocide perpetrated against the Armenian people, and it must clearly condemn it. Secondly, the Turkish government must recognize the right of the Armenian people to constitute a free and independent state on Armenian land which Turkey illegally occupies.

The Armenian Secret Army for the Liberation of Armenia has been infinitely more verbal, at times contradictory, through a variety of media, at first sympathetic periodicals like *Hay Baykar/Liberation Arménienne* in Paris and *Kaytzer* in London, but eventually in its own multilingual journal *Hayastan/Armenia*. Of all militant groups it displayed the greatest success in attracting to it the largest popular following among scattered countrymen. Since the recent split in the Secret Army into a hard-line extremists group and a moderate one, provoked by the indiscriminate, "blind" terror of the 1983 Orly airport and Latin quarter bombings, it is more difficult to summarize their respective positions. However, for a historical example from late 1979, I quote:

> Our second step was only possible due to the successful completion of our first step, which had politicized the Armenian youth enough to gain their support in the second step. This second step contains four new developments: (1) heavy assault on imperialist and Zionist and reactionary forces; (2) a much greater frequency of attacks; (3) direct communication with the Armenian masses and international opinion; and (4) strong ties with other revolutionary organizations, including operational ties with the Kurdish Workers Party [in Turkey].

Here we note the lack of reference to 1915.

Finally, a communique of 19 November 1984 issued by a new group, The Armenian Revolutionary Army,[6] after an attack on a Turkish diplomat in Vienna, provides a view of their ideological position:

> The Armenian Revolutionary Army continues to battle according to its plans.
> We remind everyone that we are the sons of the Armenian people and that we work solely to the service of its just cause.
> We reaffirm our total independence regarding the different imperialistic currents, East as well as the West, which act directly or by way of its agents, and we proclaim our attachment, without reserve, to a policy of

clearly expressed non-alignment.

Our combat which emanates from the National Liberation Struggle of the Armenian people is undertaken against the reactionary Turkish government.

It will conclude when, taking note of the legality of the Armenian Cause, the Turkish government begins negotiations with the representatives of the Armenian People.

Until then, we will continue our struggle with the same resolve expressed by our suicide commandos in Lisbon and we warn the government of Turkey as well as its representatives in the four corners of the world.

Long Live Free and Independent Armenia.

Long Live the Fighters of the Armenian Cause.

Long Live the Struggle for the Liberation of the Armenian People.

Though similar to the rhetoric of the Justice Commandos, note that reference to the Genocide has been omitted. Just as for the Secret Army, the unacknowledged crime of 1915 takes a secondary role for ARA. The Secret Army had pioneered this attitude, even proclaiming, through a series of annual posters, April 24 as Revolution Day, the day of militant struggle for a new order rather than a day for mourning or for the commemoration of martyrs.

*   *   *

What effect has ten years of militancy had on the world? No doubt a varied one, but of certain importance to Armenians, militants or not, is the impact on, or the perception of, such governments as France and the United States. Of more than passing interest, therefore, is the semi-official governmental assessment of Armenian terrorism made in the famous August 1982 article by Andrew Corsun in the *U.S. Department of State Monthly Bulletin.* Most Armenians know about this article, entitled "Armenian Terrorism: A Profile," because of the infamous note appended at the end:

> Because the historical record of the 1915 events in Asia Minor is ambiguous, the Department of State does not endorse allegations that the Turkish government committed a genocide against the Armenian people. Armenian terrorists use this allegation to justify in part their continuing attacks on Turkish diplomats and installations. (page 35)

Despite this note, even a casual reading of the entire article will demonstrate that the State Department considered the Armenian terrorist movement to have been very successful. I quote:

> Enraged over the alleged massacre of 1.5 million Armenians by Turkey during World War I, and the loss of their homeland, Armenians unlike Jews tried and failed as propagandists to focus the world's attention on

their grievances. By resorting to terrorism, Armenian extremists were able to accomplish in 7 years what legitimate Armenian organizations have been trying to do for almost 70 years—internationalize the Armenia cause.

Terrorism may not be able to ease the pain of past agonies, but it is an effective tactic in evoking international sympathy for a previously unknown (or forgotten) cause. ... Armenian extremists have waged a successful campaign against Turkish interests.   (p. 31)

In his conclusion the Corsun says:

While Armenian terrorism has evoked a greater interest in and aware-ness of the Armenian question throughout the world, the chances of Armenians attaining their major objectives through terrorism are nebulous at best. ...A viable solution to the Armenian question will only come about through political means (e.g., United Nations, lobbyist groups, etc.) and/or compromise on both sides. Yet, until such a path is followed—if ever—the issues will be kept fresh in the public's mind through acts of terrorism. (p.35)

*   *   *

The evolution from April 24 demonstrations and marches to capture public opinion in the period 1965 to 1975 to media terrorism in the decade just passed has profoundly and perhaps irreversibly changed the notion Armenians have toward their past and of their own self-image.

What effect has Armenian terrorism had on the phenomenon of the Genocide? While awakening the world to the unresolved pain of a nation, has it modified the fundamental outlook of society on the events of 1915? In short has terrorist violence had a positive or a negative effect on the Genocide?

It is hard to imagine a negative effect to either the abstract notion of genocide or the specific reality of the Armenian example which could be attributed to Armenian political violence. That there has been a negative factor on the image of the Armenian both among Armenians and the informed public is a subject which is open to discussion; it is at least a debatable topic with recorded opinion on both the negative (the majority) and the positive (minority view) of the question. Theoretically, however, terrorism cannot even affect the Genocide, an event three generations back in history. Armenians seem to have difficulty realizing this. On the other hand, a question can be legitimately posed on the effect of terrorism on how we view the Genocide, but again we would be hard put to demonstrate that any negative regard on the Genocide or our view of it, was the result, even partially, of Armenian militancy.

The worst that has been said about terrorism, again with reference to the Genocide, is that the failure of Turkey and other states, which are historically involved with the Armenian question, to acknowledge it as an irrefutable historical fact and to take measures to redress the damage caused by it, has led the third generation of survivors of the Genocide to turn to desperate methods to bring the crime against humanity—this conveniently forgot precursor of the Holocaust—to the attention of the responsible state (Turkey), other states, and world opinion through the only channel left: media terrorism. Thus, whatever terrorism may have done to tarnish the reputation of the Armenian, it has had, and perhaps intrinsically can only have, a positive effect on the universal perception of the Armenian Genocide. It is and has been by far the most influential activity to make the willful murder of the Armenian nation a topic of discussion and serious reflection, as the U.S. State Department has so eloquently told the Armenians.

*　*　*

The effect on Turkey has been equally spectacular. Today there is no Turk who does not know about the state-sponsored violence employed against the Armenians during the first World War. Ten years ago this was not the case. Then, Turks who came to the west were dismayed to hear Armenian accusations against their state. Then they could claim ignorance; today that is inconceivable. Armenians and the Genocide are discussed almost daily in the Turkish press. It has become a Turkish obsession.

Ankara has mobilized thousands of individuals for the protection of national and international Turkish institutions because of militant Armenians. It has co-opted statesmen, publicists, and scholars, both native and foreign, by the hundreds to counter Armenian charges of Genocide by rewriting the history of the period. The government through its Ministry of Foreign Affairs has sponsored international and national seminars and published hundreds of thousands of tracts of various sorts explaining their version of what happened between 1915 and 1917. A mini-industry has been created to deal with what in the final analysis is nothing more or less than Armenian history.

As I have said before, the most dangerous step the Turkish authorities have taken, from their point of view, is to engage themselves in the debate on the Genocide, even if to deny it. As Israel Charny so astutely observed in a 1983 essay directed against Turkish attempts to remove from the record their Genocide of the Armenians, "every effort they [the Turks] make [to deny the Genocide] only engraves the facts of the Genocide of the Armenians deeper into the pages of history."

This is not the place to analyze various articles and attitudes on the Genocide found in the Turkish press. The subject is now so vast that it can easily serve as a dissertation topic. Yet, one "alleged" assertion of the Turkish Prime Minister can serve as witness to the inner disruption the Armenian question is causing among Turks. On February 13, 1985, the Turkish daily Güneş, published an interview with Turgut Ozal which was quickly picked up by foreign wire services and the Armenian press. Some regarded his remarks as a "new attitude toward the Armenian question." Ozal is quoted as saying:

> The Armenians published thousands of books and brochures, and succeeded in convincing the world of the thesis of genocide. It will not serve anything to say now that is false, that the Muslim people suffered more.

Further on he directly addressed demands of Armenian militants:

> No one has the right to demand an inch of territory from Turkey or accuse the Republic of Turkey. Regardless whether something happened or not, no one has the right to demand from Turkey that she give in to demands founded on lies.

Two days later Ozal formally denied saying anything about the Armenians, explaining "Apparently someone slept [during the interview] and had a dream [that I said such a thing]." Were his remarks to be interpreted as a trial balloon to judge Turkish public reaction?

*   *   *

In conclusion, I would like the following points to serve as an assessment of ten years of Armenian terrorism and its consequences on the communities touched by it. Some of the remarks are also directed to the near future.

1. The success of Armenian terrorist organizations has made them superfluous, obsolete. For the moment informed public opinion in most western countries and Turkey knows that Armenians suffered brutal massacres constituting a Genocide perpetrated by the Turkish government during World War I. Some militant organizations may dream of constituting a standing or guerilla army for the reconquest of Armenian lands, but their actual numbers are so insignificant that without massive outside support such a possibility is a chimera. It is conceivable that a public slap in the face to the Armenian nation

could provoke a dramatic resurgence of terrorism, for example the failure to reinstate Paragraph 30 into the United Nations Human Rights report could provide the same symbolic frustration that the paragraph evoked in the period 1973-1975, which marked the inception of Armenian militancy.

2. Steps to consolidate the Armenian community for a more effective non-violent campaign toward universal recognition of the Genocide will accelerate. Organizations such as the Armenian Assembly in the United States will assume larger roles in diasporan life. The eventual success of the Armenian Congress movement, which has thus far been unable to display either charismatic leadership or clear direction, should, in one form or another, provide the Armenian community with its single most important institution.

To date, the most impressive witness to this generalized mobilization of Armenians, certainly the most concrete steps toward formal recognition of the Genocide, has come from the actions taken by international bodies, especially the Permanent Tribunal of the People and the work done concomitantly with the European Parliament. Both of these projects were pioneered by the Alliance Franco-Arménien, a small but dedicated group whose uncharacteristically and un-Armenian methods of working behind the scenes without interest in personal power or public attention should serve as an example or model for other Armenian organizations.

The Permanent Tribunal of the People has now publicly told us and the entire world that a Genocide was committed against the Armenian people by the Young Turk government according to the strictest interpretation of the Genocide Convention and international law subscribed to by most nations including Turkey herself.[7] That the United States government or the Turkish government has until now failed to publicly recognize the Genocide in no way detracts from the fact of that Genocide, as eloquently and elaborately articulated through the verdict of the Tribunal. When the governments of the world are ready to reconsider the Armenian problem, they have only to consult the verdict of the Permanent Tribunal to know how to proceed.

3. The Turkish press, the government, and academic circles in response to Armenian terrorism have, directly or indirectly, informed the Turkish people of the facts and issues of the Armenian Genocide. Even the denial of Genocide is in truth, a celebration of it.

4. Soviet Armenia, through its press and certain high-ranking officials, notably the Minister of Foreign Affairs, John Kirakossian,

has for the first time in recent years directly and consistently criticized Turkish policy and refuted revisionist assertions about the Genocide. The unprecedented April 24, 1985 article in *Pravda* entitled "Judged by Humanity" is indicative of this tendency to be more outspoken on Armenian-Turkish relations.

5. Armenians have gained a confident vigor as they see the truth of their cause prevailing. As Armenians, in our relations with the Turks today, *we know that they know that we know that they know.*

REFERENCES

1. Paragraph 30 became Paragraph 24 of the *Report of the U.N. Sub-Commission on Prevention of Discrimination and the Protection of Minorities*, adopted in Geneva on August 29, 1985. The "Ottoman" massacres of the Armenians was one of nine examples of genocide in the twentieth century cited in the *Report.*

2. With the formation of the Armenian Republic in 1990-1991, the Genocide, though still universally mourned, has ceased to be the primary focal point of Armenian life in the diaspora.

3. A recent complete listing of the incidents can be found in Francis P. Hyland, *Armenian Terrorism: The Past, the Present, the Prospects* (Boulder: Westview Press, 1991).

4. In the past six years, revisionist scholarship on the Genocide has continued despite a noticeable openness by some Turkish journalists, particularly Ali Birind, toward Armenia and the Armenians.

5. As noted above, Armenian political violence had all but stopped by 1986.

6. ARA, like the Justice Commandos, had close ties with the Armenian Revolutionary Federation and may have been an evolutionary phase of the earlier group.

7. The Permanent Peoples' Tribunal, *A Crime of Silence* (London: Zed Books, 1985).

The Image of the Turk
in Modern Armenian Literature

Vahé Oshagan

Armenian intellectual history is, in a sense, the story of a nation trying to cope with the haunting theme of evil. All the way from the fifth century, both lay and religious literatures have given very large space to recording the suffering and devastation of the country while reflecting the constant presence of death and God, evil and good, at the same time, in a world depicted as essentially hostile. By the nineteenth century, a solid spiritual tradition has been formed in which evil, because of its overwhelming presence, has lost its physical and metaphysical natures and has either been absorbed by the teachings of the church or has been accepted as an inevitable condition of life. The immense popularity of Krikor Naregatsi's guilt-ridden prayers during the last one thousand years draws its power largely from this feeling. One salient feature of this theme of evil is the almost total absence of hatred in Armenian letters towards the peoples that have successively incarnated the Anti-Christ in Armenian history—the Persians, the Arabs, the Seljuks, the Turks. Not until the twentieth century is there a call for blood, for revenge, or eternal enmity in the annals of Armenian culture. This fact might be related to the wisdom and instinct of survival, to the tradition of obedience to providence, or to faith in life and love that the generation of 1850 inherits from its past. Until the turn of the twentieth century, the Turk was not an issue.

We will concentrate our attention on the Western Armenians, living in the Ottoman Empire. Their lot, especially in the eastern provinces, is not a happy one. For close to six hundred years they have been oppressed, harassed and exploited. Around 1825 there are signs of a cultural revival, largely due to enlightened prelates of the

Apostolic church, the Mekhitarist congregations, and contacts with the West in places such as Smyrna (Izmir), Constantinople (Istanbul), Madras, Calcutta, Venice, etc. It is also the heyday of political and literary romanticism in Europe. In the Armenian world, playwrights and poets make their appearance around 1800, drawing inspiration from the tragic and glorious pages of Armenian history. The plays, mostly in classical Armenian, of Frs. M. Tchakhtchakhian, K. Avedikian, L. Injijian, E. Tomajanian, A. Pakraduni, and of E. Setian, A. Beshigtashlian, and B. Minassian, the poetry of Frs. Alishan and A. Pakraduni, the novels of Frs. T. Tornian and C. Sybilian, all from the Mekhitarist congregations, are imbued with the lofty ideals of national enlightenment and liberation as well as the ardent desire to inspire patriotism in their public. The same observation applies to the historical novels on M. Taghiatiants writing at the same time in Calcutta.

And then, suddenly, in July of 1862, a valiant rebellion erupts in Zeitun against the Sultan's taxation policy and galvanizes the entire nation. The blood spilled in the name of liberty inspires a young romantic poet, M. Beshigtashlian, to write a series of stirring emotional poems extolling the rebels in the epic style typical of classical poets.[1] Even Russian Armenian intellectuals such as M. Nalbandian and S. Shahaziz were moved by the impact and responded by writing enflamed articles and poems. Other writers in Istanbul, H. Sevadjian and S. Takvorian, actually incite their readers to follow the example of the Zeitun insurgents and struggle for freedom and dignity. A similar spirit moves other lay playwrights in the Ottoman Empire to seek inspiration in the heroic figures and events of national history, people like A. Haiguni, S. Vanantetzi, S. Hekimian, T. Terzian, Kh. Narbey, E. Yessayan, S. Laz-Minassian, S. Tghlian, and B. Turian.

By 1875 this first phase of the national awakening and liberation struggle has come to a close. Around forty-five patriotic plays, five historical novels, and countless poems and articles have been published. In all of these the implied enemy who stands in the way of recreating the free, ideal fatherland is the Turk, and yet nowhere is there any mention of him. Nor is there an image of him, either in the literature of protest or in the ordinary daily literature. Perhaps the clearest picture of the Turk in this period is supplied by the poetry of Bedros Turian. Like most other writers, Turian too has poems inspired by the suffering and humiliated Armenia. But he has one celebrated poem called *Trkuhin* (The Turkish Woman) where one can read between the lines the tyranny and frustration that these ladies imposed, through their sensuality, on the Armenian males because of the racial and social barriers separating them. With none of these writers, however, does hatred of the Turk as a symbol of oppression or pain become an issue or theme.[2]

The forty years between the romantic patriotism of the seventies and the Genocide of 1915 see a radical change in the attitude of Armenian writers to the Turk. The most important reason is the stepping up of the repression by the Ottoman regime as a result of the Treaty of Berlin in 1878, when the Armenian Question was placed, for the first time, on an international stage. The Armenian response is the organization of guerilla groups and the establishment of political parties. The second reason is the replacement, around 1875, of the traditional wealthy church leadership and its policy of conciliation by new, younger, middle-class professionals and politicians with a more aggressive policy. Finally, as enlightenment and prosperity spread and the revival gathers momentum, better communications and dissemination of information through the media creates heightened public awareness of issues.

The last decades of the nineteenth century are very trying for the Armenians in the Ottoman Empire. The paranoia of the Red Sultan and the increasing tempo of the repression by the state and by Kurdish tribes in the eastern provinces drive the Armenians to desperate, violent actions. And the escalation of violence leads to the wide-spread massacres by the Sultan in 1894 to 1896, costing the Armenians an estimated 300,000 lives. The carnage creates a furor in Europe; but in the Empire the press is muzzled and so are the writers, and the literature reflects this silence. Strict censorship has been established in 1885 and the Armenians continue as though nothing had happened! In the meantime a large and very active emigre intelligentsia which has come to life in Europe and Egypt wages a relentless war on the regime.

The literature that develops now in the newly-formed diaspora is perforce journalistic and propaganda-oriented. The most dynamic of the emigre intellectuals is Arpiar Arpiarian, who from Egypt and England attacks the Turks, calling them "barbarians." In an 1899 article he prophecies the Genocide of 1915. "The guiding principle of Turkish policy towards the Armenians," he writes, "is the total annihilation of the Armenian people."[3] He is joined by Suren Bartevian who, faced with immense human suffering, becomes the first Armenian writer to reject church, religion, and God. Finally the socialist ideologies of the political parties undermine further the power of the Church and the upper middle-class, thus reinforcing the rhetorical tendencies. All these contribute to darkening even further the already somber image of the Turk.

The year 1908 marks the downfall of the Sultan, the declaration of a constitutional monarchy, the deceptive liberalization of the new regime, the fraternization of Turk and Armenian, and the massacre of Adana in which 30,000 Armenians lose their lives. The disappointment is great, many writers return to Istanbul, and by 1912 literary life is in full swing in the capital. Rejecting the Christian West, a strong section of the literati turns to pagan values and pre-Christian origins for new inspiration. Turkish-Armenian reconciliation and public fraternization create a state of euphoria, and for many the ugly image of the Turk is forgotten. A great number of intellectuals are wary, however, and voice their suspicion of Turkish sincerity and warn the Armenians of horrible events in the making. Most eloquent among these are Zabel Yessayan, Aram Andonian, and the poets Siamanto and Vahan Tekeyan.

Yessayan, a well-known writer, was a member of the delegation of inquiry sent by the Patriarchate to Adana to investigate the 1908 massacre. Upon her return she published a book, *Averagnerun Metch* (Among the Ruins), which is both a literary masterpiece and a scathing attack, turning the Turkish image literally into that of a monster. She also published scores of short stories all inspired by the tragedy of Adana. Her book is followed by another one, *Giligian Arhavirk* (The Horrors of Cilicia), by Suren Bartevian published in 1908 which is even more damning for the Turk.

Aram Andonian's stories in the journals paint an even darker picture of the Turks. No one trusts them. "The Turks have not changed at all" is the almost unanimous opinion. Vahan Tekeyan, the least outspoken of all the poets, turns into a revolutionary in the pages of the paper *Shirag*: "The Turks have not changed. They are preparing new horrors for us" he says.[4] A. Harutunian writes in *Aztag* of "blood-drenched sunrises" and talks of the "destructive nature of the Turkish race."[5] "The Young Turks are the direct continuation of old Turkey. This race will not change—it has no creative power, it is a master of destruction."[6] Daniel Varujan writes: "We must wage battle, gun in hand, against the killer mobs."[7] Even Yervant Odian, who at first hailed with jubilation the newly-found brotherhood of the two races, voiced grave concern about the real intentions of the Turks. A. Alboyadjian says: "The crimes of Abdul-Hamid are not only his responsibility but also reflect a racial streak in the Turks that continues with the new generation."[8]

But more than anything else, more than the opinions of intellectuals, it is the stirring voice of the poets that fashions the final, terrible image of the Turk in the Armenian consciousness—and perhaps the unconscious, too. It is first the thundering verse of Siamanto, whose epic imagination, glowing idealism, and powerful words of anger and revenge not only glorify the heroes of the Armenian resistance and the Armenian revolution while branding the Turk as the Immense, the Eternal Murderer, and the Scourge of God, but succeed also in inspiring hope and faith in Justice, joining thus the old wisdom with the new realities.[9] Then Daniel Varujan, the greatest Armenian poet whose masterpiece, *Tzeghin Sirde* (The Heart of the Race), revives in the masses the national pride while castigating the inhumanity of the massacres and the infamy of their perpetrators.[10] Between them these two poets, both skinned alive in 1915, have done more than anyone else in making the image of the Turk a symbol of hate in the national consciousness.

In the years immediately following the 1915 Genocide and its horrors, three reactions can be detected among the writers. First, there is the flood of eye-witness accounts and personal memoirs that has not yet dried up. Needless to say, these narrations of the stark reality develop in the margin of literature and reflect the popular image of the Turk as a monster of cruelty. A partial list of such books from 1920 to 1970 contains around seventy titles. The shorter narratives and memoirs on the same topic published in the periodic press number in the hundreds.

Among the writers, however, the image is more varied. First the poets. Very few had escaped the carnage. Of these, the most important is doubtless Vahan Tekeyan. In his several poems written in the heat of the tragedy, the poet derides both God and mankind, but his main vehemence is directed to the Turks, whom he portrays as "human hyenas" and "executioners" deserving vengeance and everlasting hatred.[11] But within three years his whole approach changes; and by 1918 he already talks of the possibility of forgetting, of resurrecting the moral forces of the nation, of a rebirth of creative energy. And turning to God, he murmurs:

> I know, it is too early and fate is implacable
> But O God, bring near the morn when we again
> Will be able to bless you from the depths of our heart.

But Tekeyan is almost alone among the Armenian literati to speak of forgetting so soon. One writer with a track record of stark realism

in pre-1915 times is Aram Andonian. He is one of the few to have
survived the hell of massacres and deportations and accordingly to
have first-hand knowledge and experience of the Turkish mentality.
In his two books drawn from this experience, *Ain Sev Orerun* (In Those
Black Days, 1919) and *Medz Vodjire* (The Great Crime, 1920), the
image he draws of the Turk is so horrifying that it oversteps human
nature into utter bestiality. It must be said that these two books are
the only ones to have come out of the genocide experience. In any
case, Andonian's portrayal of the Turk adds very little to the image
drawn by Yessayan, Bartevian, and others. He brings nothing new to
the theme of the Turk.

The same observation is true for Mikael Shamdanjian's *Hai Mdki
Harge Yeghernin* (What the Massacres Cost the Armenian Intellect,
1919) that relates the arrest and imprisonment of some of the
intellectuals of Istanbul in April 1915 in a very affected style. By now,
the image of the Turk as the Evil has become a commonplace, almost
instinctive, fact of Armenian literature. We meet it in all kinds of
works—in the three-act play *Anmah Potze* (The Undying Flame, n.d.)
by Suren Bartevian in which the Armenian mother poisons herself
rather than yield to a Turk; in *Arunin Madyane* (The Book of Blood,
1920) by the same author, who describes in a poignant style the
tribulations of victims and survivors of the massacres; in *Anidzyal
Dariner* (Accursed Years, 1914-1918) by Yervant Odian, which depict
in a serialized form the author's experiences during those troubled
years.

Andonian is a minor figure in Armenian letters. When we pass to
the novelist Hagop Oshagan, we are dealing with one of the greatest
names in modern Armenian literature. In 1915 he manages to elude
the Turkish police and in 1930, at age 45, he is the only major writer
who has direct experience of the Turk and an intimate knowledge of
Turkish and Armenian ways of life. His fictional world is the countryside around Bursa where the two races live intermingled. His first
major novel, *Dzag Bdouge* (The Adulterous Woman), appears in 1928
and reveals a writer at grips with the most elemental drives in human
beings and village societies, Turkish and Armenian.

In the following five years, Oshagan produces eight volumes of
fiction, all dealing with the racial tensions set against a background
of rural life. These novels that cover the period from 1880 to 1915
suddenly project the Turk into the national consciousness under a
new, uncommon guise. Oshagan's world is filled with Turkish
figures—fanatical mullahs, sophisticated pashas, capricious young

women, criminals, and prison guards who are all certainly ferocious in their sadism towards the subject nation while at the same time revealing a human side to their nature that is sensitive to music, to love, to beauty. In a long, celebrated passage in *Mnatzortatz*, his masterpiece, Oshagan reconstitutes a political discussion between a German-educated Prison Superintendent and a captured Moscow-educated Armenian revolutionary in which, for the first time in Armenian letters, a Turk is shown to be a normal human being capable of holding rational discourse (although Oshagan concludes that the two races cannot coexist on the same planet). In other novels (*Suleiman Effendi, Hadji Abdullah*), Oshagan again shows that the atrocious behavior of the Turk is derived from an atavism that goes back to racial origins in the steppes of Asia, that he is but a toy in the hands of his instincts. "No man can be inhuman," says the author; and this fact humanizes, even transforms totally, the stereotyped image of a cold-blooded beast that had persisted for sixty years.

Since the Genocide, almost everything the Armenians have written has been influenced, directly or indirectly, by that horrible event. But the event itself in all its hideous details and huge span has remained unchartered, unconquered, and almost absent. Those closest to it are the bitter young men of Paris, or grown-up orphans as they call themselves, the first diaspora generation of highly gifted men like Shahan Shahnour, Vazken Shushanian, Shavarsh Nartuni, Nigoghos Sarafian at the heart of whose world is a distorted view of life, a permanent obsession to reject reality, to turn back the pages of history, and to recapture the world of innocence. In fact, theirs is a double rejection—not only that of Western civilization but also of their past and of their elders whom they hold responsible for their miserable plight and the betrayal of their homeland. At the center of this bitterness lies the unnameable, the event. The Turk is identified with this event and he, too, is unnameable, beyond humanity, beyond redemption.

Over the decades from 1920 on, this image of the Turk remains unchanged. The uprooted Armenians, burdened with nightmares, are adrift in a hostile, insecure world, a prey to constant in-fighting, humiliated at having been massacred, and with no future to look forward to. They form ghetto-like enclaves in the host countries from the United States to Egypt and everywhere are treated as "foreigners." Intolerance, authoritarianism, and xenophobia bordering on paranoia dominate large segments of social thinking.

Literature forms part of this closed world of suffering at the center of which is the Turk, the scapegoat of all failures and insufficiencies. Of course the root cause is to be found mainly in the event, but its enormity defies all talents. The vast Armenian populations of the Middle East, with fresh memories of Turkish mistreatment in Cilicia and Alexandretta, have great difficulty adjusting to the Arab Muslim culture, because the Turk is identified, in their memory, with Islam. All this reinforces the already dark image as political priorities impose themselves in the 1960s on the occasion of the fiftieth anniversary of the Genocide, and Armenian nationalism dominates the spirit. Young writers like A. Dzarugian, M. Ishkhan, Y. Boyadjian, A. Anush, Levon Sdepanian, and Vahe-Vahian tag along, identified with the popular feeling. In the United States, however, prose-writers Hamasdegh, V. Haig, P. Noorigian, A. Haigaz, and H. Assadourian adapt to the spirit of the land and fashion a new tradition of artless, popular, and folksy literature in which the image of the Turk loses some of its harshness without, however, becoming totally human.

Seventy years after the event, the Turk's image and his absence still stifle, in a certain sense, Armenian creativity. These two, the event and the image, are indissolubly tied to one another. The event is a huge block of unsolved, evil mystery, an incomprehensible segment of national history right at the center of the diaspora, severing traditions, memories, and the life of the past. Two generations of writers have come and gone, and yet no one has succeeded in transforming through art the brute horror of the event, in quality and quantity, into an experience of human proportions, into a meaningful though tragic part of life. On the other hand the pain and the grief of the massacres are very much present in almost every Armenian family, and vengeance rankles on. On the intellectual level, the usurpation of the ancestral land is another cause of distress. The whole issue is highly emotional.

But of course literature has its own rules. And the fact is that, if Armenian literature is to mature in the diaspora and gain new, higher ground, it must first tackle the experience of the event. From irrational it has to be scaled down to the rational, from the so-called "inhuman" to the human. It must be integrated into Armenian history. This means that the Turk must be humanized, demythicized, and his image, at least in the imagination of the writer, made plausible, redeemable. Perhaps a similar operation has to be performed on the Armenian, whose image has been raised to that of martyr. He, too, has to look into the mirror; he has to be humanized. Otherwise this unique, almost privileged, experience, that of going to hell and back, that befell the Armenian nation in 1915 will never reveal its secret, neither to the Armenians nor to the world. If the price is the separation of the emotional from the artistic, perhaps that price should be paid by the writers, without giving up on the political demands. The essential, for the writers, is the artistic formulation of the wisdom gained from the event. The Armenians owe it to themselves and to mankind.

ANNEX I

Death of the Hero
(Extract)

Sweet mother mine, why do you stand so lowly?
Do not tremble, come approach me,
With tearless eyes look at your son
And his wounds covered in blood.
> Let Turkish mothers shed their tears
> But you take good tidings to Zeitun.

. . . . .

Red lightnings flash from my wound
But you, mother mine, look around,
See bloodthirsty Turks everywhere
Sprawled in death by the thousand.
> They're the victims of our swords
> But you take good tidings to Zeitun.
> > — M. Beshigtashlian

ANNEX II

The Turkish Woman
(Extract)

The evening burns, the horizon is on fire
A carriage moves very slowly like a hearse
Inside is sprawled a woman of beauty gently panting.
Is she the maiden of sunsets, O Lord?
> Were she to look at you
> You'd say: Now she'll be extinguished!

. . . . .

Her bosom heaves like an ocean
She pines to love or fade away in an embrace
To fall in her tomb consumed, withered, and weary
And drain the last drop from the fiery cup of love.
> Were she to blush
> You'd say: Now she'll catch fire.

. . . . .

and she burns, she burns unquenchable,
Like the lamp of the poor woman in the Temple,
She loves to glitter as the stars at night
A flaming meteor shorn from the rib of love.
    Were she to die
    You'd say: Now she'll be born.
                — *B. Turian*

ANNEX III

The Strangulation
(Extract)

Like a herd of terrified cattle pursued by a raging sandstorm
We took refuge in a dungeon terror-stricken and trampling one
    another
We forty humans huddled in the pitch darkness.
. . . . .
Outside beast-like barbarians in the thousands
Roamed the fields and villages in ruin
Seeking our hiding-place to bring us death.
. . . . .
From corpses and bodies piled high on the dungeon's roof
Their death-rattle some ferocious others weak
Reached us below and drove us mad,
While their blood still warm streamed through the cracks
And fell on our faces drop by drop.
Suddenly a new-born babe started to cry loud and shrill
Putting to danger all of us and forcing us
To a crime as our one hope of survival.
And then we heard the sobbing voice of the mother
— God have mercy on us, my breasts are dry
Not a drop of milk, not a single drop remains. . . .
— Strangle the child, said one stretching his arms in anger
— Strangle the child whispered forty voices in unison
— Strangle me first, then my child. . . .
— They've heard us, they are digging the roof. . . .
— We're betrayed, they are digging the roof. . . .
— Some earth has fallen on me, I can see the light. . . .
— I beg of you, strangle me
  Here is my throat and my child's. . . .

The Armenian mother offered us her throat and her child's
As two arms snaked their way in the dark
Gripped the babe's neck and strangled it. . . .
                — *Siamanto*

The Massacre
(_Extract_)

I see you, O ferocious Spirit,
Hunting the defenseless and the weak
Stirring up the dust among ruins,
I see you on your white charger
Wrapped like a Viper
In your green mantle,
Crowned with the soul of Alp Aslan
While drips for ever the lukewarm blood
From the grey tassels of the saddle.
. . . . . .
O you barbarian Spirit,
The sound of crushing bones on your path
Echoing in the fiery caverns of the skies,
On your passage children are strangled
With their mothers' tresses,
While the maidens of our land are
Soiled by your lust and choked to death
With the ropes of their wells,
To what evil demon are sacrificed
The saintly virgins of our churches
Strapped to cold pillars,
And in our wondrous fields where our life
Drinks in the Sun till it is consumed in the Soul,
With the bodies of their victims
They elevate sacred Golgothas.
And then
Each and all
From skull they hold in their hands
Drink the blood of child and old
Of woman and of Christ
Crucified on the slopes of Ararat. . . .

— _Daniel Varujan_

You Will Fall

To the Turk

You will fall and this time you will never rise again
You'll remain on the ground to claw and scratch the earth
And your agony will go on and on while the ashes of your house,
Once so lively, will fall on you and bury you.

It is enough the pain and evil you brought mankind,
Cities and villages, mounts and fields that you plunged in grief,
Enough you made poor mothers weep over their homes
And filled our loving hearts with spite and hate. . . .

You will fall. . . . But in order that you feel
The greatest pain pierce your evil heart
You will be struck by those who had saved you ofttimes. . . .

And in your dying hour you will perceive, O supreme punishment,
The blossoming of our land that you once left in ruin
And our boundless merriment right in your eyes of enslaved.

— *V. Tekeyan*

REFERENCES

1. See "Death of the Hero" (Extract), 159, above.

2. See "The Turkish Woman" (Extract), 159, above.

3. A. Arpiarian, "*Medki Anotutiun*" (Intellectual Hunger), in *Nor Giank*, 1899, 306.

4. V. Tekeyan, "*Azkain Desutiun*" (National Affairs), in *Shirag*, 1909, 415.

5. A. Harutunian, "*Yerevuit Me*" (A Social Reality), in *Aztag*, 1909, 63.

6. A. Harutunian, "*Arunod Arev*" (A Bloody Sun), in *Aztag*, 1909, 130.

7. T. Varujan, "*Giligian Sarsapneru Artiv*" (On the Occasion of the Cilician Horrors), in *Aztag*, 1909, 334.

8. A. Alboyadjian, "*Hayotz Tirke Turkio Metch*" (The State of the Armenians in Turkey), in *Shirag*, 1909, 19.

9. See "The Strangulation" (Extract), 160, above.

10. See "The Massacre" (Extract), 161, above.

11. See "You Will Fall" (Extract), 162, above.

Ambiguous Legacy: Genocide and Armenian Political Romanticism

Gilbert Abcarian

The political analysis of genocide attempted here entails nine-teenth century liberalism as a starting point. To the extent that genocide constitutes intergenerational trauma, interconnections among genocide, liberalism, and contemporary American politics must be examined if that trauma is to be articulated and eased. The complexities of such examination, however humbling, cannot be avoided.

In this analysis we refer to Armenian self-determination, including statehood, as the *maximalist* position. This position is associated with the experiences and political culture of the Armenian Republic of 1918. The maximalist perspective is challenged by the *minimalist* position holding that nationhood without statehood is the more realistic option and that ethnic traditions can be secured short of sovereign independence. The conflicts between maximalist and minimalist perspectives rather nicely summarize the parameters of mainstream political thinking among Armenians. It is argued here that such thinking in *both* its expressions, but especially maximalism, constitutes an unacceptable form of political romanticism. That romanticism, in turn, is subjected to a brief critique.

I

The first task is to provide a perspective on the links between genocide[1] and aborted national independence on the one side, and American culture, foreign policy assumptions, and political values and behavior of Armenian Americans on the other. To do this we need to remember several historic factors. Liberal ideals legitimated by the French Revolution and the intellectuals who defended it provided the ideological rationale for the Armenian drive toward self-determination.[2] Those ideals remain powerfully embedded in the political-moral pronouncements of all the Armenian political parties from the late nineteenth century to the present.[3] But in the contemporary political culture of the United States, those ideals smack of mere rhetoric, suffering from stylization and abstraction from historic context. They have been trivialized by world realities and disembodied by policies and attitudes that exude liberal rhetoric while pursuing policies of imperial "realism." Thus nothing is sadder today than the cosmetic moral echoes of liberalism haunting the public speeches of recent American presidents. We are witnessing the banality of liberalism, so to speak!

Faith in the healing power of national self-determination seems rather odd at a time when liberal values in Western societies no longer constitute the governing ideological paradigm. As that paradigm recedes, the memory of genocide becomes even more painful, for thousands perished in the name of values that no longer govern our own political thinking. Conservative though they may be today, Armenians too easily forget the horrendous price tag placed on those values, even if they are in decline and do not inform contemporary political thinking and behavior. This suggests a paradox: genocide consciousness incorporates the liberal ideal of self-determination at the emotional and rhetorical levels but has little behavioral value in a world which has moved away from the promises and simplicities of nineteenth century liberal sentimentalism. Thus genocide remains problematic because Armenians have never been able to reconcile the liberal decoding of genocide with the increasingly nonliberal values that dominate their own thinking about politics in general. Why genocide occurred at all, where the responsibility for it lies, and what it signifies to survivors and their descendants alike remains a mystery. Armenians whose ethnic identification is weak may find these conflicting ideological premises simply one more good reason to throw up their hands in bewilderment and to conclude that all this is really someone else's history, an ambiguous legacy which, even when shouldered, does not redeem the original tragedy nor put it into rational political perspective.

At the root of that legacy—it is the essence of what is described here as political romanticism—lies the schismatic nature of Armenian political thinking, in particular, the following beliefs held by virtually all Armenians:

1. The Turkish state, though not necessarily the Turkish people

or government, bears moral, legal, and political responsibility for the genocide.

2. The Great Powers, after Turkey, bear the heaviest moral and historic responsibility for the suffering of Armenians from the late nineteenth century onward.

3. The Soviet Union has provided security and a large measure of cultural vitality for Armenians who live there, though not without some political limitations.

4. Armenians in the diaspora are advised to support the government and policies of the society in which they happen to live and to comport themselves as loyal citizens.

Taken separately these beliefs are certainly credible. Taken as a whole, however, they do not cohere. Partly for that reason they are described here as elements of a romantic political outlook. The elements of that belief system are highly inconsistent with one another as the basis of logical and unifying political theory. For example, conservative Armenians in the United States have little in common with Armenian terrorists from the Middle East, whose ideological orientations and political associations (e.g., Muslim radicals) are sometimes part of the anti-American or anti-Israeli political constellation of the Middle East.

The decline of liberal theory, dating at least from World War I, has diminished the possibility for an Armenian homeland and has redefined prospects for cultural self-determination.[4] It is debatable whether the disparities between liberal rhetoric and liberal possibilities already evident in the late nineteenth century were fully appreciated by the founders and leaders of the principal Armenian political organizations. Some of those organizations gambled on an international political scenario in which democracy would function as an irresistible ideological force and could be implemented by leaders who found inspiration in the West, provided they were courageous and dedicated to freedom and justice for the oppressed.[5] Thousands of Armenians, and others too, paid a terrible price for the disparity between liberal rhetoric and "liberal" actions. Then as now, liberalism as an international force was merely a moral perspective always and tantalizingly falling just short of political reality. Armenians gambled on the generous and universal impulse of humanitarian liberalism but lost to the realpolitik of national interest, Great Power rivalry, and geographic mislocation.

While some historians criticized Armenians for their overestimation of Turkish and Great Power support of the revolutionary drive for statehood, many Armenians were quite aware that their liberal goals posed dangers. But their miscalculation was to assume that once the facts about oppression were known in the West, political justice would prevail. Though empires were in transition and conflict rampant, the Armenian drive for self-determination continued even in the face of the events of 1915. The price tag for Armenian fidelity to liberal assumptions was incalculable. The gamble appeared to be a reasonable one: self-determination would be achieved because the international community supported moral principles that ensured limits on the machiavellian behavior of the Great Powers. However exaggerated, such limits did sometimes operate, but its only means of expression was State policy, which tended to respond to more "practical" interests.

Today one must ask in sadness, where is that internationalist faith, that early sensitivity toward the oppressed and the stateless? Do Armenian Americans retain faith in the liberal principle of self-determination where American foreign policy is concerned? Or do they, like millions of other citizens, support conservative policies that impose "democracy" in various parts of the world, policies that make even some conservatives wince? In far too many cases the answer is that Armenians, like other citizens, have drifted rightward, tending to everyday business as the forces of acculturation and assimilation process them through ideological implicities that distort world events. Here we must sound a note of alarm, for conservatism hardly does justice to the ideals for which so much Armenian (and other) blood was spilled. Ignorance about the Middle East is one of these simplicities. Armenian political groups in the Middle East play a pivotal ethnic role. In recent years they have been influenced by a variety of political tendencies and organizations not all of which are friendly to the United States. Some persistent western myths about Lebanon as the stable Switzerland of the Middle East have vanished in a firestorm of religious, political, sectarian, and anti-American conflicts. The area seethes with revolutionary activity, is rife with anti-Westernism, and is subject to social and military dynamics that are incredibly complex and dangerous.[6] Western distinctions between left and right are not very helpful. It is true that in a few instances anti-American means pro-Soviet. But beyond that lie disputes and cultural conflicts whose historic origins are independent of great power machinations.

However confused, Armenian Americans support policies whose logic is incompatible with the best interests of the Middle East. Western policies are anti-revolutionary, anti-Soviet, and anti-socialist.

Recent efforts by the United States to impose such policies on the Middle East have failed. In effect, Armenian Americans, like other minority groups, fail to appreciate that their own government confronts their ethnic brethren in the Middle East with policies and values that are at odds with indigenous developments in that area.

Here a classic question emerges: is it likely that specific segments of the world Armenian community can continue to support the conflicting policies of their respective governments and still maintain a significant degree of intra-ethnic political unity? Optimism is not warranted. As genocide memories fade, successive generations of Armenians will tend to subordinate the ancestral dream of self-determination to the contemporary needs and realities of life where they happen to live it. But political dreams die hard. It is likely that the generalized liberal outlook from which the idea of national self-determination was first drawn will deteriorate but survive as an "Armenian exception," an outlook seemingly compatible with prevailing conservative values. It seems obvious that American style conservatism, the dominant political value system of many Armenian Americans, fails to provide either the political or psychological context for keeping the idea of popular revolution and self-determination alive.[7]

The task of interpreting genocide in its political (as opposed to personal) meaning, which belongs to the young, depends heavily on the current social attitudes that condition their ethnic consciousness. That consciousness is not wholly controllable by the older generations. In the absence of strong empirical evidence on the matter, we shall offer several suppositions about future political orientations of those entrusted with interpretation of the genocide legacy. In doing so an attempt is made to interpret genocide as a socializing experience for young people who are removed from original events by time, place, and values.

The sobering place to start is to ask: why did Armenians suffer the genocide experience? Even more to this point, what do Armenians tell each other when that question is put? So far as the author is aware (relying heavily on his childhood experiences in California), the relevant answers include the following:

1. Turkish hostility, perhaps on the basis of economic jealousy but more likely Turkish suspicion of Christian subjects.

2. Great power duplicity and broken promises,[8] compounded by Armenian inhabitance of an area coveted by other nations.

3. Political dissension among Armenians, resulting in fatal weaknesses of leadership, ideology, military competence, and political

education and planning.

4.   Belief in a "natural" right to one's homeland on territory contested by superior powers.

In all probability the first two explanations, Turkish hostility and Great Power duplicity, would not carry great weight among the young, mainly because Armenians understand, however privately, that American security interests entail support of Turkey as an ally (formerly in the broader conflict with "communism" and the USSR and more recently as a counterweight to radical Muslim governments in the Middle East). On the other hand, the homeland-as-natural-imperative explanation runs afoul of both common sense and educational perspectives because the younger generation is probably too sophisticated to accept the underlying premise of a territorial/collective psychology of the political unconscious. That leaves the third explanation, internal dissension among Armenians. Perhaps here we come to an explanation that may produce some sympathy. Why? Because American culture strongly reinforces psychologistic modes of thinking, explaining collective failures in terms of the breakdown of personal standards and efficacy. And also because it is easy to believe, in retrospect, that late nineteenth century political sectarianism was naive and ultimately suicidal. Putting the logic of this view without qualifications, there is just a faint suggestion that the young tend to blame the victims themselves, perhaps on the assumption that because life goes to the swift, the rest, well, may perish while debating romantic abstractions.

While one cannot speak of numbers, one suspects on *a priori* grounds that a relatively large number of younger Armenian Americans simply do not get very excited when attempts are made to redeem Armenian failures or frustrations by ritual conversion of the genocide experience into a stable element of their own cultural identity. For what matters about genocide, ultimately, is not ancestral casualty figures but rather contemporary feelings and emotions; for the young, this is an older generation's experience (as, say, the Korean or Vietnam wars are to university students). Those feelings are not intergenerationally transmissible, although they are remembered in a spirit of piety. What can one say, after all, if confronted with the question recently put to me by a student: "But what am I supposed to *do* about genocide?"

There are other implausibilities about genocide as transmissible memory. For example, to the extent that religious conflict is perceived as a factor in the massacres, and to the extent that religion is viewed as the unifying framework of Armenian identity in America, one may expect a decline in the relevance of ethnic culture for many young persons. The United States is a secular society whose public life is characterized by norms and values that are pietistic and pluralistic, but hardly very religious in theological or emotional terms. One would surmise that ethnic culture increasingly will become what it is for many others in this nation: a token of family loyalty, a romantic or idealized version of one's "roots" several generations removed, and a pseudo-moral perspective which operates ritually rather than intellectually in one's personal life. Hence religion becomes an ideology of interpersonal convenience rather than a value system governing personal thought and behavior.

Without liberalism we cannot confront genocide. But the irony is that the liberal legacy of genocide is in conflict with the predominant conservatism of Armenian Americans. This contradiction manifests itself in a variety of interesting ways. We teach our children the moral and political justifications for Armenian independence, for example, but consistently fail to deal critically with those larger cultural and political forces in American society that influence our youth in the antiliberal directions of patriarchy, violence, ethnocentrism, and racism. We persuade them to condone human rights violations in right-wing regimes (for example, El Salvador) but to condemn them in left-wing regimes (such as Cuba).

II

In retrospect, liberal-socialist assumptions and values of the nineteenth century seem extraordinarily simple, if not ungenerous. The central simplicity, though this was not true of the entire left, was the notion that the freedom of the individual decreed by God, Nature, or History had its exact counterpart in the freedom of nations, on the assumption that demands for individual and collective freedom are "natural" in some self-evident moral sense. Stopping those just demands therefore is to act contrary to the fundamental forces of life. This is the belief system, however tacit and unacknowledged, that underlies the explanation of genocide given to the descendants of the original victims.

There are at least two flaws in this view: first, self-determination is far more closely related to conditions of world economy and colonialism than to nature; and second, global liberal values, whatever their abstract appeal, are much less salient in the thinking of Americans, including Armenians, than we may care to admit. If the second observation has any merit, it follows that Armenian Americans are left with a rather hollow yearning for a homeland because the idea of self-determination has been disconnected from the larger liberal outlook of which it was once a necessary part. Political independence, in short, has no consistent and compatible political theory to support it because social thought in the United States has moved powerfully toward the right. If one believes in an Armenian homeland, one should treat it as a right equally applicable to any national group that has suffered external aggression—Nicaraguans, Salvadorans, Palestinians, Greeks, Angolans, Black South Africans, and not just Poles, Bulgarians, Armenians, and other groups that are personally or ideologically convenient. It is hardly "liberal" to define and enforce selectively the idea of self-determination merely to suit one's special ethnic claims.[9]

Younger Armenian Americans, particularly those of advanced educational, artistic, or professional standing, may be pained by the disparity between their conservative political orientations and the traditional liberal Armenian belief that somewhere at the higher reaches of the international system there is a place to lodge moral grievances in the full expectation that they will be heard, adjudicated, and redressed. They know, surely like many of us, that no such court of last moral resort exists. They may also suspect that the effort to pretend otherwise by insisting on material and moral reparations is a futile exercise in political romanticism. Let us grant that genocide has shocked the "moral conscience" of humanity, that it is a "crime against humanity" as declared at the Nuremberg war crimes trials. But genocide is no less a reality today than forty-five or seventy years ago.[10] This fact suggests that moral claims are a customary but insufficient condition of policy-making; and that when they are confronted by counter claims of equal moral vehemence, the prospects for resolution are poor indeed.

The conflict between self-determination and national security is a case in point. Attention to national security is after all one means of attending to self-determination. When the legitimate security needs of one nation threaten those of another, we are confronted with moral ambiguity as well as political complexity. Since one nation does not have the right to determine another's definition of security, any hope that the principle of self-determination will resolve international conflicts is bound to confuse rather than clarify specific cases. While we may repudiate force as the ultimate arbiter of conflicting claims to national security, it is all too often force, superior force, that finally makes the "moral" determination. One specific consequence of this, it seems quite clear, is that the American military alliance with Turkey will continue indefinitely to take precedence over Armenian aspirations toward liberation, statehood, justice, and reparations.

What then *is* the legacy of genocide, what is its political meaning? Here we come to a critical juncture in Armenian political romanticism. One interpretation says that the political balm for genocide —statehood—is self-evident, while another says that in a world of political treachery, the safest and surest path is the relentless pursuit of moral justice rather than independence. What makes all this romantic is not merely that both views are often held simultaneously but that this inconsistency is followed by an even greater one that assumes Armenians have earned a collective right to practice their own particular brew of power politics, to practice selective morality, so to speak.

If Armenian self-determination has any future at all, it is closely linked with American foreign policy objectives and behavior. That policy is increasingly conservative and even less sympathetic to self-determination than it was in Woodrow Wilson's day. The outward ideological contexts of the two eras is certainly different: sporadic internationalism during Wilson's day, contrasted with constant interventionism today. But the underlying definitions of American security interests as expressed in policy terms during both periods have changed very little. The author is unwilling to support American policies that enlist the support of some of the most reactionary governments around the world in the name of freedom or anti-communism *even if prospects for Armenian statehood seem improved.* Like George Kennan and other critics of American foreign policy, the author is concerned that efforts to achieve statehood through policies aimed at the disruption of legitimate states or, say, through ethnic dismemberment of the USSR, are dangerous in the extreme and unacceptable *in purely Armenian terms.*

The first responsibility of Armenians in this country is to adopt the practice of believing and doing what is consistent with self-determination for Armenians and for all other peoples of similar circumstance, even several of the Armenians' historic enemies. Armenians should preach and practice for others what they believe is true in their own case. Unless this is done, we shall lose the services and sympathies of intellectuals, artists and others who will refuse to sacrifice their standards of truth and political credibility for dubious ethnic "gains," especially those bought at the price of a parochial political conservatism.[11] We should not alienate the best among us and turn moderate and left thinkers into ethnic marginals or political pariahs.[12] But that is happening. Failure to link Armenian self-determination to other people's freedom would suggest that genocide has no political message for any of us.

The "profascist"/"procommunist" counter charges of the last half-century in the Armenian community have the unfortunate effect of converting genocide into a weapon of psychological warfare. This is unfortunate partly because that warfare originates in historical events of decreasing salience for younger Armenian Americans. Furthermore, these sectarian conflicts must seem rather extraneous to those Armenian Americans whose understanding of genocide derives largely from family, culture, and social experiences rather than from obscure nineteenth century political-ideological debates. Such dichotomized and psychologized hostility[13] is simply not very germane to the needs and perceptions of younger Armenian Americans. Put differently, a heavy, perhaps impossible, burden lies with those who wish to continue those debates: making them relevant to the contemporary life expectancies of Armenian Americans. There are good reasons to doubt whether this will happen, for many have large emotional investments in the past.

As ethnic past and present collide, international political dynamics move even further from circumstances favorable to the emergence of an Armenian state. So long as statehood remains the political paradigm for most segments of the ethnic community, we run the danger of alienating, then losing, some of our finest minds.[14] But if we empower our intellectuals by bringing them from the margins to the center, is it possible we will have lost them anyway to the considerable seductions of traditional academic and professional rewards in a secular, conservative society? Are very many of them apt to withdraw from the ethnic culture and go the way of Murza Khan, the Persian-Armenian writer-politician who drifted away from his ethnic ties?[15] I believe the danger has been exaggerated. Recent studies by specialists in American ethnic subcultures cast doubt on the "melting pot" hypothesis that has become conventional wisdom in academic and popular circles. For example, Michael Parenti distinguishes between acculturation, involving particular life styles and customs, as contrasted with assimilation, reflecting incorporation into dominant structural-identificational group relations. By the second generation acculturation may have taken place, but not necessarily assimilation. He observes that "growing acculturation often leads to more rather than less ethnic political awareness."[16]

As he notes in conclusion, and we concur, "ethnic-oriented responses will still be found among those who have made a 'secure' professional and social position for themselves in the dominant Anglo-Protestant world."[17] If Parenti's caveat about assimilation is true, we need to rethink the kind of ethnic consciousness that we formulate and transmit to the younger generations.

III

Had genocide followed the establishment of the Armenian Republic instead of preceding it, political developments in the Armenian diaspora might have differed markedly. The massacres legitimated the idea of independence on the most dramatic of all grounds— human misery. Had statehood preceded genocide, political and moral debate among Armenians probably would have developed along significantly different lines. In any case, one fact burned itself into ethnic consciousness: the meaning of genocide and the history of the Republic were inextricably linked regardless of political ideology. Indeed, ideological differences among Armenians remain a series of footnotes to the question: what if anything have we learned about the future from the past juxtaposition of genocide and Republic? Viewed this way we are confronted above all else with political questions, but even more importantly we are forced to ask: what kind of political theory will illuminate the many relationships between genocide and the Republic? Then and only then, it seems clear, does the madness of genocide become something worthy of theoretical reflection.

That kind of political theory will not be invented by someone who is extraordinarily clever; it will come, if it does at all, from collective effort of those qualified to undertake it. This will not be easy. Perhaps the author is an example of the difficulty involved since he believes that the maximalist call for political independence has at least for now lost the debate to the minimalists who regard physical and cultural security, without the precondition of statehood, as a satisfactory standard.

There is some evidence for this view. For example, Armenian terrorist acts of the recent past[18] provide clear evidence of the waning of the maximalist position. Since it is extremely difficult to believe that the Turkish or American governments can be pressured or persuaded to implement pro-Armenian demands for statehood and reparations, it is plausible to conjecture that Armenian terrorism is basically internal in nature, aimed fundamentally at intra-ethnic consciousness-raising. Of course, terrorist acts claim to derive from standards of political rationality, but in the absence of publicly released and debated explanations one can only guess what those standards are. Whatever serious political analysis is implied in terrorist acts remains tacit and unspecified; terrorists *claim* rationality for their acts but do not *explain* them by reference to any serious theoretical conception of politics. Until this changes, serious discussion will remain frustrated.

Moral demands and precedents influence the behavior of great powers only when there is no perceived threat to national security, desired resources, or prestige interests. In the nineteenth century and earlier there were buffer zones or neutral territories to cushion such conflicts, but by the end of the present century even the remotest corners of the globe have been sucked into the vortex of great power rivalry in contexts ranging from the military and economic, through the cultural, psychological, and artistic. Small nations can no longer count on pursuing their national aspirations by looking for international nooks and crannies ignored by the powerful. In this respect the maximalist position has much less to commend it now than was the case a century, or even twenty-five years ago.

Beyond a world political scene torn by never-ending power rivalries, there is a logical context for self-determination: a world governed in essentials by an international body capable of administering and enforcing the standards of self-determination. Such a possibility is reflected in the Armenian Revolutionary Federation Credo of 1963, which states:

> The supreme aim of the Armenian Revolutionary Federation is the realization of a free, united, and independent democratic national homeland established on the territories of the historic fatherland of the Armenian nation.

> We believe that the realization of this aim can only be possible in a free democratic world context. A world in which the danger of war is permanently eliminated, and where the existing and potential international disputes can be resolved by peaceful means *through the agency of a powerful international organization which shall be endowed with the necessary means of imposing its supreme will on great or small nations alike.*[19]

With the deepest respect for the ideal described, one must reluctantly conclude that the hope for such an agency begs the prior question: how does it come into existence? Were conditions ripe for the creation of an agency that possessed such "necessary means," it is also likely that world sentiment favoring national self-determination would already exist, or alternatively, that such an agency would come into existence only as the arbitrary instrument of a world dictatorship.

These considerations taken into account, it seems clear that genocide cannot be put to rest until the idea of Armenian statehood is critically reexamined. But it must be said here, in candor, that such reexamination may be widely regarded as unnecessary at best or tantamount to renunciation of ethnicity at worst. Those who will not yield on the issue of statehood may well ask: can national identity survive very long without statehood? Of course! Armenians are world-class experts at that effort and have practiced it since the fourteenth century. Disentangling genocide and statehood from one another is a task for the new Armenian intellectuals. We do not have the right to ask the older generations to abandon positions and experiences that constituted the very fabric of their lives, yet it is imperative to modernize these traditional perspectives and move beyond an often regressive genocide consciousness.[20]

Few have put the endearing and infuriating force of Armenian political romanticism in more dramatic fashion than Arlen:

> I thought, in some ways, this has been the most miserable of stories. It made one weep for the hopes of the Armenians: those Armenians who for so many years had trafficked with the liberal sentiments of the West, attending like children to the "interestedness" of certain politicians and missionaries, watching the great nineteenth-century wave of nationalism confer nationhood on states and provinces whose own ethnic "unity" had long been fragmented. For Armenians what else had it been but an illusion, a political dream whose bridge to waking life was mainly this—the inconsistent support of the powerful constitutional democracies of Europe and America? On the other hand, what folly it has been to expect anything else of the world than what had happened! What a persistence of dreaming! Or perhaps in the end it had been a matter neither of folly nor of, let us say, victimization, for there was something quite grandly human in the Armenian experience, with its misfortunes, and pride, and survivorship, and hope: the hope of something better to come, periodically dashed. If the Armenians had been lately afflicted with self-hatred, they had also throughout their existence (like certain children) been afflicted with hopefulness. In some ways, this was probably an affliction like any other, not easily cured.[21]

Politically speaking, genocide consciousness is a dead-end; it does not tell us why the Armenians were almost destroyed, what can be done to prevent a future recurrence, nor tell us how Armenians can take their welfare into their own hands and succeed in maintaining cultural identity and political autonomy. Genocide was an historic *experience*, a collective trauma, but not a lesson; it has no didactic value of which I am aware. And yet we cling to the didactic assumption even as it leads nowhere. In this sense genocide creates a false consciousness, an expectation that if Armenians fully understood the enormity of the massacres, a clear, correct set of political premises, strategies, and goals would come into view. Armenian political history of the last one hundred years—the entire political spectrum of it— seems conclusive that the genocide has no positive or plausible lesson to teach us at the level of political life and analysis. It only appears that it does.

REFERENCES

1. Definitions of genocide tend to emphasize specific acts, the agent(s) of those acts, or a combination of both. The Convention on the Prevention and Elimination of the Crime of Genocide, unanimously adopted by the United Nations General Assembly on Dec. 9, 1948, defines genocide as "acts committed with intent to destroy, in whole or in part, a national, racial or religious group, as such." The statement goes on to give specific examples, including killing members of the group, causing serious bodily or mental harm, and inflicting group conditions of life calculated to bring about partial or total physical destruction. I. L. Horowitz, on the other hand, defines genocide as "...a structural and systematic destruction of innocent people by a state bureaucratic apparatus" (*Genocide*, New Brunswick, N.J.: Transaction Books, 1976, 18).

2. For the full story of Armenian self-determination and the Republic of 1918-20, see the following works by Richard G. Hovannisian: *Armenia on the Road to Independence*, (1967); *The Republic of Armenia*, 2 vols., (1971, 1982), published by the University of California Press, Berkeley.

3. "Liberal" in the nineteenth century meant progressive in many quarters, and perhaps the most progressive of all extant liberal ideas was that of self-determination. Even in parts of the Left this was the case. Citing the 1888 program of the Hunchaks, Louise Nalbandian notes: "Nowhere in the program is there any sign of conflict between national aspirations and universal socialism. For the Hunchaks, nationalism and socialism were mutually compatible and could be harmoniously developed together" (*The Armenian Revolutionary Movement*, Berkeley: University of California Press, 1963, 114). Needless to say, many scholars would disagree about the assumed compatibility of nationhood and socialism, unless one has in mind a hybrid "national socialism."

4. At this point in the late twentieth century even culture has become almost universally politicized and no longer constitutes an autonomous domain relatively free of government attention. Thus twentieth century efforts at cultural independence meet much the same resistance from governments as cries for political independence did in the last century.

5. Nalbandian traces the story of Armenian student fascination with and study of such writers as Chateaubriand, Hugo, Comte, Michelet, etc. These students returned from Paris as liberal "illuminati" and quickly found themselves in conflict with the older and conservative "non-illuminati" who wished to preserve the older oligarchic system (*Revolutionary Movement*, 46ff).

6. Richard Hovanissian notes that "with all their tribulations, the Armenian colonies in the Middle East are still the most vigorous national centers in the dispersion. The Armenian communities of Europe and the Americas have constantly turned to these bastions for reliance and direction. In essence, the course of world events has placed upon the Armenian of the Middle East the ponderous obligation to serve as the jealous guardian of a cultural heritage uprooted and extruded from the homeland." In view of massive religious and political upheaval in Muslim societies where these Armenians live, one may well wonder how effectively guardianship of traditional culture and political rules can be played by a Christian and ethnic minority with close ties to "enemy" states.

7. This impression can only be settled through analysis of empirical data about the political values and behavior of Armenian-American citizens; I am not aware of any major and reliable studies of that nature against which these impressions can be tested.

8. Note the following wry comment about Great Power responsibility:

   The Permanent Peoples' Tribunal was brought into existence partly to overcome the moral and political failures of states as instruments of justice. The Tribunal has inquired into the Armenian grievances precisely because of the long silence of the organized international society and, especially, of the complicity of leading Western States (with the recent exception of France) who have various economic, political and military ties with the Turkish state. (Verdict of the Session on the Genocide of the Armenians, April 13-16, 1984, Paris, 7.

9. Armenian organizations and their leaders need to encourage and get involved in other people's demands for self-determination, not just those of the Armenians. For if self-determination is not treated as a universal principle in American foreign policy, what is left amounts to no more than special pleading and may be rejected by members of the younger generation who prefer Anglo-Saxonization to the burdens of illogical ethnicity.

10. "The umbilical cord between genocidal practice and state power has never been stronger." (Horowitz, *Genocide*, 21).

11. For example, the *Newsletter* of the Armenian Assembly of America, commenting on a University of Pittsburgh sponsored symposium on Kemal Ataturk, reports that "Pittsburgh Armenians are planning to register a formal complaint with the university about the comments of Prof. Karpat and to request a clarification from the Center for International Studies regarding its endorsement of Karpat's *participation* in the symposium" (Winter 1981: 2, emphasis added).

12. A 1981 letter from the United Armenian Cultural Association of Illinois appears to recognize this problem in lamenting that "the [Armenian] intelligentsia and the professionals have remained on the sidelines leaving the helm of our leadership in the hands of "pragmatic" but biased people." The implications that intellectuals have *chosen* the sideline role is an oversimplification; I would argue that they have often been relegated to that role by unsympathetic Armenian organizations and leaders.

13. An unfortunate but pertinent example is Sarkis Atamian's recurrent reference to anti-Dashnaks as engaging in "autistic thinking." His zeal to utilize popular social-psychological models of analysis results in uncritical use of conservative social science. (*The Armenian Community*, New York: Philosophic Library, 1955, *passim*.).

14. There is a distinct possibility of intellectual alienation as the traditional

conservatism of Armenian elites and benefactors collides with the scholarship and role of Armenian academics and others. This is a very high price for a tiny ethnic group to pay.

15. See Vahé Oshagan, "The Literature of the Persian Armenians," *Ararat*, (Summer 1979: 28-36). The author unfortunately writes off Armenians "who have chosen to serve cultures other than their own and thus do not interest Armenian literature in the strict sense of the word." (36 n.9).

16. Michael Parenti, "Ethnic Politics and the Persistence of Ethnic Identification," in Harry A. Bailey, Jr. and Ellis Katz, eds., *Ethnic Group Politics* (Columbus: Chas. E. Merrill, 1969), 276.

17. Ibid., 279.

18. On March 12, 1985, an Armenian attack on the Turkish Embassy in Ottawa occurred, during which a guard was killed. The three terrorists surrendered after conducting media interviews demanding a return of Armenian lands in relation to the events of 1915.

19. Appendix of the *Congressional Record*, Feb. 13, 1963, A655-66.

20. Michael J. Arlen's comparison of Jewish and Armenian responses to the genocide experience, while anecdotal, may be instructive:

> In obvious ways, the closest parallel lay with the Jews, who had undergone, numerically, an even larger genocide in Hitler's Germany. But here, too, there seemed to be a difference. Certainly there were many Jews I knew, or knew of, who still looked back to the terrible period of the concentration camps and gas chambers as if it were an open wound, a fact of everyday consciousness. But, for one thing, the Jewish experience in Germany had been fairly recent. For another thing, it seemed to me that a majority of the Jews did not look backward in this way—in the manner of people bearing a permanently open wound. Of course, the issue might be forced; a careless or abrasive remark, sometimes only remotely anti-Semitic in intent, and even the most assimilated American Jew might respond with a flash of anger about the Six Million. Indeed, I had sometimes noticed *a curiously proprietary air on the part of Jews and Armenians alike* toward the misfortunes of their own peoples—proprietary and almost competitive, in the fashion of two insecure strangers trying to narrate two similar nightmares in an inattentive room. "Now, these Armenians," an intelligent Jewish friend had once said to me, with studied vagueness, "didn't they once have some trouble with the Turks?" Another time, I had overheard an Armenian say outright, "The way they talk you'd think the Jews invented genocide." Doubtless this was original black comedy—perverse and deeply human. But generally it seemed *to me that the Jews had handled their nightmare better than the Armenians had handled theirs: had somehow resolved it, or, at least, incorporated the trauma into everyday life—were more nearly free of it*. (*Passage to Ararat*, New York: Farrar, Straus & Giroux, 1975), 187-88, emphasis added).

21. Ibid., 268-69.

Misplaced Credulity: Contemporary Turkish Attempts to Refute the Armenian Genocide[1]

Dennis R. Papazian

Every Turkish government since the Armenian Genocide of 1915-1916, with the exception of that of Damad Ferit which came into power following the defeat of the Young Turk government by the Allies in World War I, has denied not only responsibility for the Armenian Genocide but also its very reality. In the mid-1980s, the Turkish government's denials became more frequent and more strident, in part no doubt because Armenian extremists, beginning in 1973, brought the Armenian Genocide back into public light by the assassination of a number of Turkish diplomats in various parts of the world. These attacks continued sporadically up to 1985, while Armenian public opinion crystallized against the perpetrators; very few incidents have occurred since then. In any case, the world was once more made aware of Armenian grievances, and the Turkish government apparently felt it necessary to press its own case before the bar of public opinion.

Indeed, the Turkish government went on the offensive. It hired a public relations firm, Doremus & Co.;[2] a lobbying organization, Gray & Co.;[3] and established an Institute of Turkish Studies in Washington, D.C., all for the purpose of influencing the current administration, the State Department, the Congress, and opinion makers in the apparent hope that either the Turkish denial of the Armenian Genocide would be accepted or the reality of the Genocide itself put in doubt. This Turkish propaganda offensive met with some initial success in America. The media, public opinion makers, and even a number of scholars began to speak of an "alleged" Genocide when referring to the Armenian tragedy of 1915-16, and the U.S. Department of State made an outright denial that the expulsion and murder of 1.5 million Armenians in the Ottoman Empire constituted a genocide.[4]

This denial by the U.S. State Department could only amaze the informed public inasmuch as it was American officials and civilians in the Ottoman Empire who provided Woodrow Wilson's administration with overwhelming eyewitness and photographic accounts of the tragic events,[5] and it was the Wilson administration which was the foremost champion in the world[6] of the Armenians and the Armenian cause. Over and above the official diplomatic reports attesting to the Armenian Genocide, there were also an abundance of contemporary newspaper accounts and journal articles, which appeared in the American press.[7] In fact, the Armenian Genocide was such a cause celebre in the United States at that time that there are still elderly Americans who remember giving their Sunday School pennies to help the "starving Armenians."[8]

Nevertheless, even reputable newspapers, such as the *New York Times* and the *Wall Street Journal*, were caught off guard by the Turkish public relations offensive and were quick to accept Turkish denials. Caught between Armenian claims and Turkish counter claims, these national publications were finally driven to do their own research in order to develop an informed opinion. The *New York Times* had no farther to go than its own archives, and it was confronted with the choice of either repudiating its own historical record or accepting the Armenian position. It soon dropped the word "alleged" from its articles, and a reborn sympathy for the Armenians emerged.[9]

The *Wall Street Journal*, lacking its own historic account, assigned a member of its editorial board, Dr. James Ring Adams, to conduct a three-month study of the evidence. The fruit of his research appeared in a series of three articles which were published on the editorial page in August 1983,[10] the second of which was entitled "Facing Up to an Armenian Genocide."

In this article, Dr. Adams concluded: "In this furious controversy, nonparticipants including the U.S. government take refuge in phrases like 'alleged genocide.' But humane opinion has the duty to judge whether we're dealing with a monstrous crime or a colossal fraud. Three months of extensive research leave little doubt that a horrible crime certainly did occur, that the suffering of the deportations was far out of proportion to the military threat and that Talaat and company probably did plan a genocide."[11]

Adams goes on to write: "In spite of the scholarly trapping, the Turkish defense relies on discrediting all contemporary Western accounts as war-time propaganda and all incriminating documents as Armenian forgeries. So the Turks must make liars of men like Henry Morgenthau, American ambassador to Turkey from 1913 to 1916; the great English historian Lord Bryce; and his young research assistant Arnold Toynbee."[12]

These conclusions reached by Adams, despite his strong simultaneous condemnation of Armenian "terrorism," moved the then Turkish Ambassador to the United States, Sukru Elekdag, to issue an extensive rebuttal in the form of a "letter to the editor," which was courteously published on September 21, 1983, under the title: "Armenians vs. Turks: The View From Istanbul."[13]

The Ambassador begins his letter with the statement: "Vast tragedies do, as James Ring Adams suggests, deserve 'truthful accounting.' Unfortunately, such accounting is brought no closer by his article, which by and large is a morass of misplaced, indiscriminate credulity." Elekdag continued: "A truthful accounting must, first, be factually correct. ... Second, it must be meaningful, in the sense that context and terms have some referents in reality."

The letter then goes on to deliver, point by point, the Turkish position and arguments. Since this letter comes from the pen of the Turkish Ambassador to the United States, and since the Ambassador was probably guided by his best aides and advisors, and since his letter was perhaps even approved by the Turkish Foreign Ministry, we may take it as an official statement of Turkey's version of the events of 1915-16 and deserving of attention. As a matter of fact, Elekdag has brought together in one place all the arguments proffered by his government over the decades first to deny, and then by a twist of logic to justify, the Armenian Genocide of 1915-16.

This paper will analyze the most important points made by Ambassador Elekdag to determine if they meet his criteria for "truthful accounting," being "factually correct," and being "meaningful, in the sense that context and terms have some referents in reality." I will also attempt to judge whether Elekdag's "scholarly trappings" represent obfuscation or honest scholarship.

It is surprising, in the light of Elekdag's appeal to good scholarship, that the Ambassador should have made so many errors of simple fact. The Adana massacre did not take place in 1906, but in 1909. It was Sidney Bradshaw Fay, not Fey, who wrote *The Origins of the World War*. It was Cyrus, and not Cyril, Hamlin who was president of Robert College. And, inter alia, the United States did not declare war on the Ottoman Empire, and it is impolitic, to say the least, for

Elekdag to maintain that the U.S. Ambassador considered Turkey "the enemy."

Furthermore, we should take note of the fact that Henry Morgenthau, the American Ambassador to Turkey, did not, as Turkish Ambassador Elekdag claims, "[rely] on selected missionary reports and communications translated by Greeks and Armenians who could hardly have been disinterested parties." Morgenthau, as is well known, relied primarily on official reports sent by his own experienced American consuls and consular agents stationed in various cities of Anatolia and greater Syria, reports written in English and which needed no translations.

The United States had stationed several consular officials in the Ottoman Empire, specifically at Aleppo, Kharpert (Harput), Smyrna (Izmir), Mersina (Mersin), and Trebizond (Trabzon), either within the areas of the slaughter or in the path of the deportations. Indeed, American consular officials were prime witnesses of the Armenian Genocide and did not hesitate to inform their ambassador about what was transpiring.

Since Elekdag outlines the Turkish version of the events that led to the Armenian Genocide, in order to place them in "context," let us do the same. It is true that the Tanzimat reforms of the nineteenth century, led by progressive Turks, failed, and that Turkey became the "Sick Man of Europe."[14] It is also true that various European powers had aspirations for Ottoman territories and that they used the misrule of the Sultans to justify intervention in the European provinces. None of this, as we can see, is the fault of the Armenians.

When Sultan Abdul-Hamid II, known in history as the "Damned" or the "Bloody Sultan," came to the throne in 1876, he had two alternatives to save his moribund empire in light of the aspirations of the European powers regarding Turkey: either sincerely reinstate the reforms and strengthen the Empire, or massacre his minorities and remove the major excuse for European intervention. For reasons that can only be surmised, he chose the latter. His last important minority, other than the Muslim Kurds, whom he believed he could assimilate into the Turkish majority, was the Armenians.

Abdul-Hamid created the Hamidiye, an irregular cavalry on the model of the Cossacks of Russia, to carry out pogroms against the Armenians just as the Tsar used his irregulars to persecute the Jews. Hamit massacred hundreds of thousands of Armenians during his reign, in 1894 in the Sassun villages, in 1895-1896 throughout the Turkish Empire, in 1904 again in Sassun, and there is suspicion that he was behind the 1909 massacre in Adana and Cilicia which coincided with the conservative attempted *coup d'etat* in Constantinople (Istanbul).

Enlightened Turks were every bit as distressed by the misrule of Abdul-Hamid as were the Armenians or the European powers. These Turkish patriots began to organize a revolutionary movement called, in Turkish, the *Ittihat ve Terakki Cemiyeti*, or, in English, the Committee for Union and Progress (C.U.P.). This group was known popularly in Europe and America as "the Young Turks." It was about this same time, just before the turn of the century, that young Armenians began to establish political action societies and eventually parties. Two of the more popular, the Dashnaks and the Hunchaks, had their origins in the Russian Empire,[15] but soon sent members into Turkey (in the pattern of the Russian Narodniks of the 1870s) to defend the civil rights and the personal security of the Armenian population.

The Dashnak party, realizing that reform of the Turkish government was perhaps the only genuine answer to the Armenian plight, took part in the First Congress of Ottoman Liberals in 1902, and in similar meetings after that.[16] Indeed, they even offered support to the Committee of Union and Progress in that group's effort, later to prove successful, to seize the Sultan's power by revolution and to reinstate the liberal constitution of 1876. It was the Turks who not only wanted a revolution but who carried out a successful *coup d'etat* in 1908, unaided by the Armenians or any other minority. This successful revolution against the Sultan and his government, to repeat, was carried out by young Turkish army officers and not by Armenian radicals.

Now the ironic twist: The Committee of Union and Progress, having managed a successful revolt against the Sultan, soon turned on the Armenians, their former confederates. Before their revolution, the C.U.P. had preached Ottomanism (a kind of multi-nationalism with all peoples of the Empire equal under the law). After their revolution, the C.U.P. was captured by a racist clique which demanded "Turkey for the Turks." The clear implication of the new racist policy was that the minorities, especially the Armenians, had to be eradicated.

Now let us look at Elekdag's arguments. Lord Bryce's "Blue Book," *The Treatment of the Armenians in the Ottoman Empire, 1915-1916*,[17] edited by Arnold Toynbee, is one of the most damning single early sources of eyewitness accounts of the Armenian Genocide of 1915-16.

In his letter, Ambassador Elekdag maintains that Toynbee, in the last book he wrote, entitled *Acquaintances*,[18] repudiated his earlier view of a premeditated, government-sponsored Turkish genocide of the Armenian people, repented his earlier bad opinion of the Turks, and made a final confession of his earlier error. Furthermore, Elekdag quotes from Toynbee's *Acquaintances* to show that Lord Bryce's Blue Book was intended to serve as an instrument of British "propaganda," with the implication that it was a dishonest and undependable piece of work.

Since the book *Acquaintances* must be respected by Elekdag, inasmuch as it is he who chooses to bring it forth as evidence, we may accept it as a source acceptable to the Turks. But let us look further, "in context," at what Toynbee said in *Acquaintances*. First, he does admit that the request for the Blue Book to be written came from the British government (which, indeed, might raise our suspicion of Toynbee's objectivity). But then Toynbee writes: "I believe Lord Bryce was as innocent as I was. [Otherwise] I hardly think that either Lord Bryce or I would have been able to do the job that H.M.G. [His Majesty's Government] has assigned us in the complete good faith in which we did, in fact, carry it out."[19]

Furthermore, on page 241 of *Acquaintances*, interestingly enough, we find that Toynbee writes: "In the *Genocide* [emphasis added] of the Armenians the criminals had been members of the Committee of Union and Progress—above all, perhaps, Talaat, the most intelligent of the ruling triumvirs."[20]

In Toynbee's next paragraph, which we should also quote to keep things "in context," we see that Toynbee writes: "In the course of the eight [*sic*] years 1909-15,[21] the leaders of the C.U.P. [Committee of Union and Progress] had apparently degenerated from being idealists into becoming ogres. How was one to account for this sinister metamorphosis?"[22]

Before we leave the "repentant" Toynbee, we will accept one more item of testimony from him. He says in *Acquaintances*, just as he said in the Blue Book: "The deportations [of the Armenians] had been carried out by orders from the Government at Istanbul, and the orders had been executed by gendarmes and soldiers who had no personal connection with the localities."[23] Even the "reformed" Toynbee, when read "in context," certainly is no witness for the Turkish defense. Rather, Toynbee confirms his earlier view of a purposeful Turkish-government sponsored genocide of the Armenians.

But Ambassador Elekdag, perhaps knowing that Toynbee would

not really turn out to be a reliable witness for the defense under cross examination, calls on a 1935 book written by James Duane Squires as a further witness to establish the propaganda origin of the Blue Book.[24] When we look at Squires' book "in context," however, we see that the Bryce-Toynbee book is mentioned nowhere in the narrative text of the work. On further and more careful examination of Squires' book, however, we do find the Bryce-Toynbee work listed in the Appendix among the hundreds of works commissioned by the British government during the war. Lacking any other evidence, Elekdag can brand the Bryce-Toynbee book "propaganda" only by virtue of its sponsorship, hardly a scientific gauge.

Since the Bryce-Toynbee book is listed in Squires' Appendix, and since it was commissioned by the British government and thus might be considered war-time "propaganda," let us look further into Squires' book and see how he defines "propaganda." After all, Squires was writing in 1935, before Hitler and Stalin gave the word "propaganda" such a bad name, and words do change their meaning over time. According to Squires, "propaganda" was "the one force which was to hold the far-flung millions together, which was to channel their individual energies into an immense river of national power."[25] So far, we see nothing particularly untoward.

Let us seek an even better clue to Squires' use of the word "propaganda" by looking further, "in context," into his book to see how he understood the British used "propaganda." "Men and women talked and argued and wrote," says Squires, "partly to justify the war to their own consciences, and partly to explain it to others. In most cases their writings were not struck off with studied conformance to the laws of mass psychology, but were the outpourings of immediate and hot indignation."[26] This is hardly a damning indictment, even if it could be applied to Bryce and Toynbee. Elekdag must find more significant evidence of wrongdoing on their part, otherwise the facts speak for themselves and Squires may be dismissed as a witness for the defense.

In the Turkish defense, Elekdag next submits the so-called "Langer thesis,"[27] which maintains that the Armenian revolutionary parties at the end of the nineteenth century attacked the government of Abdul-Hamid in the expectation of massacres which would elicit the concern of the European powers and their ultimate intervention on behalf of the Armenians. There is some question of the validity of the Langer thesis even as it applied to the 1890s, although we will not discuss that issue here, but it is certainly an anachronism to apply a thesis generated for the Abdul-Hamid massacres of the 1890s to the Young Turk killings of 1915-16.[28]

Elekdag uses Cyrus Hamlin, the president of Robert College in Constantinople,[29] as a witness to prove the nefarious motives of the Armenian "terrorists" who, after all, tweaked Abdul-Hamid until he massacred the Armenians. First, we should note that Hamlin, a well-informed and honest American missionary who served for many years in the Ottoman capital, died on August 8, 1900.[30] We cannot under any circumstances, therefore, accept his testimony on events after that date. Second, the actions of a few revolutionaries cannot be used, by any rational humane standard, as an excuse to destroy a whole people.

A search of the vast resources of the research collection of the New York Public Library turns up only three cataloged pieces by Hamlin. One is published by the Congregational Sunday School, the second by the *Missionary Review of the World*, and neither addresses the question at hand in a scholarly fashion. Hamlin's last article, however, published in the *Proceedings of the American Antiquarian Society*, presents Hamlin's studied, measured and considered opinion. And since the study was published in 1898, just before Hamlin's death, it should certainly contain his final word on the subject.

The article is entitled "The Genesis and Evolution of the Turkish Massacre of Armenian Subjects."[31] In it Hamlin writes: "A number of professed patriots, *Russian Armenians* [emphasis added], began to stir up revolution. They falsely claimed to have revolutionary coteries formed through the Empire. . . . The whole thing was supremely ridiculous, and the Armenian people were nowhere deceived. At a safe distance, in foreign cities, revolutionary organizations sprang up under the same name, Hunchagist, and began to belch forth their attacks upon the Sultan and his government and to call upon the people to strike for freedom. Absurd and wicked as this was, it answered Abdul's purpose perfectly. He had the papers translated and spread all over the Empire."[32]

Abdul-Hamid, Hamlin continues, tried to justify his actions "by two falsehoods. . . . First, that there had been no massacre, and second, that it was the suppression of an Armenian rebellion."[33] This statement has a familiar ring. The Turks still maintain there was never a genocide of the Armenians; and, anyway, they brought it on themselves. Hamlin, then, is hardly Elekdag's best witness; and, certainly, he cannot be used anachronistically to testify to the events of 1915-16, since, as we noted earlier, he died in 1900.

To be fair, we must admit that Ambassador Elekdag has unearthed one genuine anti-Armenian article, even in context, written by Arthur Moss and Florence Gilliam and published in the *Nation* in 1923, long after the Genocide of 1915-16. But before we can accept their testimony, we must establish the credentials of the authors: are they eyewitnesses or are they scholars who have done serious research? On investigation we discover that Moss and Gilliam are two American expatriates of the 1920s who edited a monthly magazine, called *Gargoyle*, published in Paris by Americans. They are neither eyewitnesses nor scholars. They are only writers who had become disaffected with America and its values; and, in the present case, they are only writing for a journal of opinion.

In their *Nation* article Moss and Gilliam, after denying the validity of the Bryce-Toynbee book, write, apparently in all seriousness: "In Turkey, all three main religions—Mohammedanism [*sic*], Judaism, and Christianity—are on an equal footing." "A Catholic cannot go as far politically in secular America as a Christian can go in so-called theocratic Turkey."[34] This brief piece by the editors of *Gargoyle*, less than two pages in length and unencumbered with any "scholarly trappings," is followed by a news release from the "Russian Telegraph Agency" [the press agency of the Soviet Union] regarding the "ex-patriarch Tikhon, now awaiting trial in Moscow." The editor of the *Nation* concludes, following the TASS report, "It thus becomes clear that Tikhon is no martyr; but merely a reactionary ecclesiastic. . . . He abused the privileged position accorded him under the complete freedom of conscience prevailing in the Soviet Republic. . . . It is for these offenses that he is awaiting trial, and not on account of any fancied 'persecution of religion' on the part of the Soviet Government."[35] It may be presumed, all things considered, that the opinions of the editor regarding the slandered Tikhon and that of Moss and Gilliam regarding the murdered Armenians are of equal accuracy and value, and are thus of little consequence as evidence.

If Lord Bryce's Blue Book is the first single best collection of eyewitness proof on the Armenian Genocide (and indeed that of the Christian Assyrians, of whom almost none are left to protest their own genocide), we must recognize the testimony of the U.S. Ambassador Henry Morgenthau in his book *Ambassador Morgenthau's Story*[36] as the most significant testimony in any single contemporary American book.

Henry Morgenthau was the American Ambassador to the Ottoman Empire from November 27, 1913 to February, 1, 1916, during the

Armenian Genocide of 1915-16. And, unless his testimony has some fatal flaw, he will make a good witness indeed. Since Morgenthau insists that the Turkish central government carried out a purposeful Genocide against the Armenians, Elekdag must either accept his testimony as the truth or find a way to discredit Morgenthau as a witness.[37]

Attempts to discredit Morgenthau have been made by calling him pro-Zionist—hardly a significant charge as far as Americans are concerned, whatever the Turkish view. In any case this argument has two flaws: First, as a matter of fact Morgenthau was not a Zionist; and, secondly, it would make no difference anyway. Armenians are not of the Jewish faith, and Zionism has nothing to do with the Armenian Genocide.

In case incrimination of Morgenthau by association should fail (by calling him a Zionist), Elekdag boldly declares a war *ex post facto* on the United States in order to make Morgenthau an "enemy." Henry Morgenthau's highly publicized book, *Ambassador Morgenthau's Story*, was, says Elekdag, "published in 1918 when World War I was raging and the Ottoman Empire officially the 'enemy.'"

But, as a matter of fact, Turkey did not declare war on the United States, and the United States did not declare war on the Ottoman Empire. President Wilson wanted to retain the tie in the hope of being of some assistance to the Armenians. America did not even break off diplomatic relations with Turkey until 1917, until after the Armenian Genocide was effectively completed, and then only to show its disapproval of the Turkish atrocities.

Elekdag then tells us that Morgenthau was anti-German, and quotes no less an authority than Sidney Bradshaw Fay to show that Germany was not solely responsible for World War I. Clearly, Fay argued persuasively in his book that Germany was not "solely" responsible for World War I; but this has no relevance to the Armenian question or to Ambassador Morgenthau's view of the Armenian Genocide. The Armenians have never been accused of starting World War I, even by the Turks, and the Armenians are of such little consequence to Fay's thesis on the origins of World War I that they are not even mentioned in the index to his book.

Since Elekdag has failed to discredit Morgenthau, he must look for another high-ranking American official to contradict Morgenthau's testimony. Elekdag appeals to the testimony of Admiral Mark Bristol of the U.S. Navy. Indeed, it is true that Admiral Bristol did represent the United States in Turkey sometime after World War I, but further investigation reveals that Bristol did not even arrive at his post in Turkey until 1920. Thus Bristol not only *was not* an eyewitness to our events, he was not even present in Turkey during the Genocide, as was Morgenthau and Morgenthau's successor, Abram Elkus. Bristol's intelligence came from his informants. Since the Armenians had already been eliminated from Turkey by the "final solution," Bristol could only speak with those people who remained, the Armenian executers, the Turks. The Turks, as we have seen, are hardly creditable witnesses to their own crime.

Bristol, a stern naval man, had an affinity for the military junta ruling the new Turkey, and he is eager to tell of the "bad qualities" of the Armenians and Greeks. Do "bad qualities" justify a genocide? I think not. If that were so, it might put the Turks and Americans, as well as the Armenians, at risk.

Furthermore, Bristol had a phobia against "foreigners," and was virulently anti-Semitic. "If you shake them up in a bag you wouldn't know which one would come up first. ... The Armenians are like the Jews—they have no national feeling and have low moral character." If the Armenians had no national feeling, it is certainly implausible that they could have mounted a revolt against the Turks. Thus, in a backhanded way, Bristol defends the Armenians against Turkish accusations of insurrection.

Finally, since Bristol is not a contemporary of the events, nor even a creditable witness in general (we must watch for anachronisms and scholarly dependability), and since it is not really polite for the Turks to bad-mouth the American ambassador, Elekdag tries to discredit Morgenthau's sources. Elekdag argues that Ambassador Morgenthau's account "relies on selected missionary reports and communications translated by Greeks and Armenians who could hardly have been disinterested parties."

In the nineteenth century, American Protestants inaugurated and conducted vast missionary enterprises all over the world. The "Turkish field" was one of the largest. American missionaries were, accordingly, posted all over the Ottoman Empire, and indeed had "stations" in most all the areas where the Armenians lived. They operated five American colleges, and dozens of schools, in the areas inhabited by the Armenians, attended in large measure by the Armenians.[38]

These American missionaries were the flower of the New England and Midwest American intelligentsia, products of the second Great Awakening of American Protestantism,[39] and honored graduates of such prestigious institutions as Princeton, Yale, Brown, Oberlin and Grinnell. Most of them had advanced training, and many were physicians. They also, for the most part, knew Turkish and Armenian, having translated the Bible into those languages. Yet one could safely presume, even if we did not have the documents presently in front of us, that the American missionaries would communicate with the American ambassador in their common native tongue, English, as of course they did.

Missionary reports, selected or not, all tell the same general story: Armenians all over Anatolia were expelled from their homes, slaughtered and massacred, and the remnant driven into the Syrian desert to die. Thousands of these reports are on file in the archives of the American Board of Commissioners for Foreign Missions which are now deposited in the Houghton Library at Harvard University and open to serious scholars.[40] But did the American missionaries tell the truth? One would think so. We certainly will not join Elekdag to call these God-fearing men and women liars without seeing strong evidence to support the contention. Since Elekdag presents no proof to the contrary, we must accept the missionary reports as dependable evidence, even though—in deference to Elekdag—we will not use their evidence here.

Well, we still must account for the biased "Armenian and Greek translators." All we have left for them to translate, since the American consuls and the American missionaries wrote in English, are the official Turkish documents and dispatches sent or brought by the Ottoman government to the American Embassy, materials which the Turkish government would certainly not send to demonstrate that an Armenian Genocide was taking place. But these translations could be checked in any case by the Americans, especially when they applied to serious concerns. Still, we must allow the possibility that Armenian or Greek translators made oral translations while American officials were visiting Turkish officials, and so we must deal with that issue also.

The American Embassy in Istanbul employed for over sixteen years, as legal advisor and frequent translator, an Armenian by the name of Arshag Schmavonian. Morgenthau frequently used Schmavonian as a translator when he visited with high Turkish officials and attests to the fact that Schmavonian was "held in high regard by the Turkish authorities."[41] When relations were ruptured between Turkey and the United States in 1917, Schmavonian was transferred to Washington, D.C., where he served as Special Advisor to the State

Department until his death in January 1922. The use of Greeks and Armenians as clerks and translators was not unusual in foreign embassies, and the Turks themselves used many of them in high posts before the war. Morgenthau's personal secretary in Istanbul and later in America, Hagop S. Andonian, was also an Armenian.

But Morgenthau did not rely on written reports alone. He had personal conversations regarding the Armenian killings with Talaat Pasha, the Minister of the Interior and the chief force behind the Armenian Genocide. Morgenthau reconstructs their conversations in his book, *Ambassador Morgenthau's Story*, based on his own notes, letters, and "Diary."[42] If we decide—only in deference to Elekdag and for no other impelling reason—not to use Morgenthau's book as evidence, we could examine his personal papers, his written *aide-mémoire*. Still, to be fair to Morgenthau, we must accept the distinct possibility that a man of Morgenthau's intelligence might remember certain details of his arguments with Talaat Pasha which are only loosely referred to in his notes. For example, it is quite possible that Morgenthau might remember the substance of his arguments behind the written note that, "I argued all sorts of ways with him [Talaat],"[43] and include those items in his book.

Yet, we will give Ambassador Elekdag every advantage. We will ignore Morgenthau's book, without just cause, and take testimony regarding Morgenthau from Heath W. Lowry, the head of the Institute for Turkish Studies in Washington, D.C. Lowry has written a booklet called *The Story Behind Ambassador Morgenthau's Story* in which he attempts to determine whether Morgenthau, as he stated, used only "every *legitimate* [emphasis added] step or means" for convincing the American people of the justice of fighting against the Central Powers and informing them of the Armenian Genocide, or if Morgenthau was purposely deceptive. In other words, did Morgenthau lie in his book?

Lowry's booklet, unfortunately, just as Elekdag's letter, is marred by many errors. For example, on page 7, Lowry calls the Henry Morgenthau *Sr.* papers the "Henry Morgenthau, *Jr.* Papers." For another example, on page 14, he states that Schmavonian "accompanied him [Morgenthau] in *all* meetings with Turkish officials." Then, on page 15, he writes that Schmavonian "accompanied Morgenthau *on almost every official visit* he paid to members of the Young Turk Government." Finally, he writes on page 49, quoting Morgenthau, that "Talaat told me that he greatly preferred that *I should always come alone when I had any Armenian matters to discuss with him* [emphasis added]."

While Lowry's booklet is tendentious and flawed, a full critique of it cannot be made here. Suffice it to say that since the book is published by the Turks, it must be acceptable to them as evidence. In our present analysis let us only use, then, to be ex-tremely fair to Elekdag, the evidence about Morgenthau supplied by Lowry.

First, Lowry quotes a letter written by Morgenthau to President Woodrow Wilson on November 26, 1917, in which Morgenthau informs Wilson that he is considering writing a book about Germany and Turkey: "For in Turkey we see the evil spirit of Germany at its worst—culminating at last in the greatest crime of all ages, the horrible massacre of helpless Armenians and Syrians."[44] This letter should be clear enough. Morgenthau sincerely believed that the Germans were guilty of aggression and that they were a bad influence on the Turks.

Further, Lowry quotes from Morgenthau's "Diary" entry for August 8, 1915: "I called on Talaat. He had *his man there to interpret for me* [emphasis added]. . . . Talaat told me that he greatly preferred that *I should always come alone when I had any Armenian matters to discuss with him* [emphasis added]. . . . He told me that they [the Turks] based their objections to the Armenians on three distinct grounds: 1) that they had enriched themselves at the expense of the Turks; 2) that they wanted to domineer over them and establish a separate state; 3) that they have openly encouraged their enemies so that they [the Turks] have come to the irrevocable decision to make them [the Armenians] powerless before the war is ended."

Morgenthau continued: "I argued in all sorts of ways with him but he said that there was no use; that they [the Turks] had already disposed of three-fourths of them [the Armenians], that there were none left in Bitlis, Van, Erzeroum [Erzurum], and the hatred was so intense now that they have to finish it. . . . He said he wanted to treat the Armenians like we treat the negroes, I think he meant like the Indians. . . . He said that they would take care of the Armenians at Zor and elsewhere but they did not want them in Anatolia. I told him three times that they were making a serious mistake and would regret it. He said 'we know we have made mistakes, but we never regret.'"[45]

While the Diary does not have the literary elegance of *The Morgenthau Story*, its meaning is clear enough: Talaat confesses *through his own interpreter*, not a Greek or Armenian, to Morgenthau that he wants to kill all the Armenians in Anatolia [Turkey] and that three-fourths of them are already dead. Nothing could be clearer.

But Elekdag may still consider Morgenthau "the enemy" and

refuse to accept his testimony even though it is transmitted by Heath Lowry, Elekdag's friend and head of the Turkish-supported Institute for Turkish Studies. So let us turn to testimony from the contemporary German ambassador, whose country was allied with Turkey during the war, a man who certainly could not be considered by Elekdag to be "an enemy." The Turks and Germans, as allies, were friends.

The third wartime German ambassador at the Ottoman court was Count von Wolff-Metternich, who, in a revealing dispatch of June 30, 1916, to his government, wrote: "The Committee [of Union and Progress] *demands the annihilation of the last remnants of the Armenians* [emphasis added], and the government must bow to its demands. The Committee does not only mean the organization of the ruling party of the capital; it is spread all over the provinces. At the side of each provincial governor [*vali*], and down to each *kaimakam* [kaymakam, a village mayor], a Committee member stands, with instructions either to support or supervise."[46]

Thus, we see that the testimony of the German ambassador, the representative of Turkey's ally, not only confirms the essence of Morgenthau's testimony but adds critical detail. The Turks wanted to annihilate the "last remnants of the Armenians" and are using agents of the C.U.P. to transmit their secret oral instructions to local governmental officials to ensure compliance. We have now produced, *inter alia*, the evidence of two ambassadors, one, a "friend," a German; and the other, an American, by the account only of Ambassador Elekdag, an "enemy," yet they both agree that the Young Turk Ottoman government instituted, carried out, and was responsible for the Armenian Genocide.

Next, let us grant for the moment, only for the sake of argument, that Turkish Ambassador Elekdag is correct and that American Ambassador Morgenthau is a liar. We should remember that James Ring Adams argues that Elekdag must "make liars of men like Henry Morgenthau" in order to prove his case. Were there any honest Americans, closer to events and certainly not deceitful Christian missionaries, whom we can ask instead? Fortunately, there are such men.

The American government, as we have said, had professional consular officials stationed in each of the major, and some minor, cities of the Ottoman Empire. The United States had consuls in Aleppo, Kharpert, Smyrna, Mersin, and Trebizond, and at times consular agents in Urfa, Samsun, and Erzurum, all within the areas affected by the Genocide. These men sent a constant flow of reports on the Armenian Genocide to the American Embassy in Istanbul. These reports are currently on file in the U.S. Department of State and are open for public inspection. They can also be purchased on microfilm.[47]

American Consul Leslie Davis of Kharpert, a veteran of many years service in the Ottoman Empire, for example reported on July 11, 1915: "The entire movement seems to be *the most thoroughly organized and effective massacre* [emphasis added] this country [Turkey] has ever seen."[48] Two later reports by Consul Davis were so critical of Turkish actions that the Ottoman government repeatedly frustrated his persistent efforts to wire, or even mail, them to Morgenthau.[49]

In the first reports Davis writes: "Another method was found *to destroy the Armenian race* [emphasis added]. ...A massacre would be humane in comparison."[50] The second of Davis's reports is even more pointed. Davis writes: "That the order is nominally to exile the Armenians from these vilayets [provinces] may mislead the outside world for a time, but the measure is nothing but a massacre of the most atrocious nature. ... *There is no doubt that this massacre was done by order of the Government, there can be no pretense that the measure is anything but a general massacre* [emphasis added]." Altogether, Davis sent dozens of reports to Morgenthau telling essentially the same story—mass murder on a horrifying scale.

While still in Turkey, Consul Davis made several trips into the countryside around Kharpert to see for himself if the Armenians had been merely deported or whether they were being slaughtered after they had been driven from their homes. Understanding the need for a dependable record, he took along a doctor who verified the causes of the thousands of deaths. Davis also photographed the victims and included the photographs with his report. On his return to the United States, he was asked by the U.S. State Department to summarize the findings of his personal investigation. His report has been published in a book edited by Susan K. Blair which is entitled *The Slaughterhouse Province: An American Diplomat's Report on the Armenian Genocide, 1915-1917.*[51]

In his report to the State Department, Davis writes: "Few localities could be better suited to the fiendish purposes of the Turks in their plan to exterminate the Armenian population [of Turkey] than this peaceful lake [Goeljuk] in the interior of Asiatic Turkey, with its precipitous banks and pocket-like valleys, surrounded by villages of savage Kurds and far removed from the sight of civilized man. *This, perhaps, was the reason why so many exiles from distant vilayets were brought in safety as far as Mamouret-ul-Aziz and then massacred in the 'Slaughterhouse Vilayet' of Turkey* [emphasis added]. That which took place around beautiful Lake Goeljuk [later renamed Hazar Gölü] in the summer of 1915 is almost inconceivable. Thousands and thousands of Armenians, mostly innocent and helpless women and children, were butchered on its shores and barbarously mutilated."[52]

Consul Edward I. Nathan of Mersin also describes the incredible terror created by the Turkish authorities as they expelled and massacred the Armenians in that region.[53] The seventy-seven individual consular reports on file in the U.S. State Department regarding the Armenian Genocide go on and on, giving detailed variants on the same horrifying theme—human slaughter on a mass scale, purposeful genocide.[54]

Finally, if Ambassador Elekdag will grant that Ambassador Morgenthau could read, without translations, such reports coming to him from his own consuls, and that he would not, even as "an enemy of the Turks," send false reports to his own government in Washington, we will offer the following as our final piece of evidence from Morgenthau.

Morgenthau sent a ciphered cable to Washington on July 16, 1915, which begins: "Have you received my 841? Deportation of and excesses against peaceful Armenians is increasing and from harrowing reports of eye witnesses [sic] it appears that *a campaign of race extermination* [emphasis added] is in progress under a pretext of reprisal against rebellion."[55]

But if Elekdag considers Morgenthau an "enemy," and refuses to accept his testimony, let us take evidence from the Ambassador's successor, Abram Elkus. Abram Elkus, the next U.S. ambassador to the Ottoman Empire, cabled the State Department in an October 17, 1916, report as follows: "Deportations accompanied by studied cruelties [of Armenians] continue ... forced conversions to Islam [are] perseveringly pushed, children and girls from deported families kidnapped. In order to avoid opprobrium of the civilized world, which the continuation of massacres would arouse, Turkish officials have now adopted and *are executing the unchecked policy of extermination through starvation, exhaustion, and brutality of treatment hardly surpassed even in Turkish history* [emphasis added]."[56]

These reports, and other materials from the U.S. State Department files, prove without a doubt that the Genocide of the Armenians was carried out by the Young Turk Government all over Anatolia, or in what is today Turkey. At that time, furthermore, the American president, Woodrow Wilson, the American Congress, the American people, and the U.S. Department of State were fully and correctly persuaded by the vast and incontrovertible evidence.

Indeed, Woodrow Wilson, with a plentitude of information from all sources, was so moved by the Armenian plight that he advocated an American mandate over Armenia. On May 24, 1920, the President sent a message to the Senate seeking consent to take up that duty. In his official message, Wilson wrote: [I ask this] "not only because it [the mandate resolution] embodied my own convictions and feeling with regard to Armenia and its people, but also, and more particularly, because it seemed to me to be the voice of the American people, expressing their genuine convictions and deep ... sympathies. ... the sympathy with Armenia has proceeded from no single portion of our people, but has come with extraordinary spontaneity and sincerity from the whole. ... At their hearts, this great and generous people [the Americans] have made the case of Armenia their own."[57]

Elekdag's final argument is that the Armenians were sympathetic to the Russians and had to be evacuated from the war zone in the east. A "removal of the Armenian population" from the "war zone" in the east, as Ambassador Elekdag claims, would have only included the provinces of Erzurum and Van in Turkey, and perhaps the areas of Kars and Ardahan in the Russian Empire.

As a matter of clear fact, the Armenians were driven out and annihilated not only from their historic "homeland" in the east, but across the whole length and breadth of the Ottoman Anatolia from the shores of the Black Sea to the deserts of Syria and from the Aegean Sea to the Caucasus mountains.[58] The Armenians were slaughtered in the cities, towns, and rural villages. It should be noted that the vast majority of Armenians in Anatolia were farmers, although, of course, the city dwellers were generally more visible to consular officials and visiting Europeans.

Armenians were slaughtered in the west, near Istanbul, in and around Izmit and Bursa; in the center, in and around Angora (Ankara); in the southwest, in and around Konya and Adana (which is near the Mediterranean Sea); in the central portion of Anatolia, in and around Sivas (Sepastia), Marash, Shabin Kara-Hissar, Kharpert, Diyarbakir, and Urfa; and on the Black Sea coast, in and around Trebizond (Trabzon). Only Erzurum, Bitlis, and Van in the east —where they were also massacred—might rightfully be called areas "in the war zone." Clearly the others are not.

Furthermore, the fable that "Tsarist Russia incited the Armenians to revolt by promising them an independent homeland after the collapse of the Ottoman Empire" is irrelevant. No Armenian would take seriously such a promise, inasmuch as it would be quite out of Nicholas's character. Nicholas could not be expected to give freedom to any element of the Russian Empire, and indeed he lost his throne rather than give freedom even to the Russians, his own people. In fact it was the Tsar for Tsar Nicholas II, who lost his throne rather than to give freedom even to his own people. In fact, it was the Tsar's depredations of Armenian Church properties in the Caucasus which was the immediate stimulus for the crystallization of the Armenian revolutionary movement in the Russian Empire.

Logic will not allow Elekdag to have it both ways: If "in no area of the Ottoman Empire did the Armenians constitute a majority of the population on which to build a successful break-away movement," then they should not have been feared by the Turkish government and exterminated. An "Armenian revolutionary movement" could not, in any case, have been a threat to the Ottoman government. A disarmed minority of some 3 million Armenians could hardly be a threat to 16 or more million Muslim Turks with the total power— military and bureaucratic—of the state behind them.

One by one we have called Elekdag's witnesses back for further interrogation and their testimony, in full "context," is damning indeed.

Now let us finish our narrative. The Young Turk revolution took place in 1908, but the Committee of Union and Progress preferred to stay in the background and kept Abdul-Hamid II on the throne until he conspired against them in a counterrevolution in 1909. The Committee soon lost its faith in liberalism and Ottomanism and began to turn to Pan-Turkism, a racist form of Turkish nationalism, as pointed out by Toynbee in *Acquaintances*, inspired by proto-fascistic European thought, and demanded "Turkey for the Turks." The minorities, chiefly the Armenians because of their religion and numbers, were in the way of a new homogeneous Turkish nation-state.[59]

Accordingly, the leaders of the Committee of Union and Progress decided on a "final solution" to the "Eastern Question": the annihilation of the Ottoman Armenians in a state-sponsored genocide.[60] The Armenian Genocide took place in 1915-16, conveniently under the cover of World War I, when all the Powers, with the exception of the United States, were almost totally engrossed in the conflict.

The Genocide was planned and premeditated by the leaders of the Committee of Union and Progress. It was carried out by a covert and secret Special Organization (*Teşkilati Mahsusa*) established by the

C.U.P. separate from the state structure but in control of it, similar to the way the Communist Party of the Soviet Union controlled the USSR without official status for some sixty years.[61] Brigands, as well as thugs and murderers taken from prisons, were organized into butcher battalions (*çetes*) to carry out the killings. Officials who refused to cooperate with the agents of the *Teşkilati Mahsusa* (who demanded not only the expulsion of the Armenians but also their slaughter), were dismissed from their post or even put to death.[62]

Finally, many people have said, "If there was a genocide, why was there not a 'war crimes trial' following the war as there was following World War II at Nuremburg?" Indeed, there was, and Elekdag makes reference to it.

In fact, there were special courts-martial instituted by the postwar Ottoman authorities for the trial of the C.U.P. leaders and certain members of the Young Turk cabinet, as well as a government investigative commission headed by Hasan Mazhar, and yet another established by the Ottoman Chamber of Deputies. The records of these investigations and the trials are recorded in the trial supplements of the *Takvimi Vekayi*, the official record of the Ottoman government. As at Nuremberg, so in Istanbul, the tribunal relied largely on authenticated documents rather than on courtroom testimony. Furthermore, the court accepted testimony only from Muslims. The exhibits included ciphers, telegrams, and written documents. Since they are authenticated by the Turks themselves, Elekdag must accept the fact that they reveal the truth.

The Turkish court concluded that the leaders of the *Ittihat* [C.U.P.] were guilty of murder. "This fact has been proven and verified." It maintained that the genocidal scheme was carried out with as much secrecy as possible and, accordingly, that records and written orders were kept to the barest minimum. The Ittihatists, the court further concluded, had maintained a public facade of relocating the Armenians, but it engaged in "covert and secretive" operations, relying for the most part on the use of "oral and secret orders and instructions," and carried out the killings by a "secret network." The determination to exterminate the Armenians, furthermore, was not a hasty decision, but "the result of extensive and profound deliberations."[63]

Enver Pasha, Jemal Pasha, Talaat Bey, Dr. Mehmed Nazim, and Dr. Behaeddin Şakir were convicted and condemned to death for "the extermination and destruction of the Armenians." Since they had fled and eluded arrest, the sentence was passed in absentia. Some minor officials were also convicted, sentenced and hanged. Since by January

1920, Mustafa Kemal Atatürk was gaining effective control of Turkey, and the Greeks had invaded Cilicia, the rest of the trials were aborted and those prisoners who were not allowed to escape earlier were released.[64] Justice was only partially done, and, as Mustafa Kemal Atatürk, the father of "modern Turkey," implied, the disrupted trials remain a blot on the Turkish record.[65]

Some partisans may attempt to dismiss the Turkish war crimes trials as biased because they were held while the British occupied Istanbul. In fact, this is not entirely true. It should be pointed out that the Turkish war crimes trials were commissioned under an imperial *irade* (decree) of Sultan Mohammed VI issued on December 16, 1918, well before the British occupation of Istanbul on March 16, 1920. The trials were run in series, concentrating on different geographical locations. Thus it can also be noted that both the Erzincan (Erzinjan) and Trabzon series came to a close before the end of 1919 and the British occupation; and, for example, that Abdullah Avni (one of the defendants in the Erzinjan series) was proven guilty, condemned, and hanged on July 22, 1919, again before the British occupation. In any case, all the Turkish trials were run by Turks and based only on Turkish documentary evidence and the testimony of Muslims. In contrast, it may be noted, the Allies themselves ran the war crimes trials at Nuremberg after World War II.[66]

In the light of all the available evidence, we must now ask why the United States Department of State now maintains a view contrary to that of its own officials who were eyewitnesses to the Genocide of the Ottoman Armenians by the Young Turk government? In fact, fortunately for its own reputation, it no longer does. The rejection of recognition of the Armenian Genocide was a short-lived aberration. The policy statement in the infamous "Note" of 1982 was reversed in 1983, but with no fanfare and with ambiguous public notice.[67] In a Freedom of Information Act court case filed against the State Department by Van A. Krikorian in 1988, United States District Judge Royce C. Lamberth wrote an "Opinion" which included his findings on "Facts," "Analysis," and "Conclusions." In his finding of "Facts," the Judge Lamberth placed a footnote (#1), immediately following and appended to a full quotation of the notorious "Note," which reads: "*The State Department rescinded the Note in 1983 and reinstated the US policy of recognizing the Turkish Genocide of the Armenians* [emphasis added]."[68]

The documents obtained by Krikorian show how officials in the State Department took an article which initially acknowledged the

Genocide, and literally rewrote the historical sections to reach an opposite conclusion.[69] While the State Department has made itself whole again, the nasty episode of denial is an embarrassment to many Americans.

Now we must ask some final questions, for which we as yet have found no answers. Why do Ambassador Elekdag and his government persist in attempting the cover-up of a crime in which they were not involved, and thereby become accessories, and equally guilty, under the law? Is it merely Turkish amnesia, or is there a more somber reason behind the denial? Perhaps Elekdag will come forth one day and enlighten us.

Appendix

Armenians vs. Turks: The View From Istanbul

Letter to the Editor, Wall Street Journal, September 21, 1983, page 33.

Vast tragedies do, as James Ring Adams suggests ("Facing Up to an Armenian Genocide," Aug. 12), deserve "truthful accounting." Unfortunately, such accounting is brought no closer by his article, which by and large is a morass of misplaced, indiscriminate credulity.

A truthful accounting must, first, be factually correct. Second, it must be meaningful, in the sense that context and terms have some referents in reality; lest intelligent people of goodwill be deprived of the opportunity to distinguish truth from nonsense; lest the term "genocide," so readily applied by Armenian polemicists and their supporters, be deprived of meaning.

The tragedies of 1915 during World War I, which brought such immense suffering to all ethnic groups living in Anatolia under the Ottoman Empire, were not isolated, contextless phenomena. Years before, during the second half of the 19th century, policy makers of certain European countries undertook to exploit, for their own imperial interests, the ambitions of Armenian extremist movements, whose terrorist components, in turn, sought to manipulate the Europeans.

Armenian terrorist organizations, most notably the Dashnaks and the Hunchaks, sought to establish an independent Armenian state in eastern Anatolia—an area in which the overwhelming majority of the population were Moslem Turks.

The massacre of Moslems was the main tactic of the Armenian groups. They deliberately sought to trigger reprisals by aggrieved Moslem communities against Armenian minority groupings in the Ottoman Empire. They cynically calculated that reprisals would fuel their international propaganda campaign to spur the European powers to intervene militarily to "liberate" the Christian Armenians from the Moslem "oppressors." At the same time, according to their own documents, such reprisals, it was hoped, would instill in Armenian minority populations a sense of grievance against the Ottoman government and an Armenian nationalist fervor that did not at that time exist.

Cyril Hamlin, the founder of the Robert College of Istanbul, records he was told by the terrorists that Hunchak bands would "watch for their opportunity to kill Moslems, set fire to their villages, and then make their escape into the mountains. The enraged Moslems will then rise and fall upon the defenseless Armenians and slaughter them with such barbarity that Russia will enter in the name of humanity and Christian civilization and take possession."

As with most terrorist movements, the Armenian "cause" prompted the terrorists to foreswear all inner doubts, all moral restraints. Blood-letting was the chosen instrument, their own people, by intent, the ultimate victims: Armenian riots in Istanbul in 1895; the Zeytun Revolt of 1895; Armenian raids on Moslem villages; attacks in Izmir, Ankara, Diyarbakir, Urfa, Maras, Van; the seizure of the Ottoman Bank in Istanbul in 1896; and the Adana riots of 1906.

During the period before World War I, the Armenian propaganda campaign flourished in Europe, especially in France and Great Britain. In the press and political forums, Europeans vociferously condemned Moslem communal reprisals while they ignored Armenian attacks and efforts of the progressively enfeebled Ottoman authorities to intervene and prevent bloodshed.

The sympathetic atmosphere in Europe is attributable in part to the interests of British, French, and Russian policy-makers in extending national spheres of influence in the so-called "Sick Man of Europe," the Ottoman Empire, during the latter part of the 19th century and first years of this century. Each of these powers used the Armenian cause as an instrument to further its geopolitical aims. But the attempts to incite or exploit Armenian feeling never netted tangible results for in no area of the Ottoman Empire did Armenians constitute a majority of the population on which to build a successful breakaway movement.

Armenian terrorist activities and direct involvement by European powers in the internal affairs of the Ottoman Empire reached a peak during the First World War. To undermine the Ottoman war effort on the eastern Anatolian front, Tsarist Russia incited Armenians to revolt by promising them the establishment of an independent Armenia after the collapse of the Ottoman Empire.

As a result, Armenian bands sacked Turkish villages. Other Armenians joined the ranks of the Russian army. In fact, when the Russians advanced into eastern Anatolia, barbaric excesses committed by Armenian volunteers were so severe that even Russian commanders felt compelled to redeploy these troops to the rear lines.

In response to the open Armenian uprising as well as the threat of further revolts, the Ottoman authorities concluded they had no alternative but to relocate the Armenians from the eastern front region to Syria and Palestine (at that time, southern provinces of the Ottoman Empire). Armenians in other parts of the Empire, including the capital, Istanbul, were untouched by this wartime decision.

During the war Armenian extremists and their supporters added a new dimension to their propaganda campaign by falsely claiming that the Ottoman government had embarked on a course of deliberate extermination of the Armenian people.

Allied propaganda and reporting in the press during World War I portrayed the Ottoman enemy as a ruthless, merciless foe, while the deaths of millions of Turks, men, women and children, were considered unworthy of note.

That warfare in eastern Turkey, together with famine and epidemics, resulted in the suffering and deaths of members of all ethnic groups, including 2 million Turks, is not in doubt. However, allegations that the slaughter of Armenian civilians on any scale was systematically planned, organized, or carried out by the Ottoman authorities cannot be sustained by the historical evidence.

Mr. Adams asserts that the Turkish case relies on discrediting all contemporary Western accounts as wartime propaganda and incriminating documents as Armenian forgeries. His assertion is only partially true.

The so-called incriminating documents, which Mr. Adams labels "the most damning evidence," are forgeries. Indeed, they are copies of forgeries. Even the Armenian research Mr. Adams cites is quoted as saying they can't be called fake or real because "we only have copies and the originals have dropped from sight."

The documents, purported telegrams from Ottoman government official Talat Pasha, were produced by Armenians in 1920 at the Paris Peace Conference in an effort to buttress their case for claiming the territory of eastern Turkey for a state of their own.

Curiously, they neglected to deliver the "damning evidence," originals or even copies, to the British, who immediately after the war were scouring the Ottoman Empire for evidence to convict Ottoman officials of alleged war crimes. In fact, the British released for lack of evidence, after a three-year investigation, the 100 officials they had interned in Malta. Among them was Mustafa Abdulhalik Bey, who, according to the Armenians, had received and signed for the telegraphed orders and had implemented them

Is it conceivable that the Armenians would have withheld untainted damning evidence which could have convicted their alleged erstwhile tormentors? Or is it more likely that the "evidence" was fabricated and the Armenians in whose possession it was knew it would not have survived scrutiny in court?

Examination of the copies of the alleged telegraphs reveals that neither in form, script, or phraseology do they remotely resemble the administrative records of the Ottoman government or of the ruling Union and Progress Party.

Some of the contemporary Western accounts of the events of 1915 were indeed wartime propaganda, but it is not Turkish assertions that make them so. Mr. Adams cites the writings of Lord Bryce, Arnold Toynbee and Henry Morgenthau as validating the Armenian allegations.

In his book, "British Propaganda at Home and in the United States from 1914 to 1917" (Cambridge, Harvard University Press, 1935), Professor James Duane Squires explicitly labels Lord Bryce's "The Treatment of Armenians in the ottoman Empire 1915-1919" as wartime propaganda. Also listed as propaganda are many of Toynbee's wartime works, including "Murderous Tyranny of the Turks," "The Belgian Deportation," "The Destruction of Poland," and "The German Terror in France."

Toynbee, who assisted in writing and producing Lord Bryce's book supporting the Armenian cause, disclosed in 1967 that the book was intended to serve as an instrument to further the British Government's political aims and foreign policy objectives ("Acquaintances," Arnold Toynbee, Oxford University Press, London, 1967).

Arthur Moss and Florence Gilliam, writing in a 1923 edition (June 13) of "The Nation," state: "The Bryce reports have been proved to be without tangible evidence and to have been based entirely on hearsay."

Certainly, any responsible scholar or journalist must be at least skeptical of Ambassador Morgenthau's account. It relies on selected missionary reports and communications translated by Greeks and Armenians who could hardly have been disinterested parties. The subsequent U.S. envoy in Turkey, Admiral Mark Bristol, wrote: "Unfortunately, the missionaries . . . tell only one side of the story . . . disclosing only the best qualities of the Armenians and Greeks without telling their bad qualities." He characterized Armenian propaganda in the Western World as "exaggerated, together with claims and statistics that are deceptive and misleading."

Henry Morgenthau's highly publicized book, "Ambassador Morgenthau's Story," published in 1918 when World War I was raging and the Ottoman Empire officially the "enemy," highlights an account based on hearsay of the German leadership's maneuverings on the eve of World War I. Few now deny that the account is at total variance with the facts or that Morgenthau was a victim of uncritical acceptance of hearsay (see Sidney Bradshaw Fey, "The Origins of the World War," Vol. II, 1930). Yet Mr. Adams and others are all too ready to credit his hearsay-based acceptance of Armenian allegations reiterated elsewhere in the same book.

Mr. Adams' article, as a whole, is one more proof that giving credence to Armenian allegations is by no means a function of the level of scholarship that is applied to investigation of them. Unfortunately, the potential consequences of flourishing indiscriminately smatterings of knowledge and misinformation are more than academic at a time when the very historical misrepresentations Mr. Adams seems to endorse are the insane pretext for the murders of innocents in the 1980s.

SUKRU ELEKDAG
Ambassador of Turkey
Washington

REFERENCES

1. This paper, originally written in 1985, has been revised for current publication.

2. *Parade: The Sunday Newspaper Magazine* (October 28, 1984), 2.

3. *Wall Street Journal* (April 29, 1985), 2.

4. Andrew Corsun, "Armenian Terrorism—A Profile," *Department of State Bulletin,* August 1982 (U. S. Department of State, Washington, D.C.), 35. The disclaimer was in a boxed "Note" at the end of the article, and it read as follows: "Because of [*sic*] the historical record of the events in Asia Minor is ambiguous, the Department of State does not endorse allegations that the Turkish government committed a genocide against the Armenian people. Armenian terrorists use this allegation to justify in part their continuing attacks of Turkish diplomats and installations." As it was later revealed, Corsun's original article which recognized the Armenian genocide as the first genocide of the twentieth century, was heavily edited by State Department officials to reach the opposite conclusion. See final footnote of this paper.

5. These documents and photographs can now be found in the National Archives and in the archives of the U.S. State Department. For American documentation and that of other Western powers see, Richard G. Hovannisian, *The Armenian Holocaust: A Bibliography Relating to the Deportations, Massacres, and Dispersion of the Armenian People, 1915-1923* (Cambridge, Mass.: Armenian Heritage Press, 1978). For documentation of the Armenian Genocide from Turkish sources, see: Vahakn N. Dadrian, "Documentation of the Armenian Genocide in Turkish Sources, in *Genocide: A Critical Bibliographic Review, Vol. II,* edited by Israel W. Charny (New York: Facts On File, 1991), 86-138.

6. All of the European powers, both allies and enemies of the Ottoman Turks in World War I, have a plentitude of documentary evidence in their archives attesting to the Armenian Genocide. See Hovannisian, *Armenian Holocaust.*

7. Richard D. Kloian, ed., *The Armenian Genocide: News Accounts From The American Press, 1915-1922* (Berkeley, Calif.: Anto Press, 1985).

8. Herbert Hoover wrote in his memoirs: "Probably Armenia was known to the American school child in 1919 only a little less than England . . . of . . . the staunch Christians who were massacred periodically by the Mohammedan [*sic*] Turks, and the Sunday School collections [of] over fifty years for alleviating their miseries." *The Memoirs of Herbert Hoover: Years of Adventure, 1874-1920* (New York: The Macmillan Company, 1951), 385.

9. See, "Soiling the Altar of Freedom," editorial in the *New York Times* (August 9, 1983), 22A.

10. *Wall Street Journal* (August 9, 1983), 32; (August 12), 20; (August 16), 32.

11. Ibid., (August 12, 1983), 20.

12. Ibid.

13. Page 33. The text of Ambassador Elekdag's letter is appended.

14. It was Tsar Nicholas I who coined the phrase in Russian.

15. The Dashnaks (Armenian Revolutionary Federation) and Hunchaks were strongly influenced by Russian populism and the Russian "to-the-people" movement of the 1870s. The Armenian word "Hunchak," in fact, is a translation of *Kolokol,* or Bell, the title of Alexander Herzen's underground populist publication.

16. Christopher J. Walker, *Armenia: The Survival of a Nation* (London: Croom Helm, 1980), 179.

17. *Documents presented to Secretary of State for Foreign Affairs*, By Viscount Bryce, With a preface by Viscount Bryce (London: Sir Joseph Causton and Sons, Ltd., 1916.

18. London: Oxford University Press, 1967.

19. Toynbee, *Acquaintances*, 149.

20. The ruling Turkish triumvirate included the aforementioned Talaat, as well as Enver and Jemal.

21. That is to say from the time the Armenians were cooperating with the Committee of Union and Progress until the Genocide of 1915-1916.

22. Toynbee, *Acquaintances*, 241.

23. Ibid., 240.

24. James Duane Squires, *British Propaganda at Home and in the United States from 1914 to 1917* (Cambridge: Harvard University Press, 1935).

25. Ibid., 14.

26. Ibid., 16.

27. William L. Langer, *The Diplomacy of Imperialism, 1890-1902*, 2nd ed. (New York: Alfred A. Knopf, 1960).

28. See refutation of the "provocation thesis" by Robert Melson, "Provocation or Nationalism: A critical Inquiry into the Armenian Genocide of 1915," in *The Armenian Genocide in Perspective*, Richard G. Hovannisian, ed. (New Brunswick, N.J.: Transaction Books, 1986), 61-81.

29. The name of Constantinople was changed in 1923 to Istanbul.

30. Marcia and Malcolm Stevens, *Against the Devil's Current: The Life and Times of Cyrus Hamlin* (New York: University Press of America, 1988), 467, 471.

31. *American Antiquarian Society. Proceedings*. New Series, vol. xii (October 1897 - October 1898), 288-94.

32. Ibid., 292.

33. Ibid., 293.

34. *Nation*, Vol. CXVI, No. 3023 (June 13, 1923), 705.

35. Ibid., 706.

36. Garden City, New York: Doubleday, Page and Co., 1918.

37. Seven years after the Elekdag's letter appeared in the *Wall Street Journal*, Heath W. Lowry, the director of the Institute for Turkish Studies in Washington, D.C., published a booklet entitled *The Story Behind Ambassador Morgenthau's Story* (Istanbul: Isis Press, 1990), attempting to discredit Morgenthau's book. Lowry demonstrates that Morgenthau's book was written with the help of his personal secretary and a "ghost writer," and that it was approved in detail by Robert Lansing, the American Secretary of State. Lowry argues that the authors perhaps took artistic license in recreating direct quotations from Talaat Bey, inasmuch as Morgenthau's personal notes and Diary do not have direct quotations, and that in some cases the authors merged two separate interviews with Talaat into one. We will accept the Lowry booklet as an exhibit and deal with it below, even

though he presents nothing surprising. Important political figures almost universally use secretaries and ghost writers, and administrative officials often are required to have their books approved by their responsible government agency.

38. These schools were in Istanbul, Adapazar, Bardezag, Bursa, Izmir (Smyrna), Afion Kara Hissar, Konya, Marsovan, Sivas, Cesarea, Talas, Tarsus, Adana, Hadjin, Marash, Aintab (Gaziantep), Urfa, Kharpert, Diarbakir, Mardin, Bitlis, Erzurum, and Van. See, Frank Andrews Stone, Academies for Anatolia: A Study of the Rationale, Program and Impact of the Educational Institutions Sponsored by the American Board in Turkey: 1930-1980 (New York: University Press of America, 1984), 71, for location on the map. The colleges were Central Turkey College in Aintab (1876), Euphrates College in Kharpert (1878), Central Turkey Girls' College in Marash (1882), Anatolia College at Marsovan (1886), St. Paul's Institute at Tarsus (1888) and International College at Smyrna (1891).

39. Joseph L. Grabill, *Protestant Diplomacy and the Near East: Missionary Influence on American Policy, 1810-1927* (Minneapolis: University of Minnesota Press, 1971), 10.

40. Microfilm copies of this collection, entitled "Papers of the American Board of Commissioners for Foreign Missions," have recently been made available by Research Publications of Woodbridge, Connecticut.

41. Lowry, *Story*, quoting Morgenthau, 16.

42. There are two large collections of Morgenthau papers, one housed in the Library of Congress and known as The Papers of Henry Morgenthau (which, following Lowry, we will cite as "LC:PHM"), and the other in the Franklin Delano Roosevelt Presidential Library in Hyde Park, NY, called the Henry Morgenthau Sr. Papers, and not the Henry Morgenthau, *Jr.* Papers as called by Lowry (*Story*, 7). These papers will be referred to, again following Lowry, as "FDR: HMS."

43. LC:PHM-Reel No. 5: Morgenthau 'Diary' entry for August 8, 1915, as found in Lowry, *Story*, 49-50, see *infra*.

44. Lowry, *Story*, 2. The word "Syrian" is used here by Morgenthau to refer to the semitic Christians who lived in the upper reaches of the Tigris and Euphrates Rivers. They were known more popularly as "Assyrians," to differentiate them from the Muslim Syrians of the Fertile Crescent. As noted above, the Christian Assyrians were almost completely wiped out by the Turks, a total and successful genocide.

45. Ibid., 49.

46. Christopher Walker, *Armenia: The Survival of a Nation, Revised Second Edition*, New York: St. Martin's Press, 1990), 235. See Johannes Lepsius, *Deutschland und Armenien, 1914-1918: Sammlung Diplomatischer Aktenstucke* (Potsdam, 1919), 277.

47. See, U.S. Department of State, Record Group 59, Internal Affairs of Turkey, 1910-1929 (Microfilm Publications) Microcopy 353: 88 reels, especially 867.4016/1-1011, reels 43-48.

48. R.G. [Record Group] 59:867.4016/122, Consul Davis to Morgenthau, July 11, 1915.

49. They were finally smuggled into the U.S. Embassy in Istanbul in the shoe of an American missionary.

50. R.G. 59:867.4016/269.

51. New Rochelle, New York: Aristide D. Caratzas Publisher, 1989. Hereinafter cited as Davis, *Slaughterhouse*.

52. Davis, *Slaughterhouse*, 87. The mutilations consisted mostly of the women being split open from the vagina to the belly and their gut being strewn about the ground. The killers believed that Armenian women either swallowed gold coins or hid then in their privates in order to avoid their being stolen by brigands.

53. R.G. 59:867.4016/124, Consul Nathan to Morgenthau, August 7, 1915.

54. The word "genocide" did not, of course, come into use until 1944, when it was introduced by Rafael Lemkin, so the American consuls had to use expressions such as "a general massacre" or a "method was found to destroy the Armenian race." By modern definition, the attempt to destroy a race is considered genocide.

55. R.G. 59,867.4016/76.

56. RG 59, 867.4016/299.

57. *Congressional Record. Proceedings and Debates of the Second Session of the Sixty-Sixth Congress of the United States of America*, Vol. LIX-Part 7, May 4 to May 24, 1920 (Washington: Government Printing Office, 1920), 7533-34.

58. Lord Bryce presents eyewitness testimony from Van, Bitlis, [Persian] Azerbaijan, Erzurum, Mamouret-ul Aziz [Kharpert], Trebizond, Shabin Kara-Hissar, Sivas, Caesarea, Marsovan, Angora, Istanbul, Brusa, Izmit, Konya, the area of Cilicia on the Mediterranean coast (Adana, Marash, Zeitun, Jibal Mousa [Mousa Dagh]), and Urfa. In other words, eyewitness reports from the four corners of the Ottoman Empire in Anatolia.

59. While the Kurds were used by the Turks to help carry out the Armenian genocide, the Turks were later to turn on the Kurds. The Kurdish "problem" has not yet been solved by the Turks.

60. Vahakn N. Dadrian, "The Documentation of the World War I Armenian Massacres in the Proceedings of the Turkish Military Tribunal," *International Journal of Middle East Studies*, 23 (1991), 558. In this study Dadrian used the materials from the Turkish war crimes trials organized by the government of Damad Ferit Pasha following World War I.

61. The Communist Party of the Soviet Union was finally given official status in the "Brezhnev" constitution of 1977.

62. Dadrian, "Documentation," 560.

63. Ibid., 560-63, as found in *Takvimi Vekayi.*

64. One should also add that Turkish public opinion had turned in the meanwhile from being strongly in favor of the trials to being strongly opposed to them. When the Turkish public was first made aware of the Armenian Genocide, it was scandalized for humane reasons and demanded the punishment of the offenders. But by 1920 the Greeks, Turkey's ancient and mortal enemy, had invaded Cilicia and it was becoming apparent that the Allies, excluding the United States as an Associated Power, were ready to carve up not only the Ottoman Empire but Anatolia itself. The Turks, understandably, became xenophobic and resentful of all non-Turkish peoples and foreign interference. Had the Greeks not invaded Turkey, Mustafa Kemal Atatürk himself might have continued the trials against the Young Turks inasmuch as he thought ill of the Armenian and Assyrian genocides.

65. In an interview published in the *Los Angeles Examiner* Atatürk said that the leaders of the C.U.P. "*should have been made to account for the lives of millions of our Christian subjects who were ruthlessly driven en masse from their homes and massacred* [emphasis added]." Emile Hildebrand, "Kemal Promises More Hangings of Political Antagonists in Turkey," Sunday edition, section VI, August 1, 1926.

66. Dadrian, 554, 561, 575.

67. The State Department seemed to vacillate in its position in an "Editor's Note" in the September 1982 *Bulletin*, which stated; "The articles "Armenian Terrorism: A Profile," which appeared in the feature on terrorism in the August 1982 issue of the *Bulletin*, does not necessarily reflect an official position of the Department of State, and the interpretive comments in the article are solely those of the author." It appears that the State Department finally backed out of its denial of the Armenian Genocide in its "Editor's Note" in the April 1983 *Bulletin*, which states: "The Article 'Armenian Terrorism: A Profile,' which appeared in the August 1982 issue of the *Bulletin*, and its accompanying *note* [emphasis added] and footnotes were not intended as statements of policy of the United States. Nor did they represent any change in U.S. Policy."

68. See Court Order, U.S. District Court, District of Columbia, Civil Action No. 88-3419 (RCL), dated December 18, 1990, filed December 19, 1990.

69. Below are some critical examples of the original draft text of Corsun's article immediately followed by the actual published text in the State Department *Bulletin*, as rewritten by State Department officials. The draft text was provided me by Van A. Krikorian from the documents which he obtained by his FOIA case against the State Department. The copies provided by the State Department are on file in the offices of the Armenian Assembly of America in Washington, D.C.

    Original: "Fearful of the increased boldness of the suppressed nationalities of the Empire, the Turks responded with unprecedented brutality which resulted in the killing of 300,000 Armenians from 1894 to 1896. These killings pale significantly in comparison with the full-scale attempts by the nationalistic Young Turks in 1915." (FOIA document acquired by Van Krikorian.)
    Rewritten: "In a multi ethnic state, such as the Ottoman Empire, nationalism was viewed by Turks as a serious internal threat. The result was harsher repression by the Ottoman government which led to thousands of Armenian deaths in 1895." (p. 35)

    Original: "With the advent of World War I, the stage was set for what was later to be called the first 'genocide' of the 20th century." (FOIA document acquired by Van Krikorian.)
    Rewritten: "With the advent of World War I, the stage was set for what was later *alleged* [emphasis added] to be called the first 'genocide' of the 20th century." (page 35)

70. One can only make conjectures about Turkish motives. Certainly we must allow for the possibility that the vast majority of the Turks either do not know the facts of the case or would find it embarrassing at this late date for their country to finally admit to what they have so long denied. Then some Turks claim that the Armenians want recognition of the Genocide only as a first step towards demanding monetary reparations or even, perhaps, a return of the Armenian provinces to Armenian control. A more fundamental reason is that no nation would like to admit that its very foundation is based on the crime of genocide.

The Historical Origins of the Armenian-Turkish Enmity

Michael M. Gunter

In the past decade Armenian terrorists have assassinated thirty Turkish diplomats or members of their immediate families, including four in the United States. In addition more than twenty other Turks and non-Turks have been killed, and over 300 other people around the world wounded because they happened to be in the terrorists' line of fire.[1]

When the terrorists have been apprehended, however, some Armenians have implied that they have a right to murder and should not be prosecuted. After Hampig Sassounian was found guilty of murdering Kemal Arikan, the Turkish Consul General in Los Angeles in 1982, for example, some Armenians in Boston announced: "What occurred throughout Hampig's trial was a mockery of justice, an attempt to stop the Armenian people from actively pursuing their cause. . . . We are outraged by the . . . guilty verdict." "Armenians protest misuse of judicial system," proclaimed another article in the same Armenian-American newspaper. Referring to the trial of two other Armenian terrorists, who had murdered the Turkish Ambassador to Yugoslavia in March 1983, the same publication declared: "To consider it a criminal act distorts the selfless struggles of the Armenian youth, who are pursuing the just cause of their people."[2]

What supposedly justifies this contemporary Armenian terrorism? The declared rationale is to gain revenge for Turkish massacres of Armenians during World War I and to achieve what a number of Armenian publications have summed up as the "3 R's": (1) recognition of what happened; (2) reparations; and (3) restoration of the ancestral homeland.[3]

Given the magnitude of these terrorist acts and their proffered justification, it seems appropriate to analyze objectively the historical origins of the Armenian-Turkish enmity. To do so it is necessary to study the so-called "Armenian Question" as it developed in the latter part of the nineteenth century and the deportations and massacres of Armenians which occurred during World War I. It is hoped that this process will throw some objective historical light on an important question which has all too often been the private game preserve of self-righteous apologists for one side or the other. From such an analysis, moreover, may come the understanding which will encourage those who presently support or even participate in the terrorism to terminate their involvement and enable those who are the target to take those sensible steps which may help alleviate their predicament.

THE ARMENIAN QUESTION

Into the early nineteenth century, the unique millet system of self-government for the non-Muslim minorities of the Ottoman Empire apparently satisfied the Armenian population of the Empire to the degree that they were known by the Turks as the *millet-i-Sadika*, or "loyal nation."[4] The rise of nationalism and the decline of the multinational Ottoman Empire, however, began to change this situation as the nineteenth century progressed. One by one the various Christian nations on the Ottoman frontiers in the west broke away, while in the east the Russian conquests of the Caucasus, making large numbers of Armenians subjects of the Tsar, acted as a further catalyst.

The Armenian Position.   To many Armenians, life in the decaying Ottoman Empire began to seem increasingly oppressive. According to A.O. Sarkissian, "there were four general causes of complaint: the non-acceptance of non-Mohammedan testimony in the courts; the abuses connected with the matter of taxation; oppressions and outrages committed by government officials, such as forced conversions, rapes, assaults, etc.; and oppressions and outrages committed by civilians and brigands."[5]

Non-Muslims, especially Christians, were derisively termed *gâvurs* (infidels) or *rayah* (flock) and denied equal protection of the laws. A Muslim who murdered a non-Muslim, for example, was not subject to the death penalty, while if the victim were a Muslim, capital punishment was enacted. In addition, the testimony of non-Muslims was not given the same weight in legal proceedings which also involved Muslims. As Christians, Armenians were ineligible for military service and not even allowed to bear arms, a situation filled with danger given the general breakdown of law and order in eastern Anatolia.

An unequal taxation system also burdened the Armenians.

> The Kharadj, or the head-tax, the military exemption tax, the Kishlak, or the winter-quartering tax, ... the Kurds' seemingly prescriptive right to free winter quarters in Armenian homes, ... the hospitality tax,...which meant that the Christian was bound to offer free lodging and food for three days a year to all government officials or to all those who passed as such, ... and many others were imposed and exacted from Armenians alone."[6]

Despite promised reforms, "life, property, and above all the honor of the family were always in jeopardy"[7] due to the depredations of the Kurds, Circassians, and other nomadic tribes who lived alongside the Armenians. Given this overall situation, Armenians felt "thrown outside the pale of the law."[8] As a result, some Armenians began to look to Europe as their savior and protector. Indeed, as early as the 1828-9 war between Russia and Turkey, some Ottoman Armenians supported the former, as occurred again during the Crimean War (1853-56).

The Russo-Turkish War of 1877-78 proved a major step in the development and even internationalization of the Armenian Question. Article 16 of the preliminary Treaty of San Stefano appeared to promise that Armenian reforms would be guaranteed by Russia, but the later Treaty of Berlin proffered only a watered-down Article 61 that was to be upheld by all the European powers and thus, it proved, none.

Indeed, the Armenian Question began to unfold against the backdrop of complicated European imperialist ambitions which often sought to play off the Turks and Armenians against each other. England, for example, at times tended to oppose Armenian aspirations because she feared their success would merely facilitate the Russian advance to the Mediterranean. Russia, for her part, at times sought to promote Armenian ambitions, while at other times she discouraged them, not wishing to encourage the aspirations of her own Armenian subjects. Neither, however, particularly cared when the pawns of their ambition suffered. Turks today give a great deal of weight to the influence of the European imperialists in stirring up Armenian aspirations, seeing the same sinister motives behind contemporary Armenian terrorism. Even Lord Bryce, the great friend of the Armenians, scathingly denounced the foreign intervention:

> Before the Treaty of Berlin the Sultan had no special enmity to the

Armenians, nor had the Armenian nation any political aspirations. It was the stipulations then made for their protection that first marked them out for suspicion and hatred, and that first roused in them hopes of deliverance whose expression increased the hatred of their rulers. ...[T]his is what England and Russia between them have accomplished. Better it would have been for the Christians of the East if no diplomatist had ever signed a protocol or written a despatch on their behalf.[9]

Fridtjof Nansen, the High Commissioner for Refugees in the League of Nations and also a great friend of the Armenians, expressed similar sentiments. "For the Armenians in the Turkish Empire ... it raised false hopes, and actually made things worse for them. It is the tragic truth that they would have been better off if the nations of Europe and their governments and diplomatists had never pleaded their cause at all."[10]

Conditions continued to grow worse as the newly aroused Armenians sought more, while a declining, reactionary Ottoman government offered less. Influenced by these circumstances, as well as the radical and revolutionary groups in Russia—some of them prone to violence—Armenian nationalism eventually manifested itself in the formation in 1887 of the Marxist Revolutionary Party, or Hunchaks (Bells), and in 1890 the more nationalistic *Hai Heghapokhakan Dashnaktsutiun* (Armenian Revolutionary Federation), or simply Dashnaks.

To better control his restive, eastern domains, Sultan Abdulhamid II organized a Kurdish cavalry called the *Hamidiye*. The nomadic Kurds had been the inveterate enemy of the sedentary Armenians. Deputized now as the Sultan's agents in the guise of the *Hamidiye*, the Kurds repeatedly fell upon the defenseless Armenians who, as mentioned above, were not even allowed to possess firearms legally until early in the twentieth century.

Armed conflict began in earnest when in 1894 the Hunchaks persuaded the Armenians of Sassun not to pay the extortionary, but customary, protection tax (*hafir*) to the Kurds. What the Armenians considered to be self defense, however, Abdulhamid viewed as rebellion. With brutality, he put down the insurrection in Sassun and then sat by approvingly as widespread massacres spread throughout the Armenian *vilayets* (provinces).

Unlike their fellow Christian nations in the Balkans, however, the Armenians were concentrated in the heartland of the Ottoman Empire and constituted a minority in the very land they sought as their own autonomous or even independent state.[11] In addition, the final shrinkage of the Ottoman Empire from Europe to Anatolia tended to "isolate ... the Armenians as the last of the great Christian minorities still under Ottoman rule."[12] It also helped to produce "a crucial shift from Ottoman pluralism to narrow Turkish nationalism," both of which would have "serious consequences for the Armenians."[13] For the Turks, therefore, independence for the Armenians was a logical absurdity and a threat to their very existence. As Bernard Lewis concluded: "Now a desperate struggle between them began—a struggle between two nations for the possession of a single homeland."[14] David Lang concluded that "the total death toll [of Armenians] over the years from 1894 to 1896 was not less than 200,000—some estimates put it as high as a quarter of million."[15]

The Turkish Position. Others see what occurred as a justified Turkish response to Armenian and foreign provocations. The picture they paint is very different from the one depicted by the Armenians and largely accepted in the West.

In the first place various treaties and capitulations enjoyed by the Western Christian powers enabled them to exercise a virtual protectorate over the Porte's non-Muslim subjects. Thus, the British Consul Palgrave was able to report from Trabzon in 1868 that:

> The Mahometan population is absolutely "unrepresented" at the central, irresponsible, and disseevered Government of Constantinople, where the Mahometan subjects of the Sultan have really no one to whom they can make known their interests or expose their wrongs. Meanwhile the Christians have at the capital and throughout the Empire as many Courts of Appeal and redress-demanding representatives as there are Consulates, Agencies, and, sometimes, Embassies, at hand. Indeed, not only are their complaints listened to when made, but even fabricated for them when not made.[16]

In addition, since only Muslims were permitted to serve in the Empire's armed forces, non-Muslims were able to benefit financially. The British Consul at Izmir, Charles Blunt, who spent forty years in Turkey and thus came to know the place well, explained that after the reform decree of Gulhané, issued by the Sultan in 1839,

> the Christians then came forward as cultivators; their numbers increased by new-comers, for their lives were no longer at the mercy of every petty authority; the Turkish proprietors began to fall off; population visibly decreased; their lands were no longer profitable. All Turkish proprietors have to furnish their quota for the conscription, and many, very many, of the descendants of formerly large landed proprietors, after serving their time with the army, return home to find the whole feature of their native place changed: the predominant Turkish population replaced by Christians; their heritage uncultivated lands; and if, by

chance, any of them desire to resume their former agricultural pursuits, they usually fall into the meshes of some Christian usurious banker, to whom the whole property or estate is soon sacrificed. They who return without any taste for their old pursuits, dispose of their property for what they can get, and the purchasers are either Armenians or Greeks.[17]

For the Russian ambitions to reach the Mediterranean, the Christian Armenian population was a natural fifth column to exploit. The British Consul J. G. Taylor reported from Erzurum in 1869, for example, that "it is the policy of the Russian Government, and, therefore, of its Agents ... to exaggerate real existing evils, or trump up imaginary complaints, in order to keep up that chronic dissatisfaction so suitable to the line of conduct it has always pursued in Eastern countries."[18] During each Russian invasion of the nineteenth century, Ottoman Armenians were accused of siding with the enemy. As Lord Bryce himself noted: "When foreign armies enter [the Ottoman Empire], whether it be Bulgaria or Armenia, they are welcomed as deliverers by the subject populations."[19] The commander of the invading Russian army in eastern Anatolia in 1877 was a Russian Armenian, General Mikhail Loris-Melikov. His original surname, "Melikian," had simply been Russianized.

As the Russians advanced through the Balkans towards Constantinople in 1878, the Armenian Patriarch Nerses entered into secret negotiations with them. Article 16 of the Treaty of San Stefano, which the Russians dictated to the Turks in March of that year, was the result: "The Sublime Porte engages to carry into effect, without further delay, the improvements and reforms demanded by local requirements in the provinces inhabited by Armenians."

During the same month the British Ambassador in Constantinople, A. H. Layard, reported

> that the Armenians were determined, now that self-government was about to be given to the Christian communities in Europe, to demand the same privileges for themselves in Asia. ... [I]f the Congress refused to listen to the just demands of the Armenians, they were resolved to agitate until they could obtain what they required, and if they could not succeed without foreign aid, they would place themselves completely in the hands of Russia, and even prefer annexation to her to remaining under Turkish rule.[20]

Patriarch Nerses wrote in a Memorandum to the British government that the "coexistence" of Armenians and Muslims in Turkey was "impossible." The only solution was the creation of an "autonomous Christian organization" similar to that in Lebanon.[21] An Armenian delegation headed by Archbishop Khrimian, the former Patriarch of Constantinople, pleaded its case at the capitals of the Western powers, and although it was not allowed to appear formally at the Congress of Berlin, submitted a letter to that body recommending an Armenian autonomous region in eastern Anatolia.

The outcome of this Armenian campaign was the inclusion of Article 61 in the Treaty of Berlin of July 13, 1878. This Article reiterated the commitment made by the Sublime Porte in the aforementioned Treaty of San Stefano to introduce reforms in the provinces inhabited by the Armenians and provided a pretext to allow the European imperialist powers to use the Armenians as a pawn in their power struggles in Anatolia. Many Armenian leaders were not satisfied with this treatment, arguing that while the Christian nations in the Balkans had eaten from the "dish of liberty" at Berlin, the Armenians had been denied.

The self-government which began to work for the Christian nations in the Balkans was not appropriate for the Armenians, however, because nowhere did they constitute a majority. The British Foreign Secretary, Lord Salisbury, wrote the British Ambassador in Constantinople, A. H. Layard, in August 1878, for example:

> Whatever chance of success these experiments may have, they could not be safely imitated in the Asiatic provinces of the Empire. The Mohametan races, which there constitute an enormous majority of the population, are, for the present at least, unfitted for institutions of this kind, which are alien to their traditions and their habits of thought. The Christians, to whom a representative system might perhaps be suited, are not only a small minority, but (with the exception of those in the Lebanon, who are provided for) are so scattered and intermixed with the Mahometans that any separate machinery of Government, designed for them alone, would be attended with the gravest practical difficulties.[22]

In spite of these demographic facts, the Armenians continued to bombard the foreign embassies and consulates in the Ottoman Empire with petitions which "have generally proved, on inquiry, to contain very exaggerated statements,"[23] according to the British Ambassador, Layard. Moreover, argue the Turks and their supporters, in a manner similar to what the Armenian terrorists are attempting to do today, the Hunchaks and the Dashnaks began deliberately to use terror against the Turks to incite Turkish reprisals and massacres, which would then encourage broad Armenian support for revolution and finally great power intervention. "Europeans in Turkey were agreed that the immediate aim of the [Armenian] agitators was to incite disorders, bring about inhuman reprisals, and so provoke the intervention of the powers."[24]

Indeed, this general interpretation of events has been largely verified by Louise Nalbandian who, although a confirmed Armenian patriot, wrote just before the current wave of Armenian polemical tracts began in the 1970s. Thus, Nalbandian was able to describe in a matter-of-fact way the secret Armenian revolutionary activities against the Ottoman state from 1860 on. Included in her study were references to Armenian terrorist attacks carried out in order to incite reprisals which hopefully would lead to foreign intervention, plans to strike at the Ottoman state when it was at war and to seek help from foreign governments at such favorable opportunities, Armenian publications which exaggerated Turkish atrocities, and more.[25] All in all Nalbandian's study makes it clear that the Armenians were not solely innocent victims of murderous Turks.

On August 24, 1896, for example, twenty-six Dashnaks led by a seventeen-year-old named Babken Suni seized the Ottoman Bank building in Constantinople in an unsuccessful attempt to force the Western powers to intervene on their behalf. Demands for reform were made and a threat to blow up the premises and kill its staff was issued. The terrorists were eventually talked out of the bank and evacuated to France. In reaction the Sultan ignorantly turned loose the mobs on the Armenians in the capital, and a massacre ensued. But the hoped-for European intervention did not materialize. In 1905 a Dashnak attempt on the Sultan's life failed. Kristapor Mikaelian, the leader of the conspirators, however, died when the bomb misfired.

THE DEPORTATIONS AND MASSACRES IN WORLD WAR I

World War I brought the intermittent carnage of the nineteenth century to its frightful conclusion, resulting in the extinction of Turkish Armenia in a series of deaths through disease and famine, deportations, and massacres which the Armenians and their supporters refer to as the twentieth century's first genocide. So much has been written so polemically on the subject, and its roots have become so entangled in mutual suspicions and hatreds that it is difficult to discern fact from fiction, or even where to start.

Following the Armenian terrorist attacks during the summer of 1983, for example, two different and reputable American newspapers each commissioned a three-part series on the origins of the problem. Their conclusions concerning the Armenian accusation of genocide by the Turks in 1915 were diametrically opposed. The *Wall Street Journal* series concluded that "three months of extensive research leave little doubt that a horrible crime certainly did occur. . . . Talaat and company probably did plan a genocide."[26] The *Washington Times*, however, declared that "the events of 1915 [were] distorted by fantasy into 'genocide' ... [and] are today the subject of conjecture, hype, and myth."[27]

The Armenian Position. The Armenian contention is that the Ottoman government of the Committee of Union and Progress (*Ittihat ve Terakki*) meticulously planned and then executed a systematic genocide of some one and one-half million of its Armenian citizens both by outright massacres *in situ* and by forced marches into the Syrian deserts that resulted in massacres along the way for many and ultimate death by starvation for most of the others.

Under the cover of wartime conditions and false charges of mass Armenian collaboration with the invading Russian enemy, the Turks believed that they could eliminate the Armenians who blocked their path to the east and their dreams of a greater Turan, or union of all Turkic peoples. Chief among the culprits are said to be Enver Pasha (Minister of War), Talaat Pasha (Minister of Interior), and Jemal Pasha (a military figure who held a variety of posts). Indeed, immediately after World War I, a Turkish court martial in Constantinople sentenced these three to death *in absentia*. (Subsequent Turkish governments, however, have repudiated these sentences, claiming they were handed down under duress from the allies who were then occupying Constantinople.)

"That the killings were deliberate none but dedicated Turkists deny. The horror ... was too similar in each locality for the killings to have been spontaneous manifestations,"[28] one scholar has concluded. What are alleged to be official Ottoman documents ordering the genocide have even been published by Armenian sources.[29]

Out of a plethora of pro-Armenian sources[30] two in particular are most frequently cited and stand in most damning condemnation of the Turks: (1) the Bryce-Toynbee compilation of more than 600 pages of mostly eye-witness accounts;[31] and (2) the memoirs of Henry Morgenthau, the American Ambassador to Turkey at that time.[32] In his preface, the distinguished British statesman and author, Lord James Bryce, stated that "these accounts described what seemed to be an effort to exterminate a whole nation, without distinction of age or sex."[33] The following is typical of the accounts in the Blue Book:

Harpout [Kharpert] has become the cemetery of the Armenians; from all directions they have been brought to Harpout to be buried. There they lie, and the dogs and the vultures devour their bodies. Now and then some man throws some earth over the bodies. In Harpout and Mezré the people have had to endure terrible tortures. They have had their eyebrows plucked out, their breasts cut off, their nails torn off; their torturers hew off their feet or else hammer nails into them just as they do in shoeing horses. This is all done at night time, and in order that the people may not hear their screams and know of their agony, soldiers are stationed round the prisons, beating drums and blowing whistles. It is needless to relate that many died of these tortures. When they die, the soldiers cry: "Now let your Christ help you."[34]

Ambassador Morgenthau's accounts are equally damning, as the following typical passage indicates:

It is absurd for the Turkish government to assert that it ever seriously intended to "deport the Armenians to new homes"; the treatment which was given the convoys clearly shows that extermination was the real purpose of Enver and Talaat. How many exiled to the south under these revolting conditions ever reached their destinations? The experiences of a single caravan show how completely this plan of deportation developed into one of annihilation. The details in question were furnished me directly by the American Consul at Aleppo, and are now on file in the State Department at Washington. ... All the way to Ras-ul-Ain, the first station on the Baghdad line, the existence of these wretched travellers was one prolonged horror. The gendarmes went ahead, informing the half-savage tribes of the mountains that several thousand Armenian women and girls were approaching. The Arabs and Kurds began to carry off the girls, the mountaineers fell upon them repeatedly, violating and killing the women, and the gendarmes themselves joined in the orgy. ... Finally the gendarmes, having robbed and beaten and violated and killed their charges for thirteen days, abandoned them altogether. ... For another five days they did not have a morsel of bread or a drop of water. "Hundreds fell dead on the way," the report reads, "their tongues were turned to charcoal. ... " On the seventieth day a few creatures reached Aleppo. Out of the combined convoy of 18,000 souls just 150 women and children reached their destination.[35]

Propaganda or truth? How accurate are such reports? There is no question that Lord Bryce, Arnold Toynbee, and Ambassador Morgenthau believed them. In analyzing their veracity, for example, Lord Bryce declared:

[B]y far the larger part (almost all, indeed, of what is here published) does constitute historical evidence of the best kind, inasmuch as the statements come from those who saw the events they describe and recorded them in writing immediately afterwards. They corroborate one another, the narratives given by different observers showing a substantial agreement, which becomes conclusive when we find the salient facts repeated with no more variations in detail than the various opportunities of the independent observers made natural.[36]

The Turks, however, dismiss the Bryce/Toynbee Blue Book as false wartime propaganda by their enemies (the Allies), and Morgenthau's testimony as that of a hopelessly biased and misled person. Where then lies the truth? In a later study, Professor Toynbee, although not denying the accuracy of the Blue Book, did write that it had been "duly published and distributed as war-propaganda!"[37] Based on his personal observations and studies in Anatolia after World War I, Toynbee now wrote in a more balanced light: "In the redistribution of Near and Middle Eastern Territories, the atrocities which have accompanied it from the beginning have been revealed in their true light, as crimes incidental to an abnormal process, which all parties have committed in turn, and not as the peculiar practice of one denomination or nationality."[38]   Indeed, more than a half century after he had edited the Blue Book with Bryce, Toynbee, in his final statement on the subject, declared: "These ... Armenian political aspirations had not been legitimate. . . . Their aspirations did not merely threaten to break up the Turkish Empire; they could not be fulfilled without doing grave injustice to the Turkish people itself."[39]

At the time he had compiled the Blue Book, wrote Toynbee, "I was unaware of the politics that lay behind this move of H.M.G.'s and I believe Lord Bryce was as innocent as I was. . . . [I]f our eyes had been opened, I hardly think that either Lord Bryce or I would have been able to do the job that H.M.G. had assigned to us in the complete good faith in which we did, in fact, carry it out."[40] Toynbee went on to explain that the purpose of the British government in publishing the Blue Book was to counter successful German propaganda concerning Russian barbarities against the Jews.

As for Lord Bryce's preconceptions on the subject of Armenians and Turks, his biographer, the famous historian H.A.L. Fisher, wrote that Bryce "had been ever since he voyaged in Transcaucasia in 1876, unremitting in his exertions for the relief and protection of the Armenian race."[41] Bryce "became in fact the principal advocate of the Armenian nation in England, the founder and first President of the Anglo-Armenian Society, the member for Armenia in the British House of Commons. . . . He thought them the best race in Asia Minor, superior in tenacity of will and capacity for moral and intellectual progress to their neighbors, Turks or Kurds, Tartars or Russians."[42]

As for the Turks, Bryce's "conclusion held with tenacity and passion through the whole course of his public life was the hopelessness of the Turk."[43] He believed that "wherever the Turk had ruled, he had spread desolation. The provinces of Asia Minor, once the scene of a brilliant civilization, had been emptied . . . by the lethargy, the incompetence, and the caprices of a barbarous master."[44] Indeed, Bryce himself had written that "when once the dying [Turkish] tyranny that has cursed it [the Armenian race] is dead, it may fairly hope, with its industry, frugality, and quick intelligence, to restore prosperity to countries which war and oppression have made almost a desert."[45]

Obviously Lord Bryce was hardly a disinterested compiler of the events of 1915. This however, as will be shown below, does not necessarily allow us to dismiss the Blue Book as completely false and misleading. First, however, it would be useful to examine, in his own words, Ambassador Morgenthau's preconceptions concerning the Turks.

They were, the Ambassador wrote "dull-witted and lazy."[46] He asserted: "Such abstractions as justice and decency form no part of their conception of things."[47] The author of the work so frequently cited by the Armenians and their sympathizers as definitive of their cause further opined: "Essentially the Turk is a bully and coward; he is brave as a lion when things are going his way, but cringing, abject, and nerveless when reverses are overwhelming him."[48] "We must realize," wrote Morgenthau, "that the basic fact underlying the Turkish mentality is its utter contempt for all other races. . . . The Turk may be obsequiously polite, but there is invariably an almost unconscious feeling that he is mentally shrinking from his Christian friend as something unclean."[49]

Morgenthau too, then, was hardly a disinterested observer of the Turkish-Armenian animosities. On the other hand, one should not rush to dismiss the Armenian accusations as baseless simply because Bryce and Morgenthau were confirmed Turkophobes. Prejudices notwithstanding, their testimonies, when corroborated by the wealth of eyewitness accounts cited above, as well as contemporary press accounts, indicate that several hundred thousand Armenians did die during the deportations from various causes such as sickness, starvation, and outright massacre. Certainly no one can deny that after World War I the traditional Armenian homeland in eastern Anatolia had been denuded of its Armenian population.

What is more, Toynbee himself, contrary to what the Turks and their sympathizers often would have us believe, never retracted the evidence he and Bryce presented in the Blue Book. In his final book, for example, he wrote: "After the Blue Book had been published, I could not dismiss its contents from my mind. . . . I was exercised by the question of how it could be possible for human beings to do what those perpetrators of genocide had done."[50] He declared that: "In the genocide of the Armenians the criminals had been members of the Committee of Union and Progress,"[51] stated that "the leaders of the C.U.P. had apparently degenerated from being idealists into becoming ogres,"[52] and concluded: "The Ottoman Armenian . . . deportations were deliberately conducted with a brutality that was calculated to take the maximum toll of lives *en route*. . . . My study of the genocide that had been committed in Turkey in 1915 brought home to me the reality of Original Sin."[53]

Although the Blue Book, in his own words, was "counter-propaganda ammunition," Toynbee simply meant that it was intended to arouse public opinion against the Central Powers, not that it was untrue. His own testimony made this clear: "At the very time when the Russians had been committing barbarities against their Jews, the Turks had been committing considerably worse barbarities against their Armenians. If Russian barbarities were telling against Britain and France, would not Turkish barbarities tell against Germany and Austria-Hungary? This line of reasoning in Whitehall lay behind H.M.G.'s application to Lord Bryce to produce a Blue Book on what the Turks had been doing to the Armenians."[54]

In a letter written on March 16, 1966, Toynbee similarly stated that: "It is true the British Government's motive in asking Lord Bryce to compile the Blue Book was propaganda. But Lord Bryce's motive in undertaking it, and mine in working on it for him, was to make the truth known, and the evidence was good: the witnesses were all American missionaries with no political axes to grind. So the Blue Book, together with Lepsius's book, does give a true account."[55]

Therefore, the Turkish assertion that "the Blue Book, this so-called document, contains nothing more than one-sided British propaganda, and hence is not worth dwelling upon"[56] is not warranted. Both it and the Morgenthau volume contain strong and valuable evidence of Turkish atrocities against the Armenians. On the other hand, the above analysis also indicates that both Bryce and Morgenthau held powerful and deep-rooted prejudices against the Turks which undoubtedly prevented them from seeing the entire situation. Although the Armenians did indeed suffer grievously, so too did their antagonists. It is to the Turkish position then that I must now turn before making any further attempt at arriving at a tentative synthesis.

The Turkish Position. The Turks deny that they committed genocide, arguing that the Armenian claims are a "vindictive propaganda campaign against modern Turkey ... [and] contain gross distortions and omissions of historical facts."[57] Rather, it is maintained that certain Armenians betrayed their country (the Ottoman Empire) during wartime by joining the invading Russian armies and carrying out guerrilla activities behind the Turkish lines. "Within a few months after the war began, these Armenian guerrilla forces, operating in close coordination with the Russians, were savagely attacking Turkish cities, towns and villages in the East, massacring their inhabitants without mercy, while at the same time working to sabotage the Ottoman Army's war effort by destroying roads and bridges, raiding caravans, and doing whatever else they could to ease the Russian occupation."[58]

Indeed, declare the Turks, even before the war began, Armenian groups were equipped and armed in Russia and then infiltrated across the border. Once the war started, Armenians served as guides and auxiliaries for the invading Russians. (Such units had aided the Russians in the three Russo-Turkish wars of the nineteenth century.[59]) The most famous—or infamous, depending on one's interpretation—Armenian leaders were Andranik, Dro, and Armen Garo, the latter a member of the Ottoman parliament who had joined the Armenian volunteers serving under the Russian Army upon the outbreak of the hostilities. An Armenian critic of the Dashnaks has written that: "Many Armenians believe that the fate of two million of their co-nationals in Turkey might not have proved so disastrous, if more prudence had been used by the Dashnak leaders during the war."[60]

As soon as hostilities commenced, an Ottoman document stated, "the Russians have established guerillas by arming Russian and Turkish Armenians in the Caucasus and Greeks, and anticipate expanding these guerilla organizations by sending them into Turkish land. These reports are gradually being confirmed, and realized, and Armenian deserters from military units are increasing."[61] Another document warned that "the enemy is seizing the weapons from local people in places which it has occupied, using these weapons to arm Armenians and form units."[62] A coded message to the Ministry of Defense described how "a group of 40-50 Armenian army deserters with arms at Sironik village, 2.5 hours from Mush, attacked the gendarmerie cavalrymen and police who went to the village to capture them. The clash lasted for two hours."[63] Still another message stated: "It was reported from the Province of Van yesterday that Armenians attacked several Islamic villages belonging to the afore-mentioned district on 22 March 1915; that the inhabitants of the villages initially resisted the bandits; the rebels could not hold out against the militia and gendarmerie detachments who came to help the villagers ... and that the bandits were armed with Russian rifles, small and large calibre rifles, and automatic guns."[64]

The Turks argue that as the Russian armies advanced into eastern Anatolia, they disarmed the Muslims and armed their Armenian allies who then proceeded to commit outrages against the helpless Muslim population. Behind the Turkish lines, Armenian gangs carried out acts of sabotage, staged ambushes, and attacked security posts. Armenian revolts broke out in the regions of Van, Sivas, and Marash.[65] Another pertinent document concerning events in 1915 further illustrates the Turkish position.

> Armenian gangs ... resorted to every inhuman act and atrocity toward the Moslem villages, burning the villages to the ground, murdering the people. Armenian enlisted men in the Turkish army were taking this opportunity to flee to the Russian Army with their weapons. Officers and doctors, were also joining the Russian Army, taking with them much information about the Turkish army. It was observed on many occasions that in the most critical moments of the battle, positions of ammunition, batteries or the reserve positions were shown to the Russians. In this context, Kirkor, son of Ohannes from Gumushane, was seen showing the Pazacur position to the Russians. He confessed his crime at a court-martial. Again during the most critical moments of the battle, some Armenian enlisted men were inciting Turkish enlisted men to flee, creating confusion in the battle lines. Armenian people behind the lines, did not hesitate to murder wounded soldiers who were sent back for treatment. Further, they had constant communication with Armenians in the Russian Army, informing them of the position and state of the Turkish units, and deciding their stand and position accordingly.[66]

The Ottoman government had to secure its position by removing the Armenians from strategic points where they could assist the enemy,"[67] another Turkish source states. However, "great care was taken by the Ottoman government to prevent the Armenians from being harmed during these deportations." Since "the deportations took place at a time of severe shortages of vehicles, food, fuel, clothing, and other supplies in the entire Empire ... some 100,000 Armenians ... may have died between 1915 and 1918, but this was no greater a percentage than that of the Turks and other Muslims who died as a result of the same conditions in the same places at the same time." Indeed, "far from encouraging the massacres that did take place as a result, the Ottoman Interior Minister Talaat Pasha sent repeated orders that all measures be taken to uncover and punish such acts." After the war, the British did detain several hundred Ottoman officials suspected of war crimes, but despite "large-scale searches . . . undertaken in the Ottoman archives to find proof of guilt . . . no evidence . . . was found to substantiate the accusations." In conclusion, argue the Turks: "There was no genocide committed against the Armenians in the Ottoman Empire before or during World War I."[68]

Indeed, the Turks recite atrocity stories equal to the most terrible told by the Armenians. The following testimony of Russian Lieutenant Colonel Toverdohleyov will suffice to illustrate the point.

> The killings were organized by the doctors and the employers, and the act of killing was committed solely by the Armenian renegades. . . . More than eight hundred unarmed and defenseless Turks have been killed in Erzincan. Large holes were dug and the defenseless Turks were slaughtered like animals next to the holes. Later, the murdered Turks were thrown into the holes. The Armenian who stood near the hole would say when the hole was filled with the corpses: "Seventy dead bodies, well, this hole can take ten more." Thus ten more Turks would be cut into pieces, thrown into the hole, and when the hole was full it would be covered over with soil.
>   The Armenians answered all the claims of infamy and rebukes for the murderings of Turks as follows: "Did not the Turks do the same thing to destroy the Armenians? Our deeds are nothing but the revenge for what took place in the past."[69]

Many more such stories could be recited.[70] Indeed, according to the mother of the Turkish Vice Consul, Bahadir Demir, who was murdered by an Armenian in Los Angeles in 1973, the Armenian cruelties are so ingrained in the Turkish mind that a Turkish expression for cruelty or injustice is "*Ermeni gibi*," or "like an Armenian."[71] The point, therefore, has been made. Both the Armenians and the Turks suffered horribly at each other's hands. Neither had a monopoly on total innocence or evil. Both, however, continue to maintain grossly exaggerated positions highly favorable to themselves and react negatively to contrary suggestions with vehement self-righteousness.

Synthesis? Can these two diametrically opposed interpretations be reconciled? Given the understandable passions they still evoke and the ossification of positions that has occurred, it will be very difficult. Gwynne Dyer, for example, concluded that most Turkish and Armenian scholars are unable to be objective on this issue and described the situation as one of "Turkish falsifiers and Armenian deceivers."[72]

The disparity in the number of Armenians killed during 1915 is only one example. As cited above, the Turks would have us believe that only "some 100,000 Armenians may have died," while the figure of 1,500,000 is the one most frequently cited by the Armenians. Both are probably gross exaggerations. After a careful study and necessary adjustment of Ottoman census statistics, plus a consideration of the number of Ottoman Armenians who safely reached exile, Justin McCarthy has concluded that approximately 600,000, or 40 percent of the Ottoman Armenians, perished due to starvation, disease, and outright murder.[73] Given the quality of McCarthy's work compared to other estimates, his figure is probably the most accurate accounting we have.

A recent Turkish analysis ludicrously claimed that the "documents show Armenians were almost treated like tourists during deportation."[74] Another Turkish publication declared that: "Strict instructions were issued to ensure that the sick should be attended to by a physician once a day; and that the evacuee properties should be kept in careful custody so that the owners could take possession upon their eventual return to their homes at the end of the war."[75]

When reading such statements, one is reminded of the distinction between the real and the pretend Ottoman Empire made by Sir Charles Eliot.

> If one takes as a basis the laws, statistics and budgets as printed it is easy to prove that the Ottoman empire is in a state of unexampled prosperity. Life and property are secure; perfect liberty and toleration are enjoyed by all; taxation is light, balances large, trade flourishing. Those who have not an extensive personal acquaintance with Turkey may regard such accounts with suspicion and think them highly colored, but they find it difficult to realize that all this official literature is absolute fiction, and for practical purposes unworthy of a moment's attention.[76]

Richard G. Hovannisian has commented: "The Ottoman archival material showing official plans for a humane deportation proves nothing . . . because the Committee for Union and Progress had a parallel party structure enabling it to telegraph secret orders for the genocide." He further argued that "the Turks and their supporters will go through the American . . . [and] the British archives for documents that support their position, and they will lift these and publish them and ignore 900 that have said the direct opposite."[77]

The Turkish government has further maintained that "the territory in which the Armenians lived together for a time never was ruled by them as an independent sovereign state."[78] The fact of the matter is, of course, that the Armenians lived in their historic homeland "for a time" that lasted more than 2500 years until they were virtually eliminated during the tragic events of World War I. Furthermore, although the Armenians spent much of their history as a buffer or subjected nation, it is simply not true that the territory in which they lived "never was ruled by them as an independent, sovereign state." In the course of a 2,500-year history, independent Armenian states existed in one form or another for several hundred years, ranging in size from the Armenian empire of Tigranes the Great (94-55c. B.C.) through the eras of the Arsacids (53-429 A.D.), the Bagratids of Ani (886-1045 A.D.), and the Artsruni principality of Van in the ninth century, among others. Even after the arrival of the Turks, a new (Cilician) Armenia lasted for nearly three centuries (1080-1375). Indeed, under the provisions of the Treaty of Sevres, Turkey itself initially recognized the short-lived Armenian Republic (1918-1921) immediately after World War I.

Certainly Turkish studies of the situation which describe Armenians as "robbers, deceivers and fools, . . . professional beggars, thieves and liars, . . . utterly debased, incapable of helping themselves, unwilling to help one another, and entirely lacking in gratitude,"[79] or claims that "Armenians, even if they are women, are the vilest and the wildest of people,"[80] are the product of passionately partisan polemics, not reasoned historical analyses. Finally, it should be noted that whether the Turkish atrocity stories about Armenian outrages at the end of World War I and afterwards are true or not, they are irrelevant to the accusation of genocide in 1915 because they occurred subsequently in time. (Such Armenian outrages against the Turks, however, would constitute the revenge Armenians apparently feel necessary for 1915 and, therefore, would obviate the need for further revenge in the form of contemporary terrorism.)

On the other hand, Armenian publications which explain how "out of the East came a foe unequalled in his barbarity—the slit-eyed, bow-legged Turkic nomads. . . . The Seljuks and Ottomans with their ferocious customs were determined to annihilate the whole Armenian race,"[81] or vilify "the Mongol Turk terroristic state which acquired Armenia's ancient land by genocide"[82] similarly fail to master the requirements of historical accuracy. Such racist slanders stereotype an entire nation who even at its worse has usually been respected by its most bitter foes as tough, but honorable. The grudging respect the West granted Mustafa Kemal (Ataturk) during the famous Gallipoli campaign in 1915 is an example.

What is more, Armenians diatribes against the Turks totally ignore the fact that under Ottoman rule Armenians lived peacefully and prosperously for hundreds of years and that for much of its history the Ottoman Empire itself was a haven for Europe's persecuted minorities such as the Jews.[83] The so-called "Mongol Turk terroristic state" allowed the Armenians and other Christian minorities to exist and even flourish for hundreds of years within a multinational empire. Even today the fact that there is a Greek Christian *majority* on the island of Cyprus, which the Ottomans ruled for 300 years until 1878, illustrates the racial and religious tolerance manifested by the Ottomans throughout most of their history. What, however, happened to the Muslims in Spain once the Christians reconquered the peninsula? Or for that matter, what happened to the large Muslim minorities that inhabited the Balkans into the nineteenth century?[84] When we ponder such questions it is not always clear who was "determined to annihilate" whom.

Several years ago the *International Journal of Middle East Studies* published a rare and interesting exchange between Professors Richard G. Hovannisian and Stanford J. Shaw concerning the Armenian question.[85] Hovannisian, the Armenian protagonist, concluded that the publication of Shaw's two-volume *History of the Ottoman Empire* in 1977 "by a highly reputable press causes deep consternation" and was "a disservice to scholarship in general and to the study of Armenian-Turkish relations in particular."[86] Shaw, for his part, wrote: "It is unfortunate that in presenting his view Dr. Hovannisian argues more like a prosecuting attorney seeking to denigrate or suppress information unfavorable to his position than a historian dealing with particular issues within an academic context."[87]

Christopher J. Walker, the author of a study sympathetic to the Armenian position (*Armenia: The Survival of a Nation*, 1980) denounced Shaw's work "as worthless as history as a document one is handed on a street corner during a demonstration,"[88] but saved even greater invective for an analysis by Norman Ravitch. Walker found Ravitch's study to be "a most insidious and degenerate form of historical writing" which "ends up with the idiotic, ignorant and illogical conclusion that the terrible events ... should be blamed on nationalism."[89] Ravitch had concluded that "the events of 1915 remain difficult to interpret and to resolve. ... It is, in the last analysis, unprofitable to seek to decide whether the Armenian desire for freedom was the cause or the result of Turkish repression. It was probably both."[90]

In August 1982, the *U.S. Department of State Bulletin* published an article on Armenian terrorism. At the end of it, a footnote stated: "Because the historical record of the 1915 events in Asia Minor is ambiguous, the Department of State does not endorse allegations that the Turkish government committed a genocide against the Armenian people."[91] Outraged protests from Armenian Americans, however, later forced the State Department partially to recant this statement by noting that it was "not intended as statements of policy of the United States." Ambiguously, the new statement added: "Nor did they represent any change in U.S. policy."[92] This partial State Department recantation was reminiscent of the power of the so-called "Greek lobby" in forcing a U.S. arms embargo against Turkey in the U.S. Congress after Turkey successfully occupied northern Cyprus in 1974.

Where then lies the truth in this ancient and bitter dispute? Is it even possible to locate it after all these years and so many previous attempts? While recognizing the inherent difficulties, even impossibilities, here, I feel that I have an obligation to offer, at least, my tentative judgments. Admittedly I have not experienced these events firsthand, as have the Turks and Armenians. Precisely because I am removed from the immediate passions which would have thus arisen, however, I hopefully can view what happened with a more dispassionate and, therefore, accurate perspective. Without claiming a monopoly of definitive wisdom, based on the above, I see the truth to lie somewhere between the diametrically opposed positions of the two antagonists.

First of all, there is no doubt the Armenians suffered a great wrong. No matter what the Turkish apologists argue, the fact remains that an entire nation of people virtually ceased to exist in their ancient homeland after World War I. Although the numbers of Armenians who died at this time are greatly exaggerated by the Armenians—and in addition many of the Armenians who were killed during this era died because the Armenians waged war against practically every nation they were physically able to come in contact with including not only the Turks, but also the Russians, Georgians, and Azerbaijanis—there is still no doubt that several hundred thousand Armenians perished during 1915. That even more Turks also died during World War I is both true, but largely irrelevant to the argument here, because most of the many Turkish deaths resulted from the hostilities against the Allies, not the Armenians. Gallipoli, the Russian invasion in the East, and the English-Arab drive from the South were the main arenas in which the Turks died, and the fate of the Ottoman Empire was decided. Seen from the Turkish viewpoint, then, the great Armenian national catastrophe was but an unpleasant sideshow which would have been long forgotten if it were not for the contemporary Armenian terrorism.

The Armenian claim that they were victims of a *premeditated and unprovoked genocide* does not ring entirely true, however. Rather, what appears more likely is that there was an honest, but inaccurate belief among the Turkish leaders that they were faced with a widespread and coordinated Armenian uprising from within at the very time that their state was in mortal danger from without. Decades of what the Turks saw as Armenian provocations and even treason during previous wars, armed revolutionary activity between the wars, the creation of Russian-Armenian guerrilla groups in the invading Russian army during the present one, the defection of certain Ottoman Armenians to the enemy, the armed resistance to conscription on the part of Armenians in Zeitun, incidents of revolutionary acts and sabotage in the countryside, and the Armenian uprising in Van in reaction to the unpardonable but probably unofficial policies of the local governor, Jevdet Bey—all led the Turks to conclude they were in real danger from a fifth column. (Similarly, a much better organized United States government unjustly interned its citizens of Japanese descent at the start of World War II.)

Indicative of the Turkish confusion here is a report at the start of the war in 1914 that "the Russians have provoked Armenians living in our country by promises that they will be granted independence in territories to be annexed from Ottoman land ... that they have stored arms and ammunition in many places to be distributed to Armenians and moreover, the ... Russian General Loris-Melikov went to the Van region for the same purpose."[93] Turkish fear of the famous Russian-Armenian commander in the war of 1877-78 is understandable but misplaced, since Loris-Melikov had been dead since 1888.

In addition, of course, the Ottoman Empire in 1915 was a badly decaying institution nearing the end of its long existence. In the throes of fighting a losing war, it was pushed beyond its capacities and lost control of the situation. Much of the gendarmerie who implemented the deportation orders, for example, was simply a poorly trained substitute for the original force which was now enrolled in the regular army. Indeed, some of these replacements were probably nothing more than brigands themselves. Discipline among them was certainly lax. Furthermore, under such widespread conditions of wartime disorganization, the nomadic Kurds were able to attack the deportation columns with relative impunity or even connivance on the part of the gendarmerie. An unpopular minority whom the Muslim majority considered traitors, the Armenians received little sympathy from the local population which itself was suffering grievously from the wartime conditions. Given such circumstances then, it is understandable how the deportations led to widespread massacres, disease, and starvation, all of which together cost the lives of several hundred thousands of Armenians.

Certainly, it should be clear from the above analysis that there have been two sides to the question. It behooves us, therefore, to find a genuinely just solution, not one that will simply breed further hatred and violence.

TOWARDS A JUST SOLUTION

If any minority on earth could legally claim a portion of some other state's territory, every single state on earth would be dismembered. Furthermore, while admittedly a less than perfect solution, sovereignty and independence in the form of statehood for any geographical area can be granted only to the majority, because to do so for a minority would deny the democratic ideal of majority rule. That even the Armenian apologists recognize this cardinal point is illustrated in their arguments on behalf of the Greek Cypriot majority in Cyprus against the rights of the Turkish Cypriot minority.[94] Thus, Armenian attempts to give a superficial international legal gloss to their demands for eastern Turkey[95] fail egregiously to negate the fact that to create an independent Armenia out of a portion of Turkey in an area where today virtually no Armenians live would totally violate the international legal doctrines of the territorial integrity of states and self-determination of peoples. On the other hand, for one nation to brutally wipe out the native population of a portion of its territory and then to claim that the native people have no rights in the area because they no longer live there marks the height of hypocrisy and makes a mockery of international justice.

What is generally not known is that, even before 1915, the Armenians were a minority in the very land they called Armenia. Turkish apologists stress this as an extremely important point which, when fully established, reduces even further the legitimacy of any Armenian claim to an independent Armenia in eastern Anatolia.

Justin McCarthy has made a careful analysis of the official Ottoman census, incorporating into it the necessary adjustments to correct for undercounting and other problems. His work is clearly the best available on the subject and merits the close attention of any serious, disinterested scholar. What patently emerges from his study is that in 1911-1912 the Armenians constituted a minority in the six vilayets of what was historic Armenia.[96] As McCarthy concludes: "One fact is obvious . . . all Anatolian provinces had overwhelming Muslim majorities, not simply pluralities. . . . In the centuries of Turkish rule Asia Minor had become thoroughly Islamicized."[97] What McCarthy and other pro-Turkish writers fail to mention, however, is the fact that, because of the large Kurdish population, the Turkish population was also a minority in the Eastern Provinces at the time. By not distinguishing the Kurdish population from the Turkish, and by lumping the two together as "Muslims," McCarthy ignores the complexity of the population in an area that was home to Armenians, Kurds, and Turks.[98]

The Armenian claim to eastern Anatolia is a glaring anachronism. For more than sixty years now practically none of them have lived there. Some twelve million Muslims do, however, and their right to do so has been internationally recognized since 1923 by the Treaty of Lausanne. If at this late date the Armenians were to be granted legal possession to the territory, the Cherokee Indians might as well be allowed to assume sovereignty in middle Tennessee, the English in northwestern France, or for that matter the Turks in the Balkans from which they were evicted in the nineteenth century.

It is clear, therefore, that at this late date the Armenians have no clear international legal claim to eastern Anatolia. Nevertheless, as a stateless people who suffered a wrong which has never been rectified, it behooves us to search for a possible solution to the current impasse.

In a thoughtful essay on just this question,[99] Richard Hovannisian pointed out that "there are various gradations in the . . . Armenian desiderata." Demands for financial and territorial recompense would be regarded by many as "maximalist." "Through discussion and compromise . . . intermediate positions" could be reached. However, "the one demand that is heard universally by Armenians of all walks of life and at all stages of acculturation is for an admission of wrong-doing" by Turkey. Such action would extend "recognition and dignity to the hundreds of thousands of victims whose very memory the Turkish authorities and the rationalizing revisionists would eliminate."

Professor Hovannisian's implication is that by doing this, Turkey would satisfy the vast majority of moderate, law-abiding Armenians around the world who would then disown and isolate the small group of hard-core terrorists. It also would initiate a "dialogue" through which an "ultimate resolution might be achieved."

In making this suggestion, Hovannisian pointed out that "it is not a step without serious risks and it requires enormous courage." Recognizing that the Turks are possessed of just such courage, however, Hovannisian then declared: "The Turkish government should be encouraged by its friends and allies to take the necessary first step toward the initiation of dialogue."

I too concur with this recommendation because not only do the Turks possess ample amounts of courage, but, as by far the stronger party to this ancient feud, they also are precisely the ones best situated to manifest magnanimity towards their antagonist. Certainly, an official statement that the Turkish government deeply regrets the tragedies suffered by the Armenians during World War I could be made without doing harm to the Turkish contention that they too suffered grievously during these years. In addition, since such a declaration would be made from a position of magnanimous strength, it could in no way be interpreted as giving in to terrorism.

Further dialogue should involve a more honest examination of the historical relationship between the two peoples on the part of each. Such an analysis hopefully would reveal the more positive sides of their past historical association, while admitting candidly the transgressions each had committed against the other. In time, foreign Armenian visits to Turkey, which already occur without publicity, might increase. This not only could further a positive dialogue, but promote the Turkish tourist business. Eventually, it is conceivable that the inherent Armenian genius for business ventures might be channeled into certain Turkish investments with mutual benefits for both parties. Indeed, the possibilities are endless for two long-separated, but still interrelated peoples who finally have buried their ancient feud.

That my above suggestion does not represent an impossibility is made clear by a number of statements that already have been made by both parties. Thus, numerous Armenians have repeatedly stated that if only the present-day Turkish government would admit that the Armenians suffered unfairly, the past could be put aside and the contemporary Armenian terrorists isolated. "We Armenians only request that the Turkish government admit to the atrocities committed circa World War I,"[100] wrote one in the United States. "I would like to forget and forgive, provided Turkey acknowledges that some

'Young Turks' and Ottomans wronged my people,"[101] stated another. New Jersey State Assemblyman Charles (Garabed) Haytaian added: "To this day, the fact that the Turkish government is not admitting that those things happened truly upsets many Armenians. What I would like to see is the Turkish nation say, 'Look we admit that these atrocities occurred. We are sorry.'"[102]

In an important interview with a Turkish correspondent, Charles (Chip) Pashayan, the former Armenian-American member of the U.S. House of Representatives, also agreed:

> I feel that Turkey must, sooner or latter, realize that by recognizing her guilt, she will reveal her greatness. If Turkey undertakes such a change in its position, the matter will largely end. . . . The majority of the Armenian people is willing to accept such a solution. . . . Then there will remain no ground for the terrorists to continue their activities. . . . I can assure you that once that happens, wounds of the past will heal in no time, and the issue would resolve itself once and for all.[103]

Regarding financial restitutions and the creation of an independent Armenian state on Turkish territory—two points which are unacceptable to the Turks but which they feel would inevitably arise once Turkey began to change her position—Representative Pashayan was also reasonable. (1) Financial claims "can simply by symbolic in nature. It would not become a heavy burden for the Turkish government." (2) An independent Armenian state in present-day Turkey is "simply a dream," although "most Armenians have such a dream."

For their part, a number of individual Turkish scholars have privately told me that they, as Turks, would be willing to admit that Armenians were massacred and that they regret what happened. Indeed, a Turkish group acknowledged wrongdoing by telling the King-Crane Commission shortly after World War I "that those who had been guilty of the massacres should be punished."[104]

In an amazing volume that has the ring of truth to it, the remnant of the Ottoman government itself, shortly after World War I, described what happened as "the immense wrong done to the Armenian people," but claimed "extenuating circumstances."[105] "The Turks massacred and murdered Armenians, plundered and devastated their homes. Yes. But did not the Armenians massacre and murder Turks, plunder and devastate their homes, and were they not the first to start the sinister game?"[106]

Putting aside for the moment the assignment of the guilt for first causes, the willingness of the Turks to admit their share of the blame, at least, is commendable. Magnanimous is the declaration that: "the

Turkish people bows its head. It does so in grief for the Armenian people and in shame for itself."[107]

In succeeding years, of course, the new Turkish governments have disavowed such admissions on the grounds of Allied coercion. That such statements were not made by quislings or extracted forcibly by the victorious Allies becomes clear, however, as one reads through the volume cited above. For the most part, it is a hard-hitting condemnatory analysis of the Armenian "Committees" who "in their feud with Turkey . . . raised falsehood and fraud to the rank of a science and art."[108] Indeed, the accusations it made against Armenian treachery in World War I could come right out of a standard, contemporary Turkish government publication. This Turkish volume, then, might bear careful analysis in the attempt to synthesize the conflicting Turkish and Armenian interpretations of what occurred and thus help lead to an eventual resolution of the current impasse.

As stated above, therefore, I would agree with the recent proposal by Professor Vazken L. Parsegian of Troy Hills, New York "to renounce violence in all its forms between the Turkish and Armenian versions of the events of World War I through a cooperative restudy of these events."[109] For such a study to be carried out successfully, however, "the effort must be of academic quality and objectivity, by a team of respected Turkish, Armenian and neutral historians." These scholars "would need the guidance . . . of respected international leaders," access "to national archives" and "funding . . . through an educational organization." Their work should be supplemented by meetings and studies between other Turkish and Armenian "cultural and academic groups." However, "the study cannot and must not attempt to propose solutions to the political issues." Still, such a "study, properly conducted and made available both to Armenian and Turkish readers and to the world at large can improve the historical perspective of both peoples."

On the basis of such a joint study as advocated above, the Turks may in time find it possible to surrender their position of beleaguered innocence and admit that things got terribly out of hand in 1915, causing the unjustified deaths of hundreds of thousands of Armenians. The Armenians, on the other hand, may be able to bury their hoary image of the Turks as inhuman perpetrators of genocide and see their own actions leading up to and into 1915 as at times provocative and thus, themselves, as something less than wholly innocent victims.

The Armenians and Turks were able to live in peace together for hundreds of years in the past. Even today they share many common cultural attributes. Turks, for example, have expressed to me an obvious pleasure with the fact Armenians can often speak the difficult Turkish language with them. The fact that some 60,000 Armenians live peacefully and in many case quite prosperously in Turkey today—at least if the Turkish Armenians as distinguished from others are to be believed—also indicates that Turks and Armenians can live in peace.

Whether such positive steps as these can be achieved remains to be seen. Certainly, however, there is a need for both sides to reach out beyond the present sterile diatribes. As Enver Ziya Karal, a Turkish history professor, has written: "We cannot forget those who have fallen dead both from the ranks of the Armenians and the Turks. ... [W]e should reverently bow before their memory and wish for the reinstatement and continuance of the old ties of friendship between the Turks and the Armenians."[110] If the memory of those who have suffered and died so horribly is indeed to be honored, what better way than that these hallowed dead shall have sown the seeds for a future reconciliation that would allow their children to live in mutual peace, instead of reenacting their tragic past?

REFERENCES

1. For analysis of the major Armenian terrorist groups, see my two studies: *"Pursuing the Just Cause of Their People": A Study of Contemporary Armenian Terrorism* (Westport: Greenwood Press, 1986); and *Transnational Armenian Activism*, Conflict Study No. 229 (London: Research Institute for the Study of Conflict and Terrorism, 1990). Since this paper was first written, Armenian terrorism against Turkish diplomats has ceased. The current struggle over Karabagh (Artsakh) between the newly independent states of Armenia and Azerbaijan has pushed the debate over the Armenian massacres in World War I to the background.

2. Cited in *The Armenian Weekly* (January 14, 1984), 1, 6, 7.

3. See, for example, *The Armenian Weekly* (December 10, 1983), 3.

4. On this point, see Bernard Lewis, *The Emergence of Modern Turkey* (London: Oxford University Press, 1968), 356; and Avedis K. Sanjian, *The Armenian Communities in Syria Under Ottoman Dominion* (Cambridge: Harvard University Press, 1965), 274.

5. A. O. Sarkissian, *History of the Armenian Question to 1885* (Urbana: The University of Illinois Press, 1938), 37. Sarkissian based his study on *The Records of the National Assembly* (in Armenian), which from 1860 to 1914 was "the principal Armenian deliberative body" in the Ottoman Empire. "In some 30 quarto volumes these constitute a true mine of information on Armenian affairs in Turkey." Ibid., 36n.

6. Ibid., 33-34.

7. Ibid., 33.

8. Ibid., 18.

9. James Bryce, *Transcaucasia and Ararat* (London: Macmillan and Co. Ltd., 1896), 523-24.

10. Fridtjof Nansen, *Armenia and the Near East* (New York: Daffield & Company, 1928), 283.

11. On this very important point, see Justin McCarthy, *Muslims and Minorities: The Population of Ottoman Anatolia and the End of the Empire* (New York and London: New York University Press, 1983), 46-88, 109-16, 121-30, and especially the summary tables on 110-12. For a different interpretation of the population data, see Levon Marashlian, "Population Statistics on Ottoman Armenians in the Context of Turkish Historiography," *Armenian Review* 40 (Winter 1987), 1-59.

12. Robert Melson, "Provocation or Nationalism: A Critical Inquiry into the Armenian Genocide of 1915," (paper presented at the 17th Annual Meeting of the Middle East Studies Association, Chicago, Illinois, Nov. 4, 1983), 18.

13. Ibid.

14. Lewis, *Emergence of Modern Turkey*, 356.

15. David Lang, *The Armenians: A People in Exile* (London: George Allen & Unwin, 1981), 10.

16. Bilal N. Simsir, ed., *British Documents on Ottoman Armenians. Volume I (1856-1880)* (Ankara: Turk Tarih Kurumu Basimevi, 1982), 52.

17. Ibid., 16.

18. Ibid., 65.

19. Bryce, *Transcaucasia and Ararat*, 425.

20. Simsir, *British Documents*, 161-62.

21. Ibid., xviii.

22. Ibid., 191.

23. Ibid., 267.

24. William Langer, *The Diplomacy of Imperialism, 1890-1902* (Boston: Knopf, 1951), 157. Similarly, see William Laqueur, *Terrorism* (Boston & Toronto: Little, Brown and Company, 1977), 44.

25. Louise Nalbandian, *The Armenian Revolutionary Movement: The Development of Armenian Political Parties through the Nineteenth Century* (Berkeley and Los Angeles: University of California Press, 1963), especially 97-99, 109-12, 119, 127-28, and 168.

26. James Ring Adams, "Facing Up to an Armenian Genocide," *Wall Street Journal* (August 12, 1983), 20.

27. Russell Warren Howe, "Exaggeration of a Tragic Past Provides Rationale for Terrorism," *Washington Times* (August 2, 1983), 7A.

28. Christopher Walker, *Armenia: The Survival of a Nation* (New York: St. Martin's Press, 1980), 201.

29. See Aram Andonian, ed., *The Memoirs of Naim Bey: Turkish Official Documents Relating to the Deportations and Massacres of Armenians* (London, 1920, reprinted, Newtown Square, Pa.: Armenian Historical Research Association, 1964). The Turks claim that these documents are obvious forgeries. See Sinasi: Orel and Süreyya Yuca, *The Talaat Pasha Telegrams: Historical Fact or Armenian Fiction?* (Nicosia: K. Rustem and Bro., 1986). For a defense of the authenticity of the telegrams see Vahakn D. Dadrian, "The Naim-Andonian Documents on the World War I Destruction of Ottoman Armenians: The Anatomy of a Genocide," *International Journal of Middle Eastern Studies*, 18 (August 1986), 311-60. For a critique of Dadrian's position see "Gunter Response to Dadrian Article," *International Journal of Middle Eastern Studies*, 19 (November 1987), 523-24.

30. For a listing of sources, see Richard G. Hovannisian, *The Armenian Holocaust: A Bibliography Relating to the Deportations, Massacres, and Dispersion of the Armenian People, 1915-1923* (Cambridge, Mass.: Armenian Heritage Press, 1978). See also Vahakn N. Dadrian, "Genocide as a Problem of National and International Law: The World War I Armenian Case and Its Contemporary Legal Ramifications," *Yale Journal of International Law*, 14 (Summer 1989), 221-334.

31. *The Treatment of Armenians in the Ottoman Empire 1915-16*, Great Britain, Parliamentary Papers Miscellaneous no. 31 (London: Joseph Cavston, 1916).

32. Henry Morgenthau, *Ambassador Morgenthau's Story* (Garden City and New York: Doubleday, Page, 1919). Morgenthau also published virtually the same account as *Secrets of the Bosphorus* (London: Hutchinson & Co., 1918).

33. *Treatment of Armenians*, xxi.

34. Ibid., 90 (German eyewitness).

35. *Ambassador Morgenthau's Story*, 318-21.

36. *Treatment of Armenians*, xxvii.

37. Arnold J. Toynbee, *The Western Question in Greece and Turkey: A Study in the Contact of Civilizations* (Boston and New York: Houghton Mifflin, 1922), 50.

38. Ibid., vii-viii.

39. Arnold J. Toynbee, *Acquaintances* (London: Oxford University Press, 1967), 241.

40. Ibid., 149.

41. H.A.L. Fisher, *James Bryce*, Vol. II (New York: The Macmillan Company, 1927), 143.

42. Ibid., 183-84.

43. Ibid., 181.

44. Ibid.

45. Bryce, *Transcaucasia and Ararat*, 345.

46. *Ambassador Morgenthau's Story*, 337.

47. Ibid., 334.

48. Ibid., 275.

49. Ibid., 276-77. For a further critique of Morgenthau, see Heath W. Lowry, *The Story Behind Ambassador Morgenthau's Story* (Istanbul: Isis Press, 1990).

50. Toynbee, *Acquaintances*, 240.

51. Ibid., 241.

52. Ibid.

53. Ibid., 242.

54. Ibid., 151.

55. Letter to Lillian K. Etmekjian, reproduced in "The Evidence for the Armenian Genocide in the Writings of Two Prominent Turks," *Armenian Review* 35 (Summer 1982), 184.

56. Enver Ziya Karal, *Armenian Question* (Ankara: Gündüz, 1975), 18.

57. "Let us Speak the Truth" (Statement published by the Federation of Turkish American Societies, Inc.), *New York Times*, May 18, 1975. The two most comprehensive Turkish studies in English are Kamuran Gürün, *The Armenian File: The Myth of Innocence Exposed* (New York: St. Martin's Press, 1986), and Salahi Ramsdan Sonyel, *The Ottoman Armenians: Victims of Great Power Diplomacy* (London: K. Rustem & Bro., 1987). In addition the lengthy Turkish study by Esat Uras, first published in 1950, has been published in English as *The Armenians in History and the Armenian Question* (Istanbul: Documentary Publications, 1988).

58. *Turkish Daily News* (September 9, 1982), 2.

59. See W.E.D. Allen and Paul Muratoff, *Caucasian Battlefields: A History of the Wars on the Turco-Caucasian Border, 1928-1921* (Cambridge: Cambridge University Press, 1953), 43, 51, 84.

60. K.S. Papazian, *Patriotism Perverted* (Boston: Baikar Press, 1934), 39.

61. *Documents* (Ankara: Prime Ministry Directorate General of Press and Information, 1982), 18. Turkish is an agglutinated language and is not included in the Indo-European family of languages. Therefore, it proves most difficult to translate between English and Turkish. In citing the Turkish translation into English of these Ottoman documents, I have reproduced the wording as it appears whenever the meaning was clear. To add editorial "sics" seemed pedantic.

62. Ibid., 26.

63. Ibid., 30.

64. Ibid., 50.

65. Ibid., xv.

66. *Documents*, Vol. II (Ankara: Prime Ministry Directorate General of Press and Information, 1983), 49-52.

67. "Armenian Allegations and Some Facts," *ATA-USA: Bulletin of the Assembly of American Turkish Associations*, (April, 1980), 4.

68. This and the preceding citations were taken from *Setting the Record Straight on Armenian Propaganda Against Turkey* (booklet published by the Assembly of Turkish American Associations, 1982).

69. *Documents*, 257-59.

70. See, for example, even more lurid descriptions in Ibid., 130-31, 208, 227.

71. Neside Kerem Demir, *The Armenian Question in Turkey* (1980), 78.

72. See Gwynne Dyer, "Turkish 'Falsifiers' and Armenian 'Deceivers': Historiography and the Armenian Massacres," *Middle Eastern Studies* 12 (January 1976), 99-107. Also see his letters to Ibid., 9 (1973), 129-30 and 377-85.

73. McCarthy, *Muslims and Minorities*, 130.

74. *NewsSpot: Turkish Digest* (published on behalf of the Directorate General of Press and Information, Ankara, Turkey), September, 17, 1982: 4.

75. *Facts from the Turkish Armenians* (Istanbul: *Jamanak* [Armenian Daily], 1980), 6.

76. Cited in Walker, *Armenia: Survival of a Nation*, 202n.

77. Cited in Adams, "Facing Up to an Armenian Genocide."

78. *The Armenian Issue in Nine Questions and Answers* (Ankara: Foreign Policy Institute, 1982), 3.

79. Salahi R. Sonyel, "quoting with approval a selection of American relief experts who had low opinions of the Armenians," in Dyer, "Turkish 'Falsifiers' and Armenian 'Deceivers,'" 100-1.

80. Demir, *Armenian Question in Turkey*, 83.

81. *The Armenian Weekly* (special issue, June 1, 1983), 42.

82. *The Armenian Reporter* (June 30, 1983), 2.

83. See Werner Keller, *Diaspora: The Post-Biblical History of the Jews* (New York: Harcourt, Brace & World, Inc., 1969), 269-77.

84. On these points, see in general, Pierre Oberling, *The Road to Bellapais: The Turkish Cypriot Exodus to Northern Cyprus* (Boulder: Social Science Monograph, 1982).

85. "Forum: The Armenian Question," *International Journal of Middle East Studies* 9 (1978), 379-400.

86. Ibid., 387. An editor at the Cambridge University Press recently told me how certain Americans of Armenian descent tried to pressure and even threaten his press against publishing the Shaw study.

87. Ibid., 388.

88. Christopher J. Walker, "The Armenian Holocaust in its Modern Historical Context," *Ararat* 24 (Spring 1983), 45.

89. Ibid.

90. Norman Ravitch, "The Armenian Catastrophe: Of History, Murder & Sin," *Encounter* (December 1981), 72, 77.

91. Andrew Corsun, "Armenian Terrorism: A Profile," *U.S. Department of State Bulletin* (August 1982), 35.

92. *U.S. Department of State Bulletin*, April 1983. See also Ibid., September 1982.

93. *Documents*, 1.

94. For a much fuller development of these important points, see my "Self-Determination in the Recent Practice of the United Nations," *World Affairs* 137 (Fall 1974), 150-65; "Self-Determination or Territorial Integrity: The United Nations in Confusion," *World Affairs* 141 (Winter 1979), 203-16; and the many citations to other scholarly analyses therein.

95. See, for example, Shavarsh Toriguian, *The Armenian Question and International Law* (Beirut: Hamaskaine Press, 1973), 74-86.

96. McCarthy, *Muslims and Minorities*, 46-88, 109-16, 121-30. For a different interpretation of the population data, see Levon Marashlian, "Population Statistics on Ottoman Armenians in the Context of Turkish Historiography," *Armenian Review* 40 (Winter 1987), 1-59.

97. McCarthy, *Muslims and Minorities*, *115*.

98. Levon Marashlian, *Politics and Demography: Armenians, Turks and Kurds in the Ottoman Empire* (Cambridge, Mass.: Zoryan Institute, 1991).

99. The following discussion is based on Richard Hovannisian, "The Armenian Case: Toward a Just Solution," *The California [Armenian] Courier* (December 1, 1983), 9.

100. Edward Hatchadourian of Pompano Beach, Florida, letter to the editor, *Christian Science Monitor*, (September 12, 1983), 22.

101. Levon K. Topouzian, *The Chicago Tribune*, reprinted in *The Armenian Weekly* (September 17, 1983), 3.

102. Cited in *The California [Armenian] Courier* (October 20, 1983), 3.

103. This and the following citations are taken from the transcript of the interview which appeared in *The Armenian Reporter* (October 11, 1984), 1, 12.

104. Cited in Harry N. Howard, *An American Inquiry in the Middle East: The King-Crane Commission* (Beirut: Khayats, 1963), 165.

105. *The Turco-Armenian Question: The Turkish Point of View* (Constantinople: The National Congress of Turkey 1919 [reprinted]), 83, 85.

106. Ibid., 117-18.

107. Ibid., 116.

108. Ibid., 94.

109. Vazken L. Parsegian, "April 24, 1985—A Time for Change," *The Armenian Reporter* (October 4, 1984), 3. The following citations are taken from this article.

110. Enver Ziya Karal, *Armenian Question* (Ankara: Gündüz, 1975), 26.

A Contribution to
The Psychology of Denial of Genocide

Denial as a Celebration of Destructiveness, an Attempt to Dominate the Minds of Men, and a 'Killing' of History

Israel W. Charny

Truth will come to light, murder cannot be hid long.
—Shakespeare, 1596

Any man's death diminishes me because I am involved in Mankind. —John Donne, 1571-1631

There is one phenomenon of genocide that in its own grotesque way can shed more light on the psychology of genocide than we may be able to see when we look at the actual events of mass murdering and understandably are blinded by the Satanic horror of what we are looking at; and this is the strange phenomenon of denials of genocides that have already indisputably taken place in history.

"The last victim of any genocide is truth," wrote Richard Cohen in the *Washington Post* in a column entitled "Rewriting History - Killing Truth" in 1983, after he had heard the Ambassador of Turkey explaining at the Embassy in Washington that "there never was a policy to exterminate the Armenians." Cohen concluded: "And so year by year, person by person, the genocide blurs, doubt corrodes it, and the easy word 'alleged' creeps in to mock the Armenian anguish."[1]

Gerard J. Libaridian has summarized two important developments which identify contemporary Turkish governments more closely with the policy of the regime that actually committed the genocide so many years ago.

First, the government of Turkey has developed a totalitarian attitude toward this issue: all means of communication and mind control, from school textbooks, university seminars, radio and television programs beamed toward neighboring countries, to embassy personnel, are used by the Turkish government to promote the denial of an historical fact. The mechanisms being created for the promotion of the new truth are no different from the official history which is adopted in the U.S.S.R. at the highest level and then promoted, without allowance for dissent, throughout schools, newspapers and other media, encyclopedias, and monographs.

The second important development ... is the role the Turkish government has assigned to some historians and academics, in the U.S. and in Europe: to rewrite that history according to the image which present-day rulers have decided Turkey should project. The Turkish government, using its embassies and newly created institutes, promotes its official position through Turkish but also non-Turkish scholars, particularly in the U.S. Thus, political considerations for the distortion of history are covered with the legitimation which academics alone can provide.[2]

I remember very well my own first exposure to denials of the Armenian genocide. Back in 1964, I was a consultant at a psychiatric hospital for emotionally disturbed children, and we hosted at a day-long clinical conference two visiting Turkish mental health professionals. By sheer chance, I was seated next to them, and as the day wore on a pleasant and friendly ambience was developing between us. During a recess later in the day I remembered to ask them—as fellow mental health professionals who in my sense of what our professions represent obviously cared about human beings—if they could tell me something about the history of the massacre of the Armenians about which I had just learned from Marjorie Housepian's important article in *Commentary* magazine, "The Unremembered Genocide."[3] My two colleagues froze, turned away without a word, and never spoke to me again.

THE TRAGIC PLEASURES OF GENOCIDE

Before we proceed with an analysis of the meanings, satisfactions, and rewards of denials of genocide, it behooves us to touch on the original events of mass murders to realize, painfully, that many human beings and societies derive great satisfaction from the destruction of great numbers of human lives. I regret very deeply to say that rounding up men, women, and children, marching them away mercilessly on death marches, or killing them outright gives many, many people pleasure, satisfaction, and a sense of strength and triumph. This terrible statement is true of many of us human beings who are not at all, technically, sadists, perverts, or mentally ill, but rather are, according to conventional standards—which incidentally I otherwise propose should be changed[4]—"normal" human beings, if you will "born in the image of God."

It is difficult to acknowledge that no few men achieve ecstatic transcendental moments and spiritual fulfillment standing above piles of corpses whose very wretched non-beingness confirms for them their own pseudo-deity and invincibility.[5] Were it not this way, there would be millions more Armenians, and Jews, and Ukrainians, and Cambodians, and Gypsies, and countless other peoples alive. Although I as a person enjoy and love life and people, I have to acknowledge also that the basic psychological organization of our species includes powerful tendencies to seek power over others, intoxication and addictive pleasures from the suffering of others, deep comfort in sacrificing others as substitutes for one's own mortal vulnerability, and a sense of triumph and omnipotence from the powerlessness and excremental nothingness of one's victims. In other words, notwithstanding the myths of our western civilization about man's basic good nature and love of his fellow man, evil is also a *natural* part of the human soul; not only an alternative wrongfully chosen by some few people, but a natural alternative inherent in life. The same miraculous life source that makes us capable of duty, caring, and helpfulness also makes us capable of delighting in spectacles of men being torn apart in the Coliseum, obliterating villages in Armenia and Vietnam, or burning piles of human flesh in Auschwitz incinerators. It is a fact that I hate, but a fact, nonetheless, that many human beings validate and glorify their own lives in the corpses they make of others.

THE DENIAL OF GENOCIDE

What possible benefits can there be to denials of genocides that have already actually taken place years before? What can be the rewards or payoff for those who years after a genocide they themselves have not committed deny that the genocide ever took place?

It is understandable that any actual murderer would seek to deny his actions lest he be brought before the bar of justice for his actions. But it hardly makes sense that the children and grandchildren and totally unrelated people of the same nationality that committed the mass murder years and even generations before need to deny the history of the genocidal acts by their anonymous forefathers.

Are there perhaps political advantages to be gained from the denial? In the case of the Armenian Genocide, for example, there can be *some* reason to think that the Turks are concerned over the political ramifications of the continuing yearning and groping towards possible political organization by the Armenian people to seek a reconstitution of an independent homeland. Even so, it is far from clear that an acknowledgement of the genocide committed by a much earlier regime would enable a more significant political process towards national self-determination so many years later—as was the impact of the Holocaust immediately following World War II on the United Nations process which did give birth to the State of Israel. The latter event took place in the context of a strong international Zionist movement that preceded the Holocaust by many years, as well as significant political undertakings toward the creation of the Jewish State such as the Balfour Declaration by the British government. There is no corresponding momentum of nationalism among the Armenian people, and one might even speculate that a less psychotic policy by the Turks might stop enraging Armenians and possibly would even have the opposite effect of lessening the need for a renewed Armenian nationalism. An outstanding Armenian scholar, Richard G. Hovannisian, observes that although some Armenians insist on financial or territorial restitution, the aggrieved party which demands some form of compensation is "disorganized and scattered" and "many of the aggrieved would be satisfied with a simple Turkish admission of wrongdoing and the end to efforts to erase the historical record."[6]

If we turn to denials of the Holocaust, where we also see an incredible array of people and resources committed to the madness of denying that the Holocaust ever took place, we are also hard-pressed to find a political explanation of the value of the denials, although there is some truth to the idea that discrediting the reality of the Holocaust is a way of weakening the moral justification of the State of Israel.

In both cases, political explanations go just so far, and on balance it becomes clear that we must turn to motivations that go beyond whatever weakening of the respective people's political positions might be gained by denying the genocidal tragedy that befell them to seek explanations on other levels.

There is another possibility: that the descendants and the adherents or believers in the national identity or ideology that previously committed mass murder may be fighting for a precious quality of national pride when they devote themselves to trying to erase the record of evil committed by their nation. This possibility would gain some credence if these same sources also issued statements denouncing mass murder, or if they made statements of concern for the suffering of the respective victim populations (in both the Armenian and Jewish cases, nobody has yet denied that these people at least suffered forcible removal from their natural habitats and were taken elsewhere under great hardship).

There is some such protestation of caring about the Armenian people in Turkish propaganda, but it is essentially in a cynical context of denying the genocidal crimes and not very likely to be taken as real concern for the victims. Thus, the forced marches of the Armenians are typically relabeled a "relocation." Writing in the *Wall Street Journal* in 1983, the Turkish Ambassador to the United States said: "The Ottoman authority concluded that they had no alternative but to relocate the Armenians from the eastern front region to Syria and Palestine,"[7] and a pamphlet on "Armenian Propaganda" published by a Turkish group insists that "great care was taken by the Ottoman government to prevent the Armenians from being harmed by these deportations."[8] In the Jewish instance, in a trial of a rabid anti-Semite in Canada, a witness who is also a rabid anti-Semite, who was previously convicted of racial hatred in Sweden, testified that "the prisoners in Auschwitz dined and danced to bands, swam in an Olympic-size swimming pool, and attended live theater."[9]

All of these are hardly statements to elevate the national moral image and pride of the peoples who are accused of murder, but are patently cynical mockeries of the victim peoples.

I have read a considerable variety of documents denying the one or the other genocide, ranging from the puerile and blatantly anti-Armenian or anti-Semitic to the most sophisticated gentlemanly or scholarly presentation, and I am quite convinced that there is little evidence of any real concern for the victim peoples. I do see in these presentations a certain effort to add or build the national pride of the peoples who committed the genocide, but these efforts are based on continuing to attribute a basic superiority to that nationality, a justification of a philosophy that might makes right, and an unquestioning obedience to the nation-state.

To sum up the argument thus far: There appear to be some political motivations in trying to suppress the history of past genocidal events, and there appear to be some motivations towards rescuing the positive image of one's people who stand condemned by history for having been mass killers, but the major purposes and motivations of denials of past events of genocide seem to be to get away with another lie, another coverup. Thus, symbolically, the denials add new deep insults to the original terrible injury. *Denials of genocide make no sense unless one sees in them renewed opportunities for the same passions, meanings, and pleasures that were at work in the genocide itself, now revived in symbolic processes of murdering the dignity of the survivors, rationality, truth, and even history itself.*

It is my strong opinion that to understand the insanity of denials of the facts of a genocide years later is not only an academic exercise in the analysis of another distorted and ugly human behavior, but should be used to give us new insights into developing more effective policy positions in response to such denials. If we understand that what is at stake is not simply argumentation over facts of history—which are so clearly established that one also ought to think in response to each instance of denial if there is not some sort of victory for the deniers when we agree to argue with them about the facts—it might be much more effective to couple our restatements of the hard historical evidences with statements which confront directly and powerfully the motivations, tactics, and meanings of the acts of denial.

So long as we are in the fortunate position of operating within democratic societies, we are in a position to characterize blatant lies about history as lies, and the liars as liars. Our argument is not only with the pseudo-facts, distortions, and outright falsehoods, but with the cold-blooded, mocking, arrogant rearrangement of known historical truths. The false witnesses who deny that a genocide recorded in history ever took place are killers of the knowledge process, and in effect accomplices to the past destructiveness they deny as well as to future destruction of human life. In effect, these apologists for evil years later are celebrating the past destruction of the victims, and while throwing bitter salt on the memories of the victims they are implicitly calling for future renewals of spilling the blood of the same or other hapless victims—who can also be consigned to the indifference of a falsified historical record.

DENIAL AS A NATURAL AND NEEDED PSYCHOLOGICAL PROCESS

To understand the pathology of denial of genocide, it behooves us to understand the psychology of denial as a natural and frequently utilized defense on behalf of the sanity of man.

Were we, any of us, to face the full blinding truths of our existence; the ultimate given of reality that we are all slated to die; that we are people on a planet within a universe whose dimensions we do not understand and which, in all probability, is also slated for destruction by nature itself, let alone by the wanton destructiveness

FIGURE 1

A Continuum of Constructive and Pathological Uses
of the Defense Mechanism of Denial

Existential condition in response to which denial is employed	Denial as a helpful and psychologically acceptable defense	Dysfunctional or disturbed use of denial to an exaggerated or unrealistic extent	Denial coupled with projection or assignment of denied condition on to other
Weakness in one's personality or character	Denial as not facing weakness in one's personality or character	Unavailability to criticism, inability to learn from repetition of one's faults, evasions of responsibility, arrogance	Projection of same or equivalent weakness on to other, e.g., *You are stupid/ weak/impotent/ dirty/bad/ worthless*
Illness and injury	Denying as avoiding acknowledging the illness or injury or the implications for one's life	Inability to seek or receive needed care	Projection of illness or injury or equivalent condition on to other, e.g., *"making another person sick,"* or *"driving the other crazy"*
Death vulnerability	Denying as avoiding awareness of one's imminent, possible, or ultimate death	Neglectful, careless, dangerous, daredevil, and self-hurting behaviors that ignore risk of death	Projection of death vulnerability on to other, e.g., *concentration camp guard or kapo, and ideologues of mass murder: "YOU die, not I! For I control life and death like a God!"*

and evil of our species;

—were we to look fully in the face of the essential insignificance of virtually everything that virtually all us do a good deal of the time, and the near impossibility of our ever contributing significantly to the real betterment of human welfare;

—were we to be honest with ourselves about the considerable gaps between the personal dreams many of us have for our own lives and what we are able to create, our personal stories of deep disappointments in marriages or with certain children whom we loved so deeply, our disillusionments in movements, beliefs, and ideologies we held so dear or in groups, organizations and communities to which we gave ourselves;

—were we to look realistically at the trail of dread illnesses and crippling disabilities that we and our loved ones encounter throughout our lives, and the never-ending losses and deaths of everyone we treasure and hold dear;

—were we to recognize, moreover, the fact that in our stay on earth there is never an era when we are not in the midst of terrible personal and historical demonstrations of unfairness, injustice, evil, and destruction; that almost everywhere we turn, torture, imprisonment, and mass murder are the way of life; and that these are committed by titled academicians and professionals, learned physicians, as well as leaders of holy churches, no less than by militarists, criminals, perverts, and madmen...

In short, were we truly to look at the human condition, we would likely be burned up—destroyed—for having looked at the unbearably ugly side of the countenance of God as it were, i.e., the terribly tortured realities of suffering and premature death that are the fates of *millions* of us.

So nature has made it possible for us, as another part of the wondrous mystery of our minds, to deny—that is to be consciously relatively unaware of if not completely unaware of—this and that pain, humiliation, disillusionment, impotence, and agony, as well as the rage and hate exploding within us at the injustices of life.

There are countless examples of denial. Men who lose limbs can make themselves virtually unaware of their loss for some time; marital mates who are betrayed and even scandalously cuckolded under their very noses can pretend unknowingness for years; parents who cannot bear their ugly, ungrateful children can pretend that they are beloved and loving.

Denial is within limits a way of not taking a full look at the too much that is truly too difficult to look at and bear at any given point. When news comes of the death of a loved one, one of the first reactions often is denial that it could be true. When the dread news of serious life-threatening or terminal illness is brought to the knowledge of people, there is often a period of shock that involves an inability to comprehend and know the facts; the shock is then often followed by another period of fighting back desperately at any cost to prove the unprovable, that one's life is not threatened and death is not at the door. It has been reported that when certain ecological disasters descend on a community such as a flood that wipes out whole communities, there is a period in which many of the survivors remain as if unknowing and apathetic to the calamity, so much so that in teaching young mental health practitioners intervention in crisis situations, we emphasize that such denial responses are, in fact, the expected and desirable norm, and that, paradoxically, the ability to look too fully and too intensely at reality can blow out the mind of the observer who dares to see too much or too rapidly. Finally, we not only deny what is done to us, we also deny so much of what we ourselves are and cannot bear in ourselves, our own fearfulness and insecurity, pettiness and jealousy, negativism and hostility, narcissism and grandiosity, our annoying habits and failures, and our destructiveness to others.

On the other hand, if we defend ourselves against truth too long or too intensely, the denial often saps our remaining strength and reduces our ability to cope with what has happened, and with the situation as it now is, and what must be done. For example, temporarily cushioning the blow of a death is useful, but keeping oneself unaware and unfeeling about the loss of a loved one means that mourning cannot be completed, and reconciliation with the reality of the loss and reconnection with others will not be possible. Similarly, temporarily remaining as if unknowing about an illness or damage to one's body can be helpful, but the more one holds on to escaping the truth, the slower one's body is naturally able to heal and the slower one is able to learn the marvelous ways of compensation and reorganization that might serve as a basis for rehabilitation. Moreover, to bolster unknowing, one must often engage in various rituals and behaviors that are necessary to maintain one's ignorance but which in themselves are seriously damaging—such as drinking oneself into oblivion, narcotizing oneself into unknowingness, or losing oneself in the non-being of a cult.

Even when one is denying an apparently inevitable verdict of one's

death, there are good reasons for many people to be able to acknowledge that they are going to die, even if only implicitly; for undesirable
and unpleasant as the end of life must be, it has been found that the
process of taking leave from life can be less wretched, perhaps less
painful physically, and in its own right even a rewarding final
experience, when truth is accepted with dignity and simplicity.

For our purposes, perhaps the most important aspect of pathological denial is that the need to deny undesirable information also forms
the basis for many projections of highly undesirable characteristics
on to others; and it is projections which, ultimately, are the machin-
ery for delivery of the worst damages we human beings do to one
another. Many acts of destruction which are now allowable become
legitimate in the eyes of their doers "because" the others are cast in
the light of monstrous, alien, inhuman creatures.

Figure 1 shows how denial can serve constructive psychological
defense purposes, but also how it becomes a basis for disturbances
in oneself and for disturbing and doing harm to others. If I cannot
face the fact that I am very concerned about whether I am sufficiently
intelligent, it is likely that I will call you stupid. If I am afraid that I
am inferior, it is tempting for me to create definitions of you as
subhuman and valueless. If it is the fear of craziness that haunts me,
you will do well to be careful that I not drive you into madness instead
of me. If I cannot bear to acknowledge that death terrifies me, I may
very well turn to wishing on you and possibly creating the actual
conditions for your death, so that, magically, I continue to deny that
I will have to die. As I have written earlier:

> Much of the incomprehensible cruelty of genocide issues from the
> gripping power of the genocider's own fear of death, which are projected
> onto his victims. The guiding motif of the genocider's proclamation to his
> victims: "Better you should die than I!"[10]

In sum, in the psychology of the individual, the defense mechanism
of denial serves as a thermostatic or regulatory mechanism to control
the flow or intensity of informations that are too painful, threatening
or overwhelming to the human psyche. Denial can be a useful
sedating force; it is a pacemaker which establishes a tolerable rhythm
for experience and allows for the regrouping of remaining strengths
and regenerative forces within us. However, used to excess, over
protracted periods of time, and translated into projections of the
weaknesses we fear in ourselves on to others, denials of facts and
realities sap our strength and leave us either flailing and absurd in
the face of what must be acknowledged and dealt with in our lives, or

lead us to become cruelly dangerous to others on whom we seek to cast our burdens so that they become the victims instead of us.

THE VIOLENCE OF IMPOSING DENIAL ON OTHERS

Those who seek to impose on a people and on mankind in general denials of the historical truth of a past genocide are using their attempted rewriting of history to do several psychological violences to others.

Denial of a known event of genocide is, first of all, denial that a crime was committed, and denial that there were/are any criminal governments or people responsible. The blatant denial of the mass murder of a people is also promoting a powerful meta-message of celebrating the deaths of the victims, and the agonized, tortured final treatment they suffered on their way to their deaths at the hands of those who were devoted to their murders. The deniers in later years are, in effect, "one" with the Talaat's and Eichmann's who originally issued the administrative orders to deport the victims on forced marches and torture-chamber trains; they are one with the bayonet and machete-bearing killers, and the soldiers with machine guns who indifferently executed their victims on top of the ravine; they are continuers of the obedient guards who clambered up on the roofs of the barracks to pour Zyklon B into the death room where naked people stretched and gasped agonizingly for their last breath. I fear the deniers are also one of those who, some horrible day that lies ahead, may order or press the levers and buttons which will insanely dispatch nuclear missiles to a Boston, Leningrad, Baghdad, or Tel Aviv—whatever place where millions of human beings will stretch and gasp agonizedly for their last breaths in a raging inferno of death.

To deny a people their right to remember, mourn, protest, and plan for their overcoming, continuity and re-creation is also to impose psychological illness, weakness, humiliation, and madness on that people. It is to victimize them again in another way. The deniers are terrorists who are out to kill the feeling, sensibility, and attachment of a people. They are would-be killers of the collective identity, culture, peoplehood, and national aspirations of a people already tortured and massacred.

To seek to impose on the world that two plus two equals six, black is white, or that a mass murder that took place and is etched in the personal and collective memories of a people never happened is also a far-reaching test of the ability of a few to command the blind obedience of all the others. It is an attempt to exploit the same

FIGURE 2

An Analysis of the Meta-Messages of Denials of Known Events of Genocide

THE DENIAL OF A KNOWN GENOCIDE IS A CHALLENGE NOT ONLY TO FURTHER VERIFICATION OF THE HISTORICAL RECORD, BUT ALSO TO CONFRONT RENEWED EVIL

Denial of responsibility, wrongdoing, or evil by those who were responsible—or by those who now identify unashamedly with the murderers	To deny that a crime was committed is to deny there were criminals: the alleged perpetrators of an alleged genocide that never took place can have no responsibility for any wrongdoing or evil
A celebration of the destruction of the known victims, and a celebration of renewed destructiveness in the future	To deny the countless deaths of a known event of genocide is to celebrate the deaths of the same victims and to intimate cynically that the doctrine of power which brought about their destruction is still in force, to be used when opportunity permits
Humiliation and mocking of the sensibilities and memorial of the survivors	To seek to erase agonizing vivid memories and pictures from the eyes and minds of survivors, their descendants, and relatives is to mock their sensibilities, memorial needs, and personal attachments—in a sense once again to victimize the victims
An attack on the collective identity, peoplehood and national and cultural continuity of the victim people	To deny a cataclysmic holocaust in a people's history is to seek to abort the re-grouping and re-creation of that people's historical process and national and cultural continuity
Unabashed use of the big lie proclaims a new attempt to dominate the minds of men by dictators and/or ideology	To promote blatant lies about major events of history is to demand power over the minds of the masses and their blind obedience to dictators of their minds
Killing the record of a known event of genocide is also to "kill recorded human history"	To "kill" the ability of men to differentiate between what is known and unknown is to write a final chapter to mass murder by murdering truth, reality, and human memory and history

mechanisms of blind obedience and conformity which are tragically and decisively at work in the execution of genocide, for we now know, without any doubt, that within a framework of an authoritative structure, certainly in an army, but also in a civilian setting when citizens are given instructions by their government, and even in rarified university or research settings, *most* people, from all walks and standings in life, will accept orders to do just about anything to whomever they are told to do so (see Stanley Milgram's classical study).[11]

Those who seek to deny history such as the Armenian Genocide or the history of the Holocaust are also arrogant killers of truth. They are attempting to write a final chapter to the original genocide—now by "mass murder" of the recorded memories of human history. If being alive as human beings means some basic sense of knowing the record of history, the "killing" of objective history is also the killing of human consciousness and evolution.

Political scientist Herbert Hirsch identifies three conditions under which mass murder occurs: (1) cultural conditions, myths, and stereotypes provide the environment within which victimization may occur; (2) psychological conditions involve obedience to authority to carry out the orders; (3) political conditions involve a giving of orders and justification for the acts of destruction.[12] When revisionists speak their lies, whether rabidly or sophisticatedly, they are out to shape or recreate the very cultural conditions under which victimization may occur, to command the blind, unknowing, stupid, conformist, submissive sides of human nature, and they are out to gain the kind of political control which, in other eras, is used to justify actual acts of destruction. To deny the facts of a past genocide is to celebrate its destructiveness, minimize the significance of human life, and subordinate people to blind obedience to government and authority.

We must fight denial of past genocides, not only to set the record of the past straight, but to fight evil in our time, relentlessly, courageously, and toughly.

PRACTICAL MEASURES TO FIGHT DENIAL

If we recognize that the meanings of denial of genocide go beyond a battle for historical veracity, then we need to address these other meanings when we fight back against the revisionists. It is largely an illusion that the battle is over the facts whether a known genocide ever took place. In fact, when we reply to revisionists only with "knee-jerk" responses to their lies and try again and again to prove events that really are incontrovertibly known, there is also a serious danger that inadvertently we are confirming their power to humiliate, dominate, terrorize, and "kill" our minds.

If the no less important issue is whether liars can control the minds of all of us and kill the human historical record, this is what we ought to consider saying, intelligently and effectively, even to urbane ambassadors in black-tie diplomatic settings, in deceptively quiet church settings, or in pseudo-academic institutes that manipulate the trappings and authority of western academia while cynically violating every known standard of western scholarship and science.[13]

Understanding the psychology of denial and genocide should lead us towards formulating a series of practical proposals for fighting denials, and to building new, more effective tools that will exact a toll from those who deny a past genocide and thereby celebrate its occurrence.

1. We need legislation in democratic societies to define blatant lies about the non-occurrence of an established event of genocide such as the Armenian Genocide and the Holocaust as felonies on the grounds that they are abusive of freedom of speech. Such extreme distortions of history are no less misleading than false advertising which is not allowed under many laws, or violations of food and drug laws, or a variety of other failures to provide accurate and accountable information that democratic societies insist upon. Denials of genocide are also barely-concealed rationalizations of and incitements to renewed discrimination and persecutory behaviors, and these too are often outlawed in a democratic society. It is good to note that some such legislation is already in force in some parts of the world. In Germany, for example, it is a violation of the law to deny that the Holocaust ever took place, and it is a violation to speak contemptuously of a people. I learned of one initiative by a German scholar to bring charges against Turkish newspapers which are brought into Germany for their continuous incitements against Armenians, who are referred to as "dogs," "heathens," and the like.[14]

2. The argument against historical revisionism should not be simply an academic one to present over and over again the facts of a genocide which took place, but should be a moral argument against all those who lie about history, that in so doing they join forces with the events about which they are lying and become celebrants of mass murder. The full weight of collective values of decent and responsible people should be pressed against those who show contempt for history and celebrate the deaths they deny ever happened but which

everyone knows took place. Religious leaders, educators, health professionals, and jurists, for example, all have ample reason within the guiding philosophy and values of their professions to speak out against rationalizations and justifications of mass murder. Those who deny the history of a genocide should be labeled accomplices to the murders of that genocide. We should try to enlist a wide variety of people and organizations in condemning the revisionists.

3. The fuller underlying meanings of denial should be identified for what they are. Those who would offend and enrage the intense sensibilities of the relatives and compatriots of the victims are torturers, and those who seek to impose blatant historical untruths on the masses of people are fascists seeking blind obedience to their use of power. There is no reason we cannot mount powerful condemnations of the deniers and expose them to ridicule for trying to manipulate entire societies and the record of history itself.

4. We need to be clear that the denial of any one people's genocide is an affront to all other people. Many scholars have pointed out the profound relationship between the Armenian Genocide and the Holocaust to the Jewish people that took place later in the same century. One Jewish scholar refers to the Armenian Genocide as a "dress rehearsal" for what came later.[15] Moreover, the Germans themselves were implicated in the Armenian Genocide. The great-granddaughter of Henry Morgenthau, the American Ambassador to Turkey from 1914 to 1916, wrote to the *Los Angeles Times* in 1985 that her great-grandfather "blamed the tragic events in part on German government, as Turkey was then a vassal state of Germany in World War I. He, of course, had no inkling of the even larger genocide that the twentieth century held in store."[16] Marjorie Housepian Dobkin shows how the Armenian Genocide was progressively denied in the years afterwards and how the fact that Germany was implicated was soon forgotten by the world. The implications are clear that the denial of the one instance was the precondition that made possible the later disaster of the Holocaust. Moreover, Housepian Dobkin cautions us that "the day could come when—if the world survives—all but a handful of Jews will find the revision outside of Israel complete."[17]

I am convinced today, as I was in 1982 when we faced the pressure of the Israeli government to close down the International Conference on the Holocaust and Genocide to surrender to the Turkish government's blackmail and even threats against the lives of Jews, that to give in to the pressure to deny the Armenian Genocide is dangerous to the welfare of the Jews, let alone an offense against values all decent people hold dear.[18]

The same value must apply to each and every instance of the denial of the murder of any people whatsoever: If the United States turns its back on the history of Pol Pot's genocidal campaign against his own people which cost between one to three million Cambodian lives because Pol Pot has been fighting America's historic enemy Vietnam; if far-away China denies its systematic extermination of Buddhists in Tibet; if Christians in Lebanon deny their massacres of Muslims in refugee camps; if the government of Iran denies its execution of Baha'i and the possibility the persecutions could mount into a more extensive campaign of death; if lucrative trade agreements with certain South American countries which are destroying their indigenous Indian population are dependent on closing one's eyes to these events—any and all of these instances require the peoples of *all* ethnic, national, and religious groups to insist on awareness of what is happening and to use our individual and collective influences and power in whatever ways we can to try to prevent further mass killing.

5. To aim at implementation of the above, we should bring together a serious group of talents from the public relations industry, including advertising professionals, mass media experts, social scientists, and scholars of genocide in a Task Force or Commission which will be charged with creating effective public relations and media techniques for combatting denials of genocide. These professionals can help us create messages that label the deniers for what they are, panderers of murder and hate, and to create messages that speak to the dignity of the lives of all peoples, without exception.

There is no reason that we cannot employ the finest resources and talents to win more peoples' allegiances to the value of life and to condemn the deniers as accomplices to genocide. The deniers should be made the objects of a profound consensus of criticism, as well as objects of ridicule that they dare to pretend that they can rewrite past events any way that they see fit without regard for the objective record of known history. Instead of fighting the deniers only in repeated efforts to re-marshall the evidences of past events, we should use the fullest range of talents that we can organize to push the deniers into an untenable position before public opinion around the world.

REFERENCES

1. Cohen, Richard. "Rewriting History - Killing Truth," *Washington Post*, May 31, 1983.

2. Gerard J. Libaridian, "Genocide and Politics: A New Role for the Academic Community," *Armenian Assembly Journal*, Winter 1985 (12:1), 6.

3. Marjorie Housepian, "The Unremembered Genocide," *Commentary*, September 1966.

4. Israel W. Charny, "Genocide and Mass Destruction: A Missing Dimension in Psychopathology," *Toward the Understanding and Prevention of Genocide: Proceedings of the International Conference on the Holocaust and Genocide*, Israel W. Charny, ed. (Boulder and London: Westview Press, 1984), 154-74; and Israel W. Charny, "Genocide and Mass Destruction: Doing Harm to Others as a Missing Dimension in Psychopathology," *Psychiatry*, 1986: 49 (2), 144-57.

5. Israel W. Charny, in collaboration with Chanan Rapaport, *How Can We Commit the Unthinkable?: Genocide, the Human Cancer* (Boulder: Westview Press, 1982), Chapter 9, "Sacrificing Others to the Death We Fear Ourselves: The Ultimate Illusion of Self-Defense," 185-212. See also an earlier presentation of this concept in Israel W. Charny, "A Contribution to the Psychology of Genocide: Sacrificing Others to the Death We Fear Ourselves," *Israel Yearbook on Human Rights*, vol. 10, Yoram Dinstein, ed. (Tel Aviv: Faculty of Law, Tel Aviv University, 1980), 90-108.

6. Richard G. Hovannisian, "Genocide and Denial: The Armenian Case," *Toward the Understanding and Prevention of Genocide*, 84.

7. Sukru Elekdag, "Armenians vs. Turks: The View from Istanbul," *Wall Street Journal*, September 4, 1983.

8. "Armenian Propaganda," pamphlet published by a Turkish group, no date.

9. Allan Mendelsohn, "Canadian Jurors Ponder: Did the Holocaust Occur?" *Jerusalem Post*, March 1, 1985.

10. Charny, *How Can We Commit the Unthinkable?* 192.

11. Stanley Milgram, *Obedience to Authority* (New York: Harper & Row, 1974).

12. Herbert Hirsh, "Why People Kill: Conditions for Participation in Mass Murder." Paper presented at 1984 Annual Meeting, American Political Science Association, Washington, D.C.

13. See, for example, an engraved invitation "to a special meeting of the diplomatic corps and friends" to hear "Dr. Arthur R. Butz, Associate Professor, Northwestern University and author of *The Hoax of the Twentieth Century*" at the "Church Center for the United Nations" on Friday, January 12, 1979. Butz' book denies there was any program of mass murder of the Jews by the Germans, "only" one million Jews died and as a result of wartime conditions, and Zyklon B was merely a disinfectant used to combat typhus.

14. Personal communication from the wife of Dr. Frank Boldt, *Landeszentrale fur politische Bildung*, Bremen, West Germany. Parenthetically, it can also be noted that Dr. Boldt had been the object of intense attacks by the Turks for planning a conference on the Armenian Genocide and the Jewish Holocaust in April 1985.

15. Pinchas Lapid, "The 'Dress-Rehearsal' for the Holocaust," *Bulletin of Bar-Ilan University*, Summer, 1974, 14-20 (in Hebrew).

16. Lucy Eisenberg, *Los Angeles Times*, February 5, 1982.

17. Marjorie Housepian Dobkin, "What Genocide? What Holocaust? News from Turkey, 1915-23: A Case Study," *Toward the Understanding and Prevention of Genocide*, 110.

18. Israel W. Charny, "The Turks, Armenians, and the Jews," *The Book of the International Conference on the Holocaust and Genocide: Book One, The Conference Program and Crisis*, Israel W. Charny and Shamai Davidson, eds. (Tel Aviv: Institute of the International Conference on the Holocaust and Genocide, 1983), 269-316.

The Religious Element in Genocide

Leo Kuper and Gary Remer

Religion and Genocide are intimately related. This relationship was most marked in the annihilation of the members of religious sects deemed heretical (as in medieval Europe) and in the religious wars (as in the sixteenth and seventeenth centuries in Europe), and in the recurrent massacres of Jews over many centuries in both Western and Eastern Europe. But it is a significant element also in many of the twentieth century genocides,[1] where the conflicts and motivations appear to be purely secular, raising no issues of differences in religious belief or ritual practice.

In emphasizing the significance of religious difference, we do not mean to imply that they are a necessary element in, or a sufficient cause of, genocide. People of different religions live together harmoniously in many contemporary societies; and if there are conflicts of interest between them, they are certainly not resolved by massacre. And conversely, there are large scale massacres, genocidal and other, which are not grounded in religious difference—for example, the massacres of ethnic groups in Rwanda and Burundi, and of economic classes in Russia under Stalin, and in Kampuchea under the Khmer Rouge. But in most cases of genocide, differences in religion, and the associated meanings attached to them, contribute in some measure to the genocidal process.

Religious beliefs, and the perspectives they foster in believers, are, of course, quite variable in their implications for the tolerance of other religious groups. In his analysis of variations in the affinities of different types of religion for different forms of tolerance and intolerance, Gustav Mensching[2] comments that the supra-confessional communities are by their very nature tolerant, and he cites *inter alia* the Baha'i International Community. (This Community teaches the oneness of God and of religion and of mankind, conceives of divine revelation as a continuous and progressive process, and strives to bring about the unity of mankind). Mysticism, drawing on the individual experience of unity with the divine, also tends to be inherently tolerant of the beliefs of other groups. Polytheistic religions have the capacity to incorporate foreign deities and their associated religious practices, along with a corresponding flexibility in their relations with different religions. By contrast, "all universal religions raise a general claim to absolute truth . . . founded, explicitly or implicitly, upon the conviction that one's own religious community is the sole possessor of truth." Particularly in prophetic religions with a religious claim to absoluteness, "the battle against those who are steeped in the darkness of religious error or have departed from the truth of their own religion is particularly passionate, being waged in the name of truth."[3]

The forms of tolerance and intolerance also vary, and Mensching distinguishes two categories of attitudes, pertaining respectively to form and to content. Formal tolerance is mere non-interference with members of another faith, whereas in the contrasting attitude of formal intolerance there is a suppression of deviation in the interests of formal unity. Tolerance of content (intrinsic tolerance) is based not only on non-interference with other religions, but also on the "positive acknowledgment of a foreign religion as a genuine and legitimate religious possibility of encounter with the sacred." The corresponding negative attitude (intrinsic intolerance) is marked by opposition to other faiths and religions on the basis of what is regarded as truth. A further distinction is made between inner and outer tolerance and intolerance, depending on whether these attitudes are directed inwardly to the accepted religion or outwardly to another religion.[4]

These brief extracts from Mensching's work greatly simplify his argument and are included to suggest some of the issues that call for investigation in the analysis of the religious element in genocide. The problem is not that of an objective interpretation of the sacred writings (if that were indeed possible), but rather the directions for action which are derived from them. And the history of religious dissidence in general provides abundant testimony to the great diversity of prescriptions for action which can be derived from the same religious revelation. Thus, Christians may derive from their sacred writings the conviction that Jews must bear, through a long history of suffering, a curse for their role in the crucifixion of Christ[5]—

a seemingly perpetual communal guilt extending through unborn generations—or exceptionally, they may find some encouragement to benevolent tolerance of Jews in the biblical references to the "chosen people" and in the revelations of their prophets. And they may also feel some affinity for the patriarchal structure of their ancient societies.

In addition to the many ambiguities in the sacred writings and the inconsistencies in the revelations and sayings of the founders of religious movements, there is always change over time in the interpretation and salience of religious doctrines. What significance can we now attach to the special horror of idol-worship in Judaism and Islam, which was clearly a response to the specific historical situation of new monotheistic movements seeking followers among peoples still attached to the tangible and immediately accessible manifestations of their deities in a great variety of images. Clearly, the revelations of the founders are to be interpreted in the context of particular social situations, and these revelations—and the traditional meanings attached to them—are themselves responsive to changing historical circumstances and to varied social contexts. Geertz demonstrates this very effectively in a comparison of the different social consequences, in Indonesia and Morocco, of a radical fundamentalism seeking a return to the original Islam of the Days of the Prophet.[6]

Hence, in our preliminary exploration of the religious element in genocide, which we confine mainly to the inter-related monotheistic religions of Judaism, Christianity, and Islam, we start from the obvious premise that the religious factor does not operate in isolation from the general social context, but in association with other social forces. The annihilation of the Cathar sect in thirteenth century France would seem to be a relatively "pure" case of religious genocide. But the popular fervor of its adherents and the support of some of the southern nobility threatened the power of the organized Catholic Church. And the Northern barons, "though many of them were sincerely religious, were all anxious to enrich themselves at the expense of the wealthy Southern lords."[7]   Still, it is possible to differentiate between those genocides in which the religious difference operates directly, and often as a primary element, and those in which it contributes indirectly, and in a subsidiary, though significant, role.

HERESY

We assume that, irrespective of other motives and precipitating events in the annihilation of heretical sects, the religious differences are highly significant, and we take as our starting point the concepts of heresy, and the precepts relating to heresy, in the three monotheistic religions of Judaism, Christianity and Islam. Of course, as noted above, the practical implications of these concepts and precepts change over time. Moreover, practice may diverge from precept. Lewis comments that "Islamic practice on the whole turned out to be gentler than Islamic precept—the reverse of the situation in Christendom."[8] And in any event, the relevance of these precepts for the genocidal annihilation of the members of heretical sects is dependent on the power to carry out an exterminatory mission. In Islam, there has been an interpenetration of faith and power, of religion and authority, throughout most of its history,[9] as is true also of Christianity, whereas in Judaism there was only a brief period in which the Jewish state had the power to suppress heresies.

At first glance, the use of a common set of terms to describe Jewish, Christian, and Islamic religious intolerance appears artificial. Judaism, as a practice-oriented religion, was most clearly intolerant of non-orthodox practices. Islam too is oriented to orthopraxy rather than orthodoxy, Muslims being allowed considerable freedom of belief as long as they accept a basic minimum of doctrinal conformity.[10] Christianity, on the other hand, having abandoned most of Judaism's ritual, is noted for its persecution of dogmatic errors. Thus, the Church convened the Council of Nicaea early in its life (325 AD) to arrive at doctrinal orthodoxy, in particular on the nature of the Trinity, in contrast to Judaism's lack of any official formulation of dogma. Even what is accepted today by Orthodox Jews as the "Thirteen Articles of Faith" was first formulated by Maimonides in the twelfth century, some fifteen hundred years after the completion of the Hebrew Bible.

While valid, this distinction between practice-oriented versus dogma-centered religions is by no means absolute. Talmudic literature records a number of terms—min, apikoris, kofer and mumar—all referring to individuals whose errors are doctrinal. The Tora itself obliges Jews to both worship and believe in God. Moreover, Korah's rebellion against Moses, as described in Numbers, was not only over the institution of the priesthood, but also over the broader doctrinal issue of the equality of the whole congregation of Israel before God.

Religious dissent in Christianity was not only grounded in doctrinal disputes, but it also revolved around the proper practices of the faithful. Disputes over what should be considered sacraments, how they should be performed, and in the case of baptism, the appropriate time for its performance, have been longstanding. So too have been the debates over the proper organization of the Church (i.e., what should the Church hierarchy look like, or should it even have a hierarchy at all). Yet these issues are clearly different from doctrinal questions relating to the source of evil, whether it is to be attributed, as for example in the dualist heresy, to the existence of a second and evil god, the lord of material creation and of darkness.

In Islam, however practice-oriented the religion, the main divisions (between Sunnis, Shi'ites, and Kharijites) rested on doctrinal differences, notably in theories of the nature of the Caliphate and the criteria for succession to this supreme office. The combination of spiritual and political authority in the Caliphate was the counterpart of the religious penetration of all aspects of social and political life, with the result that dissident social movements would tend to express themselves, and find legitimation, in doctrinal innovation.

Indeed, it is clear that religious disputes over practices and beliefs, while theoretically distinguishable, are inseparable in the real world; heterodoxy usually has practical consequences, and open opposition to accepted practices requires doctrinal justification. Heresy, as we shall define it here, describes beliefs which run counter to either accepted doctrine or practice. While weighted toward the former in Christianity, and toward the latter in Judaism and Islam, heretics and heresies of both varieties are to be found in the three religions.

There are, to be sure, many difficulties in comparing tolerance and intolerance of heretics and heresies in these religions. The social contexts are quite varied. Heresy is defined in relation to authoritative orthodox doctrine. In the Christian Church, as mentioned above, there was an early authoritative formulation of orthodoxy, as well as the power, after the third century, to enforce it. But Judaism in the diaspora did not command the necessary sanctions to enforce orthodoxy or to suppress religious dissent. The revered sage of Vilna, the Gaon Elijah, might fulminate against the heresy of Hassidism; he could do little to restrain this heretical sect.[11] As for Islam, Lewis comments that in the absence of an apostolic tradition and of a supreme pontiff, orthodoxy and heterodoxy "could at first sight be determined only by making the teachings of one school the touchstone for the rejection of the others."[12]

Even the terms used to express the concept of heresy are hardly synonymous. The Bible does not have a specific Hebrew term for the heretic, but it regards as a heretic one who "whores after strange gods," a conception which does not fall within our own definition of heresy. In the later Talmudic and Rabbinic literature, several terms are used for heretics. *Kofer* may be translated as "freethinker." *Mumar* refers to the convert, the apostate, "but in the Talmudic tradition it sometimes means heretic." *Apikoris*, skeptic, has applications overlapping with heresy. However, the term which is most commonly used, and which corresponds closely to heresy, is *min*. The word *minim* in the Talmudic literature is applied by some to the Judeo-Christians and to those who deny the coming of the Messiah, or Israel's divine status as the chosen of God; it is applied also to belief in an independent divinity of evil and the portrayal of God as a cruel jester.[13]

Islam offers a variety of terms for religious divergence: *bid'a*, innovation; *ghuluww*, expressing the idea of excess; *zandaqa*, which is most commonly translated as heresy; *ilhad*, deviation from the path, subversive doctrine; *Kafir* and *Kufr*, unbeliever and unbelief.[14] Lewis, whose discussion of Islam we have been following, considers *Kafir* and *Kufr* the nearest approximation to heresy. However, they do appear to have a much wider connotation, extending to relations with other religious groups, whereas we are restricting the concept to the internal sectarian divisions within the different religions. In any event, whatever the semantic difficulties, the phenomenon we are discussing is relatively clear—the deliberate destruction of a dissenting religious sect.

THE PERSECUTIONS OF HERETICS

It is particularly in Christianity that the concept of heresy, the justification for its suppression, and the annihilation of heretical sects were most highly developed. The intimate association of the Roman Catholic Church with the power of the state, its own development as an imperial church, and the authoritative determination of doctrinal orthodoxy laid the basis for the campaigns against heresy. And this was systematically and zealously pursued through Inquisition against the medieval heretical groups (Albigenses, Cathars, Waldenses, Bohemian Brethren) and in the attempt to suppress the heresies of the Reformation. Nor were the Protestant territorial churches exempt from the religious intolerance toward heretics of which they themselves had been the victims; but their persecution of heretics did not extend to the annihilation of heretical groups.

The Christian treatment of heresy is startling in its deviation from the Christian ethnic. As Elton comments in this introduction to a collection of papers on *Persecution and Toleration*, the Christian religion of all religions,

> being the most sophisticated and therefore that productive of most variety, has worked out most thoroughly the principles and practice of destroying the heretic... It should cause more disquiet than one commonly encounters that a faith whose founder seemed resolved to transcend the denominational boundaries should have taken so enthusiastically to the rooting out of deviation. Even the experience of being itself the victims of persecution, which filled the first 300 years of its existence, seems only to have sharpened its capacity to do unto others as it itself had been done by. At any rate, it is certainly fascinating to discover that a faith which created the most remarkably complex theologies ever invented should also have given so much deep thought to the cleansing of a hearth which really only its passion of philosophy had dirtied in the first place.[15]

In contrast to Christianity, Islam, as noted above, had been relatively tolerant of divergences in belief. The required minimum of conformity was readily accessible. Lewis comments that many definitions were attempted of this basic minimum, "but most inclined, in practice if not always in theory, to accept as Muslims any who testify to the unity of God and the apostolate of Muhammad."[16] Nor were the minimum ritual requirements particularly onerous. It was excessive divergence, in breach of tradition and disruptive of the social balance, which might be punished by exclusion from Islam. And given the intimate relationship between the structure of rule and religious beliefs and practices, with struggles for power expressed in sectarian deviation, it was subversive doctrine in particular that invited the most repressive action.

Regimes varied in their repressive tendencies, and we read of extreme persecution and indeed annihilations from time to time—an inquisition in which the Manichean heresy provided most of the victims; repression of the Anatolian Shiites;[17] the extermination of the Barghawata, who were treated as heretics;[18] and the virtual extinction of Sunnism in Persia.[19] And in contemporary Iran, there has been a deliberate campaign to eradicate the Baha'is. Founded in the mid-nineteenth century, the Baha'is were viewed as a heretical sect, disruptive of the social order, and they were violently suppressed, with perhaps as many as twenty thousand victims.[20] Further massacres followed from time to time, with Baha'is cast in the role of scapegoats. They are still perceived as heretics. They are not recognized as a religious minority, in contrast to Christianity, Judaism, and Zoroastrianism, though they are the largest religious minority in the country, with some 300,000 followers; they are special anathema to the Islamic fundamentalist theocracy.

The persecutions recall the early stages in the genocide against Jews in Germany—the incitement of mobs, the dismissals from government employment, economic boycotts, exclusion from schools, desecration and destruction of holy places, expropriation of property, and judicial murder directed against the leaders of the Baha'i faith. In addition children are abducted, and girls forced into Muslim marriages. It is essentially on grounds of religious faith that the Baha'is are exposed to the threat of genocide. But this is not the justification advanced by the Iranian government. Instead it charges that the Baha'is are a treacherous political party, affiliated to imperialism, allied to international Zionism, and plotting against the Islamic Republic. These charges have been made at the United Nations on many occasions, including the meetings, in August 1983, of the Sub-Commission on Prevention of Discrimination and Protection of Minorities, when a forty-page document was circulated under the title, *Baha'ism: Its Origins and Role.* This must be one of the most disreputable documents ever presented to the United Nations, quite startling in its moral depravity and intellectual puerility. And the fact that Baha'i leaders accused of treasonable activities could readily secure a pardon by converting to Islam is sufficient commentary on the perfidious nature of the charges and their religious motivation.

In Judaism, in the vulnerable communities of the European diaspora, and in part under the influence of the Christian Church, there was an increasing resort to the punishment of heresy by excommunication. Quite apart from its religious significance, this served the political function of protecting the unity of the community in a hostile environment, where dissidence provided the opportunity for destructive intervention. But in periods of fragmented jurisdiction, excommunication was a much less effective weapon against religious dissent.

The practice of excommunication goes back to biblical times. It can be a fearsome punishment. But this form of persecution is generally remote from genocide. Not so the biblical injunctions of Jehovah against idol worship and other abominations in the eyes of the Lord—injunctions which specifically proscribe certain groups.

IDOL WORSHIPPERS, INFIDELS AND OTHER NON-BELIEVERS

In Judaism the religious proscription of idol worshippers and other non-believers is conveyed in the concept of *herem.* This contains within it the ambiguity inherent in many taboos, between the sacred and the profane, the beneficent and the malevolent. It is defined as "the status of that which is separated from common use or contact either because it is proscribed as an abomination to God or because it is consecrated to Him."[21] The Tora applied the destructive form of *herem* to Israelites who worshipped other gods, whether individual Israelites or an entire community. This was the most destructive form of *herem.* Human beings were to be put to the sword and their possessions burnt. The term was also applied to the seven nations inhabiting the land promised to Israel. Not a soul of these was to be left alive "lest they lead you into doing all the abhorrent things that they have done for their gods and you stand guilty before the Lord your God." However, the spoil of these nations was not *herem.*[22]

There was a further form of *herem* which did not derive from divine injunction and which might be proscribed as a votive offering to God, designed to secure his favorable participation in the coming battle. It seems plausible, as suggested in the Encyclopaedia Judaica, that this was the original form of the enemy *herem* and that it was later transformed into a blanket proscription of the seven nations inhabiting the land promised to Israel and rationalized as a protection of the purity of Israel's religion.[23] Colonizing zeal would have intermingled with religious faith. But whatever the relationship between these motivations, there were a number of genocidal massacres in the early period of the wars of settlement.

Divine intervention in warfare is deeply shocking even to our hardened modern sensibilities. It was a common feature of ancient warfare. The Gods participated very actively in the wars of the Greeks and Romans, and the tutelary god of a besieged city might be adopted by the besieging army so as to secure divine neutrality. The Crusades and the jihads are holy wars, and divine blessings accompanied the troops in the world wars of the twentieth century. Indeed, the propitiation of the gods, and their intervention in warfare, are widely reported—a reminder of the significant role of religion, not only in the civil violence of "domestic" genocides, but also in the mass killings of international war.

Islam, in its policy toward other religions, distinguished between lands where Muslims ruled and Islamic laws prevailed (the Dar al-Islam, the House of Islam) and the outside world, inhabited and governed by infidels (the Dar al-Harb, the House of War). Between the realm of Islam and the realms of unbelief, there was "a canonically obligatory perpetual state of war," the jihad, which was to continue until either the whole world accepted the message of Islam or submitted to its rule. With the realm of Islam, toleration was extended to Judaism, to Christianity, and to Zoroastrianism in Persia, "as earlier, incomplete, and imperfect forms of Islam itself, and therefore as containing a genuine if distorted divine revelation."[25]   These tolerated believers were allowed to practice their religions, they were accorded a measure of autonomy, and they enjoyed protection of their lives and property.

The toleration was however conditional upon submission and acceptance of inferior status. Discrimination took many different forms: the payment of higher taxes, sumptuary regulations, distinctive clothing, limitations on the height of places of worship, and the requirement of an appropriate humility toward Muslims.

Lewis writes that "on the whole, in contrast to Christian anti-Semitism, the Muslim attitude toward non-Muslims is not one of hate or fear or envy but simply of contempt." While "the negative attributes ascribed to the subject religions and their followers are usually expressed in religious and social terms, very rarely in ethnic or racial terms . . . the language of abuse is often quite strong," the conventional epithets being apes for Jews and pigs for Christians.26 And in the Ottoman Empire, a reform decree of 1856 stipulated that abusive and derogatory references to non-Muslims were to be banned from official usage, and the common appellation of ra'aya (grazing cattle) was dropped from official documents.[27]

Toleration and persecution fluctuated over time. In periods of security, notably in the flowering of Islamic civilization in the High Middle Ages, non-Muslim subjects enjoyed great tolerance. In periods of contracting dominion, economic decline, and external threat, their situation generally deteriorated.

There were fluctuations in tolerance and repression in different countries and variation between Islamic sects. Morocco and Iran were particularly repressive. "Expulsion, forced conversion, and massacre—all three of rare occurrence in Sunni lands—were features of life in Iran up to the nineteenth century."[28] Different regimes varied in their toleration of other groups. The Messianic movement of the Almohads was highly intolerant of deviations from its version of Islam, and it was probably in the period of Almohad rule "that Christianity was finally extirpated from North Africa. Jews, too, suffered badly in North Africa and Spain—and exceptionally in Muslim history west of Iran—were given the choice between conversion, exile and death."[29]

There were differences too between rulers—at times an oscillating balance, with alternation between tolerance and the rigid reinstitution of traditional discrimination. There might also be retaliation against religious groups whose members had collaborated with a previous regime overthrown by revolution; and it is interesting to note that in contemporary Iran, this traditional charge of collaboration with the previous ruler is made against the Baha'is. On occasion the populace engaged in the massacre of religious groups whose members had attained too high an office or prestige or otherwise overstepped the bounds of acceptable behavior, as in the genocidal massacre of the Jewish inhabitants of Grenada in the eleventh century.[30]

In the modern period Arab countries received an infusion of Christian anti-Semitism, with Christian Arabs playing a leading role but supported at times by European diplomats, as in the Damascus affair of 1840, when Jews were accused of the ritual murder of a Franciscan father by his fellow monks and the French consul. There are now more versions and editions of the notorious Protocols of the Elders of Zion in Arabic than in any other language, as well as works charging a Jewish conspiracy against mankind, bloodlust, and ritual murder.[31]

In the years between 1941 and 1948, even before the establishment of the State of Israel, there were numerous outbreaks of anti-Jewish violence in Iraq, Syria, Egypt, Southern Arabia, and North Africa. And the Palestinian conflict, though secular in origin, draws on ancient religious prejudice as elaborated over time and has brought about the final destruction of the ancient Jewish communities in Arab lands.[32]

This history then is one of religious prejudice and discrimination, punctuated by genocidal episodes, but relatively tolerant for a universal, militant, proselytizing religion in possession of the absolute ultimate truth, becoming increasingly intolerant however in the modern period of Islam now resurgent.

Christian intolerance of other religions was especially marked in the Middle Ages, in the wars of the Counter-Reformation, and with some variability in the colonization of the Third World.

The Crusades against Islam were not genocidal in intent. They were not directed toward the extermination of Muslims. They were a defense, in general, against the expansion of Islam into Christian lands and, more specifically, a response to grievances concerning the plight of Christians in Islamic lands, the molestation of pilgrims, and the desecration of holy sites. The first Crusade, launched under Papal authority in 1095, granted the plenary indulgence of the remission of penance for sins to all those who came to the aid of Christians in Eastern lands. It aroused intense religious fervor and massive support.

Between the years 1095 and 1291, eight major crusading expeditions were launched. They were Holy Wars, not entirely comparable to the Jihads of Islamic history, but they did result in a number of genocidal massacres of the Muslim inhabitants of besieged cities, seemingly following acceptable norms of warfare in those days.

Jews were not the specific targets of the Crusades. But periods of religious Christian exaltation in Europe were always threatening to Jews, and the Crusades were regularly accompanied by extensive genocidal massacres of European Jews, perpetrated by frenzied hordes, or military bands, or both. This exterminatory factor even extended to the abortive Crusade of 1309.[33] The primary source of this murderous hatred was the accursed theological status of Jews associated with the central sacrament of Christianity and its symbolic representation in the Cross. The role of Jews was continuously represented, and indeed misrepresented, in Christian teaching and in the mystery plays as contemporary reality and as communal guilt extending to unborn generations.

This accursed theological status of Jews in Christianity has evolved further over the centuries, in response to changing historical circumstances. In the Middle Ages in Europe, there were the accretions of medieval beliefs in the Devil and in sorcery, and a corresponding demonization of Jews. Already in the twelfth century, the myth of the conspiracy of the Elders of Zion was foreshadowed.[34] Jews were accused of profanation of the Host, of practicing the ritual murder of Christian children, of pacts with the Devil, of conspiring to destroy Christendom, and of engaging in sorcery and other malevolent practices. They were assumed to be guilty of the Black Plague (1347-1350) and freely murdered throughout Europe. And they remained hostages to the fortunes of the societies in which they lived, conveniently vulnerable targets for periodic pogroms. Later, in the period of the enlightenment and the development of scientific thought, the theological license for persecution and massacre was transformed into racist theories and then ultimately into the Final Solution of Nazi Germany.

It is only in recent years that many of the Christian Churches have begun to modify their teaching in relation to Jews. But the demonization of Jews and evolved forms of the theological curse persist to the present day and contribute in some measure to the special anathema directed against the State of Israel.

TWENTIETH CENTURY GENOCIDES

The more specifically religious conflicts have now receded in significance. For the most part the major issues of contention in the twentieth century genocides are not differences in belief. There continues to be some persistence of the older forms in the religious massacres of Jews, as notably in Russia, and particularly in the Ukraine at the end of World War I. In Germany, under the Nazis, the theologically accursed status of Jews, with all its medieval accretions, persisted in a modern ideology of racial hierarchy and racial survival. And it now contributes to an almost world-wide delegitimation and dehumanization of Israel, centered in the United Nations, and threatening the survival of the state.[35] In Iran the survival of the Baha'is is threatened by an old style genocide against dissident sects, reproducing some of the more modern elements of the Nazi persecution of the Jews in the 1930s and masquerading as the suppression of treacherous political dissidents, organized as a political party with imperialist affiliations and conspiring against the Islamic revolution.

If one views the Communist commitment as somewhat analogous to religious faith, then one might argue that the eradication of religious groups in Communist states corresponds to the religious genocides of earlier times. The Legal Inquiry Committee of the International Commission of Jurists reported in 1959 that, in addition to other massive killings of Tibetans, the Chinese had killed Buddhist monks and lamas on a large scale, destroyed Buddhist monasteries, desecrated holy places, and publicly humiliated religious leaders in a manner calculated to shock the people out of their age-old religious faith.[36] And in a further report the Committee concluded that acts of genocide had been committed in Tibet in an attempt to destroy Tibetans as a religious group.[37] In Kampuchea the Pol Pot regime sought to eradicate the national religion of Buddhism, and members of a Muslim tribal group, the Cham, were victims of genocidal massacres. The Soviet Government systematically persecuted religious groups, seeking, unsuccessfully, to eliminate religious belief, affiliation, and ceremonial from Soviet life. Its victims included members of the majority Orthodox Church, Catholics, Jews, and

Muslims. The campaigns against Islam and Buddhism were said to have resulted in the virtual elimination of religious leaders, mosques, and lamaseries.[38] There was some relocation of groups, notably in the deportation of Muslim nations from the North Caucasus and the Crimea to penal exile under conditions inimical to survival.

However, over and above communist doctrinal rejection of religious commitment, other considerations would certainly have been of crucial significance. Tibet was a theocracy and a border state: effective Chinese colonization of the country (or recolonization, depending on one's interpretation of the constitutional position) certainly called for the effective dismantling of the religious center of power. The Khmer Rouge revolution could not conceivably have been more radical in its commitment to the total restructuring of the society and the eradication of all social strata which might possibly oppose its totalitarian regime. In Soviet Russia, quite apart from the consolidation of absolute rule, considerations of *realpolitik* were clearly significant in the genocidal deportations of Muslim peoples from the border areas of the Northern Caucasus and the Crimea.

Leaving aside the communist eradication of religious groups, and leaving aside also the genocides in the course of international warfare, genocide is essentially a phenomenon of plural societies;[39] and the superimposition of issues of conflict in these societies, and of differences between the plural sections in their history, culture, status, and role, renders it difficult to determine the significance of the religious element in the final catastrophe.[40] The Turkish government's genocide of its Christian Armenian subjects illustrates this difficulty.

Viscount Bryce, the distinguished British jurist, author, and statesman, who sponsored the major documentation of the genocide and consistently pleaded the Armenian cause, declared in a speech in the House of Lords on October 6, 1915, that "there was no Moslem passion against the Armenian Christians. All was done by the will of the Government, and done not from any religious fanaticism, but simply because they wished, for reasons purely political, to get rid of a non-Moslem element which impaired the homogeneity of the Empire, and constituted an element that might not always submit to oppression."[41] Toynbee, in his historical summary, described the increasing chauvinism of the ruling Young Turk party and commented further, when presenting estimates of the number of Armenians who perished in the genocide, that "this immense infliction of suffering and destruction of life was not the work of religious fanaticism. Fanaticism played no more part here than it has played in the fighting at Gallipoli or Kut, and the 'Holy War' which the Young Turks caused to be proclaimed in October 1914 was merely a political move to embarrass the Moslem subjects of the Entente Powers."[42]

There is general agreement that the Young Turk government was not motivated by religious fanaticism. But this does not mean that the religious differences and animosities were not significant in the genocidal process, and the eyewitness accounts assembled by Toynbee, and his own analysis, offer abundant evidence to the contrary. The government was not operating in a vacuum, but in a society in which religious affiliation had been the basis for administrative and social and political differentiation. The genocide was not perpetrated only by party officials, their regional and local representatives, the criminal bands they specially recruited, and the Kurds, traditional enemies of the Armenian people. There was also extensive participation in the genocide by the most varied strata of Turkish society. In the same way that one cannot understand the German genocide of Jews without taking account of the role of the major bureaucracies and the involvement of every segment of organized German society, so too it is necessary to take account of the involvement of the Turkish people themselves, peasants and townsmen, in the execution of the genocide.

The Turks, in their four hundred years of rule over the Armenians, might have pursued a policy designed to integrate them as full members of Turkish society. Instead, under the *millet* system, religious affiliation was emphasized and elevated into a basic principle of administration. On the one hand Christians were denied political participation in the dominant Muslim government; and on the other hand they were organized as separate units, under a patriarch, thus conferring an ecclesiastical character on their corporate identity and extending appreciable autonomy in spiritual matters, in schooling, and in the exercise of certain limited judicial functions.[43] Hence the system tended to maintain, and indeed to enhance, the plural divisions in the society. Differences were superimposed—ethnic, religious, administrative, political, and cultural. And to these differences there must be added an occupational differentiation in the nineteenth century, with the entry of Armenians into industry, commerce, and finance (though the overwhelming majority continued in their traditional occupations, as farmers and artisans).

In addition to the superimposition of structural differences, there was a superimposition of issues of conflict, punctuated by massacres and related to religious discrimination against Armenians and their struggles for greater security and equality of participation. The discrimination against the Christian subjects of the Ottoman Empire provided occasion for intervention by outside powers, motivated, one supposes, both by humanitarian concern and a predatory interest in the benefits to be derived from the dismemberment of the empire. The combination of internal resistance to oppression and external intervention precipitated the massacres of between one hundred and two hundred thousand Armenians during 1894-1895.

Johannes Lepsius, a dedicated representative of German mission-ary interests, in his authoritative study of the massacres, dismisses the suggestion that they were caused by a conflict of race or a national rising by the Armenians and concludes that "without any question their origin was purely political, or to state it more exactly, they were an administrative measure." But then he adds that "the facts go to prove that, considering the character of the Mohammedan People, whose very political passions are roused only by religious motives, this administrative measure must, and did, take the form of a religious persecution."[44] His study documents in detail the religious fanaticism of the massacres: the forced conversions under threat of death, the atrocities against priests—humiliated, tortured, mur-dered—and the desecration and destruction of holy places.

These genocidal massacres had unleashed social forces generated from the plural structure of the society and inimical to the Arme-nians, with demonstrations of religious hatred in terrible atrocities against priests and in the desecration and destruction of churches and forced conversions.

The religious differentiation and discrimination, and their ramifications in social structure and attitudes, were too recent to be suddenly effaced in 1915 as a significant element in the genocide. Moreover there are many accounts of religious fanaticism and persecution and atrocity.[45] In some areas, conversion to Islam might be offered as an alternative to deportation. In July 1915 the German consul at Samsun reported that the government had sent to Armenian homes fanatical and rigorously orthodox Muslims to propagate Islam under threat of the most dire consequences for those who remained faithful to their religious beliefs.[46] There were forced conversions of women, children seized and sent to orphanages or Turkish homes to be brought up as Muslims, and forced circumcisions. Lepsius refers to constant reports by consuls from December 1915 onwards that the Turkish government planned the forcible conversion to Islam of the survivors of the genocide, a charge the government denied.[47]

It was to be expected that priests would be massacred as part of the campaign to deprive Armenians of their leaders. Toynbee, in his book *Armenian Atrocities, The Murder of a Nation*, reproduces a formidable list of ecclesiastical victims up to September 22, 1915, with the following comment: "It is an amazing list, yet it is wholly consistent with the program of the Ottoman Government. The Armenian Church has been the bulwark of the Armenian race, and the race is marked down for extermination."[48]

But the massacres reproduce the atrocities of the 1894-1895 massacres and demonstrate a special animosity against the Armenian church and its priests. Morgenthau reports that "nothing was sacred to the Turkish gendarmes; under the plea of searching for hidden arms, they ransacked churches, treated the altars and sacred utensils with the utmost indignity, and even held mock ceremonies in imitation of the Christian sacraments. They would beat the priests into insensibility, under the pretense that they were the centers of sedition. When they could discover no weapons in the churches, they would sometimes arm the bishops and priests with guns, pistols, and swords, then try them before courts-martial for possessing weapons against the law, and march them in this condition through the streets, merely to arouse the fanatical wrath of the mobs."[49] Moreover, the government declaration of a *jihad*, however cynical a strategy to embarrass their enemies in the First World War, would inevitably have the effect of inciting religious fanaticism.

We can accept the argument that the precipitating events were the extreme Turkish nationalism of the ruling party and its perception of the Armenians as a threat to the integrity of the state, already greatly diminished by the secession of the Greeks and Balkan Christians. This is essentially the thesis of Melson in a recent article[50] in which he draws attention to the antecedent factors preceding the genocide, mentioning first the historical experience of "some persecution and contempt." This is an aspect on which we have placed much greater emphasis in our discussion of the significance of the religious differentiation.

Clearly religious differences were significant in the Croatian massacres of Serbs, as they were also in the mass killings upon the partition of India. The Croatian genocide of Serbs in the Second World War arose out of a long history of conflict, fueled later in the newly constituted state of Yugoslavia by Croatian resentment of Serbian hegemony and repression and Serbian resistance to Croatian demands for autonomy. The defeat of Yugoslavia by the Axis powers, the partition which followed, and the establishment of the satellite Croatia provided Croats with the opportunity to slaughter hundreds of thousands of Serbs in a genocide which bore a strong religious stamp, reminiscent of earlier wars against the Schismatics. It was a genocide by Croatian Roman Catholics, with Muslim support, against Serbian followers of the Orthodox Church. Some Catholic priests participated in the killings and conducted ceremonies of forced conversion by which thousands of Serbs escaped massacre. And there was participation also, or at any rate condonation of the massacres, at higher levels of the Catholic hierarchy. Serbian forces themselves engaged in counter massacres of non-conformists, especially Muslims.[51]

In India, Hindus were in a great majority and separated from Muslims not only by religion but also by caste prohibitions on intermingling. In addition, there was some occupational differentiation, with Hindus more strongly represented in government administration, the professions, business, and finance. Inevitably in a politically unified but communally divided India, Hindus would have dominated the society.

Partition into a Hindu India and Muslim Pakistan solved this problem. But the distribution of populations, with substantial religious minorities in areas dominated numerically by members of other religions or with much intermingling of peoples of different religions, did not permit of an easy severance into a Hindu India and a Muslim Pakistan. The relocation of groups on the basis of religion provided the opportunity for massacre and counter-massacre in a continuous spiral of escalating violence. This was particularly extreme in the Punjab, where Hindus and Sikhs massacred Muslims, and Muslims massacred Hindus and Sikhs. Estimates of the numbers slaughtered range from 200,000 or less to half a million or more, with ten and a half million refugees engaged in the gigantic exchange of population.[52]

Pakistan proved unstable, disrupted by discrimination against East Pakistan and by inadequate response to demands for greater autonomy, leading to an escalation of conflict in a process quite characteristic of plural societies. The pluralism was extreme, comprising West Pakistan, with its Punjabi, Baluchi, Pathan, and Sindhi peoples, and East Pakistan, separated by 1,000 miles, and incorporating the eastern half of Bengal, a portion of Assam, and the tribal areas of the Chittagong Hill Tracts. They were in fact two distinct countries in terms of culture, language, economy, and geography, the bond between them being the common religion of Islam. But even in this respect there was diversity, with between ten to twelve million Hindus in a population of about seventy-five million in East Pakistan. Discrimination by West Pakistan, which Bengalis perceived as an internal colonialism, fueled demands, which West Pakistan finally sought to suppress by a massive armed onslaught. This was directed against leaders and potential leaders, indiscriminately against civilians, including women and children, and with special animus against the Hindu population. The International Commission of Jurists expressed the view that there "was a strong prima facie case that the crime of genocide had been committed against the Hindus of East Bengal."[53]   While the Hindus were suspected of inciting a movement for secession, it seems inconceivable that, given the history of communal conflicts in India, the religious differences were not a significant element in the attempt to exterminate or drive out a large portion of the Hindu population.

In Lebanon, carved by the French out of its mandated portion of the Ottoman Empire, the constitutional solution to religious pluralism made provision for a unified legislature and administration, with structural balance between the religious sections based on a formula for differential participation. The effect was to maintain, and probably to enhance, the significance of religious division in a society, with appreciable geographic concentration of sects and the recognition of religious courts having jurisdiction in matters affecting personal status; in 1958 there had been an outbreak of civil war between Christians and Muslims-Druzes. Conflict over the original terms of incorporation, which increasingly ceased to correspond to the numerical distribution of religious groups, and the involvement of Palestinian refugees in the communal conflicts, finally led to the civil war of 1975-6 in which religious groups freely engaged in mass murder. Many different elements have contributed to the final massacres, but religious affiliations have been certainly basic, defining both the murderers and their victims.[54]

Among the remaining four cases we have classified as twentieth century genocides, two can be interpreted readily without reference to religious differences. The first, the annihilation of the Herero people by the German rulers of South West Africa in 1904, was essentially an exterminatory reprisal for rebellion. The second, the massacre of Ibos in Northern Nigeria in 1966, was precipitated by ethnic conflict and resentment of the Ibo presence.[55]

In two cases, the massacres of Tutsi by Hutu in Rwanda in 1963 and of Hutu by Tutsi in Burundi in 1972-73, there were no sharp religious divisions. Indeed, religious communion seems to have been no particular obstacle to massacre.

> The massacres were accompanied by unspeakable brutality. But a Christian touch was not altogether wanting. Thus, Lemarchant refers to the courageous action of Catholic Fathers in refusing to surrender Tutsi who had found asylum in their mission stations. In a bizarre episode on Christmas day a band of Hutu, armed with clubs, machetes, and lances, screened a congregation at Christmas service, removing the Tutsi worshippers, whom they led to a rocky promontory above a river. The Tutsi asked the grace of a last prayer, whereupon both Hutu and Tutsi, in a similar reflex, fell upon their knees, praying loudly. Then, according to the narrator, the Hutu proceeded rapidly and with propriety (propre-ment) to the execution of the victims, consigning their bodies to the river.[56]

These four cases are a reminder that religious differences between murderers and victims are not a necessary element in genocide.

CONCLUDING COMMENT

We started from the premise that there is an intimate relationship between religion and genocide. The argument and documentation we have presented substantially support this thesis. If it is accepted, then a number of implications follow for the prevention of genocide and related mass killings.

Religious groups have often been involved in genocidal massacres, either as perpetrators or as victims. The involvement as perpetrators may be quite direct, as in the annihilation of heretical sects or the genocidal massacres of non-believers. Often the religious element operates indirectly, encouraging a dehumanization of the victims. In either case responsibility attaches to religious leaders to examine the role of their religious teaching in encouraging an exclusion of other groups from a common humanity and in providing a theological license for mass murder. For the victims, their own suffering might be sublimated by seeking to extend to their endangered religious groups the support and protection which they had been denied in their own holocaust.

One hopes that, if the support of religious groups were enlisted, some significant progress could be made in the prevention of genocide.

REFERENCES

1. We are following the definition of genocide in Article 2 of the United Nations Genocide Convention. For the text see page 112, above.

2. Gustav Mensching, *Tolerance and Truth in Religion* (University of Alabama Press, 1971), especially 9, 14-17, and 64 ff.

3. Ibid., 126-127.

4. Ibid., 11-13.

5. See Emil L. Fackenheim, *The Jewish Return to History* (New York: Schocken Books, 1978), 75, fn. 17.

6. Clifford Geertz, *Islam Observed—Religious Development in Morocco and Indonesia* (New Haven: Yale University Press, 1968).

7. Steven Runciman, *The Medieval Manichee* (Cambridge University Press, 1960), Chapter 6 and discussion on 132 and 141.

8. Bernard Lewis, *The Jews of Islam* (Princeton University Press, 1984), 24.

9. Ibid., 5.

10. Ibid., 53.

11. See Leon Poliakov, *The History of Anti-Semitism* (New York: Vanguard Press, 1965), I: 264-69.

12. Bernard Lewis, *Islam in History* (London: Alcove Press, 1973), 231.

13. This follows the account in the *Encyclopaedia Judaica* (Jerusalem: Keter Publishing House, 1971), 359.

14. Lewis, *Islam in History*, 226-32.

15. G. R. Elton, in W. J. Sheils, ed., *Persecution and Toleration* (Oxford: Basil Blackwell, 1984), xiii, xiv.

16. Lewis, *Islam in History*, 233.

17. Ibid., 229, 234.

18. Roger le Tourneau, *The Almohad Movement in North Africa in the Twelfth and Thirteenth Centuries* (Princeton University Press, 1969), 13. In a discussion of a rebellion against Almohad power, he also writes of a purge of enormous dimensions which, according to one source, resulted in 32,780 deaths (p. 54).

19. Lewis, *Islam in History*, 234-35.

20. The *Baha'is in Iran* (New York: Baha'i International Community, 1982), 35. See also the following additional sources: Amin Banani, *Religion or Foreign Intrigue: the Case of the Babi-Baha'i Movements in Iran* (31st Congress of Human Sciences in Asia and North Africa, September, 1983); Roger Cooper, *The Baha'is of Iran* (London: Minority Rights Group, 1982); John Ferraby, *All Things Made New* (London: Baha'i Publishing Trust, 1975); Christine Hakin, *Les Baha'is ou victoire sur la violence* (Lausanne: Favre, 1982); and William Sears, *A Cry from the Heart* (Oxford: George Ronald, 1982).

21. *Encyclopaedia Judaica*, 344.

22. Ibid., 346.

23. Ibid., 350.

24. Lewis, *The Jews of Islam*, 21.

25. Ibid., 20.

26. Ibid., 23.

27. Norman A. Stillman, *The Jews of Arab Lands* (Philadelphia: The Jewish Publication Society of America, 1979), 97.

28. Lewis, *The Jews of Islam*, 40.

29. Ibid., 52. See also Stillman, *The Jews of Arab Lands*, 77.

30. Stillman, *Ibid.*, 57-59 and 211-25. More generally on the historical record, see Lewis, *The Jews of Islam*, 44-58; also Abraham L. Udovitch and Lucette Valensi, *The Last Arab Jews: The Communities of Jerba, Tunisia* (Harwood, Academic Publishers, 1984).

31. Lewis, *Islam in History*, 143; Stillman, *The Jews of Arab Lands*, Epilogue, 108ff.

32. Lewis, *The Jews of Islam*, 191, and "The Return of Islam," in Michael Curtis, ed., *Religion and Politics in the Middle East* (Boulder, Colorado: Westview Press, 1981), 27-28.

33. Poliakov, *The History of Anti-Semitism*, I: 50.

34. Ibid., 58.

35. Ehud Sprinzak, "Anti-Zionism: From Delegitimation to Dehumanization," *Forum* 53: 1-12.

36. *The Question of Tibet and the Rule of Law* (Geneva: International Commission of Jurists, 1959).

37. *Tibet and the Chinese People's Republic* (Report by the Legal Inquiry Committee on Tibet, International Commission of Jurists, Geneva, 1960), 3.

38. Robert Conquest, *The Nation Killers: The Soviet Deportation of Nationalists* (New York: Macmillan, 1970), 97-99.

39. See Leo Kuper, *Genocide* (New Haven: Yale University Press, 1982), 142-46.

40. Ibid., 57-59.

41. Arnold Toynbee, *Armenian Atrocities: The Murder of a Nation* (London: Hodder and Stoughton, 1915), 7.

42. *The Treatment of Armenians in the Ottoman Empire, 1915-1916* (London: His Majesty's Stationery Office, 1916), 651-52.

43. Ibid., 617-19.

44. Johannes Lepsius, *Armenia and Europe* (London: Hodder and Stoughton, 1897), 34-37, also section 4 and details in Appendix. In his book on Genocide, *op.cit.*, Kuper described the massacres as "a sort of ambassadorial note to the European Powers to refrain from intervention in the domestic affairs of Turkey, and a most bloody warning to the Armenians themselves against seeking the intercession of these powers on their behalf or aspiring to autonomy" (116).

45. *Treatment of Armenians* Documents 7, 11, 12, 57, 59, and 76.

46. Permanent Peoples' Tribunal, *A Crime of Silence: The Armenian Genocide* (London: Zed Books, 1985), 133 and ff.

47. As quoted in *A Crime of Silence*, 82. On forced conversions see also Lepsius, *La rapport secret du docteur Johannes Lepsius* (Paris: Payot, 1918), 282-88.

48. Ibid., 104-5.

49. Henry Morgenthau, *Ambassador Morgenthau's Story* (New York: Doubleday, 1918), 305.

50. Robert Melson, "Provocation or Nationalism: A Theoretical Inquiry into the Armenian Genocide of 1915," in *The Armenian Genocide in Perspective*, Richard G. Hovannisian, ed. (New Brunswick: Transaction Books, 1986), 61-84.

51. Kuper, *Genocide*, 89 and fn 8.

52. Ibid., 63-68.

53. Ibid., 78-80, and International Commission of Jurists, *The Events in East Pakistan 1971: A Legal Study* (Geneva, 1972).

54. Kuper, *Genocide*, 80-83.

55. Ibid., 74-76.

56. Kuper, *The Pity of It All* (Minneapolis: The University of Minneapolis Press, 1977), 197.

Dilemmas of Transnational Defense of Minorities

The Movement for Armenian Rights (1876-1915) and the Contemporary Movement for Soviet Jewry

Helen Fein

PREFACE. Since this conference paper was written (1985), enormous changes have taken place in the Soviet Union. *Perestroika* has led to both democratic and anti-democratic movements: towards decentralization and independence, ethnic conflict within and between states, pogroms against Armenians instigated or overlooked by central authorities in Azerbaijan (and against Armenians and others in other republics), officially sponsored anti-Semitic movements, and a mass exodus of Soviet Jews. These changes appear to date some of the data analyzed but do not challenge the central theme or dilemma presented.

The dilemma is that minorities in oppressive states who have global links to an ethnic or religious collectivity abroad are sometimes able to appeal to the great powers to respond to their plight, but this action may provoke further repression rather than protection as the minorities become dependent on the consistency of the intervention of these patrons for their safety. These patrons' conception of their interest is often capricious, depending on their relations with the governments involved, other great powers, and the political clout of the domestic constituencies petitioning to help these minorities in other countries. War between the patron states and such oppressive states annuls the influence of the patrons and may endanger the minority further, as war both triggers genocidal intentions and masks genocide. Civil wars and imperial decline may also lead the ruling elite to consider genocide as a means to "solve" a minority problem or to terrorize other minorities and the majority to comply with their rule.

With the break-up of the Soviet Union and the resulting ethnic conflicts in many parts of the former empire, genocide remains a possibility. The action by the center and the Communist Party in stirring up pogroms against Armenians in Azerbaijan, in instigating Pamyat to threaten a pogrom in Moscow, and the publication of Hitler's *Mein Kampf* by the Defense Ministry show that central forces, possibly using these issues to enlist popular support for a military dictatorship, are willing to ignite group hatred and violence for their own ends. Whether they have the organizational ability now or can acquire it in the future to commit genocide remains an open question.

The goals and strategies of Armenians and Jews, and other national groups, will differ, depending on their different existential opportunities and interests. However, given these possibilities, it seems to me imperative that all minorities and patron states defend the basic human rights of all groups in the former USSR as well as the right of emigration, regardless of the political solutions to questions of states' independence, autonomy or confederation, and ethnic conflicts over sovereignty.

* * * * *

Protests against killings, persecution, and oppression of subjugated minority groups in other states have been organized for over a century in Britain and the United States. Although the questions in the nineteenth century which drew most participants to rights movements on both sides of the Atlantic revolved around domestic issues, foreign issues—such as the persecution of the Christian minorities and nationalities within the Ottoman Empire and the Jewish subjects of the Tsar in Russia—also elicited concern. In some cases the Western public identified with minorities involved in successful movements for national liberation. Local revolts and foreign aid brought about the independence of Greece and Bulgaria. But the Armenian reform movement led not only to defeat but to annihilation in 1915 when the ruling troika—a chauvinistic faction of the Committee of Union and Progress, or "Young Turks," who organized the 1908 coup—authorized the deportation and murder of the Armenians under the cover of World War I, which made potential allied sanctions difficult if not impossible.

Many have remarked on the consequences of the failure of the victorious allies to punish the perpetrators of the genocide, award the Armenians any compensation, and keep their promises of an Armenian protectorate (guaranteeing its autonomy), as well as the reading of these failures by Adolf Hitler.[1]

It may be just as important to examine the precedents of that genocide in order to consider what we can learn from the interaction of the perpetrators, the victims, and outside states which may influence them. The strategies of transnational human rights movements and limits of power (or willingness to use power) of one state to intervene in the arena the other prefers to label "internal affairs," despite international human rights covenants, in order to protect minorities—and majorities—are ever-present issues.

We ask: How did the centuries-old discrimination endured by the

Armenians escalate to massacre and genocide? What were the goals and strategies of the Armenian movements within the empire? What was the role of the great powers and how did this interact with the expectations of the Armenians? What were the goals pursued by the Sultan and the subsequent Turkish elites ruling the empire and how did they perceive the Armenian and other minorities? What interests and strategies were considered by the great powers and especially the Triple Entente (England, France, and Russia) for introducing change in the Ottoman Empire? What anticipated costs conditioned their calculus of means? What was the cost of their non-intervention? To better consider the implications the Armenian experience may yield for contemporary use, I then turn to the history and strategic dilemmas of the American movement for Soviet Jewry.

THE ARMENIAN QUESTION AND THE OTTOMAN EMPIRE, 1876-1915

The Ottoman Empire began declining in its ability to rule and retain territory in the seventeenth century, two centuries before Nicholas I of Russia labelled it, in 1853, the "sick man" of Europe. The Ottoman governing class was unable to conceive of any way of transforming the empire that would offer its many aspiring nationalities a credo to compete with that of national liberation of the nineteenth century. There was no basis of solidarity among its subjects to legitimate Ottoman domination, no notion of a common nationality, no representative mechanism, and no common bond of belief or language within the Empire, which stretched in mid-seventeenth century from Persia to Hungary. The Ottomans, after war and massacre failed, had acceded to Greek emancipation, Bulgarian self-rule, and the independence of Romania and Serbia by 1876. By 1908, they had withdrawn from continental Europe except for Salonica and Albania.

The British helped the Turks to check the process of imperial disintegration in the nineteenth century, fearing Russian penetration of the Straits. Britain viewed with alarm the Tsar's expansion into Asia, his declarations of concerns for the Christian subjects of the neighboring empire, and rushed to defend the Turks against Russia in the Crimean War. But the Turks' oppression of their Christian minorities, which justified European intervention, obliged the Turks' allies to press them to institute reforms. To accommodate or to anticipate such great power demands, the Sultan issued edicts or accepted peace treaties in 1839, 1856, 1863, and 1878 which granted all subjects equal rights, opportunities, and justice under the law.

Never implemented, these became empty promises.

Regardless of wealth or status, the minorities had neither civil nor minority rights. The prototypical Armenian was the oppressed peasant or *rayah*, subject to special taxes and the depredations of Kurdish nomads whom they were obliged to board during the winter. In the late eighteenth and early nineteenth centuries the Armenians had appealed to the Russian Tsar, who claimed to be the protector of Orthodox Christians in the Ottoman Empire; but after 1876 other European powers entered the scene, legitimating the results of the Russo-Turkish War in the Treaty of Berlin (replacing the earlier Treaty of San Stefano between the Turks and the Russians alone). Equal rights were granted in the constitution of the new Sultan, Abdul-Hamid (1876), but that document was quickly withdrawn. The appeals of Armenians in 1876 for specific implementation of their rights with European oversight to check Turkish and Kurdish local officials were disregarded in the Treaty of Berlin; the Armenians had attended the Berlin conference with only a "paper spoon," and came away with an open-ended funnel in which promises and remonstrances were poured platitudinally and periodically. The English did obtain the right to appoint military consuls within the interior of the Ottoman Empire, but these officials could only investigate Armenian complaints. As they usually arrived during or after the massacres and had no authority, they could (at best) confirm their suspicions, but could neither deter nor prosecute the perpetrators.

The dynamics of British pressure, Turkish persecution, and British nonresistance were explained in 1890 by the British Consul, Clifford Loyd:

> All the Christians asked for was protection, but this was the one thing the Government failed to provide. ... The result is that this summer the valley has again been overrun by the Kurds, *who here, as elsewhere, openly declared that their action meets with the approval of the Turkish government.* ... England's responsibility towards Armenia is attested by a triple bond of obligation. Together with France, she contracted through the Crimean War a special obligation towards all the Christian subjects of the Porte. ... The Crimean War convinced the Porte that the integrity and independence of the Ottoman Empire were absolutely essential to the balance of power in Europe. The Porte ... immediately fastened on the diplomatic advantage which the policy of the Crimean War had given it. ... From that day to this England has done nothing to fulfill her solemn obligation under that convention. And the Armenians, meanwhile, have been enduring the life of agony which the Consular Reports reveal.[2]

Armenians developed a new collective consciousness in the latter half of the nineteenth century as Western missions in the Armenian provinces inspired Armenian cultural, educational, and political self-organization. Stimulated by the Balkan movements for national independence and contemporary European revolutionary movements, their aspirations and yearning for self-assertion rose. Educated Armenians within and outside of the Ottoman Empire established secret (but too well-advertised) self-defense and revolutionary organizations in the last quarter of the century: the Black Cross (1878), Protectors of the Fatherland (1881), the Armenakan Party (1885), the Hunchakian Revolutionary Party (1887), and the Dash-naktsutiun (Armenian Revolutionary Federation) in 1891. Although some organizations were infiltrated and aborted, they drew upon the Armenian peasants' cognizance of their impotence and degradation, inciting instances of self-defense against Kurds and government troops, anti-government rebellion (or acts of local resistance to demands of authorities labelled as rebellion), and later assassinations (of Muslims and Armenians) and random collective violence against Kurds.[3]

The Sultan responded to self-defense and resistance with officially sanctioned state and popularly executed massacres. Officially he organized the Hamidiye, regiments of Kurdish tribesmen modeled after the Russian Cossacks, who perpetrated massacres of the Armenians similar to the pogroms the Black Hundreds in Russia committed against the Jews during the same period. The Hunchaks next (in 1895) tried mass protest in the capital, seeking implementation of European-sponsored reforms; some members came armed, and the result was a Turkish massacre. The next year a small group of Dashnaks took over and threatened to blow up the foreign-owned Ottoman Bank if their demands for redress, guaranteed by the European powers, were not met. European diplomats persuaded them to retreat and guaranteed them sanctuary, but the Armenians of Istanbul had no similar protection as marauding Turkish mobs almost instantly set out to slaughter Armenians without police hindrance in another officially sanctioned massacre, leading to 5,000-6,000 Armenian deaths and mass emigration, estimated by one source at 75,000 persons.[4] The slaughter of Armenians in the capital was accompanied by a wave of massacres of Armenians in the provinces; from 1894 to 1896, an estimated 100,000 to 200,000 Armenians were slain, while thousands more suffered material ruin.[5]

The strategies of Armenian revolutionary parties are viewed by some historians as rationally calculated attempts to secure their demands—although the romance of revolutionary militancy often deterred a pragmatic self-assessment—by instigating the intervention of the European Great Powers with a policy of provoking Turkish massacres in reprisal to Armenian "provocations." Langer views this as cynical exploitation of the hapless Armenian victims, but Walker considers it a desperate but legitimate tactic:

> Certainly, they did act provocatively, and in that sense did "want" reprisals; but only in the sense of wanting to show to the world in one brief, dramatic flash the lingering inevitable horrors which they had to suffer more slowly, year in, year out. Quantitatively there was nothing to choose between a long-drawn-out massacre or a quick one. ... Almost all of the massacres of the 1890s occurred without provocation; and to blame Armenian revolutionaries for the killings which occurred after the action of a revolutionary . . . is to confuse provocation with executive decision.[6]

Under terms of the Treaty of Berlin, Britain could not exert pressure on the Sultan without backing from the other powers, most of which had self-interested motives to object to "coercion." Britain, having lost all faith in the Sultan's willingness to reform, considered a plan to invade Turkey in 1895, sailed their ships into the Dardanelles, and invited Russia to join its partition of the Empire. France, having a large financial investment in the Empire, resisted all plans to dismember it, directly and indirectly. Russia first rejected the plan in 1895, reversed itself in 1896 (making plans for a preemptive invasion of the Bosporus), and then reversed itself again after the French disclosed the plan publicly, arousing opposition within the Russian government.

The great powers, having rejected invasion, collaboratively spun hypothetical plans for reform, completing a sixty-four page scheme in February 1897 that was never implemented by the Porte. Thus, by the turn of the twentieth century, Armenians in the Ottoman Empire were seen by the Turks as a foreign ward that could be ravished periodically when her European great-aunts and uncles were not looking. But Great Power protests only stirred resentment against the ward, instigating the warder's lust, which was never effectively sanctioned by her protectors.

Besides massacre, mass rape and forced conversion were other means the government sanctioned to eliminate the Armenian people in the 1890s. Bryce observed: "As has been said by the writer who knows Asia Minor better than probably any other European, 'The Turks attempted to ensure by a system of outrage that over a large tract of country no Armenian woman should become the mother of an

Armenian child.'"[7] Sexual violence thus reinforced the ethnic hierarchy.

There was little domestic instigation to protect the Armenians when foreign policy interests were posed in Britain. British policy was no different when Gladstone was in office than when the Tories governed, despite the Liberal espousal of moral crusades. Public opinion on the Armenian question apparently was articulate only in England (and the United States), and the public was essentially reactive and, for the most part, uncommitted to an enduring organized movement to change British policy. The Evangelical Alliance and similar groups had little impact on state policy when competitive national interests were anticipated and weighed by the British Foreign Office. Langer argues that it was rational for the continental powers to dismiss the Armenian question:

> After all, if the Turks were massacring the Armenians, so were the Russians massacring the Jews. If the Turks oppressed the Armenians, did not the Russians oppress them too?... One might sympathize with these people, but one could not start a great European conflagration for their sake, and everyone understood that a reopening of the Turkish question might very well result in such a conflagration.[8]

Despite the European legal tradition justifying humanitarian intervention of states against other states perpetrating massive crimes against their people, then—as now—genocide was considered an internal affair.

The Armenian revolutionary movement increasingly turned toward cooperation with other ethnic movements for reform within the Empire. In 1908 the Young Turks of the Committee of Union and Progress (Ittihat), headed by a central committee (Cemiyet), after two years of army mutinies demanded and secured the Sultan's restoration of the 1876 constitution. The party's slogan was "Freedom, Justice, Equality, Fraternity." Its victory was welcomed by Muslims, Christians, and Jews. Armenian revolutionary committees in exile cooperated with the CUP, anticipating that Armenians would obtain civil rights and proportional representation, as had been promised. In the first national Parliament, the Turks had only a slight majority: 141 of the 288 seats were held by minorities.

But early promises of rights and "Ottomanization," as well as the decentralization of administration, were forgotten as a chauvinistic faction became dominant in the CUP after 1911, when the political situation became more desperate. The rout of the Turks accelerated as Austria-Hungary annexed Bosnia and Herzegovina in 1908 and

Italy attacked Tripoli in 1911. A coalition of Bulgaria, Serbia, and Greece attacked and defeated Turkey in the First Balkan War of 1912. However Turkey regained some territory against a divided coalition in the Second Balkan War of 1913.

The Young Turks who made the revolution "did not want only to save the state in its existing form . . . (but) wanted to revive it and make it a going concern in the modern world."[9] The new men of power conceived of no way to retain their dominion and accept the demands of minorities—the emerging pan-Arab movement, the Maronite Christians, the Greek Christians, the Macedonians, the Albanians, and the Armenians. To justify their domination, they adopted a credo based on Pan-Turanianism, which alleged a prehistoric mythic unity among Turanian peoples based on racial origin which was to be implemented by "Turkification," instituting the Turkish language throughout and Turkish supremacy over Muslim masses, centralizing rule from Constantinople.[10] This implied a strategy of moving toward Central Asia to unite Turkic peoples stretching to China. But the Armenians were situated in the middle of this broad swath, in Anatolia.

In 1912 Russia's perception of her interests changed. The Tsar tried to pacify the ethnic minorities and stabilize the Armenian provinces adjoining Russia to stave off unrest, Hovannisian asserts.[11] After protracted negotiations, the European powers which had signed the Treaty of Berlin agreed to a reform scheme which the Turkish government was pressed to sign (with the Russians alone who were to enforce it) in February 1914. For the first time, means of implementing equal justice were enacted: there were to be two European Inspector-Generals observing the tax collectors, courts, and schools, and local officials, and a mixed police force.[12]

World War I gave the ruling Turkish troika, allied with Germany, the opportunity to retract this promise, establishing Turkish hegemony as it annulled the Armenian question by annihilating the Armenians. The British official White Paper, prepared by Arnold Toynbee but authored by Lord Bryce, best documents the background events and the segregation, stripping, deportation, and massacre of the Armenian population; it estimated that two-thirds of the 1.8 million Armenians in the Ottoman Empire in 1914 were annihilated or deported to the Arabian desert in 1915, concluding that:

> It is evident that the war was merely an opportunity and not a cause—in fact, that the deportation scheme, and all that it involved, flowed inevitably from the general policy of the Young Turkish Government.[13]

The only government with any potential means of sanctioning Turkey to make it stop killing was Germany, but it had been indifferent or opposed to earlier sanctions proposed among the Treaty of Berlin signatories. German ambassadors first tried to overlook the policy of their ally, but later protested the massacres to the Turkish government, first in an equivocating voice and then bluntly. The Third German Ambassador, Count Paul von Wolff-Metternich, sought unsuccessfully in December 1915 to persuade the Turkish government to issue a statement disassociating Germany from the Turks' crimes in order to repudiate allegations abroad that Germany had instigated them, but concluded that it was impossible without the threat of sanctions. And Berlin was unwilling to risk alienating a wartime ally by making a public protest or applying strong pressures.[14]

Although the war served as a cover, a pretext for annihilation, it did not do so primarily by diminishing the visibility of the victims. The Turks could cover up neither the massacres nor the mass participation in expulsion and looting by Muslim villagers. There was a repertoire, a tradition of collective violation of the other, upon which the Turks could draw. The repertoire specified that the actors would perform the scenario on an open stage. The massacres were reported promptly in the British and American press. Perhaps some concern for the reactions of neutrals could be seen by the exemption of Armenians in major cities where foreigners were concentrated —Constantinople and Smyrna—from expulsion after the protest of U.S. Ambassador Morgenthau.[15]

World War I altered the calculus of deterrents and costs of genocide once the ability of the allied powers to intervene was annulled. Britain, France, and Russia were now enemies; indeed, Turkey had been thrust back in the winter of 1915 by a Russian force including Russian Armenians—a circumstance used to charge the Armenians with being enemies, too.

Can we separate consideration of the responsibility for the genocide of 1915 from the failure of the strategy of the Triple Entente regarding the Armenians which had proved to be a disaster by 1895? Dr. Johannes Lepsius, testifying for the defense of the Armenian assassin of Talaat Bey (an architect of the genocide) in Germany in 1911, charged that

> In the game of chess between London and Petersburg the Armenian was the pawn, sometimes pushed forward, sometimes sacrificed. The humanitarian causes, "protection of Christians," were pretexts. When in

1895 Abdul-Hamid was forced to sign the plan of reforms presented by England, Russia and France, he had already set in motion a number of Armenian massacres. Lord Salisbury announced that, as far as England was concerned, the Armenian question had ceased to exist. Prince Lobanov indicated to the Sultan that he had nothing to worry about because Russia pays no attention to the execution of reforms. The Sultan drew his own conclusions.[16]

Bryce believed that in 1896 the Triple Entente had endangered the Armenians by transforming them to an irritant, seen as a disloyal, Western-oriented minority; the Sultan, Abdul-Hamid, decided to remove any grounds for power—sharing by decimating the Armenians in the Armenian *vilayets*, so there were no Armenian majorities there.[17]

Although the European warranties and European movements undoubtedly raised the Armenians' expectations, the source of national self-consciousness was latent in the Balkan national programs and the Russian revolutionary movements. What threatened the Armenians was not the extent of great power interventions, but the lack of sanctions and/or actual intervention, the ineffectuality of protest without sanctions. When competitive interests were at stake, no state would sacrifice its national interest to aid the Armenians.

The strategy of the Armenian revolutionaries between 1890 and 1896 increased the provocations (violations of the status quo likely to evoke collective reprisals) in Turkish eyes without increasing the civil rights or physical security of the Armenians except in instances where preparations for self-defense enabled them to hold off marauding mobs and government troops. Given the structure of ethnic domination in the empire and the ability of the Sultan to appeal to Muslim solidarity and to use the Kurds against the Armenians, any challenge to the order of domination might provoke vengeful retaliation against the Armenians. Insofar as Armenian violence was directed against local oppressors and may have turned into anti-Kurdish collective violence, it made collective reprisals more likely, fortified the authority of the Sultan, and negated revolutionary appeals for unity. The strategy of the Armenian revolutionaries became one of the interacting causes increasing the likelihood they would be perceived as a threat.

After 1908, this strategy was nonviolent and political. The Armenian nationalists and revolutionaries, believing the promises of the Young Turks, joined with them in 1908. But once the World War was started, the alternatives before them all led to deadly endings. Had they taken up arms against the government, they would have been hunted down and killed. Had they encouraged defections among the Russian Armenians or flight to Russia, they would been condemned and killed as traitors by one side or the other. The time to deter the genocide had passed; the powers that could have deterred it had rejected using sanctions (and incentives) consistently or to intervene to protect the rights of the Armenians. Now the Armenians found themselves the objects, not the subject, of their history.

THE AMERICAN MOVEMENT FOR SOVIET JEWRY AND THE FUTURE OF RUSSIAN JEWS

We turn to examine the plight of Soviet Jewry up to 1985, a powerless minority in a relationship to the imperial state with suggestive parallels to that of the Armenians in the Ottoman Empire. The Armenians were, and the Jews are, viewed as enemies by the dominant elite in multi-ethnic empires with symbolic kin—other Armenians, other Jews—in states with which the empire is in conflict. Both minorities depend on their kin and on public opinion in such states to protect them.

There are significant differences in the culture, organization, control of violence, and role of minority groups in these empires. The norm of Islamic life was toleration of the *dhimmi* (protected peoples of the Book) as long as they accepted subordination—never equality—while the alleged norm of Soviet society is the equal rights of all peoples. The Soviet Union was (prior to the Gorbachev era) an organized, stable, and expansive totalitarian state, easily suppressing rebellion in neighboring Communist states. Most often it relied on bureaucratic violence, in contrast to the disintegrating Ottoman Empire, which had a limited bureaucracy, was challenged by subjugated nationalities on its periphery for nearly a century before 1915, and regularly used mass collective violence to punish the Armenians and other rebellious groups.

Until 1967 most Soviet Jews appeared passive, "the Jews of silence," as Eli Wiesel called them,[18] showing few signs of collective identification as Jews, despite discrimination and widespread belief they were alien.

The definition of Jews as alien in Russia is not new. The Russian state exploited popular anti-Semitism in the nineteenth century in response to threats to its autocracy. The state sanctioned pogroms after the assassination of Alexander II (1881), with popular participation which served both to ventilate and to divert popular unrest. The populist *narodniks* congratulated the peasants for attacking the Jews, seeing this as a first step towards a social revolution.

By contrast, Marxist movements generally disdained using anti-Semitism to appeal to the people. Although Marx was stridently hostile to the Jews in his only writing on the Jewish question, equating them with capitalism, the Marxists' view evolved. Succeeding Marxist and Social Democratic theoreticians—Engels, Kautsky, Lenin, Trotsky, and Bebel—repudiated anti-Semitism, viewing it as a tool of reaction—"the socialism of fools," as Bebel put it. The Bolsheviks rejected Jewish nationalism (Zionism) as a diversion of the Jewish working class from the class struggle in Russia, as did the non-Bolshevik Jewish Workers' Bund. From 1917, the Soviet Constitution and subsequent Soviet law guaranteed Jews equal rights, punished discrimination and overt anti-Semitic acts, and recognized Jews as a nationality with collective national rights, including cultural expression. They enjoyed Yiddish schools, publications, and theater until 1939.

Although Jews in Russia were associated with many parties and movements, many early Bolsheviks came from Jewish backgrounds but disdained Jews and Judaism. These "non-Jewish Jews," as Isaac Deutscher put it,[19] and the over-representation of Jews in revolutionary movements became the basis of stigma and stereotype of the Jews, fortifying anti-Semitism. Secularized Jews were attracted to communism, because it promised a universalistic community without discrimination or exploitation. Instead of waiting for the messiah, they awaited the revolution. Thus, members of the Jewish bourgeoisie as well as the working class initially welcomed the revolution.

Given this background of promises and the general hostility of communism to organized religion, secularized Soviet Jews did not protest religious discrimination in the first two decades of Soviet life.

Changes in the status of the Jews, later seen to be cumulative, began before World War II. Since the late 1930s, Jews were eliminated from positions of influence and denied entry to the diplomatic corps, political bodies, higher bureaucracy, and the military. Some have related this to increasing ethnic competition and a wartime appeal to Great Russian nationalism. The ideal of Jewish cultural autonomy was nullified during Stalin's last decade by the murder of leading Jewish cultural figures and by the Soviet failure to resurrect Yiddish schools, the press, and cultural institutions after 1945.

Stalin's late crusade against "cosmopolitans" and accusation of a plot among Jewish doctors appeared to be a portent of state violence against the Jews which was aborted by his death in 1953. Despite de-Stalinization, cultural discrimination against Jews as a religious and ethnic collectivity and individual discrimination increased during the 1960s. Under Khrushchev, hundreds of synagogues were shut down and the state prohibited the baking of matzos for Passover, the holiday of Hebrew liberation.

Although Jews were still more likely to be employed in scientific and administrative roles in the 1960s than other Soviet citizens, their opportunities for entry to such posts were increasingly limited; the authorities justified quotas as a means to aid the development of other peoples.[20]

At the same time, the Soviet Union revived classic anti-Semitic propaganda in the 1960s. Previously, attacks against Jews collectively were veiled by labelling the target as "cosmopolitans" or "cosmopolitanism"; now the target was unveiled. Soviet press coverage pertaining to Jews and Zionism more than doubled from 1966 to 1968: "at least 62 books and pamphlets" on Zionism were published between 1962 and 1980, "a few...in editions of over 100,000."[21] Its salience is demonstrated not only by the numbers of publications issued but by the contexts in which it is reiterated: army and factory lectures, schools, films and television, fiction, and "scientific criticism." This propaganda stresses traditional (and non-Marxist) themes of pre-World War II anti-Semitic propaganda and also adds new ideological elaboration, equating Judaism with Zionism with racism—indeed, Judaism is declared to be the cause of Zionist crimes. By rewriting history, Jews are shown no longer as victims of Nazi crimes but responsible for Nazism.

The plot lines of major Soviet anti-Semitic tracts depict the Jews as a united body in an international conspiracy, recalling the spurious and discredited *Protocols of the Elders of Zion*, portraying *the Jew* as a betrayer, an exploiter, a venal, sadistic, and sexual violator, guilty of unthinkable brutal crimes. Judaism is purported to be the doctrine which educates Jews to entice, manipulate, and violate *the qoyim* (literally: Hebrew, "other nations").[22]

The desperation of Soviet Jews was raised not only by discrimination and disproportionate judicial prosecution for economic crime but by the Soviet Union's escalated anti-Semitic and anti-Israel propaganda campaign after the 1967 Arab-Israeli War and the breaking of diplomatic relations with Israel. Some Soviet Jews began making public appeals and petitions to the government in the late 1960s to emigrate to Israel, later adding sit-ins. Their nonviolent publicity-generating tactics of confrontation—appealing to the authorities but not deferring to them to set the scene—were adapted from the

Russian dissident movement.[23]

In the initial years of the movement, the Soviets first stonewalled, reacting negatively to appeals, which caused some Jews to try desperate means, such as sky-jacking an airliner to go to Israel. The government arrested and tried them in Leningrad in 1970, imposing two death sentences which aroused international protest, increasing support for the nascent American movement for Soviet Jewry.

The Jewish coordinating superstructure of American Jewish organizations—the Establishment—had protested routinely to American officials about the persecution of Soviet Jewry for years. Elite protests by prominent representatives are a traditional tactic of the Jewish Establishment. In 1963 the Establishment created a nominal paper organization—without officers, members, or resources—to issue more protests. Grass-roots Jewish community councils and student groups (predecessors of the Union of Councils for Soviet Jews and the Student Struggle for Soviet Jewry) arose which were moved in part by the activist repertoires of the 1960s in the United States. These groups prodded the Jewish Establishment to endow this new organization with resources to enable it to become more effective and vied with the Establishment to get resources independently in order to take over control of the direction of the movement; they differed on goals, strategy, and tactics. The Israeli Consulate at times encouraged the movement and at other times worked through the Jewish Establishment, concentrating on its goals and strategies, which changed over time.

Israel, which represents interests both as a state and a Jewish community, was subject to diverse pressures and conflicting conceptions of interest. Israel in the 1960s identified with Soviet Jewry both on moral and political grounds. Further, it viewed Soviet Jews as potentially desirable immigrants. It often protested the plight of Soviet Jewry in the forums of the United Nations and covertly supported immigration without publicity. In the 1960s, when the protests of the Jewish Establishment were routinized and ineffectual, it encouraged the grass-roots American movement. The government of Israel began to view the American movement (which had become worldwide by 1976) and the militancy of Soviet Jews in Israel (which it tried to curb unsuccessfully) as a threat to its relations with the Soviet Union. However, Israel is handicapped in these relations by its links to the United States, so it cannot strategize or signal the Soviet Union independently.

Although in its earliest days the movement's protests reflected a wide range of concerns, in time its goals became strategically constricted to increasing Soviet Jewish emigration, assuming that the best way to preserve Soviet Jews was to enable them to become Israeli Jews or, increasingly, former Soviet Jews in the West.

As this goal emerged, strategies of the movement changed, moving from protest to politics. The Jewish Establishment maintained its discrete protests to the U.S. Administration despite evidence of State Department hostility to raising Jewish issues.

But increasingly the Establishment had to react to a strategy that it had not chosen. The Jackson-Vanik Amendment (introduced in the U.S. Congress in 1972 and passed in late 1974) to the Trade Bill, tying Most Favored Nation trading status to freedom of Jewish emigration, was sponsored by Senator Henry Jackson at the request of the Union of Councils for Soviet Jews, reacting to a recent Soviet decree imposing usurious exit taxes on prospective emigrants linked to their education. Since Congress had become the instigator of American human rights policy in the early 1970s, the Amendment, once introduced, rapidly gathered sponsors. Senators, representatives, and their aides began cooperating with the grass-roots movement enthusiastically, ignoring the Jewish Establishment. Richard Perle, Senator Jackson's legislative aide, "recognized Jewish organizations as 'incompetent and unrepresentative, indecisive, preoccupied with other areas.'"[24]   The Jewish Establishment, responding to pressure by the Nixon Administration (which opposed the Amendment) and believing attempts to sanction the USSR would be counterproductive, waffled on supporting the Amendment. "Now, Jewish hesitancy infuriated congressional leaders ... Perle contacted friends, who prompted the 'more ethnic Jews' to pressure the Jewish leadership."[25] This led to enough grass-roots Jewish pressure to move the Presidents' Conference (of major American Jewish organizations) to reaffirm support for the Amendment.

The conflict between the Administration and Congress over Jackson-Vanik was prolonged. The Soviets tried to undermine chances of its passage by retracting the exit tax; President Nixon resigned; and the Yom Kippur War led to new Israeli requests: these put off its passage. Finally Jackson and Secretary of State Henry Kissinger agreed to a negotiated solution based on a letter of understanding to Congress by the Administration regarding Soviet assurances and a benchmark number of Jewish emigrés allowed out annually, accepting the firmly expressed public Soviet position that they would make no deals conceding that another state might intervene in their internal affairs.

The Amendment to the Trade Reform Act was passed by both Houses of Congress in December 1974 and was signed by President Gerald Ford in January 1975. But the implicit understanding with the Soviet Union unravelled as the Kremlin abrogated the 1972 trade agreement that month, perhaps in response to the Stevenson Amendment to the Export-Import Bank Bill, limiting credits to Moscow without Congressional approval—which the Administration tried but failed to squash. According to this interpretation, the Stevenson Amendment drastically reduced the incentive of the USSR to cooperate in an exchange by diminishing the reward.[26]

What has been the effect on the emigration of Soviet Jews of the Jackson-Vanik Amendment? My reading of the decline from 1972 to 1975, sharp increase to 1979, and radical decline beginning in 1980 is that the release of Soviet Jewry depends on the total context of relationships between the United States and the USSR, especially the balance or prospect of positive exchanges which were established while linkage of U.Ss policy to rights issues advanced. For it was during the Carter years when Soviet dissidents were welcomed to the White House that the greatest flow of emigrés was let go.

Why, one may ask, does the Soviet Union allow Jews to depart in large numbers at all, given the restrictions on emigration to family reunification (which allows only Jews, Volga Germans, and Armenians to exit)?

Gitelman believes that originally the anti-Zionist campaign was intended to dissuade Jews from trying to leave the USSR but it became "a vehicle for those motivated purely by anti-Semitism or by careerist ambitions and other considerations" and, rather than deterring Jews, convinced them that they had no future in the USSR, a recognition reinforced by university and professional discrimination. This led to a vicious cycle, enabling the authorities to justify denying higher education to this "unstable element," now seen as a "fifth column," which, in turn, moved more Jews to emigrate. Depending on their predispositions, other Russians viewed their departure either with jealousy, puzzlement, and defensive patriotism, or positive feelings about their departure (saying "good riddance" to them).[27]

At the same time, as immigration of Soviet Jews increased, repression directed against the refuseniks and dissidents also increased and discrimination continued. Many Hebrew teachers and Jewish activists were imprisoned on trumped-up charges of drug-dealing, arms possession, and the generalized catch-all of "anti-Soviet agitation."

More significantly, on the level of Soviet ideology and propaganda, there has been continued and unremitting hostility toward Jewry and Judaism, demonizing the Jews and promoting the notion of a Jewish conspiracy standing behind the United States, Israel, and world capitalism which is threatening the Soviet Union. Few involved in the movement for Soviet Jewry really consider Soviet motives for mobilizing anti-Semitism, many concurring with the assumption that the government's end-in-view is the forced assimilation of the Soviet Jews. The mobilization of anti-Semitism serves four functions, according to Nudelman:

—To replace the former "Russian-Jewish" intelligentsia by a new nationalist intelligentsia which will become a mainstay of the nationalist-imperialist regime in its fight with dissidents and national movements in the Soviet empire's outlying regions.

—To fortify the position of the Soviet regime in the Eastern European bloc in order to suppress national-dissident movements in socialist countries, and to consolidate them into an effective military force.

—To undermine the positions of independents, such as dissidents, intellectuals, and nationally-oriented elements in other Communist parties in order to turn them into a reliable force in the struggle for hegemony in Europe.

—To win over anti-Western national-totalitarian Afro-Asian regimes in order to create a unified camp in the struggle against the United States and China.[28]

To be sure, these are rationally calculated ends in an ongoing conflict within and between Communist societies. Just as Jews were overrepresented in Soviet scientific and administrative elites, they are now overrepresented in the "Soviet democratic dissent movement—60 to 70 percent of whose members are Jewish or married to Jews."[29] So it would be easy to stigmatize dissidents as Jews once Jews are collectively stigmatized not only as enemies of the people but enemies of all peoples. Communist regimes in Czechoslovakia, Hungary, and Poland have also blamed purported subversion, dissidence, and rebellion on Jews even after the majority had fled—the remainder mostly never identified as Jews or were aged and apolitical—leading credence to Nudelman's analysis.

Chronic competition and strains within Soviet society cause the ruling elite to depend on repression. Nationalist movements have arisen in the Ukraine, the Baltic states, Armenia, and Georgia which challenge Russian domination, while pan-Islamic sentiment among the growing Muslim population might be even more threatening. The Soviet elite may now view anti-Semitism as a unifying ideology to create solidarity; were there a real threat of internal breakdown along national lines, it would stigmatize this as a Jewish plot and simultaneously warn other nationalities—as the state makes the Jews disappear—what might be their fate were they to be similarly labelled. For the collective attack on Jews as Jews does not justify their assimilation but their elimination. Defining a group outside the universe of obligation of the dominant group is a prerequisite for annihilating its members. In Communist states, to become an enemy of the people is the first step to becoming a non-person. When Lev Korneyev (whose books have sold over 100,000 copies) declares that, since all Jews are citizens of a Jewish nation, this "automatically puts Jews into the role of a fifth column in any country," all Soviet Jews are potential victims.[30]

Some Soviet activists have concluded "A 'final solution' is being prepared." This is not an idle remark, but the sober conclusion of veteran Jewish activists in the USSR in the face of an assault on Judaism unmatched since the death of Stalin. The "solution," activists say, will not be physical annihilation, but perhaps the reactivation of the plan of mass deportations of Jews to remote areas of Russia which was canceled only by the sudden death of the dictator in 1953."[31]

The potential for genocide cannot be facilely dismissed. The Soviet Union not only has an ideology which justifies elimination of the Jews, it has the bureaucracy and facilities (prisons, camps, Gulags) in place and the victims defined and registered by the passport system. Furthermore, it deported eight suspect nationalities between 1941 and 1943; while their toll is low compared to the total of Soviet victims—"probably little over half a million people died as a result of it"—imposing conditions leading to mass death of a national or ethnic group is an indictable offense under the Genocide Convention.[32] Government measures also led to a mass famine and the deaths of millions in the Ukraine in 1933, measures designed to squash nationalist tendencies there by destroying the peasantry.[33] This, too, can be considered genocide. Thus, the USSR has much experience in eliminating suspect peoples as well as persons.

Yet a necessary condition for genocide is not a sufficient condition to instigate the perpetrator. Insofar as the Jews are conceived of as symbolic representatives of the West, their plight is visible, and they have instrumental value in negotiations with the United States; they are protected by the very conditions that stigmatize them. The threat of a war between the US and USSR would annul the conditions protecting them and alter the calculus of genocide in the same way that World War I altered the calculus of costs inhibiting the Ottoman Empire before 1915 from wholly annihilating the Armenians.

Thus, the American movement for Soviet Jewry needs to recognize its dependence on the global strategy of the United States. While on the domestic level, the movement can use threat and exchanges, on the international level the United States can effect changes within the Soviet Union only by exchanges benefitting both states.

The only positive outcome for Jews and others would be to advance disarmament, mutual security, and human rights, promoting exchanges with linkage which can be tracked. Were the threat of world war or internal breakdown imminent, the Soviet Union would have a motive and could readily cloak the deportation and/or annihilation of Jews and dissidents labelled as Jews.

However the movement is at a strategic disadvantage in converting goals to specific demands when it confronts Soviet anti-Semitic propaganda. Jews internationally have been put on the ideological defensive since the 1975 United Nations General Assembly declaration that "Zionism is racism," which has obscured the fact the Soviet campaign of Jew-hatred might be considered "direct and public incitement to commit genocide," a punishable offense under the Genocide Convention.

It would be appropriate for intellectuals and representatives of Soviet Jewry and democratic movements in the West to confront the Soviet Union publicly with the charge it is issuing a new warrant for genocide, reviving the discredited charges of *Mein Kampf* and *The Protocols of the Elders of Zion*, charges which have led to millions of murders in this century. For forty years after the Holocaust and seventy years after the Armenian Genocide, one does not have to wait for the curtain to be drawn when the playbill tells us the plot outlines; to cry out in advance might cause the actors to change the script.

REFERENCES

1. Louis Lochner, *What about Germany?* (New York: Dodd, Mead, 1942), 2.

2. Dikran H. Boyajian, *Armenia: The Case for a Forgotten Genocide* (Westwood, NJ: Educational Book Crafters, 1972), 126.

3. Louise Nalbandian, *The Armenian Revolutionary Movement: The Development of Armenian Political Parties through the Nineteenth Century* (Berkeley, CA: University of California Press, 1967); Gerard J. Libardian, "The Changing Armenian Self-Image in the Ottoman Empire: *Rayahs* and Revolutionaries," in *The Armenian Image*, 155-71.

4. Christopher J. Walker, *Armenia: The Survival of a Nation* (New York: St. Martin's Press, 1980), 167-68.

5. Richard G. Hovannisian, *Armenia on the Road to Independence, 1918* (Berkeley, CA: University of California Press, 1967), 28.

6. Walker, 171, William L. Langer, *The Diplomacy of Imperialism 1890-1902* Sec. Ed. (New York: Knopf, 1968), 157, 163.

7. James Bryce, *Transcaucasia and Ararat* (New York: Arno Press and the New York Times, 1970; reprint, 1896), 514.

8. Langer, 163.

9. Feroz Ahmad, *The Young Turks: The Committee of Union and Progress in Turkish Politics, 1908-1914* (Oxford: Clarendon, 1969), 156.

10. Zaravend (pseud.), *United and Independent Turania: Aims and Designs of the Turks*, trans. V. N. Dadrian (Leiden: Brill, 1971), 37-38.

11. Hovannisian, 31-32.

12. Roderic H. Davison, "The Armenian Crisis (1912-1914)," *The American Historical Review*, 53 (April 1948), 481-505. See also William J. van der Dussen, "The Westenenk File: The Question of Armenian Reforms in 1913-1914," *The Armenian Review*, 39: 1-153 (Spring 1986), 11-89.

13. Bryce, *The Treatment of Armenians in the Ottoman Empire*, 633.

14. Ulrich Trumpener, *Germany and the Ottoman Empire, 1914-1918* (Princeton, NJ: Princeton University Press, 1968), 204-47.

15. Henry Morgenthau, Sr., *Ambassador Morgenthau's Story* (Garden City, NY: Doubleday, 1918), 336-39.

16. Boyajian, 287.

17. Bryce, *Transcaucasia and Ararat*, 523-24.

18. Eli Wiesel, *The Jews of Silence: A Personal Report on Soviet Jewry* trans. Neil Kozodoy (Toronto: Signet Books, 1966).

19. Isaac Deutscher, *The Non-Jewish Jew* (Boston: Alyson, 1968).

20. This theory of equality is that of a Soviet sociologist, V. Mishin, cited in I. Domalski, "New Developments in Anti-Semitism," in *Anti-Semitism in the Soviet Union: Its Roots and Consequences*, 1 (Jerusalem: Hebrew University, 1979).

21. Zvi Gitelman, "Moscow and the Soviet Jews: A Parting of the Ways," *Problems of Communism* 29: 1 (1980), 26.

22. V. Begun, "Invasion Without Arms," in Dr. R. Nudleman, "Contemporary Anti-Semitism: Forms and Content," *Anti-Semitism in the Soviet Union*, 48, 38, 40; see also *Soviet Anti-Semitic Propaganda* (London: Institute of Jewish Affairs, 1978) and Allan L. Kagedan, "Soviet Anti-Jewish Publications, 1979-1984" (New York: American Jewish Committee mimeo., 1985).

23. For description of the origin of the Soviet Jewish movement and of conflicts among the movement, organized American Jewry (referred to herein as the Jewish Establishment), and Israel, see William Orbach, *The American Movement to Aid Soviet Jews* (Amherst, MA: University of Mass. Press, 1979).

24. Orbach, 132.

25. Orbach, 139.

26. William Korey, "Jackson-Vanik: it has worked well," *Christian Science Monitor*, October 20, 1983: 22. Korey's observations, however, are contradictory: "But the evidence is overwhelming that Jackson-Vanik made possible the emigration of large numbers of educated Jews and in no way was responsible for lower emigration figures. The vagaries of Soviet emigration policy cannot be seen as directly or even indirectly related to the congressional amendment."

27. Gitelman, 25.

28. Nudelman, 26.

29. Orbach, 43.

30. *Soviet Jewry Action Newsletter*, Rosh Hashanah 5744 (September 1983), 1.

31. *Ibid.*, Chanukah 5745 (December 1984), 1.

32. Robert Conquest, *The Nation-Killers: Soviet Deportation of Minorities* (New York: Macmillan, 1970), Introduction.

33. Robert Conquest, *Harvest of Sorrow: Soviet Collectivization and the Terror-Famine* (New York: Oxford University Press, 1986); *Commission on the Ukraine Famine, 1932-1933; Report to Congress* (Washington, DC, USGPO, 1988).

Genocide in the Twentieth Century

George Wald

The Armenian Genocide in World War I was the first such episode in a century in which genocide and its accompanying phenomena have unhappily become commonplace.

We must recognize that such operations are by no means confined to what some might regard as undeveloped or backward societies. On the contrary, they have at times involved nations that are commonly thought of as among the most developed and sophisticated in the world.

One has only to recall that at the turn of the century the United States government had barely completed its genocidal depredation of its own aboriginal peoples, the American Indians.

Also the most impressive example of the thoroughly twentieth century application of high technology and sophisticated management to genocide involves the Nazi German attempt to exterminate the European Jews, an operation that involved an almost unimaginable amount of human suffering and degradation, and took a toll of some six million helpless persons.

Perhaps a quite incomplete listing will help to convey an idea of the extent to which the phenomenon of genocide has taken hold:

1915-16. The Genocide of Armenians in Ottoman Turkey. About 1.2 million killed, and another 600,000 dispersed as refugees throughout the world.

1932. El Salvador. A minor Indian peasant uprising was crushed with 4,000 killed, followed by a general massacre of 30,000 within a few weeks.[1]

1939-45. The German Genocide of Jews, the "final solution" (a phrase earlier used in the Armenian Genocide), conducted in highly organized and equipped *Vernichtungslager* (extermination camps and factories). Some six million victims.

1939-40. Following the German attack on Poland, Sept. 1, 1939, an attempt to wipe out the Polish elite (intellectuals, government officials, military officers), in order to leave behind a leaderless subject people. Estimates of about 20,000 killed.

1965-69. Indonesia. Following a military coup in October 1965 that replaced the far-left dictatorship of Sukarno by the far-right dictatorship of Suharto, a long orgy of killing of alleged "communists," officially estimated at 500,000, with other estimates ranging to over one million. Also 750,000 imprisoned without trial.

1975. On Dec. 7, 1975, Indonesian troops invaded the former Portuguese colony of East Timor. By 1979, estimated deaths, by killing and starvation, reached 120,000 (about one-sixth of the population). Organized resistance by Fretilin. Operation still continuing, with country sealed off from objective foreign observation by Indonesian government.[2]

1975-78. Cambodia (Kampuchea). Under Khmer Rouge regime of Pol Pot. Forced evacuation of the principal city, Phnom Penh, driving inhabitants to forced labor in the countryside, with widespread official and unofficial executions of supposed bourgeois, in part as reaction of peasantry to years of deprivation, exploitation, and secret U.S. bombing and invasion. Estimates at least 500,000 dead.

1980. Guatemala. Genocide of village Indians in the highlands. An indiscriminate terror practiced on defenseless peasants, accompanied by wide-spread torture and mutilation, and given maximum public exposure. Under a succession of military dictators: Garcia, Rios-Montt, Mejía. About 40,000 to 50,000 killed.[3]

That is just a sampling of genocide in this century. Unhappily it has become a more and more common procedure by which governments deal with opposition, real or imagined.

There are attendant phenomena of high interest, virtually all of them already apparent in the Armenian Genocide of 1915-16:

Rhetorical Euphemisms. No government ordinarily wishes to display its genocidal practices abroad, even when they may serve useful political ends at home. Hence it is common usage to disguise such practices with a special euphemistic phraseology. Thus the Ottoman policy of extinction of Armenians was always spoken of as "relocation." During the recent Vietnam War the United States Phoenix program of assassination in the villages was described as "dissolving the rural infrastructure". What has been called "land reform" to the peasants in Vietnam, the Philippines and El Salvador, is spoken of more frankly inside their governments as "rural pacification". And so on, endlessly.

Genocide and International Relations. In World War I, the German and Austro-Hungarian governments were deeply embarrassed by the genocide practiced by their ally, Turkey, upon their Armenian fellow Christians. In spite of the great distress expressed by German consuls, missionaries, and nurses stationed in Turkey, who reported in detail the horrors being experienced by the Armenians, the Central European governments hesitated to publicize these events or object to them, being more concerned with not irritating their Turkish ally, and at all costs keeping Turkey in the war. Along the same line their adversaries in the war (England, France, Russia, eventually the U.S.) gave maximal publicity to the Armenian Genocide.

One finds throughout the history of genocide all kinds and degrees of involvement with Great Power politics. The British government, susceptible of Palestinian Arab sensibilities, would not permit a shipload of Jewish refugees from the Nazi holocaust to land and discharge its passengers in Palestine.

The United States government looks aside as its client government of Indonesia engages in genocide internally, as in 1965, or in East Timor as from 1975 to the present.

Sometimes the great power relationship is more direct. We are told that during genocidal killing of Indian peasants in El Salvador in 1932, American warships patrolled the coasts of that country. And the American government now supports with arms, funds and the training of troops the succession of military dictatorships (at present euphemistically described as an "elected government") waging war against a peasant insurrection in El Salvador.

Genocide and the General Public. Perhaps the most serious and ultimately most destructive effects of genocide—except of course for its immediate victims—is its degradation and brutalization of all humanity.

The repeated genocides throughout the present century have dulled the sensibility of people everywhere. They become *accustomed* to genocide, and cease to respond. The news of a new genocide may be received impersonally, without emotion, as a mere statistic. It is another instance of what the psychiatrist, Robert Lifton, has called *psychic numbing*, in this case worldwide.

It is that realization that makes genocide, wherever it occurs, of universal importance. Those brutalities—the killing, torture, starvation, expulsion—are not only happening to others elsewhere, they are happening to us wherever we are. Permitting them to happen, indeed merely knowing of them, makes us accomplices. Inevitably they brutalize us—and without end.

If for that reason alone, beyond our compassion for its victims, genocide anywhere is a crime against humanity everywhere.

REFERENCES

1. See also the Peoples' Permanent Tribunal on El Salvador, Mexico, Feb. 11, 1981, in *Un Tribunal pour les Peuples* (Paris: Berger-Levrault, 1983), 142-67.

2. See proceedings of Peoples' Permanent Tribunal on East Timor, 21 June 1981, in *Un Tribunal pour les Peuples*, 227-57.

3. See Peoples' Permanent Tribunal on Guatemala, Madrid, Jan. 29-31, 1983.

Critical Thinking and Teaching About the Armenian Genocide

Phredd MatthewsWall

I am very proud and honored to be here as an educator of today's young people. Before beginning my talk, I would like to share with you an original poem written by one of my eighth grade students. The poet's name is Juliana Conrad; the poem is entitled "The Armenian Genocide":

When the wind blows ...
I can hear your voice calling ...

When the wind blows ...
I can hear your voice calling out to
whomever can hear you ...

When the wind blows ...
I can hear your voice calling out to
whomever can hear you or save you
from the awful things they do ...

When the wind blows ...
I can hear your voice calling out to
whomever can hear you or save you
from the awful things they do,
for reasons we don't have time to figure out ...

When the wind blows ...
I can hear your voice calling out to
whomever can hear you or save you
from the awful things they do,
for reasons we don't have time to figure out ...
because we're too worried about
our own execution ...

Juliana wrote this poem during a course I taught on the Armenian Genocide this school year. She has captured an understanding of the pain, fear, confusion, and helplessness of a people slaughtered for no apparent reason. It is the innocence, knowledge, and willingness to understand that makes teaching and learning so beneficial for all of us.

Well, you might ask, how did I come to teach about an event in history that I had never heard of until about a year ago? I have been associated with members of the Facing History and Ourselves Curriculum Project and National Foundation of Brookline, Massachusetts, on the topic of the Holocaust, which occurred prior to and during World War II. I was intrigued by the methodology used to approach the teaching of this horrible event in history. There was and is a commitment to provide students with a wealth of material, both printed matter and audiovisual, in the form of documents, letters, telegrams, posters, videotapes of survivors, films, and the like. These materials have the added importance of being primary sources recorded at the time in which many of the events being studied were taking place. They gave rise to many of the questions you may ask yourselves as adults: How could so many people be killed and no one do anything? Did anyone try to stop the massacres? What possesses people to be so cruel to fellow human beings? Did anyone know this was about to happen? Why didn't everyone try to escape? These very same questions came from the lips of the children we see and teach every day—if we allow them to ask these questions. That last statement is extremely important. We must provide a vehicle not only for adults to ask these complicated questions, but for children as well. How else will they learn?

During the time I had prepared an eight-week unit on the Holocaust, I had to do a tremendous amount of reading to become knowledgeable enough to assist the students in asking, and discussing possible answers to, many of their complex questions. In this way we all grew in understanding not only of what happened to the victims of the Nazis but how a seemingly insignificant loss of rights can turn into an unsuspected monster, in the form of a genocide. Another very significant result of the teaching of this unit was the understanding by a majority of the students about their own lives and responsibilities to one another. Examples of this occurred when I would make connections to ostracism, being a part of the "in group," name calling, watching or instigating fights, and the role one plays in daily decisions. When I presented students with the idea of three roles, i.e.

victim, victimizer, and bystander, they tended to feel initially that these were very clear roles with no overlap, the bystander being the least disagreeable. As we progressed through the study, we realized that these roles had much overlapping and that the "bystander" who ostensibly doesn't become involved is in fact accountable for action not taken. When one is looking at responsibility to inform people of danger or to help prevent a potentially explosive situation, the bystander carries a heavy burden.

During the summer of 1984 I attended a workshop at the Facing History Center. There I met Richard Hovannisian, who gave me tremendous insight into the occurrence of another horrible atrocity of the twentieth century, the Armenian Genocide. It was Professor Hovannisian's presentation and the following statement, which I read from *The Facing History and Ourselves* text, that encouraged me to teach about the Armenian Genocide:

> Adolf Hitler made the following statement in a speech to his commanding officers before the invasion of Poland in 1939:
>
>> Our strength is in our quickness and brutality. Genghis Khan had millions of women and children killed by his own will and with a gay heart. History sees in him only a great state builder. What weak western European civilization thinks about me does not matter. ...I have sent to the east only my "Death Head Units," with the order to kill without mercy all men, women, and children of Polish race or language. Only in such a way will we win the vital space that we need. Who still talks nowadays of the extermination of the Armenians?

I immediately saw that my curriculum unit on the Middle East was greatly lacking an extremely important issue: the acknowledgement of the first genocide of the twentieth century, perpetrated upon the Armenians. I spent the rest of the summer reading, writing, and digesting as much material as possible to prepare myself and my students for another learning experience which would again force them to think critically about past events in history and their own futures.

I began the six-week unit by having my students look at headlines from the *New York Times* newspapers printed from 1914 to 1921. Immediately students were shocked by the headlines that read "Turks Lock Them in a Wooden Building and then Apply the Torch," "Armenians' Heroic Stand in Mountains; All Finally Exterminated," "500,000 Armenians Said to Have Perished; Washington Asked to Stop Slaughter of Christians By Turks and Kurds," "Only Power That Can Stop the Massacre is Germany, and We Might Persuade Her to

Act." When my students sat for a discussion after looking at these headlines, they were surprised that they had known nothing of the events that were obviously known by many Americans as witnessed by the headlines. They were equally shocked that these events happened prior to the well-known Holocaust of World War II. This experience made them immediately want to know more. It also brought back the memory of the list of reasons we had previously discussed about why we study history: to learn from the past, to learn from the mistakes made in the past and not to repeat them, to help prepare for our future by understanding the past, to gain an understanding about people who lived at a different time under similar and very different pressures from those facing us today. The very clear thought that came to mind was that, had more people been aware of or tried to do something about the Armenian Genocide, there may never have been a Holocaust in Europe.

After starting with the headlines, I had students read poems written by Armenians who survived the Genocide or descendants of survivors. This was to give the students some insight into the feelings of the people living during the period being discussed. I then proceeded to give students a sense of Armenian culture and its historical background. We also looked at the life of minorities under the government of the Ottoman Empire, as ruled by Sultan Abdul-Hamid II. This gave the students an understanding of the hardships faced by Armenians and the attempts at some reform. We then dealt with the coming of the new government in Turkey by the "Young Turks." It was then that we looked more closely at the issue of discrimination and singling out of the Armenians in an effort to push the "Young Turk" concept of "Pan-Turkism," which seemed little more than a racist policy. Next we discussed the resistance posed by different groups of Armenians and also the response of other nations to what was occurring in Turkey. We also discussed the fact that there are Turks today who continue to deny that a genocide ever took place. We talked about why a people would attempt to deny something like this. Students responded that not all Turks were involved, that some may have been frightened of retaliation by the government, and others may not want to be held responsible; also some may have been taught that the genocide never took place, or they may have been given a different viewpoint of what happened.

This year I had a very interesting discussion about judgment, which was videotaped with the help of the Facing History Project. It was a successful attempt to get the students to deal with the issue of how to decide if anyone should be punished now for what happened to nearly an entire culture. Students felt that there should be some recognition by the Turkish government that there was a horrible tragedy like the Genocide, but they had trouble with deciding what kinds of retribution should be allowed, because so many years have now passed and the perpetrators themselves can no longer be dealt with. The students felt it unfair for present Turks to suffer for mistakes their ancestors made; nevertheless, they believe that something should be done. This brought the students to another point: thinking about how we can try to prevent things like this from happening in our future.

Suggestions students had were: to try to communicate to as many as possible about the events that are occurring, don't let too much time go by before saying something, don't discriminate against others because they're different, work toward coexistence, stand up for your rights, and—most importantly—respect each other's cultures.

I would like to conclude my presentation by making a plea to you and to future generations. That plea is to not stay silent about things that you know deep in your heart are unjust to humanity. Don't remain quiet about things that affect you personally because you feel no one is interested in what you have to say. If we continue to isolate ourselves from one another and to see our histories as unconnected, we sow the ground for future discrimination and atrocities—and, yes, genocides to occur again to new victims. No event in history that affects a whole culture should be allowed to be seen as an isolated event. We are all human beings and deserve dignity, self-respect, and the right to life and liberty.

Genocide and Deterrence

John Loftus

The missing link between the Genocide of the Armenians and the Holocaust of the Jews may have been a German diplomatic official, the vice-consul in Erzurum, in Turkey, during the Genocide. The man's name was Max Erwin von Scheubner-Richter. He came from a very aristocratic background. His fraternity brother was no less than Alfred Rosenberg, the Nazi ideologist. In fact, it was Rosenberg himself who introduced von Scheubner-Richter to Hitler, only a few years after the Armenian holocaust. Rosenberg became the editor of the *Volkischer Beobachter*, the original newspaper of the Nazi party. He chose as his manager the former vice-consul in Armenia, von Scheubner-Richter.[1]

Von Scheubner-Richter joined the Nazi party in 1920. He was, if you will, a midwife at the marriage between the Hitlerian ideology and the monied industrialists in Germany. It was at his house that von Scheubner invited Hitler to meet with Fritz Thyssen, the prominent German industrialist who was to finance the growth of the Nazi party. Through von Scheubner's connections, the young Hitler received the money to build a potent political force. It was this marriage between the German industrialists and the fledgling organizers of the Nazi party that brought Hitler to power. For three years, between 1920 and 1923, von Scheubner worked closely with Hitler. In fact, when the Beer Hall Putsch was arranged, it was von Scheubner who arranged to have General Von Ludendorff march with Hitler. Von Scheubner marched arm and arm with Hitler that day, and on that day, in 1923, von Scheubner was one of the thirteen early Nazi party members who were killed. Hitler called von Scheubner "irreplaceable," and had a plaque in his office ever afterwards with von Scheubner's name and the names of the other early Nazis who died in the putsch.

When von Scheubner returned from Armenia, he did not return with revulsion at what had gone on. Only five years after a Genocide in Armenia, he spoke "of the necessity to fight Jewish Bolshevism and to eradicate ruthlessly all elements foreign to the body national of the Germans." Did von Scheubner teach the lessons of Armenia to Hitler in these early days, or was this something that Hitler learned only in 1941 and 1942, at the time the final solution was being prepared? In 1931, ten years before the final solution was implemented, Hitler gave a secret background conversation with a German correspondent. The transcripts of this talk were recently declassified and released. In the conversation, it is shown that, at a very early stage, in 1931, Hitler knew of Armenia. Let me read you what he says (this is Hitler speaking to a German newspaperman): "Everywhere there is discontent; everywhere people are awaiting a new world order. We intend to introduce a great resettlement policy. We do not wish to go on treading on each others' toes in Germany. In 1923 little Greece could resettle a million men. Think of the biblical deportations and the massacres of the Middle Ages. Rosenberg refers to them, and remember the extermination of the Armenians. One eventually reaches the conclusion that masses of men are mere biological plasticene."

There is a strong circumstantial case that the vice consul to Armenia, von Scheubner, was the man who carried the lesson of the holocaust forward from the Armenians and transmitted it to Hitler, that Hitler recalled it and formulated it as part of his foreign policy as early as 1931, a decade before the Holocaust was to be released in full fury. The essence of what Hitler understood was indifference. To put it crudely, it takes one hundred people to kill each child in a genocide: one to pull the trigger, but ninety-nine to shrug their shoulders. It was this legacy of indifference, this lack of deterrence, that led Hitler to make his famous statement, "Who now remembers the Armenians?" The courts did not, the governments did not. There was no deterrence to using genocide to achieve popular domestic aims.

This thread of indifference runs from the Genocide of the Armenians to the Holocaust of the Jews and other peoples during World War II—the thread of indifference runs through the holocausts in Bangladesh and Cambodia. Genocide is not an aberrant condition; the circumstances giving rise to it are with us always. They are with us in this country today. Like most children growing up, I knew very little of holocaust and genocide. The average American student today reads only six sentences about the Jewish holocaust in his textbooks, and virtually nothing on Armenia. There are children growing up today who do not know who Hitler was. Perhaps the underlying reason for this indifference to genocide as part of our history in America is that it hasn't happened here, that we really don't feel involved, and quite frankly neither did I. I was a career prosecutor with the Justice Department in 1979 when President Carter created the Office of Special Investigations to look into allegations that Nazi war criminals were resident in our country. I thought it might not be a bad job for a few months, so I volunteered to go over. Because of my military intelligence background, I was asked by the Justice Department to see if we might have some old files buried in our classified vaults that might assist us in reopening some of these cases forty years later. So for the first time in forty years, someone was given security classification to go through all of the vaults of the U.S. intelligence community to research the contents of American files. It was an overwhelming task. There are twenty vaults in Suitland, Maryland, where the records are stored; each vault is underground and is one acre in size, four or five hundred feet deep, fifty to seventy-five-feet tall, and crammed from floor to ceiling with classified records about the Holocaust and its aftermath in Europe that were put away by our government, along with our other secrets. And no one had the faintest idea of their contents. In order to speed up the search, I decided to concentrate on a particular pilot group, White Russian Nazi collaborators, because their country was very significant for intelligence interests.

No one has tears enough to cry for the millions who died in the Holocaust and no one has time enough to hear all of their stories. But I would like to tell you about one individual whose dossier I read in our classified vaults to argue, if you will, that there is an American connection. Stanislaw Stankievich earned his Doctor of Humanities in the best Western universities in Europe before World War II. But his little country of White Russia was divided in half between Russia and Poland by the Hitler-Stalin Pact. Doctor of Humanities Stankievich enlisted in the winning side, and joined the elite intelligence service of the German SS. Two years later, in the summer of 1941, when the Third Reich invaded Russia, the armies had to move through White Russia, the traditional invasion route for everyone from Napoleon to the Teutonic Knights. Stankievich was made mayor of a county under Nazi rule. The SS had recruited intelligentsia from each of these European countries to assist them in maintaining control over the native forces. There was a German administrative staff of only 500 to govern a country of ten million people in White Russia. Men like Stankievich were indispensable. He organized a police force of native collaborators. They incarcerated the Jews in ghettos and extorted all of their property and belongings.

In the fall of 1941, the Nazi invasion of Russia was stalled. Winter was coming along. The SS was desperate about this huge population of Jews immediately behind their rear lines. This was the settlement in the Pale, the traditional sanctuary ground for Jews fleeing pogroms in western Europe. So the cities and towns were ninety percent Jewish. In Stankievich's county alone, there were 8,000 Jewish men, women, and children. In the fall of 1941 a young SS officer named Adolf Eichmann sent a telegram to Mayor Stankievich making a suggestion: that Stankievich should carry out an experiment. Could Stankievich arrange to take his native police force and massacre the entire Jewish population of this county in a single day? On the night of October 19, 1941, Doctor of Humanities Stankievich threw a wild party for his police force, to get them properly drunk for the work that was to come. At three o'clock on the morning of October 20, the raid began. Stankievich's policemen took the Jews out in groups of one hundred on trucks and busses, out on a road near the airport where the ditches had been dug. Dr. Stankievich was very clever. He figured he could save time digging ditches by having the Jews lie head to toe. That way his troops could also shoot through two layers of bodies and save ammunition. A layer of dirt was shoveled over the wounded, and as they suffocated to death another double layer of Jews was put in the pits, and so on. Dr. Stankievich called it the sardine method. The worst part of the sardine method wasn't discovered until after the war, when American Red Cross officials were conducting autopsies. They could find no wounds on the children. Apparently to save the price of a bullet, Dr. Stankievich had the babies buried alive.

After the massacre of the 8,000 in Borissow, Dr. Stankievich became promoted to become the head of the city of Baranovitche, the second largest city in White Russia, and it was here that Eichmann began shipping the Jews of Western Europe on cattle cars. Eichmann himself was revolted by the crude and cumbersome method of slaughtering in the pits. He noted in his diary on the way back to Berlin that he would have to find a more "humane" method of killing the Jews; perhaps he should try an experiment with poison gas. What kind of man was Stankievich and these others, to nauseate Eichmann? To have him construct Auschwitz, Treblinka, and Sobibor as more "humane" alternatives of genocide?

The White Russian collaborators did very well under German rule. They were even allowed to have their own Nazi puppet government. They raised a special SS brigade called the Belarus (Byelorus) from all the police executioners. And the Belarus Brigade fought against the American forces in Italy at Monte Cassino, and again against the Allied forces in France. Dr. Stankievich and the other collaborators were evacuated to Berlin by the SS and were given special quarters. They were set up as a Nazi government in exile. But Stankievich and the others weren't fools. They realized that they had joined the wrong side after all. And they opened negotiations with the British government, successfully. Shortly before the fall of Berlin, the entire Nazi puppet government of White Russia marched 300 miles westward from Berlin to the town of Hoexter, in what was to become the British zone of West Germany. There they were given sanctuary; the British secret intelligence service allowed them to re-form their government in exile. The British at that time viewed these Eastern Europe nationalists, if you will, as an antidote against Communist rule in Eastern Europe. They intended to take these fugitive armies of (in many cases) war criminals and train them as secret commando groups to go behind the Iron Curtain.

The Soviets weren't exactly oblivious to all this. The genius in the British government who thought up this program was Sir Harold Adrian ("Kim") Philby, the highest-ranking Soviet spy in the British government. In fact, there are many people in the world who were aware of Dr. Stankievich and his atrocities in particular. For example, at the Nuremberg war crimes trials, Dr. Stankievich, the massacrer of Borissow, became part of the legacy. There was a German soldier who was so revolted by what he saw that he became a witness for the prosecution. Dr. Stankievich's name appears in the Congressional Record of the United States. In 1947 he was one of the few war criminals singled out on the floor of the Congress as an example of the sort of person who should be hunted down, who must never be allowed into America. It was therefore with some surprise that Dr. Stankievich's name surfaced again in 1947 when the Soviet delegate to the United Nations rose and accused the governments of Great Britain and the United States of hiding thousands of Eastern European war criminals in our war camps in West Germany. Americans thought the accusation preposterous. President Roosevelt and President Truman had given strict orders that Nazis were not to be used as intelligence sources, that war criminals would be hunted down. Congress had passed very strict laws.

Nevertheless the Army went out to investigate. They were particularly looking for Dr. Stankievich, the butcher of Borissow. They didn't need much time to find him; our State Department had put Dr. Stankievich in charge of a refugee camp in the U.S. zone. Dr. Stankievich was helping to select persons who were worthy to receive visas to the United States. The army arrested Dr. Stankievich and he gave them a full confession, copies of which are in his intelligence files in the vault. The State Department had him released. Our State Department had decided, with the urging of Mr. Philby, that these Nazi collaborators were simply too valuable as anti-Communists to be ignored, that they should be protected and recruited. On six different occasions, the CIA and the Army tried successfully to block Stankievich's immigration to America. They pointed out that, apart from being a war criminal, Stankievich had actually worked for the Communists before the Nazi uprising, and was now believed to be a double agent for the Communists again. The State Department ignored the warnings, because after all their good friend Kim Philby vouched for Dr. Stankievich's credentials. Stankievich was smuggled to America. He was given a job as a broadcaster with Radio Liberty, in New York City, spreading information about the American way of life behind the Iron Curtain. The Soviets in response simply told their population who the announcer was.

The State Department arranged for Dr. Stankievich to become a citizen of the United States. He worked on the taxpayers payroll for twenty years, and retired in New York City. He dropped dead two weeks before I could file charges against him in Federal District Court in New York. At that time, part of me wanted to get out of the vault and forget what I had seen, and return to my job at the Justice Department. But there are some nightmares that aren't easily forgotten. You see, buried in Stankievich's file in the classified vaults were the memoirs of a Jew, Solomon Schiadow. He was one of 50,000 Jews in Baranovitche under Stankievich's command. Of the 50,000, only 5,000 survived the first year. Of the 5,000, five hundred were selected as skilled laborers to be sent to the Kuldichvo concentration camp; the rest were slaughtered. Of the five hundred, only one hundred and twenty-five remained alive after six months. Sol organized a breakout. They dug a tunnel that enabled the Jews to escape from Kuldichvo; many of them made it through the Nazi lines and joined up with the Russian partisans. They went back and fought the men who had slaughtered their families. When the war was over Sol shot his way out of the Soviet Union and made his way to Italy, and then to America. He had lost his first wife, three children, and all one hundred and twenty-seven members of his family. He sat down and wrote his memoirs so that no one would ever forget the 50,000 Jews of Baranovitche or what had happened to them. He gave a copy of his memoirs to the FBI, who put them in the classified vault. At the request of the State Department, the FBI had recruited the men who had tried to murder Sol Schiadow and they were living less than an hour away from him, in South River, New Jersey.

South River is an interesting town. They have a private cemetery there for the White Russian SS. And in it is the grave of the Nazi President of the White Russian Government, a government that presided over the massacre of nearly three-quarters of a million Jews and some two million of the civilian population, a government whose combat arm, the Belarus Brigade, fought against Allied forces during World War II. I tried to locate Sol as a witness when we were preparing for the Stankievich trial. We were told by the U.S. Government investigators that he could not be found and was presumed dead. And so I dedicated my book (The Belarus File) to him: "To Sol, a Jew, who bore witness to the Holocaust" and "To Meg, my newborn, so that she may never have to." When my manuscript was declassified by the CIA, I called the television program "Sixty Minutes," and they aired a special half-hour segment on the Belarus connection. Shortly afterwards the Justice Department received a call from Sol. They had made yet another mistake; he certainly was not dead. He was put in touch with me; we became very close friends. My wife and I were the only ones on earth who knew anything about his background or his history in that part of the world.

A year ago, I flew down to meet him. It was a Conference on the Armenian and Jewish Holocaust and I had been asked to speak. We had asked Sol to keep his identity a secret because of his proximity to the men and women of South River. He is an old man; he is entitled to his privacy. And speaking that day—and there were many children in the audience of Eastern European descent—it was obvious that their parents had given them an entirely different view of the Holocaust: that only the Germans killed Jews; that there were no Hungarians or Poles or White Russians or Ukrainians involved. And I was telling them otherwise. But who was I to say this? I wasn't even born in World War II; I certainly wasn't there. All I had done was to read the intelligence files. The kids wanted a witness, and suddenly Sol stood up in the audience and said: "Tell them, tell them who I am." It was an act of final courage; he was surrendering his anonymity to bear witness to the truth.

You have made an act of courage by coming here today. You also bear witness to the truth. The sacrifices of the Armenians, the Jews, the Gypsies and Gentiles, and Cambodians will not be forgotten so long as one of us remembers the truth and we teach it to our children. Because out of the maelstrom of the twentieth century, I believe, will come a fundamental law of civilization: that men who murder little children will be hunted for the rest of their lives; that we will pierce the legacy of indifference that led Hitler to say: "Remember the extermination of the Armenians," but in a different context than we remember it today. I do not think that any of us are speaking about vengeance. What we are talking about is deterrence. If we are to keep our children safe from the next holocaust, and there will always be the threat of another, we must establish this iron law that there is no statute of limitations for genocide. Ten years from now, when the last Nazi dies of old age in this country, I hope that there is someone from the Justice Department there at his desk trying to take his citizenship away from him. But I fear that the average American doesn't really care if a Nazi war criminal lives next door as long as he keeps his lawn mowed. World War II was long ago and far away, and who remembers the Armenians.

The crimes of the last generation and of the generation before were the holocausts; the crime of our generation is indifference. Here in the United States we must bring forward not just the Nazis, but the Nazi recruiters, the men and women in our government who took the law into their own hands, who lied to the President, and who made this country a rest home for war criminals. We cannot put these old politicians and bureaucrats in jail, but we must bring them forward into the light of publicity and expose them for what they were. We can thus teach our children never to forget, or we can send a warning to the bureaucrats of this type in the future who may consider being accomplices after the fact in someone else's genocide that the risks are too high. They will be caught.

If we do nothing, the classified records of the Holocaust will be available forty years from now when the seventy-five year time ban on our agents' files has expired, and our children will come to us and say: why didn't we do anything when the Nazis were still alive? I fear that we shall give them Dante's answer: The seventh circle of hell is reserved to those who had the ability to prevent evil, but did nothing. We cannot stand by for another Armenian Genocide, for another holocaust in Europe; we must not be silent. I believe that this is the only country on earth where the truth about the Holocaust will be preserved, that this century will be remembered for two things: as the century of atomic power and the century of genocide. This is the only country in the world where my book could have been declassified. This is the only nation on earth today where you and I would be free to speak about these issues today. When my daughter is old enough, I'm going to give her Sol's diary and let her read it. I'm going to tell her about the Genocide, about those brave Armenians and Jews and Gentiles who came forward years later so that it would not be forgotten. And I will tell her about meeting you. And I will tell my daughter that there are still heroes in the world: her father met some.

REFERENCES

1. See Barkadjian, Kevork B., *Hitler and the Armenians* (Cambridge: Zoryan Institute, 1985) and Lauffer, Max M., "A Tale of Two Genocides," *Journal of Armenian Studies*, Vol II, No. 2 (Fall/Winter 1985-86), 75-86.

The Genocide Convention
and the Prevention of Genocide

Senator William B. Proxmire

[Ed. Note] The United States officially became a party to the Genocide Convention in February 1989, forty years after President Truman submitted it to the Senate for ratification. The Convention itself was ratified by the Senate in February 1986, by a vote of 83-11. The necessary implementing legislation, making genocide a crime under Federal law, was approved in October 1988: it is known as the Proxmire Act, in recognition of the Senator's tireless efforts over a period of almost twenty years to secure ratification of the Convention.

Senator Proxmire's address to the Conference took place almost a year before the Senate ratified the Genocide Convention, but in explaining the importance of the Convention, the reasons for the long delay in ratification, and vividly indicating the uncertainties over the form ratification would take, it is a document of continuing importance.

Genocide, as you know, is the planned, premeditated extinction of an entire racial, religious, or ethnic group. It is as vicious a crime as any of us can conceive. We have had a Treaty, a Convention, that makes genocide a crime under international law, pending in the United States Senate since 1949—for thirty-six years. It has not passed.

This is a Convention that should pass. For one thing, it is a Treaty that was drafted by United States delegates to the United Nations; it is a Treaty that passed the United Nations unanimously; it is a Treaty supported by seven presidents—four Democrats and three Republicans, including of course President Reagan; it has been reported five times by the Foreign Relations Committee, the last time by a 14 to 0 vote (Senator Jesse Helms abstained—perhaps he is against it, but he abstained). It has now been ratified by ninety-six nations, including every developed country in the world except the United States.

The documentation supporting the Treaty is overwhelming. We have had more testimony on that Treaty than on any other treaty in our history, with the possible exception of SALT II. We have had many, many days of hearings, we have had eighty-seven witnesses, 200 submissions for the record, and 1,500 pages of testimony. The Treaty is supported by every major religious organization, by the American Bar Association, by every major fraternal, civic, and labor organization—and it has not passed the Senate. Who opposes it? Well, it is opposed by the John Birch Society; it is opposed by the Liberty Lobby; it is opposed by the Klu Klux Klan and Phyllis Schlafly's Eagle Forum. That's about it. And we fail to act. Why?

There are three major forces shaping the Convention—they are moral forces. There are Americans and others who recognize that genocide is the most vicious kind of crime against human life; and a top priority for any civilization, any government, should be the preservation of human life. There is a second force, the development of human rights as international law, that has been advancing. It is a tough struggle and it is a quite recent one; it is very difficult to achieve because in all countries there is a great pride and concern about the sovereignty of the nation and a reluctance to give up any fragment, any part, of that sovereignty. And then there is a force—perhaps the most serious energizing force behind the Genocide Convention—which is the recognition of the heartbreaking individual human struggle for survival and life. None of us can truly understand genocide unless we see it through the eyes of the children and the women and the men who have been imprisoned, tortured, and killed, literally by the millions, or unless we have a brother, or sister, or child, or parent who has perished.

Genocide is not a recent crime; it is something that has gone on throughout human history. In ancient Rome there was the incredible genocide against the Carthaginians after three Punic Wars. The Romans decided, as the Roman Senator Cato used to say at the end of every speech: *Carthage must be destroyed.* (He didn't give as many speeches as I have given for the Genocide Convention, incidentally; I have spoken every day the Senate has been in session since January 11, 1967 in favor of the Genocide Convention—that's over 3,000 speeches.) And the Romans did destroy Carthage. They killed every able-bodied male there; they carried the women and children into slavery; and they sowed the land with salt so that nothing would grow there again. It was a vicious, terrible genocide of a kind that you would think, in this day and age, we would no longer engage in, but as you know we have. The genocide of Christians by the Romans was another dramatic episode; it has gone on with Genghis Khan; Adolph Hitler's slaughter of Jews in Germany and throughout Europe during World War II; Pol Pot's actions in Cambodia; and, of course, what you are very conscious of and rightly so, and what more people in the world should be conscious of, the Turkish slaughter of a million Armenians.

I was impressed by one of the pieces of your literature that was headlined "A Debt Yet To Be Paid: The Armenian Genocide—Seventy Years Ago." It is so important to recognize that the first great genocide of this century was the genocide committed against the Armenians. Let me just give you a few fragments from the *New York Times* of 1915. On March 20, 1915, the *New York Times* reported as follows:

> Whole Plain Strewn by Armenian Bodies ... Turks and Kurds Reported to Have Massacred Men, Women and Children ... When the Russian forces retreated from this district the Kurds fell upon the helpless people and shut them up in mosques. The men were killed and the women were carried away to the mountains. The organizers of the Red Cross Fund says there are 120,000 destitute Armenians now in the Caucasus.

Then, a little later, appearing in the *New York Times* of August 30, 1915, a Reuters dispatch states:

> In one village one thousand men, women and children are reported to have been locked in a wooden building and burned to death.

On September 5, 1915, a letter from Constantinople was reprinted in the *New York Times*:

> It is impossible to read or to hear, without shedding tears, even the meager details of these deportations. Most of the families have traveled on foot, old men and children have died on the way, young women in child-birth have been left on mountain passes, and at least ten deaths a day are recorded among them, even in their place of exile, victims of hunger and sickness.

Then, on September 16, 1915, in the *New York Times* there is a report from a Times correspondent lately in Salonika that

> all the reports from Turkey are agreed as to the terrible character of the Turkish atrocities against the Armenians. It is believed that it is the official intention that this shall be a campaign of extermination, involving the murder of 800,000 to 1,000,000 persons. Christians can escape murder by embracing Mohamedanism, in which all of the female members of the convert's family of marriageable age—wife, sisters, or children—are distributed around to other Turks, making the revision to Christianity in the future practically impossible.

The terrible thing about genocide is that people are killed not for some crime that they have committed, not for some threat that they represent, but simply because they belong to a particular ethnic, racial, or religious group.

Then, on September 21, 1915, in the *New York Times*:

Accounts from different sources agree that over the whole of eastern and northern Asia Minor and Armenia, the Christian population is being deliberately exterminated, the men of military age being killed, and the younger women seized for Turkish harems, compelled to become Mohammedans, and kept, with the children, in virtual slavery.

On October 11, 1915 the *New York Times* reported:

Spare Armenians, Pope Asks Sultan ... Following Report from Constantinople, Benedict XV Writes to the Porte.

October 13, 1915, again in the *New York Times*:

Armenian massacres in Asiatic Turkey have been renewed with vigor since Bulgaria's practical entrance into the war as Turkey's ally. This information reached the State Department today from Ambassador Morgenthau, who stated that the majority of Armenians in Asiatic Turkey have been killed.

July 27, 1919, Letter to the Editor in the *New York Times*:

The refugee has his two children torn from him, and he saw his wife sold into slavery. He saw his countrymen beaten or stabbed to death, and hundreds left to die from hunger and sickness as they were being driven from place to place. "Long before the time we were given in which to make our preparations, the Turkish gendarmes came. With whips, and by beating, they compelled us to leave everything and go to the railroad station."

Now that genocide should have been a warning to the world, but it was not. People didn't talk about it; they didn't have the kind of meeting that you are having here on this campus. They didn't have the kind of remembrance that we are having elsewhere on the Genocide Convention. They should have, because there was a meeting in July 1938, about twenty-three years after these atrocities, this terrible genocide, when thirty-two nations met in France to determine what could be done for Jewish victims of Hitler's anti-Semitic campaign. No nation offered refuge, no nation offered asylum, none. There was a cable from the French Foreign Office to Germany after this meeting took place that said the following: "None of the States would dispute the absolute right of the German government to dictate with regard to its citizens such measures as are within its own sovereign powers." No wonder Hitler went ahead. No wonder he dismissed the outrage of foreigners and in 1939, less than twenty-five years after the Armenian Genocide, he asked: "Who remembers the Armenians?"

The story of genocide is not told by the millions; it is told by the stories of individuals. I suppose the most graphic account that most of us have is the story of that wonderful child, Ann Frank. I think all of us are familiar with the terrible murder of this child of love and forgiveness. Few people know of Raphael Lemkin, whose concept of genocide led to the creation of the Genocide Convention in the United Nations. Raphael Lemkin was a man who lost seventy relatives to Hitler's gas chambers. He and his brother were the only survivors of a very large Jewish family. Lastly I think many Americans are familiar with Raoul Wallenberg, a remarkable Swedish Protestant, who risked his life, and apparently perished in a Russian prison, but saved tens of thousands of Jews from the genocide during World War II.

The Jewish Holocaust is the genocide that is most familiar to most people. But the end of World War II did not bring the end of Genocide. Only a few years ago, in Nigeria, there was a slaughter by the Government of one million Ibo tribesmen; in Bangladesh, three million Bengalis were slaughtered; in the 1970s a million lost their lives in Cambodia.

What do we do about this horrible situation? Lemkin, the Polish Jew mentioned earlier, who had lost so many relatives, really went to work in a remarkable way. It was he who coined the term "genocide" in 1944, and called for action to declare it a crime under international law. He went to the United Nations, lobbying everybody he could talk to. He spent all of his time, all of his energy, all of his money, trying to persuade the United Nations to adopt a Genocide Convention. The American delegation was moved and impressed, I'm proud and happy to say. In fact, in 1946, the American delegate, John Maktos chaired the committee that drafted the Genocide Convention. The head of the American delegation, Ernest Gross, demanded positive action "now," as he put it. In 1949 that Treaty went to the United States Senate—an American treaty in its drafting form, an American treaty supported vigorously by our President at the time, Harry Truman. But there has been no action since, and I think it is an absolute moral outrage. It's a disgrace.

Why did that happen? Well, the man who preceded me in the Senate was Joseph McCarthy of Wisconsin. Unfortunately, Joseph McCarthy was able to paralyze the moral action of this country in some important respects. Somehow international cooperation became discredited as being associated with Communism and equated with disloyalty and conspiracy against the Republic. McCarthy and McCarthyism were part of the way that view was disseminated and distilled into too many people in high office, including the Congress of the United States and including our Presidency. Another strain was the argument that the Genocide Convention would challenge and diminish our sovereignty. It would threaten American citizens who might be called before a foreign court. This is absolute nonsense—there is nothing in the Convention that would ever have an American citizen called before a court. The country could be called before a court if we adopt the Convention in its present form. In addition to that, there was the Bricker Amendment, which was being pushed very hard, which was very popular in the country, and which appealed to our isolationist instincts; it argued that human rights treaties with other countries, when those countries are socialistic or communistic, were steps toward socialism.

And then President John Kennedy gave a remarkable speech at American University on human rights and revived the spirit of those who felt we could have a Genocide Treaty. He said that, after all, peace itself, in the last analysis, is a matter of human rights. But neither Kennedy nor President Johnson at the time could muster the support to push the Treaty through Congress. After all, the Treaty was opposed by the American Bar Association, a very prestigious, very powerful, highly respected association of top lawyers in the country. The Bar Association took a hostile position against the Treaty until, in 1968, Supreme Court Justice Tom Clark put together a blue-ribbon panel and studied the Treaty very carefully. The panel concluded that there were no Constitutional impediments, none, to treaty-making power for the promotion of human rights. The Bar Association reconsidered the Treaty and rejected it again, but by a very narrow vote, and then we were on our way, because then the people recognized more and more the critical importance of the United States leading the way on human rights and the ridiculousness of the opposition.

The American Bar Association officially withdrew its opposition to the ratification of the Genocide Treaty in 1976, and now I can tell you that it is the best ally we have. It has been fighting very hard for the Treaty. Even before its official reversal of policy, members of the Bar Association persuaded Richard Nixon, who is not recognized by many as a great moral hero in this country, to submit the Treaty to the United States Senate. The Bar Association vigorously urged him to do so, and he did that. When the Treaty was submitted to the Senate in 1970-71, the Foreign Relations Committee reported it favorably. Senator Jacob Javits and I went to Senator Mike Mansfield, who was then Majority Leader in the Senate, and we urged him to bring the Treaty to a vote. Mansfield was reluctant to do so, because he did not wish to tie up the Senate in a lengthy debate on the issue when there were many other pressing matters to be considered. Senator Sam Erwin did threaten a filibuster; Erwin, as you know, was the man who did such a fine job in the Watergate situation, but he was absolutely dead wrong on this issue—a fine gentleman and a Senator of great prestige, but in great error on the question of the Treaty. We could have defeated Sam Erwin, in my opinion, but it would have been difficult and time-consuming.

Finally, however, the dam broke during the last election. In October President Ronald Reagan came out in favor of the Genocide Treaty. This was remarkable, because this is the most conservative Administration that we have had in many years, and it was a terrific break for us—it demoralized and isolated the opposition. The Foreign Relations Committee reported the Treaty to the Senate by a 14 to 0 vote, with only one abstention, that of Jesse Helms. Senators Simms and East, however, stalled it—it came out with only a week to go, and you can't pass anything with only a week to go in the Senate. It's very easy to filibuster—all you have to do is to be willing to talk for a day or two, and that's not hard for most Senators—and you can delay almost anything. Now, in spite of that situation, however, we got a Resolution passed in the closing days of the Senate. Let me read you what that Resolution says: "The Senate hereby expresses its support for the principles embodied in the Convention of the Prevention and Punishment of the Crime of Genocide and declares its intention to act expeditiously later on in the first session of the Ninety-ninth Congress." That Resolution passed 87 to 2. There were only two Senators who voted against it. We thought we had a juggernaut.

But now there is a new obstacle. That new obstacle is something that makes this a very difficult issue. The Genocide Convention comes up next Thursday in the Foreign Relations Committee. It will be the sixth opportunity for the Committee to report it out, and I'm sure that they will do so. What the issue now involves is the fact that Senator Helms has persuaded the Chairman of the Foreign Relations Committee, Richard Lugar, and the Administration to support an amendment. What that amendment would do is to provide for a reservation saying that in any charge against the United States for violating the

Convention, we would not submit to the World Court unless we agreed to submit to the World Court in the instant charge.* That's like saying we can have a court and we can have a law alright, but we are not going to abide by it unless we want to abide by it. And in the view of every Democrat on the Foreign Relations Committee, that is wrong. But the Administration supported the reservation, and I think that it is going to be very hard for us to win. My expectation is that it will probably lose in Committee by one vote.

Now, why did the Administration take this position? The Administration just last year had a run-in with the World Court. As you know, the CIA authorized the mining of the harbor in Nicaragua. With Nicaragua we have peaceful relations, theoretically, at least; we have ambassadors, we were technically at peace, yet we mined their harbor. So Nicaragua did what you might expect them to do, they went to the World Court. And they won. Now the Administration considers that to be an insult and a rebuff. So they do not want to submit to the World Court again. I think the World Court was right. I hate to say that my country was wrong, and usually it is right, but in this case we were wrong. The Administration, however, isn't in a forgiving or forgetting mood, so when Helms came to them with the amendment with a reservation about the World Court for the Genocide Convention, they accepted it, although last year they thought the reservation wasn't necessary. This year it's a different ball game.

I'm happy to say that your Senators are on the side of those who oppose that reservation: John F. Kerry and Edward F. Kennedy [of Massachusetts], Christopher Dodd [of Connecticut] and Claiborne Pell [of Rhode Island], and other Democrats are opposed to it. We're going to have a tough fight over it. And, of course, what makes this so hard is that if the Helms amendment introduced by Lugar and supported by the Administration knocking out the World Court wins, we could have an easy battle after that for ratification of the Genocide Convention. We can easily invoke cloture, which means cutting off debate, and come to a vote. But we get a Genocide Convention that is long in noble rhetoric and symbolism—it's worth passing—but it's weak in real significance. If Helms loses, we face a tough, hard, bruising,

---

*[Ed. Note] The amendment did pass; as incorporated into the U.S. ratification of the treaty, it states: "before any dispute to which the United States is a party may be submitted to the jurisdiction of the International Court of Justice, ...the specific consent of the United States is required in each case."

uphill fight and a filibuster—a filibuster that I know, I absolutely know, after twenty-seven years in the Senate and having fought on both sides of filibusters, that we can win because we have the votes. We've demonstrated that in Committee, by 14 to 0; we've demonstrated it on the Floor, by the vote of 87 to 2 on the 1984 resolution. For that reason I feel we should go forth and go all the way for it. It's going to be a very exciting fight, and I hope that when you watch it you will recognize that.

Unfortunately, in most speeches, mine included, there has been concentration on only one genocide in the past, that terrible genocide that Hitler perpetrated in Europe. The Armenian Genocide was absolutely heartbreaking, and was a Genocide that we should never forget.[*] As I pointed out, if we had remembered it, called it to the attention of the world, as we should have, it is possible that Hitler would have recognized the terrible thing that he was about to do and it is conceivable that we would have been able to stop him. We have an opportunity now, and I want to congratulate you for meeting here, and devoting your time and attention and your weekend to the cause of international human rights in this great and meaningful way.

---

[*] [Ed. Note] In 1985, when Senator Proxmire spoke, the Reagan Administration was urging the ratification of the Genocide Convention and, at the same time, attempting to defeat a Congressional resolution that recognized the Armenian Genocide.

Genocide and Governmental Responsibility

A Panel Discussion
with Irving Louis Horowitz, Vartan Hartunian, Israel W.
Charny, Richard G. Hovannisian, and Set C. Momjian
Chairman: Herbert Sawyer

GOVERNMENT RESPONSIBILITIES TO JEWS AND ARMENIANS:
THE NAZI HOLOCAUST AND ARMENIAN GENOCIDE RECONSIDERED[*]
Irving Louis Horowitz, *Professor of Sociology and Political
Science, Rutgers University*

The subject of government responsibility for genocide evokes a
certain clinical perspective. This subject is so clearly laden with
emotional impact and touches many of us personally and auto-
biographically. On the other hand, an analytical framework, some
kind of rational model for rationalizing madness, is a task more akin
to psychoanalysis than history. Genocide is not the kind of subject
that is easily dealt with scientifically. Yet that is precisely the
requirement of our age.

The initial problem in the determination of genocide and government responsibility is a certain ambiguity inherent in the question of
state obligation. If we are talking about requiring governments or
states to bear responsibility for a particular genocide, at the time it
occurs, we enter the realm of wishful thinking. To request or implore
of the victimizers that they somehow accept responsibility for those
victimized, at the very moment when the ruling elites are engaging in
what they consider to be a national redemption or a national purge,

---

[*] A slightly revised version of this paper appeared in the *Armenian Review*,
Vol. 39, No. 1/153 (Spring 1986), 1-9.

is a piece of dangerous mythmaking. Thus, when the issue of government responsibility is raised, it cannot possibly mean the genocidal state itself accepting responsibility for a genocide or for a holocaust. To make such an assumption would be tantamount to legal cretinism.

We are talking about a series of events beyond a point in time when the particular genocide initially took place. The victims and their allies are asking for a redress of grievances by a new government that takes over from a genocidal regime. Thus, an essential ambiguity resides in an appeal for government responsibility by a subsequent group in authority. What is usually solicited is a retrospective sense of responsibility on the part of victimizing nations and states. The problem is that, perhaps even more than individuals, states are reticent to accept retroactive responsibility of any kind.

Second, the behavior of leaders in a post-genocidal state has varied greatly. For example, even though the United States bore no responsibility for the Holocaust, American leaders from Presidents Truman to Reagan have taken measures which assume a level of responsibility. More important, Germany from the days of Chancellors Adenauer to Kohl has made declarations and has given reparations to Israel, in the name of the six million Jewish people who died in the Nazi concentration camps. There is a restoration of property rights to individuals who can identify themselves as having had stores, property, or valid contracts under the old order; or reparations to those who desire to return to Israel and be part of the Jewish community. Thus, Germany in its post-Nazi phase took specific as well as general responsibility for the Holocaust.

The same sense of responsibility has not been assumed by Turkey. Recognition of the genocide is virtually absent in Turkish regimes in terms of policy toward Armenia. There was in fact a continuity of Turkish genocidal policies from 1896 to 1915 to 1922. In other words, the character of the regime in Turkey, however it changed from the old Ottoman Empire to the new Kemalist state, did not shift until relatively recently in its genocidal policies. Therefore, the continuous pattern of denial by Turkey for the Armenian massacres is a denial in some measure fueled by virtue of the fact that no Turkish regime ever had to account for its actions to subsequent governments. There have been many governments, but only one state. The obligations and the commitment to either restore property or reform a regime never happened. Simple oral admissions were never forthcoming. Indeed, the genocide continues to be denied today by Turkey and its officials.

The third point is a difficult one to face. All who do research and writing on mass deaths carried out by or on behalf of regimes know that data is hard to establish or recover. Locating responsibility for genocide is in some measure a function of evidence, or to document key events. One is struck by the fact that the Armenian community is at a considerable disadvantage in this regard. Armenian scholars for a long time lacked ready access to key sources of documentation. Presently, there are a great many research efforts going on, primarily by Armenian and Jewish scholars, to correct this situation. But these are not easy efforts by any stretch of the imagination. Turkey continues to offer little support to archivists and researchers concerned with the Armenian Question.

Fourth, there are problems of backwardness and underdevelopment that uniquely determine patterns of genocide. One should not forget that communications networks were very well developed in Germany between 1933 and 1939. The levels of assault on Jews were journalistically documented. The evidence on the photographic side is quite extensive, much higher for the Jewish Holocaust than for the Armenian Genocide. The Nazis in their thirst for political order and their sense of moral certainty themselves inadvertently provided damning evidence. To be sure, source documents did not prevent the Holocaust; nor did backwardness prevent the Turkish destruction of Armenians. But it is more difficult, in terms of historical memory, or the restoration of memory, to establish the factual ground of genocides which take place in pre-industrial economies.

Assessing responsibility by governments is thus complex. Placing responsibility, evaluating damage, monitoring levels of mass executions, all become extremely difficult when dealing with events that are nearly a century old. The technological order shapes both the character and magnitude of genocide, and no less affects the levels of response. Between the Ottoman Empire and the Nazi Wehrmacht stand a thousand years of technology compressed in a hundred years of time.

That brings us to a fifth point: Germany and Turkey were at different stages of development at the time of the mass destruction policies. Whether industrialism was under Nazi control or not, or agrarianism under Ittihat control, the different developmental syndromes are key. Turkey is still a relatively backward country with respect to European networks or industrialism and urbanism. The "Guestworkers" of Germany are largely comprised of Turks, who are indeed called the Black Jews, the *Schwarze Juden* of West Germany.

With Turkey, one is not dealing with an advanced industrial network; rather it is a state and a people which still suffer considerably from economic backwardness. Whether or not this helps or hinders the genocidal political strategy is not the issue at the moment. It is enough to say that the character of the Turkish Genocide vis-a-vis the refinements of the Nazi Holocaust were in part determined by the economic levels of development sustained by each of these two systems of government.

This creates a dual outcome: in Germany, the genocide was highly systematic and rationalized; in Turkey, genocide was random, sporadic, and episodic in character. Types of genocide are determined by levels of economic development, genocidal policies are determined by state power. The Nazi genocide, with its engineering of death, was a supremely modern concept, involving a high level of sophistication in weaponry and death-making hardware. The Nazis solved technological problems such as disposing of bodies; i.e., they resolved questions such as how few people are required to dispose of how many corpses how rapidly by the hour. The Nazi phenomena, the phenomena of engineering death, represented the highest evolution of the banality of evil; and alas, it was quite modern.

In contrast, with respect to the Turkish annihilation of Armenians, the impression given throughout the documentary literature is that this monstrous genocide remained highly personal. It involved traditional forms of assassination: mass killings through physical dismemberment rather than fast-working noxious gas baths and biologically sanitized techniques. It is not necessary to assert which is the more horrible of the two traditional modalities of assassination and liquidation or engineered modes of assassination. This aspect of the philosophy of genocide is beyond my analytic capacities.

The sixth point that I would make is that the determination of governmental responsibility is often influenced by relationships between states in the present era. The Turkish involvement with Islamic politics, Israel's desire to protect its 20,000 to 25,000 Jews still living in Turkey from any further harassment, the commonality of Turkey and Israel as two singular non-Arab states whose leadership is essentially secular and tied to the Western Alliance—these items, among others, tend to subdue levels of Israeli support for Armenian reparation and restoration, even though it is clear that Jewish support for Armenian claims on a worldwide level is relatively high. We are dealing with multiple levels of policy analysis: not just with peoples who were assaulted, Armenians and Jews, but rather with a quadratic relationship of peoples and states: Turks and Germans, Turkey as a nation and Germany as a nation, Jews as a people, and Israel as a nation. These cross-cutting variables and structures make the question of responsibility a ready sacrificial lamb on the Altar of diverse national policies.

The seventh point that needs to be raised is the degree to which state or government acceptance of responsibility for a genocide is the function of the power of overseas or exiled minority communities. The concentration of Jews after World War II (and in some measure before World War II) in the United States, in Israel as a nation, in Western Europe, and in some of the more advanced nations of Latin America, such as Argentina, Brazil, and Chile, created a high level of awareness of the Jewish Holocaust. Jewish community life in these countries created some measure of influence. Interest groups and voluntary associations are factors in the national structures of all democratic societies. The Armenian communities have not been as fortunate in this geographical location, certainly in terms of redressing grievances. It is extremely difficult for the Armenian community to exert equal influence over Turkey. Armenia lost its national independence five hundred years ago, and its people are concentrated in the Soviet Union and in Lebanon. Neither of these host nations have been especially hospitable to Armenian claims, since they entail a large nationalist component.* Armenian resistance and demands for restoration of rights are directly tied to the role of the Armenian communities throughout the United States: in Philadelphia, Boston, Los Angeles, and other areas, where Armenians have created a power base within a democratic network.

What first appears as a matter of legal concern: namely, the rights and responsibilities of governments for acts of genocide, on closer inspection appears to be a consequence of the respective position of Jews and Armenians in democratic societies, in relation to global actors who largely determine "parochial" outcomes. Thus, the fixation of state responsibility is largely made possible by the relative strengths and weaknesses of the protests by offspring of victimized groups, no less than the horrific nature of the events being retrospectively described. It should be plain that Armenian protest has increased rather than slackened as Armenian power in the United States increases and as Turkish political needs remain mired in an

---

*[Ed. Note] This paper was written in 1985, well before the breakup of the Soviet Union and the establishment of the independent Republic of Armenia in 1991.

historically conditioned backwardness. In this mortifying environment, concerned citizens should speak loudly as individuals and as members of interest groups. Victims must define research areas clearly and responsibly. They should work to develop a cultural climate of unity, a context in which restoration of memory no less than land are priorities. In that sense the Jewish community is a model to the Armenian community—from its fund raising to its consciousness-raising activities, and it has been so recognized by leading Armenian figures. On the other hand, the model of Jewish community life cannot be followed in a mechanistic way since there are considerable historical differences between the two peoples. These religious, ethnic, and national differences should be frankly and seriously addressed by those interested in moving beyond the apocalypse in human history and toward some sort of shared political behavior among victimized groups.

It has been stated by Set Momjian, an Armenian-American member of the U.S. Holocaust Council, that the visit of an American president to a German military cemetery that houses the graves of forth-nine Waffen SS soldiers constitutes a denial of the Holocaust itself, and at least in possibility may contribute to rationalization of the mass slaughters perpetrated forty years ago. While a denial of historic memories—"let bygones be bygones"—hangs over the rhetoric of both Ronald Reagan and Chancellor Helmut Kohl, these leaders took pains, under broad public pressure to be sure, to reassert the awful reality of the Holocaust. Indeed, the "Bitburg flap" stimulated the West German Chancellor to speak out more forcefully than ever before in recognizing Germany's governmental responsibility for the Nazi Holocaust. Historical memory may not be as fleeting or as flimsy as cynics of mass communications suggest.

The Presidential policy of *gleichbedeutend*, of making the sufferings of Jewish victims and Nazi victimizers synonymous, may be viewed as morally obtuse and historically indefensible, but it does not constitute a denial of the Holocaust. It does lean toward a denial of the special place of the Holocaust in the twentieth century. The very levels and intensity of this debate over the Presidential visit, not to mention the capacity of the Jewish people to respond with vigor to such an issue of vital sensitivity, is precisely what is absent in the Armenian situation. The fact of the Turkish Genocide, as an event, or better, a series of events stretching over a quarter century and more, is precisely what remains in contention. There is no Turkish official willing to acknowledge what the German Chancellor readily admits to:

that remembrance of the Holocaust represents "the revelation of national shame." And until such a time occurs, the assumption that Jews and Armenians are in the same moral condition vis-a-vis their tormentors will remain a dangerous presumption.

It may seem an eccentric conclusion to these remarks on governmental responsibilities to Holocaust and Genocide victims to plead for more careful research, but I think not. Unit historic memory is restored through massive penetration of the cultural forces in Western societies, the Turkish regime will be able to ignore or disregard Armenian claims. The efforts of a William Saroyan in literature, an Alan Hovhaness in music, and yes, a Richard Hovannisian in history, must become the tip of an iceberg, and not simply the entire range of cultural expression. The brilliance of the Armenian people—in business, commerce, and industry—is beyond question. But without a strong cultural component, random acts of terror become a vehicle of expression without chance of much success at the level of mass influence or elite policy. Without a strong cultural component, frustration of goals followed by aggression to retrieve some measure of respect, ending in disillusionment with the cause itself, becomes the natural history not only struggle, but of failure.

I am not arguing the case for passive acquiescence in the face of historic wrongs. Quite the contrary, even strategies of paramilitary actions must be based on a careful consideration of the chances of success and strategies being advanced. For otherwise, the Armenian cause, however just and righteous, will become a part of a laundry list of failed movements which themselves become episodic, sporadic, theatrical, and eventually simply forgotten. The question of statist obligations must not be severed from those of individual obligations, to conscience no less than to action. That is a lesson burned deep in the memories of the Jewish and Armenian peoples alike.

THE MORAL IMPLICATIONS OF THE ARMENIAN GENOCIDE

Vartan Hartunian, *Pastor, First Armenian Church, Belmont, Mass.*

The Genocide of the Armenian people (1915-1923) by the Ottoman Turkish government was of such horrendous proportions in its evil as to shock the world conscience of that era. It led the United States Ambassador to the Ottoman Empire, Henry Morgenthau, to state:

I am confident that the whole history of the human race contains no such horrible episode as this. The great massacres and persecutions of the past seem almost insignificant when compared to the sufferings of the Armenian race in 1915.   (*Ambassador Morgenthau's Story*, 1919)

These horrors also led the spokesman for the Sublime Port, during the post-Genocide Military Tribunal proceedings in Istanbul, to write in the *Alemtar Daily*:

Our only means of salvation is to cry out loud to the civilized world that we are determined to bring to just and open trial all offenders. . . . We Turks are charged with a crime and are infected with an incurable disease which is more horrible than the plague. This is precisely why we set up a special military tribunal in order to punish the offenders so that due justice is carried out.   (*Renaissance*, No. 128, January 5, 1919)

These moral sentiments were soon forgotten, the victorious nations became enemies of each other, the Turkish government changed color and was forgiven, and the world witnessed "The Great Betrayal" of the Armenian People. Abraham H. Hartunian, who survived the Genocide, makes the following statement in his memoirs:

Oh, that we had realized from the start that all the European powers were thinking only of their own gain and were ready to sacrifice the Armenians!

Oh, that we had known they were not our saviors, but murderers more cruel than the Turks! They had not declared war to save enslaved and powerless nations but to buy oil, mines, and land by giving these same nations in exchange!

Oh, that we had understood they were deceivers! They had not prepared to preserve the peace of the world but to preserve their own imperialism at the price of the peace of the world!
(*Neither to Laugh Nor to Weep*, Armenian Heritage Press, 1968, p. 126)

Because of this great betrayal by the so-called Christian powers of the world (Britain, France, Germany, Italy, and Russia), Abraham H. Hartunian continues:

The blood of the Armenian will protest to the God of Justice! And either the result will be our murderers' repentance, and just compensation for the Armenian fragment, or else the thunderbolt of righteousness of the just God will strike Europe and destroy her!
(*Neither to Laugh Nor to Weep*, p. 127)

Whether or not one believes in divine retribution, I must point out that the above statements were written in 1924. During World War II (1939-1945), whether by diabolic coincidence or fulfillment of this prophecy, Europe and Russia indeed did experience wide and horrible destruction.

* * *

The thesis I am proposing is that, just as individuals cannot commit crimes without due consequences for themselves, neither can nations do so without due consequences for themselves. Nations that commit genocide are in greatest peril. And since no nation commits genocide without the silence approval or cooperation of other nations, the world itself is under judgment. The threat of nuclear destruction which hangs over humanity is God's warning to the nations.

During 1985, the seventieth anniversary of the Armenian Genocide, we are beginning to hear "the waves of Armenian justice pounding on the shores of humanity." The governments of several nations—in particular Turkey, France, Israel, and the United States—are becoming increasingly involved in the *Armenian Question.* Although there are attempts at revisionist history with regard to the Holocaust (1933-1945), such revisionism is limited to individuals or self-appointed organizations. In the case of the Armenian Genocide, Turkey and the United States are attempting official governmental revisionism precisely for the same reasons that the original great betrayal took place. Such attempts, I submit, will have dangerous consequences not only for these two nations but for all mankind.

We are all aware, I believe, of our State Department's position on the Armenian Genocide. In the face of overwhelming documentary evidence in its own archives, we have been told that this Genocide is "alleged" and that the events of 1915 and subsequent years in Turkey have not been reliably documented. (*State Department Bulletin, NOTE,* August 1982)

Secretary of Defense Caspar W. Weinberger went beyond revisionism to the perversion of facts in an address to the Foreign Affairs Committee of the U.S. House of Representatives

> I would like to address another congressional issue of importance to our relations with Turkey: the so-called "Armenian Genocide" Resolutions. H. J. Resolution 37, introduced in January, would, among other things, designate a National Day of Remembrance with Reference to "Armenian Genocide" in Turkey between 1915 and 1923. Whatever the merits of such remembrance, we believe such resolutions are counter-productive in that they serve to encourage Armenian terrorists who have killed more than 50 Turkish citizens, mostly diplomats, over the past years. Some murders have occurred in the United States. We also believe that consideration of this resolution would embarrass the United States and strain relations with this critical ally. For these reasons, I hope you give your support to preventing favorable action on this resolution, and preventing the introduction of others like it.

The following is my response to Secretary Weinberger:

> Regarding your statement to the House Foreign Affairs Committee on February 21, 1985, in opposition to H. J. Resolution 37, may I respectfully point out that the political relationship between the United States and Turkey would be greatly improved if the United States took the initiative in recognizing not only the historical truth of the Armenian Genocide but also that the present Turkish government bears no direct responsibility for it except in its denial of this tragedy perpetrated by the Ottoman Turkish Government of 1915-1918.
>
> May I also point out that the unfortunate assassination of Turkish officials, which began long before resolutions of the type you oppose were submitted to our Congress, was the result of the Turkish denial that the Genocide ever took place and its official program to rewrite the history of those years and to interfere in the memorial services for the victims of this Genocide.
>
> It is also sad to note by your comments, that the United States Government is embarrassed by historical truth. As Secretary of Defense, you certainly know that truth creates moral power and that embarrassment is the result of blackmail. You should also ponder the fact that denial is the last stage of genocide and that your statement and your support of the Turkish position is a tacit approval of genocide as an instrument of government.   (March 1, 1985)

It is my observation that most nations, particularly the powerful ones, are secretly ready and willing to commit genocide. Their excuses for committing this crime simply abet the crime since there cannot be any excuse or reason for killing hosts of the innocent —children in particular. It is sad to recall that in the case of the Japanese on our West Coast, the United States committed the first two stages of Genocide—*identification* and *segregation*. The last two stages, which are *extermination* and *denial*, would possibly have taken place if the Japanese had attacked our Western shores.

MORAL AND SPIRITUAL FOUNDATIONS OF GOVERNMENT

Since governments are part of the mystery of creation, they have a spiritual basis; since they are involved in the inter-relationships of persons, they are bound and guided by moral principles. Morality involves judgments concerning the goodness and badness of human actions. Spirituality is consciousness of a Divine Presence (God) with knowledge of past, present, and future events directed by moral law. Spirituality sees ultimate responsibility in the actions of individuals and governments and in this knowledge makes morality meaningful and possible.

In discussions of *genocide* and *holocaust*, when spiritual and moral considerations are removed, we have left only a jungle of power, an evolutionary tooth and claw, the survival of the fittest (perpetrators of genocide) and the destruction of the unfit (victims of genocide). Both the *Young Turks* and the *Nazis* were essentially atheists. Once the spiritual basis for their decisions was removed, their actions were directed not by moral considerations but by the full use of immediate power for immediate ends. The Turkish government of 1915 deliberated and decided to carry out the Armenian Genocide, since the leaders were convinced that no outside force could intervene (Turkish borders were militarily secured) and that no inside force could prevent it (Armenians were unarmed). Assuming that there would be no moral consequences for their acts, they released some ten thousand criminals from their prisons and trained them to carry out the Genocide. A similar process operated in Germany during the Holocaust:

> In Hitler-Germany, a highly developed people devised the rationale and methodology for exterminating six million human beings—over a million of them children—and for converting them into fat for soap, hair for mattresses, and bone for fertilizer. ...This new formulation enabled mass murderers to think of themselves as technicians following orders and to call mass murder "special treatment." The accompanying obliteration of all customary human feelings—remorse, guilt, or pity—created a new phenomenon in history which defies human understanding.
>
> (*The Holocaust*, Nora Levin, p. xii, Schocken Books, New York)

Events following the Armenian Genocide and the Holocaust clearly indicate that the crimes of nations will come to judgment in time, because there is something in creation that does not like the sadistic torture and killing of innocent children. A German eyewitness during the Armenian Genocide has reported the chopping off of the hands of hundreds of children and letting them bleed to death as they ran to and fro howling in pain and anguish. Elie Weisel has written:

> Never shall I forget that night, the first night in camp, which has turned my life into one long night. Never shall I forget the smoke. Never shall I forget the little faces of the children whose bodies I say turned into wreaths of smoke beneath a silent blue sky.
>
> (*Time*, March 18, 1985, p. 79)

THE BIBLICAL VIEW OF GOVERNMENT

The Bible tells us that governments are from God for the purpose of ruling society in such a way as to prevent evil and to realize the greatest possible good (Romans 13). The Ten Commandments were given not only to individuals but to peoples and governments.

Governments, therefore, are to obey God's law:

> Do not commit murder.
> Do not commit lust.
> Do not rob and steal.
> Do not lie.
> Do not desire the property of others.
>   (Exodus 19, 20, 21)

Governments are also to have positive programs of service to the people:

> Bring good news to the poor (welfare).
> Proclaim liberty to captives (prison reform).
> Open the eyes of the blind (medical care and education).
> Set free the oppressed (give minorities full human rights).

Above all, governments are to give priority to children:

> Children are the foundation of a future society of justice and love.
>   (Luke 18: 15-17)

Consider in the light of the above, the 300,000 Armenian children and the 1,000,000 Jewish children who were mercilessly killed during the Armenian Genocide and the Holocaust.

THE SIGNIFICANCE OF APRIL 24, 1985 FOR ALL MANKIND

Genocide is a crime against humanity. The Genocide of the Armenian people during World War I was of such proportions in its evil and pain as to penetrate not only the marrow of the bones of civilization but its continuing conscience which has been mortally disturbed for the past seventy years. This "first genocide of the twentieth century" took the lives of one and one-half million Armenians and scattered the survivors throughout the world. Perpetrated by the Turkish government from 1915-1923, its unrestrained evil gave rise to the Holocaust of World War II and subsequent genocides such as in Cambodia and presently in Iran against the Baha'is. Because of the universal scope of this tragedy which, if not forgotten, is being systematically denied with dangerous consequences for humanity, the US House of Representatives in September 1984 passed by a two-thirds majority a resolution designating April 24, 1985 as a "National Day of Remembrance of Man's Inhumanity to Man, and in particular recalling the Armenian Massacres."

During April 1985 Armenians are commemorating this event worldwide. In the conviction that the integrity of historical events provides moral power and the honoring of the victims of genocide is a moral force for peace, the Armenian people feel that the time has arrived when non-Armenians should join Armenians and Jews in remembrance of the victims of genocide. This moral force, we believe, would stand strong against future threats of wholesale destruction of the innocent.

April 24 is an opportunity for all peoples who love justice, freedom, and truth to bring to the attention of the United States and the United Nations the fact that the Armenian Genocide was a crime not only against the Armenian people but against humanity itself. It established a pattern of terrorism on a wholesale basis which has since poisoned the political life of the twentieth century. Hitler was inspired by the Turkish success. The Turk has never acknowledged guilt and given compensation. If a small civilized nation can be virtually eliminated by terror and the survivors driven from their land, what hope is there for mankind in the future to raise its super-structures on foundations of justice?

GENOCIDE AND NUCLEAR WAR

If nuclear war does come, most of humanity will suffer what the victims of genocide have already suffered without the knowledge and often without the concern of those who were not partakers of their suffering and death. The present growing outcry against nuclear war seems to have its basis in the fact that all classes of individuals in our generation clearly sense that they can no longer insulate themselves from the horrors that have been inflicted upon defenseless and innocent men, women, and children during the Armenian Genocide, the Jewish Holocaust, Hiroshima or Nagasaki. The fact remains that under the nuclear threat of destruction, every individual throughout the world, like victims of genocide, is being identified, segregated, and classified for extermination. If the unimaginable should happen, the only difference from the genocides of the past would be that there would be no government left to deny it.

It behooves us all to begin studying carefully the injustices of the past, expose them to international scrutiny, memorialize them in repentance, make reparations where possible, and pray that the God of Justice will forgive these crimes of individuals, religions, and nations, and not "blot out this adulterous generation" in the fires of nuclear retribution.

BIBLICAL PROPHECY

I began this paper with a prophecy of Abraham H. Hartunian regarding the destruction of Europe and Russia during World War II.

Here is a prophecy from II Peter: 3 regarding "Nuclear War":

> The day of the Lord will come as a thief in the night; in the which the heavens shall pass away with a great noise, and the elements shall melt with fervent heat, the earth also and the works that are therein shall be burned up.

St. Peter does not leave us in despair: "Let us look for a new earth where dwelleth righteousness."   (II Peter 3:13)

Maintaining Moral Values

Israel W. Charny, *Director, Institute of the International Conference on the Holocaust and the Genocide, Jerusalem*

I want to take this opportunity to express my pleasure at being with you at this Conference. Were the Conference devoted entirely to the subject of the Armenian Genocide, I would have been only too glad to participate. The fact that the Conference was from the outset defined also as devoted to consideration of the process of genocide as it has affected other peoples is important to me, both as a matter of principle and as a preliminary step in our attempt to understand and prevent genocide. As many of you know, the Institute that I direct, which continues the work of our Conference of 1982 and which is called the Institute of the International Conference on the Holocaust and the Genocide, is devoted to just that universalization through, and together with, our particularizations. Each of our peoples which has suffered genocide has an obligation, a mission, to remember, to memorialize, to study, and to religiously continue the ceremonies, the caring about our past. At the same time it is very much the conviction of many of us that the story of what happened to our own peoples, the story of what happened to many other peoples—and it is the same story, whatever the differences—that the stories of all our peoples who suffered are the stories of peoples of the future. Perhaps we again, either in our separateness or as part of a great mass of humanity, as Rev. Hartunian has emphasized so beautifully, face the continuation of mass murder, and it seems to me that one of the most fitting ways that we can memorialize our own past is by devoting ourselves to the study of genocide and especially efforts at prevention.

I'd like to address my remarks not to governments as perpetrators of genocide, but more to governments as accomplices, governments as bystanders, governments when they are in situations where they are confronted with a choice between their own continuing self-interests—in whatever management or leadership functions they serve their particular peoples—and taking a clear-cut moral position about genocide that is taking place, or has taken place, to another people. And in that connection, I thought it would be relevant, and of considerable interest to many of the participants, to go back to the Conference in 1982 and to share with you some of the story of those events. One way I can begin is by telling you a current story that sounds very familiar, but I have the impression that very few people know about it.

I almost wasn't here in Massachusetts for this particular remembrance because earlier in the year I was invited to a conference that was to take place—I hope it has—at the University of Bremen, in Germany, a Conference that was specifically to be devoted to the Armenian Genocide and the Holocaust, both simultaneously. I wrote back to that invitation—it was before I heard from our hosts here—that I'd be very glad to attend, and then I heard nothing more. When the invitation arrived from the group here, I needed to clarify what was happening with the Conference in Germany. Frankly, I was a bit annoyed that the organizers had not replied to my last letter. To learn more about the arrangement processes, I picked up the phone and called the home of the organizers there. A woman answered, the wife of the gentleman who was organizing the Conference, and she said, "Ah, you are calling from Jerusalem, then let's speak Hebrew." And she swung into a beautiful Hebrew. I replied with pleasure—it's nice to speak Hebrew with someone in Germany—and I also thought to myself (and this remark is intended for those of you who are Armenian and have too many doubts about your own value as a people) "Ahaa, I should have known why they didn't answer my last letter; she's Jewish." There's a real wrinkle to the continuation of the story. She promised me that her husband would call me back; he didn't; I made my decision; and I'm here.

A few weeks ago I had a call from the same woman, who was in Israel. She said her husband had asked her to be in touch with me; he wanted to apologize for the breakdown in communication. I had written to them already that I was coming here to Massachusetts. They were trying to go ahead with the Conference, but they were having serious trouble. She in the meantime had to come to Israel because, this in Hebrew again, her mother was dying, and she had to be with her. Her mother, it turns out, and she are Armenian. Her mother was a survivor of the Armenian Genocide who settled in Palestine, as so many Armenians did. She grew up in Israel, hence her beautiful Hebrew—don't worry, I'm not angry about the letter any more. Her mother had undergone brain surgery in an effort to save her life, and the poor woman was lying in this world of transition, and what was she remembering? There are so many stories like this, but each one can only more us to tears—she was reliving the Armenian Genocide. It was all happening for her again in that last flow of memories. In the meantime, what is happening back in Germany? "My husband is being persecuted by the Turks. They are out to cancel the Conference." Is that familiar? And to whom have they gone? To the various German government administrators, officials, on the state level, on the federal level, and the pressure is on. "We're terrified," she said, "the burden is tremendous. No matter what, I'm going back to him in a few days." I hope that we will hear and learn that they were able to stand up to the pressures and conduct a meaningful conference.

The story of government in the case of Israel in 1982 is particularly poignant, particularly meaningful, because we are dealing with the officials of a people who have been victims, a people that cares very deeply about values of justice; and yet, as the story unfolded, we saw in relation to this government also some of the same dynamics which I suggest are crucial for us to understand in the unfolding story of evil. When we are talking about a government that itself commits destruction, there's not very much else to be seen. You see the ugliness of the Ottoman Turkish government, you see the ugliness of the Nazi killing. When we look at governments in action in these other, indirect situations, I believe that we are given an opportunity to see some of the dynamics that may very well be at work in the actual situations of destructiveness. We see the turn to a kind of opportunism and the blind devotion to pragmatism. A government sees its own self-interest in certain terms. I believe that a certain government leader—and we will be hearing about it shortly from Mr. Momjian—who's concerned pragmatically with relationships with a certain other country, is getting himself or has gotten himself into quite a value dilemma as to how one takes a stand in regard to value issues when, after all, one has to maintain good relations with this other country. We see the blindness of the bureaucratic process.

I will never forget the meetings held with Israeli officials as we moved towards the Conference in June 1982. The sense that we had was that here were people busy doing their job, and their job at that time as they determined it was that they didn't want to have any trouble with Turkey because it was important for Israel to maintain good relations with Turkey. Also there was indeed a matter of serious threats by the Turks against certain Jews. But I hardly have the feeling at times that these officials even remembered the Jews that they were concerned about. What they were remembering was their jobs. And when the tyranny of getting their jobs done, especially as groups pull together—groups of officials each one supporting the other—to push even further towards that pragmatic goal, then people and values seem to disappear from the situation. There is a tremendous dulling of sensitivity to the purposes of government for the people that government is supposed to serve.

In 1982 the story, in brief, was that the Israeli government, continuing the policy that it had followed, I'm sad to say, for many years of trying to maintain good relations with Turkey, responded to serious Turkish threats by calling us in and saying, in effect, "Don't have the Armenians participate" in what was to be the first international conference on Holocaust and Genocide. We said, "That's not possible." The Israeli officials answered, "All right, we understand that you have to be true to your values. Then, why don't you simply hold the conference on the Jewish Holocaust and forget about the genocides of all other peoples?" And we said, "Well, the point of this Conference is that we want to make the linkage between these events in the histories of all peoples on this planet and to work at concepts of prevention of genocide." The government position then was "Well, if that's the case, then cancel the Conference."

And as you know we decided not to cancel the Conference, and then came a series of steps by the government designed to force us to cancel the Conference. Here was a small laboratory for seeing the way governments take positions. People who had committed funds were approached and told that their position would be compromised if they gave the Conference funds. We had one check for $10,000 which had arrived from a foundation in the United States. We deposited it in the bank, but before it cleared in the bank in New York, that particular foundation leader was told in no uncertain terms that he would have trouble doing business in Israel in terms of government support if that money cleared. Participating institutions were told to withdraw their support. In the case of my home institution, Tel Aviv University, which was scheduled to be on a certain level of sponsorship, I was told in the men's room, as I recall, by one of my senior colleagues, that the University would not participate and what the hell kind of trouble was I making anyway. The government remembrance authority, Yad Vashem, where we were supposed to open the Conference, withdrew. The participants were sent cables, individual cables, that informed them that the government of Israel requested them not to participate in the Conference. And for many of us, and here I move to my identification as a Jew who cares very deeply about Israel, the first reaction of course was "I don't do something that compromises the interests of a government I care about." Pressures were brought on the press. Those of us who made the decision to go ahead made the judgment that, (a) yes, there were serious threats made against Jewish lives, but they were largely on the level of terrorism or a kind of bullying that (if one submits to it) strengthens the hands of the bulliers and terrorists and, (b) that the moral issue involved called for some serious degree of risk-taking.

Now I'm going to take a jump ahead and tell you a recent story. I contacted the Foreign Ministry of Israel earlier this year on behalf of two members of the International Council of our Institute with the request that we be given information about the position of Israel with regard to the killings of the minority in Sri Lanka who are known as the Tamil. For our purposes, they are the local Armenians, or the local Jews—it doesn't make any difference, does it, which analogy we use? *The names change, the game is the same.* The story there very briefly is that Israel, in a perfectly legitimate way, has developed a certain number of commercial and political relationships with Sri Lanka which are kosher and to the advantage of Israel, a small country. I happen to know one of the people who is involved in a very beautiful agricultural project; there is another project I don't like, because it reminds me of George Bernard Shaw's remarks about trading in certain security matters—but that's part of this world as well. Government troops of Sri Lanka were reported in the world press—I sent the Foreign Ministry clippings from the Hebrew press and from the *New York Times*—to be directly involved in the killing of some 5,000 Tamil in the recent outbreaks. We asked what is the position of the government of Israel as a party that is doing business with this other government when killings of that sort erupt towards their Jews or Armenians. The answer that I received from the Foreign Ministry was as follows: We do not know of the alleged events; we do not make policy decisions on the basis of newspaper reports. To which our Institute replied as follows: "Your reply was frivolous and unacceptable to us. The enclosed information will call to your attention the seriousness of the question raised, and we do request a further reply." And what we enclosed was as follows: a copy of a telegram that was sent from Europe in 1942 by a Jew, which he managed to get to the United States State Department, telling of the mass extermination that was being organized and taking place in the various Nazi death camps; and along with that we sent a copy of the State Department internal memo in which a State Department official ruled that this was not sufficient evidence to confirm the alleged events taking place against the Jews in Europe and, as a further consequence, the information would not be passed on to the leader of the American Jewish community, Rabbi Weiss.

What I'd like to conclude with is that, with regard to all governments, and with regard to many other institutions in human life, it seems to be that one of the first levels of commitment that we all need to come to—Armenians, Jews, every individual attorney, every individual physician, every individual educator, engineer, whoever and whatever we are—is that, at the least, while we are on this planet, we all try to stand up clearly for these moral issues regardless of who the victims are. Pastor Neimoller wrote: "First they came for the Jews, and I did not speak out because I was not a Jew. Then they came for the Communists, and I did not speak out because I was not a Communist. Then they came for the Trade Unionists, and I did not speak out because I was not a Trade Unionist. Then they came for me, and there was no one left to speak out for me."

HUMAN RIGHTS AND THE ROLE OF THE PRESIDENT

Set C. Momjian, *Member, U.S. Holocaust Memorial Council*

Last Monday [April 15, 1985] there was an emergency meeting of the United States Holocaust Council. The meeting was held in New York. The subject was President Reagan's trip to Germany, and specifically the President's trip to Bitburg Cemetery, a cemetery where some of Hitler's SS troops are buried. For those of you who do not remember, the SS were Hitler's elite soldiers, considered by many as a symbol of international crime against the Jewish people and against humanity. After listening to the outrage expressed by Council member after Council member, I had my chance to speak. And I said that for the past five years that I had been on the Council, I have talked about the much more serious problem that the Armenian community has faced, and has faced for the past seventy years. I told them I knew they had listened to me, but it was not until that day that the Council fully understood. But with the events of the past week or two, I've been in meetings morning, afternoon, and night with the Council, and the members are worried about the future not only of the Council but of the Jewish community. There was another emergency meeting last night—I was in Washington until about 9 o'clock—this time over a statement issued by the President just hours before. I would like to read to you the President's statement that we were handed as we walked into the meeting:

> I think there is nothing wrong with visiting that cemetery where those young men are victims of Nazism also. Even though they were fighting in the German uniform, drafted into the service to carry out the hateful wishes of the Nazis, they were victims just as surely as the victims in the concentration camps.

I would now like to read you the response by the Council that was given to the President today.

> Members of the U.S. Holocaust Memorial Council, meeting last night following a most moving Holocaust memorial ceremony in the rotunda of the Capitol, were confronted with reports of the comments you made earlier today equating the deaths of Nazi soldiers who fought for Hitler with the victims who were murdered by Hitler in concentration camps. We were shocked to learn that a President of the United States could utter such a distortion of what took place during the Holocaust. If no immediate correction is offered by you, it will mean you see no difference between war and genocide. The whole meaning of the Holocaust, which this Council is mandated by Act of Congress to articulate and to explain, would be corrupted if these words of a President of the United States remain unchallenged and unchanged. We are saddened at having to communicate this expression of shock, but our conscience permits us no less. We are compelled to do everything possible to undo the harm your words have caused. This statement was adopted unanimously by all Council members present, including representatives of every religious faith.
>
> *Elie Weisel*, Chairman
> U.S. Holocaust Memorial Council

Part of the discussion last night was that perhaps the Council should resign *en masse*. The longest part of the evening was devoted to the question of whether Elie Weisel should accept a medal from the President today [April 18, 1985]. The Congress had awarded Elie Weisel a Gold Medal a year ago, and it was to be presented by the President. Two weeks ago Elie Weisel had received a telephone call from the White House saying that the presentation would take place in the East Room, and that Elie Weisel could invite 125 of his friends, including all the Council members, and the White House would invite 125 people, for a total of 250 people in the East Room while the President presented the medal to Elie Weisel. Earlier this week, Elie Weisel got a call from the White House saying that the location of the award ceremony had been moved from the East Room to the Roosevelt Room, and because the room was small, Elie Weisel could invite two guests: his wife and his son. So the Holocaust Council's discussion centered on whether or not he should accept the medal. I had to come home to Philadelphia last night—I took the 10:30 p.m. train—but many of the Council members met with Congressmen and Senators late in the evening to make a decision on accepting the medal. They decided that Elie Weisel should accept it, and he should make a statement, but they were sure that the President would apologize for the sentiments he had expressed in the afternoon.

When I arrived in Boston, I called Elie Weisel from the airport. I learned that, when the President handed him the medal, he turned it over immediately to his wife. There was no apology; if anything there was a determination that there would be no retraction of the statement and that the President indeed would go to Bitburg cemetery. The Holocaust Council is now deciding whether the Council should go to the cemetery and, if so, they will be met by the Jewish communities from all over the world, who will not enter the cemetery with the President. So there are many problems. What does it all mean?

It means that the Jewish community is in the same boat the Armenian community has been in for the past seventy years, a result of the fact that, when governments deal with governments, principles somehow become negotiable. Never before has the Jewish community been treated like this. The fear that I sense at the Holocaust meetings revolves around the question of "what next?" Israel Charny mentioned the Tel Aviv conference in 1982. And when you talk about principles being negotiable, could anyone in this room ever have imagined that the State of Israel would lobby the U.S. State Department and the U.S. Holocaust Council members to keep Armenians from attending a Conference on genocide so as not to embarrass Israel's ally, Turkey? It happened. Elie Weisel, who was chairman of the Conference, issued a statement from Paris pointing out that in the Bible it is said that to humiliate is to murder. And he would not humiliate the Armenians by banning them from the Conference. He said that he would resign, and he did. The bottom line is: if the Israeli government has not learned the lessons of the Holocaust, if they try to muffle the screaming voices of another genocide to appease an ally, what really can we expect from nations whose people have never experienced anything approaching a genocide? I do not make this statement to be critical of Israel, nor am I being critical of the United States or our President. I am simply stating a fact that, with governments, you have to be alert for hidden problems; government responsibility does not always mean what we think it should mean.

The White House is against the pending resolution in Congress setting aside April 24 as a day of remembrance for man's inhumanity to man, in particular, the Armenian Genocide. The reasons given by the President *a few months ago* are the following: 1. The events happened a long time ago, few people are still alive who were living then; 2. It's time to emphasize friendship, rather than remind countries about their guilt; 3. Turkey is an important ally and we should avoid insulting her. *Now* the White House is against canceling the trip to the German cemetery in Bitburg. The President the other day said the following: 1. The events happened a long time ago, few people are still alive who were living then; 2. It's time to emphasize friendship, rather than remind countries about their guilt; 3. West Germany is an important ally and we should avoid insulting her.

Thus, as I pointed out earlier, the Jewish and Armenian communities are now in the same boat. For the past forty years, the Armenian Genocide and the Jewish Holocaust have been going along parallel lines, with the members of each community doing our own thing. This past week, the parallel lines crossed, and I predict that you will find, in the future, a much closer relationship and a much better understanding between Armenians and Jews. Of major importance for Armenians and Jews is the Holocaust Council and Museum. The Council can speak on issues as it is doing now. If you've been reading the papers and watching television, you know how effective the voice of the Council has been. There will be a Committee of Conscience, to speak up for all groups. It is in the process of being formed.

In terms of responsibility, the United States has done more than any other country in establishing the U.S. Holocaust Council and Museum to be erected on one of the most desirable pieces of land in Washington. It will be only the second national museum on the Holocaust in the world, the other being in Israel. The museum should be completed in 1989* and will include material and exhibits of all genocides. Make no mistake, it is basically a museum on the Jewish Holocaust, but again all genocides will be included, and I assure you,

---

*The Holocaust Museum in Washington is now scheduled to open in April 1993.

as an Armenian on the Council, that Armenians will be pleased with the amount of space and the presentation of the Armenian Genocide when it is completed.

Government support is a fleeting thing, especially in the United States, where we have a change of administrations and a democratic government and where very little is not subject to change if the majority of people will it. In a recent speech I said that the United States had been blessed with good men as presidents, and I mean it. I don't think we've ever had a president who did not do what he honestly thought was in the best interests of this country. Herein lies the problem. What is in the best interests of the Jewish or Armenian communities is not always in the best interests of the United States. A president will put the interests of the United States government on one side of the scale, and the interests of the interest group on the other. Sometimes they balance. In that case a decision is easy. Oftentimes the interest group may have help from key Congressmen on balancing the scale. And then, once in a while, we get a president who devotes his life to human rights, like President Carter; and he, like the proverbial butcher, will put his thumb on the scale to make sure it balances on the side of human rights, morality, and moral principles. I will be with President Carter this Tuesday, April 23, and I'm proud to call him a very close personal friend; more than once has he used his thumb on the scale for Armenians.

I would like to touch on ethnic responsibility. As an Armenian, every time an Armenian issue comes before the government, I and all other Armenians feel the Armenian side of the scale should hit the ground. All other ethnic groups react in the same way when it comes to their interests. What we have to learn is that, if the issue is not of vital interest to us and it is important to the United States, we have to say, "We are against it, but if it is important to you, Mr. President, we'll understand." Then, when a really important issue comes along, we have to hang tough and say, "Mr. President, we backed you last month, and now we need your help." In politics it's known as building up points, something we Armenians very seldom do.

Governmental responsibility is not easily defined; it means different things to different groups. To those of us gathered in this room, it means human rights and morality. To a group dedicated to the defense of this country, it means something completely different. Ethnic responsibility lies in sometimes convincing the government as to what *its* responsibility is. To do that successfully you have to have it all together; that is, have clearly defined goals, a united community—not always easy—and of course it helps if you have the ear of a president, especially if the president is committed to human rights.

ON BUILDING BRIDGES
Richard G. Hovannisian, *Professor of Armenian History, UCLA*

Let me make a few comments in response to points made by the speakers this evening. I'd like to focus, if I may, on comments made by Professors Horowitz and Charny in particular. Professor Horowitz began with a very appropriate statement that this issue of genocide is so emotional that it almost seems to be a contradiction in terms to sense the emotionality of the subject and yet demand the scholarly, cold, scientific research that has to be undertaken to study it and to understand the madness. How true that is. It is regrettable, I think sorely regrettable, that in seventy years after the Armenian Genocide the kind of scientific studies that should have been taken regarding the understanding and analysis of the perpetrators of the Genocide and the victims of the Genocide still has not been done. Christopher Walker addressed himself to this deficiency in a letter to one of the Armenian newspapers recently in which he pointed out that, while it is all well and good that we should go back and look at the memoirs of Ambassador Morgenthau or the British government's Blue Book, those sources were of 1915, of contemporaries: what about the scientific investigation that should have been continued in the subsequent seventy years, in the current time, according to current standards of the social sciences?

It is true that the destruction of the Genocide was so great that the first generation at least was too devastated to do anything but get its families back together and try to pick up the pieces. But this is not in any way an excuse for the second and third generations and the scholarly community at large, and I would certainly support and strengthen the concept of our need for this kind of investigation. The question of accessibility is important. In the case of the Jewish Holocaust, the German Archives are open, the German documents have been available, the Germans have supported a study of the subject. The same does not hold true for the Armenians. Perhaps the greatest document that the Armenians have is vanishing from their hands, and the greatest document that they have is the survivors, the thousands of survivors, each with an eyewitness account, each with an eyewitness story, giving details of that person's existence and suffering that none but the most intense denier could repudiate. In a few years we will no longer have the survivor generation in our midst. That is an enormous loss, a great loss, the possibility of which I cannot even begin to think of, and of course whatever can be done to preserve the remnants of that generation are important. But let us imagine ten years from now being told, "You weren't there, how do you know what happened?" And you say, "I heard it from my parents, or my grandparents." Well, what's that, that's hearsay. That's what we're coming to.

With respect to the question of international community responsibility and governmental responsibility for the punishment of the perpetration of genocide, various governments moved in that direction in the Armenian case, but they weren't bold enough to carry it out. Although the word genocide was not used, the Treaty of Sevres specified the punishment of the perpetrators of what today would be called the crime of genocide: the massacres and deportation of the Armenian population. The Treaty specified the restoration of property to those who had it confiscated. It committed the Turkish government to help the Western forces, the Allies, to recover Armenian women and children who had been sequestered and taken away into Turkish households. But we know that the Treaty of Sevres was supplanted by the Treaty of Lausanne in 1923, at which time the word "Armenia" or "Armenian" did not even appear, let alone any of these other stipulations that had been made in the Treaty of Sevres. The problem of abandonment of the Armenian Question, therefore, makes a heavy statement about the question of governmental *responsibility*, and that word, as has been stated, has many connotations: the responsibility of the Turkish government to face, to acknowledge, and to do whatever possible to overcome this terrible barrier, this terrible malaise, in Armenian-Turkish relations; the responsibility of the governments that were in the war and promised and pledged themselves to see to it that the provisions of the Treaty of Sevres would be respected, yet, ultimately, opted for the abandonment of Armenia and the Armenians.

Israel Charny reminded me of the traumatic days in June of 1982 when a group of us finally, after many crises, after not knowing three days before we were leaving actually whether the Conference was going to take place or not because of all the pressures that had been brought to bear on its organizers, the kind of blackmail to which no academic forum should be subjected, yet did take place, and I was reminded of the great bravery of the organizers and the nearly two hundred or more participants who defied everybody and said: "My human conscience, my belief in humanity and this cause, and my academic freedom demands that I attend the Conference and participate in the Conference and not submit to blackmail of any kind or even the urging of my own beloved government." That takes courage and it raises the whole question of conscience, and the questions of relationships, Jewish and Armenian relationships. The problem of blackmail has not ceased. Since Tel Aviv, in many forums to which I have gone, I have been faced by a delegation of the Turkish-American Association, protesting either my presence or protesting the discussion of the Armenian Genocide. Here in Boston this last June, at a Facing History and Ourselves Workshop, I was again confronted by a delegation. The Workshop organizers were confronted by that delegation, who were protesting the mixing of the Jewish Holocaust and the Armenian Genocide in the same agenda. A member of that delegation is here tonight, recording us, and I'm sure all the information here will go back to wherever it is, and that's fine, because we have nothing to hide. The fact that a genocide occurred, we proclaim, we know it, and if you need to record it in order to say that we said so, you're welcome to do so.

The question of Armenian-Jewish relations is a fundamental and very complex issue. It is a very difficult one for both sides. There are suspicions that exist; people do not want to share their tragedies, each wants to come here and say, ours was worse: what were the scorching deserts compared to what we went through? The Armenians say sometimes: the ovens—that was very kind compared to what we went through. Why do we have to compete in the suffering and not accept one another's suffering? The Jewish community has a great deal to give us, as an Armenian community; we have a great deal to learn from that community; we can only admire and hold in awe their organization, their strength and unity, when it comes to issues such as we face today, despite the internal divisions that they may have. The ability to get on every national newscast, early morning and late night, and to be into the media—that takes an enormous amount of strength and organization and commitment, and we can only learn from it. The Jewish community has problems with the Armenians today; it has problems with the Armenians not because it does not like Armenians, but because it is under pressure, it is being black-mailed, if I may use the term, by the authorities or the deniers, to not even give the Armenians a forum. I spoke before the Jewish Federation in Los Angeles in October 1984; it was preceded by telephone calls from the Turkish consul with both veiled and unveiled threats regarding the Jewish community in Istanbul, followed by a three-page telegram from the Grand Rabbi of Istanbul, begging the Conference organizers to cancel Hovannisian in order not to cause them problems. This type of situation understandably causes problems for the Jewish community which has its own difficulties, which has its own loyalties to Israel, and which gets very nervous when it gets telephone calls from upstairs in the Jewish organizational headquarters in New York or wherever saying: back off, this is really not our issue, we have enough problems as it is. At the same time there are thankfully the individuals, as we've seen this evening, who are willing to come forth and maintain that there is a morality in politics and even as a Jew, or especially as a Jew, there is a morality that must be maintained. I can only leave you with these remarks. I thank all the participants and urge us to establish bridges. We are remiss in the establishment of bridges with many communities, and I think this evening may be a beginning. I would hope so.

Q: As a comment on Prof. Hovannisian's remarks, it is a mistake to overemphasize Jewish cohesion. In fact the Jewish community gets itself together only on a very narrow range of interests. The question is for Prof. Charny: After the threats made by the Turkish government, what was the impact of the 1982 conference in Tel Aviv on world Jewry?

CHARNY: I waited a few months and then I called the Israeli Foreign Ministry and asked to speak to the Turkish Desk. There was a long silence at the other end. I said I wanted to know if anything indeed had taken place following our holding the Conference. There was a long silence again, and that's where my good old psychoanalytic training came in. I outlasted his silence. And then the Turkish Desk voice said, "No, nothing happened." He sounded angry that he had nothing to report. "Nothing happened. But that doesn't mean something couldn't happen the next time." No, there were absolutely no repercussions, which is obviously deeply gratifying to report because it was terribly important to all of us that there be no repercussions, but also deeply gratifying because many of us had the conviction that it was a real bully kind of terrorism that had nothing behind it.

Q: What is the governmental responsibility for current situations, for example the genocide of 350,000 members of the Baha'i in Iran?

MOMJIAN: Originally, when the Holocaust Council was formed, President Carter had visualized a Committee of Conscience, and that Committee of Conscience would have outstanding leaders from throughout the world who would look out for possible genocides and then, when these eminent figures spoke, people would listen. We are trying to start it up, but I do not think that it will be created until after the next election.

HOVANNISIAN: In relation specifically to the Baha'i, I should say that they have organized very strong international committees to support the Baha'i, and perhaps making notoriety of potential genocide is one of the best ways to stop it, at least in some cases. And the indications are that (either by coincidence or not by coincidence), since the hearings and since the widespread publicity in newspapers about the Baha'i by renowned individuals of many nationalities and religious groups, the persecution of the Baha'i has gone down significantly. Advertisement and public interest can make a difference, even in such regimes as that of the Ayatollah Khomeni in Iran.

Q: What are the consequences and the true meaning of forgiveness in the Christian sense, when you forgive somebody who does not admit that he is guilty?

HARTUNIAN: I think the question of forgiveness of the perpetrators of the Genocide who have never asked for forgiveness, who have never admitted it, or who have never regretted it, is an academic question. We cannot forgive when the context for forgiveness, which is repentance or a confession and a request, is absent. Without that context, forgiveness is meaningless. We as Christians simply can rid our hearts and minds of hatred. My position on this is that we should first of all, as Armenians, in relation to the Turks, distinguish between the average Turk who is living today and the Turkish government. I see no sense in creating tensions between ourselves and the average Turk in America, or even in Turkey. Our quarrel is not with the average Turk—in fact I would go so far as to say let's create relations of communication with them. Our quarrel is with the Turkish government, and there is no question of forgiveness there or forgetfulness. It would be a sin, first of all, to forget the enormous crime of genocide, and forgiveness without confession or a setting the record straight or a request for it would itself be a kind of sin; it would belittle the whole moral process. I think forgiveness must come at the proper time, and I think it may come only in the future, when the entire question of genocide and the historical facts are resolved and there is a process of discussion, of confession, forgiveness, reconciliation, and perhaps the building up of a new world.

Q: In psychiatry, a person who has attempted to commit a homicide or a suicide and won't admit guilt is considered to be still homicidal or suicidal. Do you consider the government of Turkey to be genocidal as long as it denies the Armenian Genocide?

HARTUNIAN: I touched on that when I said that there are four stages of genocide: identification, segregation, extermination, and denial. A nation that has committed genocide and denies this is actually preparing the way for the next genocide. My answer to your question would be "yes."

CHARNY: My answer would be the same. It doesn't necessarily mean that they are preparing to murder once again, but it certainly means that they are mocking every value that we have about the evil, the wrongness, of murder, and they are confirming murder in their response. At the very least they are standing up as accomplices to all possible future murders by their denial of murder in the past.

Q: How do we as individuals bring our concerns about human rights to the attention to our government? Look at the neglect of the Indian in the United States? What can be done?

MOMJIAN: That's why we have elections every four years. If the majority of the people have a certain feeling, with the next election, they can ask the candidates the questions. When I was at the United Nations at Geneva, we had the American Indians always coming there. For some reason, they have never had a voice in this country. If people like yourselves organize, the situation may change. They will have a place in the programs of the Holocaust Museum, as will Gypsies and all other groups who have been victims of genocide.

HERBERT SAWYER (Bentley College): I'd like to make an observation about the question. It seems to me that the response about elections every four years is a very important one. A follow-up observation or question might be: what about the interim period? Of course it does seem quite clear that governments, particularly in democratic societies, don't exist in a vacuum and such observation about the need to organize is quite clearly critical. It's easy to stand here and talk about organization, but what is required is very much more than that. A conference such as the one we have this weekend is certainly a very good beginning, not only because we are talking about a genocide, but because we are talking about a couple of genocides, which suggests a common interest. And what is really required is not only that Jews and Armenians understand what genocide means, but rather that human beings understand what genocide means, and that the potential is there across the board, as it were, both in terms of the peoples who can perpetrate it and in terms of the people who might be the victims of genocide. The crucial thing here, it seems to me, is that Conferences such as this do not happen in a vacuum, that they have an effect, and that that effect results in some kind of organization, some kind of effort, some kind of recognition that what is really at stake and what is really necessary is a vision of the long-term as opposed to short-term interests.

HOVANNISIAN: That's a very sensitive question, and a very good question, and I don't think any of us have answered it to your satisfaction. I think that the bottom line is that we are responsible for our government, and if our government is wrong and punished, we must be punished also whether we had anything to do with that government or not. It is unfortunate but it happens. Many Germans were not involved, but they had to pay reparations, they had to lose territory. Many Japanese may not have been involved but they suffered the losses of war. In the same way we as a people, for whatever wrong our government does, must also be answerable for those wrongs whether we immediately committed them or not. In that way also, the Turkish people, although we hold nothing against the people, must understand that their responsibility, and also the guilt, trickles down through it; it has to absolve itself of that guilt.

The Legacy of Genocide

Richard L. Rubenstein

For those who were trained to believe that the traditions of civilization constitute both a defense against and an overcoming of obscene barbarism, the twentieth century's record of genocide constitutes an unprecedented historical crisis. In the past soldiers have spontaneously pillaged, raped, and murdered members of defeated communities. Political leaders have subjected their enemies to calculated mass violence, such as the extermination of the Melians by the ancient Athenians and the fire bombing of Hamburg and Dresden during World War II. Nevertheless the Armenian Genocide, the Jewish Holocaust, and the slaughter in Kampuchea by the Pol Pot regime were different from these. These actions can be seen as perhaps the most "successful," but by no means the only, programs in which modern, legally-empowered governments have deliberately and cold-bloodedly targeted a portion of their own citizens and/or citizens of occupied nations for extermination. Never before in history had depersonalized, bureaucratized, systematic mass death been carried out on so vast a scale against unarmed civilians or as a function of a government recognized as legitimate by the overwhelming majority of its citizens.

According to historian George Kren and social psychologist Leon Rappoport, a historical crisis may be said to occur

> . . . when events make such an impact upon people that the apparent continuity of their history seems drastically and permanently changed.[1]

Among the more important symptoms of the historical crisis is the undeniable fact that the principal institutions which in the past have protected human beings against unwarranted assault and destruction have proved wholly impotent in the case of state-sponsored genocide. On the contrary religious and legal institutions played a significant role in facilitating the state's program of extermination. This is not the occasion to examine the failure of religious institutions in preventing genocide save for consideration of a single issue, the extent to which religious leaders have regarded the elimination of a religious minority as a desirable political objective while failing to confront seriously the issue of implementation before the fact of genocide and responsibility after the fact.

In the case of the Armenian Genocide, the declaration of Grand Mufti (Şeyhulislam) that Turkey was engaged in a Holy War in defense of Islam constituted a deliberate attempt to arouse religious passion in the service of genocide. The singling out of priests for special degradation, the systematic desecration of Armenian churches, and the attempts at forced conversion all had the effect of giving mass murder an aura of holiness.

In the case of the destruction of the European Jews between 1933 and 1939, the anti-Semitic policies of the ruling National Socialists met with overwhelming official Catholic and Protestant approval, although there were acts of kindness by individual German Christians to Jews.[2] Until the actual implementation of the wartime extermination program, the leaders of both the Protestant and Catholic churches of Germany openly sympathized with the National Socialist aim of eliminating the Jews as a religious, cultural, and demographic presence in Germany. Hitler's anti-Semitism was seen as fostering a genuinely Christian Germany.

There was, however, a very important difference between Hitler's approach to the elimination of the Jews and that of church leaders in both Germany and Poland. From 1919 on Hitler gave much thought not only to the objective of eliminating the Jews but to the *method* by which they were to be eliminated. As is well known, Hitler's rhetorical question to his generals before the invasion of Poland in 1939, namely, "Who still talks nowadays of the extermination of the Armenians?" indicates that the Armenian Genocide played a role in convincing Hitler of the feasibility of his own project. The Jews were a community with a continuity of domicile in German lands extending back to Roman times. It would not have been easy to uproot such a community even in the best of times. However the years between 1933 and 1939 witnessed the greatest worldwide economic depression of modern times. In an era of global mass employment, few governments anywhere were willing to accept more than a token number of Jewish immigrants. Beginning in May 1939, the British government prevented more than a trickle of Jews from entering Palestine. Thus emigration has ceased to be a viable method of population elimination. Hitler understood this and did not flinch from employing the most extreme methods of elimination when the war provided the opportunity.

In Germany both the Protestant and Catholic churches wanted a nation that was wholly Christian and Germanic. In Poland the Catholic Church wanted a Poland that was wholly Roman Catholic. Unlike Hitler few (if any) of the church leaders faced the all-important question of implementation, at least not openly. During the war, when German church leaders became privy to the secret that was no secret —namely, that the Jews were being murdered in the East—they were caught between their desire for a wholly Christian and Germanic Fatherland and the fact, clearly understood by Hitler, that this could be accomplished only by genocide. In modern times, when emigration is impossible, those who seek cultural, religious, or ethnic homogeneity are likely to find that their objective can be achieved only by mass murder. After the war, when the German method of eliminating the Jews became public knowledge, there were expression of regret on the part of some church leaders concerning *how* the Jews were eliminated. Few Germans expressed pride in the extermination camps. Even neo-Nazis have tried to invent a myth that the Holocaust never happened. Nevertheless one may ask whether there was much genuine regret about *what* the camps accomplished. Germany was finally free of Jews. For all practical purposes there were no longer any demographic impediments to a Christian and Germanic Fatherland.

The situation was not very different in Poland. Before the war both the government and the Polish church regarded Poland's 3,250,000 Jews as an unwanted "surplus population."[3] In 1939 both institutions sought the total elimination of this "surplus population." They thus shared a common political objective with the National Socialists. That objective was not achieved by emigration but, as we know, by extermination. It cannot be denied that the Germans gave the Polish church what it wanted.

Under the circumstances we must ask whether either the Polish and German churches can entirely wash their hands, Pilate-like, of responsibility for fostering a political objective that could be achieved *only* by genocide? What is the moral status of an institution that fosters a political objective without considering the question of implementation? Alternatively, there is the possibility that responsible elements within the German and Polish churches fully understood the requirements of implementation, but deemed it unnecessary or unwise to specify the method required since they would not be required to carry out the dirty work of extermination. In either case the leaders of both the German and Polish churches were unwilling or unable to do anything to prevent genocide.

When we turn from the German and Polish churches to the world center of the Roman Catholic Church, the most important single institution for the fostering of religious and moral values in the western world, we find the same wartime silence. With its tens of thousands of priests and its religious and academic institutions throughout Europe, the Vatican had one of the best intelligence networks in the world. The Vatican was in a position to know more and to know it earlier than any other non-German institution. Yet in spite of that knowledge, on no occasion during the war did Pope Pius XXII utter an unambiguous, explicit, public condemnation of the extermination process or the death camps. (In fairness to the Catholic Church, it must be recorded that thousands of Jews survived in Slovakia, Hungary, and elsewhere because of protests emanating from the Vatican.)

Whatever the reasons for the silence, the historical record is clear. The government of Europe's most powerful nation during World War II employed its agencies of law and order systematically to enslave, gas, burn alive, and shoot to death tens of thousands of men, women, and children daily without any effective, public protest by the churches. If the churches did not wholly approve of the dirty work of National Socialism, there was always some reason why silence was more important than protest. *Thus, religion as an institution was neither able to prevent nor even to express verbal opposition to the rise of a wholly novel state-sponsored institution in the heart of Christian Europe; the industrialized, assembly-line, depersonalized, mass extermination camp.*

By the same token, legal institutions have failed completely to provide any protection for the victims. In the case of Turkey, before coming to power in 1908 the Young Turks promised that the older tradition of corrupt, inefficient personal rule would be replaced by a modern, rational, legal political system in which all citizens would enjoy equality before the law, religious toleration, and the abolition of cast privileges. What was not understood by the Armenian minority at the time was that a rational, legal system of government could be an infinitely more effective instrument of genocide than the older system. An important reason for this development is that political modernization has often involved the legitimation of state power in the service of social, cultural, and ethnic homogenization. In his celebrated essay on bureaucracy, which he identified as "rational legal" domination, Max Weber observed that one of the most important consequences of such domination is a tendency toward the "leveling" of the population.

> Bureaucratic organization has usually come into power on the basis of a leveling of economic and social differences. . . . Bureaucracy inevitably accompanies mass democracy, in contrast to the democratic self-government of homogenous units. This results from its characteristic principle: the abstract regularity of the exercise of authority, which is the result of the demand for "equality before the law" in the personal and functional sense—hence of the horror of "privilege," and the principal rejection of doing business from case to case.[4]

There was a fundamental difference in the political perceptions of the Young Turks and the Armenians. For the modernizing Young Turks, democratization and legal rationalization meant homogenization; for the Armenians and other minorities it was taken to mean the promise of equal opportunity and the retention of a distinctive cultural and religious identity. It was the terrible fate of the Armenians that the power to define social and political reality in Turkey was in the hands of those who were determined to achieve homogenization through extermination. In reality, there was no other viable method of homogenization either in Turkey in World War I or in occupied Europe during World War II. Regrettably, both the Armenians and Jewish tragedies demonstrate the risks entailed in cultural or religious diversity under a system of rational legal domination, especially in times of acute social or political instability.

In the case of National Socialist Germany, some of that nation's best legal minds accepted the task of creating the basis in law for depriving millions of citizens of Germany and the occupied lands of their rights, their jobs, their property, and finally their lives. Put differently, the law became a singularly effective device for transforming citizens with political rights into "non-persons" devoid of the most elemental human rights. As early as September 1919, Hitler called for the "removal" (*Entfernung*) of Germany's Jews by legal means. He expressed his opposition to "purely emotional anti-Semitism" and called for a "rational anti-Semitism" which would carry out a "systematic and legal struggle" against the Jewish presence in Germany.[5] When one compares the destructiveness inflicted by the legally empowered agents of the state in Turkey and Germany on human beings who had committed no crime with the violence inflicted by outright criminals, it is painfully obvious that the officers of the law were the infinitely greater danger.

In the past the social contract between ruler and ruled carried with it the implicit understanding that, if the ruled were reasonably law-abiding, they could normally expect at least minimum protection of life and property. Normally sovereignty did not include the right to mete out unmerited punishment in the form of abusive incarceration, torture, and death without cause. By contrast, in Turkey the willingness of Armenian men to serve in the wartime defense of Turkey even after the massacres instigated by Abdul Hamid from 1894 to 1896 was used by the state as a means of facilitating its extermination project. In the Third Reich even wounded war veterans who had risked their lives in World War I and had been awarded the Iron Cross were burned alive or sent to the gas chambers. The social contract has proven null and void, not only for Jews and Armenians, but for any group targeted as victims by state authorities. Nor has this been true of Turkey and Germany alone. The list of states which have targeted human beings for extermination in the twentieth century is too well known to be repeated in this context.

In *the Cunning of History*, this author argued that the fate of Europe's Jews demonstrated that rights do not belong to men by nature, that men have rights only insofar as they are legally certified members of a political community willing and able to defend their rights.[6] *The Cunning of History* was published in 1975. In that book the author indicted that he expected further acts of genocide in the future. Little did he imagine that his apprehensions would materialize so speedily. On April 17th of that year, the communist Pol Pot regime conquered Phnom Pehn, capital of what was then known as Cambodia and now is known as Kampuchea. Within one week the entire population of that city was forcibly evacuated and deposited in the jungle regions, where the majority perished. Out of a population of 7,000,000, the Vietnamese communists estimate that the new regime was responsible for the death of 3,000,000. American authorities estimate that the new government was responsible for the death of 2,000,000. In either case the proportion of human beings put to death by their own government staggers the imagination.

Like Turkey in World War I and National Socialist Germany, the Pol Pot regime was determined to use state terror and mass murder so to restructure society as to achieve a fully homogenous community.

The Turks aimed at religio-ethnic homogeneity; the Nazis aimed at "racial" homogeneity; the Pol Pot regime aimed at class homogeneity. The regime sought to create a self-subsistent, agrarian communist state. Its leaders were convinced that the population of Kampuchea's cities had been too corrupted by capitalist ideas and foreign influences ever to be integrated into the communist community they proposed to create. As in the Armenian regions of Turkey and in National Socialist Germany, any citizen whom the government regarded as unassimilable automatically became a right-less, nonperson. The Pol Pot regime resorted to the same methods against its unwanted citizens as did its genocidal predecessors.[7] One again, it became painfully apparent that, if there is an uncontested right, it is no longer the "inalienable" right of the citizen to "life, liberty, and the pursuit of happiness," but the god-like right of the state to do anything it wishes with its citizens, provided they are incapable of effective resistance.

The terrible right of a modern state to exercise genocidal sovereignty was implicitly confirmed in September 1979 when the United States, Great Britain, Australia, and Canada joined the majority of seventy-one nations that voted to recognize the Pol Pot regime's right to membership in the United Nations as the *legitimate* government of Kampuchea. Only thirty-five nations were opposed; thirty-four abstained.[8] The regime's seat had been challenged by the Vietnamese-dominated puppet regime which had dislodged Pol Pot from Phnom Pehn. At the time of the United Nations vote, the facts of the Pol Pot program of extermination were known to the governments of the world. When the United States supported Pol Pot's bid to retain United Nations membership, its intention was not to approve of genocide but to prevent Kampuchea's U.N. seat from going to the puppet government sponsored by Vietnam. Nevertheless the U.N. vote did show that the practice of genocide does not disqualify a sovereign state from recognition as a legitimate member of the family of nations. This author does not point to this dreary example because he feels that the government of the United States had a reasonable alternative. Nevertheless the incident is yet another example of the failure of the time-honored categories of politics and law to provide a defense against genocide.

The philosopher Thomas Hobbes distinguished between the state of nature, in which the condition of men was one of "war of all against all," and that of civil society, in which men banded together and submitted to the authority of a sovereign in order to put an end to the radical insecurity of the same state of nature. We have now learned that, for groups threatened with or targeted for elimination, life in civil society can be far more dangerous than life in the state of nature. At least in the primitive state of nature each person had some chance to defend himself against potentially predatory neighbors.

Men born into civil society are educated to believe in the implied social contract between the state and its citizens, between the ruler and the ruled. If they keep their part of the social contract, they do not expect to be the prey of an adversary infinitely more dangerous than a predatory neighbor: the organizational and technological power of the modern state. Confronted by its power, individuals or groups targeted for elimination find themselves in a far more hopeless condition than they would have been in the state of nature. Under modern conditions, both flight and self-defense on the part of the victim are likely to prove useless. If the victim is unwanted by the state in which he is domiciled, there is a very good chance that he will not be wanted anywhere, no matter what his talents may be, as indeed was the fate of the Jews during World War II. Such victims find themselves in a novel form of the state of nature, the state to which those cast out of civil society are condemned.

Thomas Hobbes' state of nature *preceded* the formation of civil society. The genocidal programs of the twentieth century have revealed a vision of the state of nature which *follows* civil society. Long before World War I, the epithet most commonly used by the Turks for their Christian subjects was "dog." During the war, the Turks were to demonstrate the extent to which they were willing to deny human status to the Armenians. The Nazis characterized their victims as subhuman, using the German word *Tiermenschen*, literally, animal men, as a way of so degrading them that no guilt would be felt for any violence done to them. Perhaps intuitively the Nazis understood that their victims had been condemned to the very modern form of the state of nature which they had created, namely, a condition in which civilized human beings are expelled from civil society and denied all traditional human rights. Given the Nazi penchant for saving everything but the victims' lives, even the stripping naked of the victims before killing them had an economic purpose, since it cost less to launder and recycle clothes unsoiled by involuntary defecation. Yet there may perhaps have been another reason for the stripping. There is something artificial about membership in civil society. If Hobbes is correct, symbolically if not historically, the creation of the social contract is an act of artifice designed to protect men from amoral nature. By stripping the victims of their clothes and by searching the orifices of their bodies, thereby denying them any remnant of privacy or dignity, the Nazis emphasized how completely they had rendered their victims *Tiermenschen.*

In any event, traditional legal institutions offer no remedy for people in such a condition. The few victims who survived were saved only by the *destruction* of the National Socialist legal system and the passing of sovereignty from the Third Reich, a state that sought to destroy them, to states that permitted them to return to normal civil society.

In addition to the failure of religious and legal institutions to prevent mass murder, a failure partly due to the role of science in reducing the credibility of religion with its assertion of a universally binding moral standard, Kren and Rappoport regard the Holocaust as evidence of "the failure of science." They argue that "the scientific mode of thought and the methodology attached to it were intrinsic to the mass killings."[9] Not only was industrialized mass murder facilitated by scientific methods of research, organization, and implementation, but "the rational-abstract forms of conceptual thought required and promulgated by science provided the basis for systematic and efficient identification of people by race, transportation of large numbers of concentration points, killing, and body disposal."[10]

Ambassador Morgenthau was one of the earliest observers to note the influence of scientific modes of thought upon the implementation of genocide:

> For centuries the Turks have ill-treated their Armenians and all other subject peoples with inconceivable barbarity. Yet their methods have always been crude, clumsy, unscientific. ...But the Armenian proceedings of 1915 and 1916 evidenced an entirely new mentality.[11]

Morgenthau goes on to credit Germany, especially Pan-German thinkers, as the source of the newer, more scientific organizational methods employed by the Turks to deport and exterminate the Armenians.

Science also fosters an emotionally-detached, depersonalized professionalism in which technical expertise comes to be wholly divorced from moral values. This attitude was already evident in the way in which the Armenian Genocide was planned. It was especially manifest in Germany among the SS personnel responsible for the killings. After the war these men insisted that they were under no obligation to evaluate the rightness of their behavior, but they did have an unconditional obligation to carry out the responsibilities delegated to them by their superiors. Value-free, scientific profession-alism took on a new meaning when the daily destruction of tens of thousands of human beings become no more than a task to be carried out as efficiently, impersonally, and unemotionally as possible.

Nor, when we consider the role of science in twentieth century genocide, can we ignore the importance of the eugenics movement or the medical professionals who staffed Hitler's euthanasia project for the implementation of the Final Solution. The eugenics movement provided scientific legitimation for mass murder. Trusted medical symbols took on a new meaning. What began as medical advocacy of eliminating "unworthy lives" for "racial health" ended with the delivery of Zyklon B gas to the death chambers in vehicles carrying the insignia of the International Red Cross and the pouring of the gas crystals into the chambers by a "sanitation officer." In the Third Reich medical science fostered the idea that the killings were nothing more than a health measure. Moreover the national committee of the German Red Cross was headed by such SS medical luminaries as Dr. Ernst Grawitz and Professor Dr. Karl Gebhardt. Gebhardt was condemned to death by the U.S. Military Tribunal and executed in 1948 for his part in medical "experiments" which included using female prisoners at Ravensbruck concentration camp as human guinea pigs and deliberately infecting them with gas gangrene. Grawitz committed suicide in 1945.

One way of confronting the historical crisis is to deny its relevance to more fortunately situated human beings. The simplest expression of such denial is to say to oneself, "It happened to them, not to us." This is especially tempting if one does not share the religious or cultural background of the victim. Undoubtedly an important reason why the Armenian Genocide has elicited so little public response over the years is that most Americans have felt comfortable distancing themselves from an event which took place in a faraway land to a people thought to be strange in appearance and custom by an American population of predominantly Northern European ante-cedent. The National Socialist encouraged the same tendency toward denial and distance both in Germany and occupied Europe. Before and during World War II, German propaganda used every conceivable device to convince the peoples of Europe of the wholly alien character of all their victims. In the case of the Jews, the German government flooded the world with all manner of anti-Semitic propaganda. The Jews were not alone. German propaganda stressed that the Russians were "truly subhuman." The SS publications house even published a propaganda magazine entitled *Untermensch*, "Subhuman," which was filled with pictures of Soviet prisoners of war in the most pathetic condition as proof of their want of humanity.[12]

The propaganda succeeded. When the killing time came, with few exceptions, the best the Jews could hope for from the majority of the peoples of Germany and occupied Europe was indifference. Nevertheless denial is not an entirely functional response. When the government of perhaps the best educated people in the heart of Christian Europe creates, as a new state institution, the industrialized death camp, and when governments as disparate as the regimes of Talaat Bey and Enver Pasha, Joseph Stalin, and Pol Pot, resort successfully to mass extermination as a legitimate state function, the entire human moral and political universe is irrevocably altered.

As obscene as were the Armenian Genocide and the Jewish Holocaust, from the point of view of the perpetrators these were almost wholly successful programs of population elimination. From the point of view of the leaders of Turkey during World War I as well as the leaders of the Third Reich, their victims were *surplus peoples*. The conception of a surplus people is not absolute. Regardless of talent or ability, a group become "surplus" if, for any reason, it has no viable economic or political role in the community in which it is domiciled.

The Armenians and the Jews became surplus because those who intended their undoing had the power to define social reality in their places of domicile. In the modern era other groups have become surplus by the action of the market place as well as by government fiat. Among the most important factors leading to the rise of a surplus population of significant size are the following:

1. The rise to power of a modernizing political movement determined to create ethnic, class, or religious homogeneity among its citizens. Those persons who are incapable of being "homogenized' find themselves in danger of being defined a surplus by a state capable of enforcing its political definitions. This was the fate of the Armenians in World War I, the Jews in World War II, anti-communist Russians during the Russian Civil War, the middle-class Kampucheans in 1975, the Vietnamese boat people, and a host of other groups and classes in the twentieth century.[13]

2. An unprecedented increase in population without a compa-

rable increase in resources capable of sustaining the population growth.

3. Rationalization of the means of agricultural and industrial production with the result that ever fewer workers are capable of producing an ever-expanding volume of goods.

4. Radical alterations in the demand patterns of a market economy that render millions of workers economically redundant. This condition was especially prevalent during the Great Depression of the 1930s, which led to the rise of Hitler.

5. The vocational displacement of a powerless minority community by unemployed members of an indigenous majority community. This indeed was the plight of the Jews in many parts of Europe under Hitler. This has also been the plight of other minorities, such as the ethnic Chinese in Southeast Asia and the Indians and Pakistanis in Uganda in recent years.

6. The appearance of famine or other types of large-scale material scarcity in which too many people compete for too few goods. This indeed has been the plight of millions of human beings in Ethiopia and sub-Saharan Africa.

One of the most disturbing aspects of twentieth-century genocide is that none of the economic or political factors leading to the growth of massive surplus populations throughout the world has been alleviated since the end of World War II. On the contrary the intensified, worldwide competition in international trade compels almost all producers, whether in agriculture or industry, to shift from labor-intensive to automated, computer-assisted methods of production wherever possible. Throughout the world tens of millions of human beings have been uprooted from the land and from simple craft production to face an uncertain future in urban centers that offer little hope of employment to the unskilled and the unlettered. When we read of famine in Africa or of the debt crisis of some Third World country, we do not normally link these phenomena to the problem of surplus people. Yet that is the context in which the phenomena must be understood. Throughout the world the modernization of agriculture and industry have rendered millions of human beings hopelessly redundant for the foreseeable future. For the technologically sophisticated, modernization has been the source of unprecedented wealth and opportunity. For the millions displaced by "progress," modernization has meant loss of a meaningful place in the world.

This loss is the Sword of Damocles hanging over contemporary civilization. No one can predict that there will be yet more state-sponsored extermination programs as a means of "solving" the problem of surplus people. Neither can we be certain that in times of stress, such as war or other social catastrophe, government elites will study the Armenian Genocide and the Jewish Holocaust as programs that worked rather than as supreme examples of man's inhumanity to man.

REFERENCES

1. George Kren and Leon Rappoport, *The Holocaust and the Crisis of Human Behavior* (New York 1982), 13.

2. On the German churches and the Jews in the Hitler period, see John Conway, *The Nazi Persecution of the Church: 1933-45* (New York: Basic Books, 1968), 1-44, 261-67.

3. See Celia S. Heller, *On the Edge of Destruction: Jews of Poland Between Two World Wars* (New York, 1977).

4. Max Weber, *Economy and Society*, eds. Guenther Roth and Claus Wittich (New York, 1968), vol. 3: 983.

5. See Hitler's September 16, 1919, letter to Staff-Captain Karl Meyer in Werner Maser, ed., *Hitler's Letters and Notes* (New York: Harper and Row, 1974), 211.

6. Richard L. Rubenstein, *The Cunning of History: Mass Death and the American Future* (New York, 1975), 89.

7. See Richard L. Rubenstein, *The Age of Triage: Fear and Hope in an Overcrowded World* (Boston, 1983), 165-67.

8. See Leo Kuper, *Genocide* (New Haven, 1981), 173.

9. Kren and Rappoport, *The Holocaust and the Crisis of Human Behavior*, 133.

10. Ibid., 134.

11. Henry Morgenthau, *Ambassador Morgenthau's Story* (New York: Doubleday and Page, 1919), 365.

12. See Alan Clark, *Barbarosa: The German-Russian Conflict* (New York, 1966), 233-35.

13. The subject of the rise of surplus people and the way governments have dealt with them is discussed extensively in Rubenstein, *The Age of Triage*.

Scholars Press

The Armenian Version of Daniel

S. Peter Cowe

This work offers a diplomatic edition of the Armenian version of Daniel on the basis of practically all extant evidence and then provides the raw material for a re-investigation of the version's origin, textual affinities and translation technique. In addition to the Massoretic text and various Greek recensions, the Armenian text is also compared with the Peshitta and Georgian versions.

In a separate chapter, the reliability of the text of the medieval Armenian biblical manuscripts is evaluated from the perspective of earlier citations in the works of Armenian authors and the lections found in the diverse liturgical books. The conclusion seeks to locate the Armenian translation of scripture within the ecclesiastical and intellectual currents of the fifth century A.D.

Code: 21 02 09
Cloth: $64.95   1-55540-687-4

The Armenian Minority Problem

Mary Tarzian

This study analyzes enduring issues of minority rights, using the Armenian experience in the first decades of this century as a case-study. Written shortly after the events and informed by first-hand accounts and research in archives in the United States and Europe, this book captures the international mind-set in the age of self-determination following World War I in a way that is nearly impossible for a researcher today. As world leaders revisit the compromises made in the post-World War I era, this book will help keep the discussion honest.

Code: 21 02 11
Cloth: $49.95   1-55540-705-6

The History of Lazar P<arpec<i

Robert W. Thomson

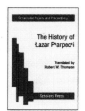

This is the first translation into English of Łazar P<arpec<i's *History of Armenia*. Written circa 500 CE, the *History* provides insight into the events and society of 5th Century Armenia and reflects Armenia's position between Sasanian Iran and the Eastern Roman (Byzantine) Empire. An accompanying *Letter*, also included in this edition, contains details of Łazar's own career and the early years of his patron Vahan Mamikonean.

Code: 00 19 07
Cloth: $59.95   1-55540-579-7
Paper: $29.95   1-55540-612-2

From Humanism to Rationalism

Armenian Scholarship in the Nineteenth Century

Rouben Paul Adalian

This work of intellectual history describes the modernization of Armenian culture that occurred during the 19th century, especially as that process was reflected in changing Armenian language and literature. Of particular interest to this study is the contribution to Armenian culture of clerics in Venice and Vienna who, collectively, were known as the Mekhitarians. The work includes an extensive bibliography, and a general index.

Code: 21 02 10
Cloth: $34.95   1-55540-724-2

Scholars Press
800-437-6692 or 404-442-8633
P.O. Box 6996, Alpharetta, GA 30239-6996

Selected Recent and Forthcoming
Studies on Genocide

Prepared by Roger W. Smith

BOOKS

Alexander, Edward. *A Crime of Vengeance: An Armenian Struggle for Justice.* New York: Free Press, 1991.

> A dramatic and moving account of the Genocide told through its effects on Soghomon Tehlirian.

The Armenian Genocide: Documentation. Munich: Institute for Armenian Studies. Vol. 1 (1987), Vol. 2 (1988), Vol. 8 (1991).

Chalk, Frank and Kurt Jonassohn. *The History and Sociology of Genocide: Analyses and Case Studies.* New Haven, Conn.: Yale University Press, 1990.

Charny, Israel W., ed. *Genocide: A Critical Bibliographic Review*, Vol. 2. New York: Facts on File, 1991.

> Topical essays, with critical bibliographies. A major portion of the book is on denial and includes chapters by Israel Charny, "Psychology of the Denial of Known Genocides," Vahakn N. Dadrian, "Documentation of the Armenian Genocide in Turkish Sources," and Roger W. Smith, "Denial of the Armenian Genocide."

Davis, Leslie A. *The Slaughterhouse Province: An American Diplomat's Report on the Armenian Genocide, 1915-1917.* New Rochelle, N.Y.: Aristide D. Caratzas, 1989.

> An American Consul's report to the State Department; contains photographic evidence of the Genocide. The entire document is of major importance.

Derogy, Jacques. *Resistance and Revenge: The Armenian Assassination of the Turkish Leaders Responsible for the 1915 Massacres and Deportations.* New Brunswick, N.J.: Transaction Publishers, 1990.

Hovannisian, Richard G., ed. *The Armenian Genocide: History, Politics, Ethics.* New York: St. Martin's Press, 1992.

> A major new work that examines the historical, cultural, and political conditions that led to the Genocide and subsequent claims that it never took place. With a foreword by Governor George Deukmejian.

— ed. *The Armenian Genocide in Perspective.* New Brunswick, N.J.: Transaction Publishers, 1986.

> An extensive review appears in the *Journal of Armenian Studies,* V (1) Winter/Spring 1990-91.

BOOKS (cont)

Jernazian, Ephraim K. *Judgment Unto Truth: Witnessing the Armenian Genocide.* New Brunswick, N.J.: Transaction Books, 1990.

> The most recent in a series of excellent survivor memoirs published by the Zoryan Institute in Cambridge, Mass. Others in the series are: Bertha Nakshian Ketchian, *In the Shadow of the Fortress* (1988), John Yervant, *Needle, Thread and Button* (1988); and Ramela Martin, *Out of Darkness* (1989).

Kazanjian, Paren, ed. *The Cilician Armenian Ordeal.* Boston: Hye Intentions, 1989.

Kirakossian, John S. *The Armenian Genocide: The Young Turks Before the Judgment of History.* Madison, Wisc.: Sphinx Press, 1992.

> A translation of this original work by the late scholar and former Minister of Foreign Affairs of Armenia (1975 to 1985).

Marashlian, Levon. *Politics and Demography: Armenians, Turks, and Kurds in the Ottoman Empire.* Cambridge, Mass.: Zoryan Institute, 1991.

Mazian, Florence. *Why Genocide? The Armenian and Jewish Experiences in Perspective.* Ames, Iowa: Iowa State University Press, 1990.

> A thoughtful sociological analysis of genocide that focuses on "outsiders," social strife, ambitious leaders with goals of territorial expansion, propaganda, a system of destruction, and the failure of social controls.

Melson, Robert. *Revolution and Genocide: On the Origins of the Armenian Genocide and the Holocaust.* Chicago: University of Chicago Press, 1992.

> A systematic comparison of the Armenian Genocide and the Jewish Holocaust, based on an innovative theory of genocide that links ideological, total genocide with social change, revolution, and war. This decent and humane book is scholarly, yet accessible to any interested reader.

Miller, Donald and Lorna Touryan Miller. *The Armenian Genocide of 1915: An Oral History of the Experience of Survivors.* Berkeley and Los Angeles: University of California Press, 1992.

> A deeply moving study, based on interviews with one hundred survivors. The first book of its kind, it contributes significantly to our understanding of the Genocide, the experience of those subjected to it, and the long struggle that ensues for survivors to make sense of the world and their place within it.

Staub, Erving. *The Roots of Evil: The Origins of Genocide and Other Group Violence.* Cambridge: Cambridge University Press, 1989.

> An important study that examines the psychological and cultural bases of genocide. Case studies include Armenia, Nazi Germany, Cambodia, and the "disappearances" in Argentina.

ARTICLES

Armenian Review, 42 (4), Winter 1989.
   The entire issue is on the Genocide.

Dadrian, Vahakn N.   "The Documentation of the World War I Armenian Massacres in the Proceedings of the Turkish Military Tribunal." *International Journal of Middle East Studies*, 24 (4) 1991: 549-76.

— "A Textual Analysis of the Key Indictment of the Turkish Military Tribunal Investigating the Armenian Genocide." *Armenian Review*, 44 (1), Spring 1991: 1-36.

— "Genocide as a Problem of National and International Law: The World War I Armenian Case and its Contemporary Legal Ramifications." *Yale Journal of International Law*, 14 (2) 1989: 221-334.

— "The Naim-Andonian Documents on the World War I Destruction of the Ottoman Armenians: the Anatomy of Genocide." *International Journal of Middle East Studies*, 18 (3) 1986: 311-60.

— "The Role of Turkish Physicians in the World War I Genocide of Ottoman Armenians." *Holocaust and Genocide Studies*, 1 (2) 1986: 169-92.

Dinkel, Christoph.   "German Officers and the Armenian Genocide." *Armenian Review*, 44 (1) Spring 1991: 77-133.

Sanasarian, Eliz.   "Gender Distinction in the Genocidal Process: A Preliminary Study of the Armenian Case." *Holocaust and Genocide Studies*, 4 (4) 1989: 449-61.

Smith, Roger W.   "Genocide and Denial: The Armenian Case and Its Implications." *Armenian Review*, 42 (1) Spring 1989: 1-38.

Social Education 55 (2) February 1991. With a special section on "Teaching About Genocide" edited by Samuel Totten and William S. Parsons.

CONTRIBUTORS

GILBERT ABCARIAN was educated at Fresno State College and the University of California, Berkeley, where he received his PhD in political science. He teaches political theory courses as professor of political science at Florida State University, having taught previously at the University of Tulsa and Bowling Green University.

GREGORY H. ADAMIAN recently retired after 21 years as president of Bentley College and now serves as its first Chancellor. A graduate of Harvard College, he also holds degrees from Harvard Graduate School of Public Administration and Boston University Law School.

RICHARD ASHTON, a survivor of the Armenian Genocide, attended the University of Massachusetts and the University of Wisconsin, Milwaukee. Now retired, he has served as executive secretary of the Armenian General Benevolent Union, Western District, and Vice-Commander of the Knights of Vartan. His short articles and commentaries appear in newspapers and Armenian publications.

ISRAEL W. CHARNY is executive director of the Institute on the Holocaust and Genocide, Jerusalem, and associate professor of psychology at the Bob Shapell School of Social Work at Tel Aviv University. He is the author of *How Can We Commit the Unthinkable?: Genocide, the Human Cancer*, and several other books and articles dealing with genocide.

HELEN FEIN, a historical sociologist, is author of *Accounting for Genocide: National Responses and Jewish Victimization during the Holocaust*. She received the Sorokin Award of the American Sociological Association in 1979 and serves as executive director of the Institute for the Study of Genocide.

SOL GITTLEMAN is provost and professor of German at Tufts University, where he also holds the Alice and Nathan Gantcher Chair of Judaic Studies. He received his doctorate in comparative literature from the University of Michigan and teaches courses on the literature of American immigration.

MICHAEL M. GUNTER is professor of political science at Tennessee Technological University and author of *The Kurds in Turkey: A Political Dilemma* and *"Pursuing the Just Cause of Their People": A Study of Contemporary Armenian Terrorism.*

VARTAN HARTUNIAN is pastor of the First Armenian Church in Belmont, Massachusetts, and translator of the genocide memoir by his father, Abraham Hartunian, entitled *Neither to Laugh nor to Weep*.

IRVING LOUIS HOROWITZ is Hannah Arendt Distinguished Professor of Sociology and Political Science at Rutgers University and author of *Taking Lives: Genocide and State Power* (now in its augmented third edition). In his capacity as president of Transaction Publishers, he has supervised a series of books on the history and people of Armenia.

RICHARD G. HOVANNISIAN is professor of Armenian and Near Eastern History, Holder of the Endowed Chair in Modern Armenian History, and Associate Director of the G. E. von Grunebaum Center for Near Eastern Studies at the University of California, Los Angeles. He is author of a multivolume study on the Republic of Armenia and editor of *The Armenian Genocide in Perspective* (1986) and *The Armenian Genocide* (1992).

ALICE ODIAN KASPARIAN, a genocide survivor, is a graduate of the Massachusetts College of Pharmacy, Michigan State, and the University of Michigan. Author of *The Armenians of Angora and Istanos* (in Armenian and in English), *Armenian Needlelace and Embroidery*, and other publications, she lectures on various topics in Armenian culture and the arts.

DICKRAN KOUYMJIAN is the Haig and Isabel Berberian Professor of Armenian Studies and Director of the Sarkis and Meliné Kalfayan Center for Armenian Studies at California State University Fresno. His current research is devoted to Armenian literature and manuscript studies; he is a member of a team preparing a comprehensive album of Armenian paleography.

LEO KUPER is professor emeritus of sociology at the University of California, Los Angeles. A native of South Africa, he directed the UCLA African Studies Center for four years and recently has been active in human rights groups of the United Nations. His publications include *The Prevention of Genocide*.

JOHN LOFTUS is a former Justice Department prosecutor who now writes about the history of intelligence. His books include *The Belarus File* and (with Mark Aarons) *Unholy Trinity: How the Vatican's Nazi Networks Betrayed Western Intelligence to the Soviets*.

PHREDD MATTHEWSWALL is a former teacher at the Martin Luther King School in Cambridge, Massachusetts, and is now a Program Associate at the Facing History and Ourselves National Foundation.

BARBARA J. MERGUERIAN teaches 20th century Armenian history at Tufts University. She majored in international relations at Brown University and received her PhD in Russian history from Harvard. Her current research interests focus on the relations between Americans and Armenians in the nineteenth and twentieth centuries.

SYBIL MILTON is Senior Historian of the United States Holocaust Memorial Museum and has published numerous books and articles about Nazi Germany and the Holocaust. She is co-editor and contributor to *Holocaust: Ideology, Bureaucracy and Genocide* (1980); *Genocide: Critical Issues of the Holocaust* (1983); and co-author of *Art of the Holocaust* (1981), which received the National Jewish Book Award in Visual Arts in 1982.

SET C. MOMJIAN has been a member of the United States Holocaust Memorial Council since its establishment in 1980. A noted art collector, he is a former member of the United States delegation to the United Nations and has served as White House Representative to the United Nations Human Rights Commission in Geneva.

VAHÉ OSHAGAN was born in Bulgaria and received his doctorate in comparative literature from the University of Paris. He has taught humanities at the American University of Beirut and Armenian culture at the University of Pennsylvania and the University of California Berkeley. He has published six volumes of poetry and two volumes of stories. He edits the annual of Armenian poetry *Raft*.

DENNIS R. PAPAZIAN is professor of history and director of the Armenian Research Center at the University of Michigan, Dearborn. A specialist in Russian history, he is a frequent commentator on current foreign policy issues and serves as president of the Board of Directors of the Michigan Ethnic Heritage Studies Center.

WILLIAM B. PROXMIRE is the former United States Senator from Wisconsin. He now practices law in Washington, D. C.

JAMES J. REID is with the Speros Basil Vryonis Center for Hellenic Studies in Sacramento, California, and a former faculty member of Lehigh University and fellow of the Institute for Mediterranean Studies in Crete. His publications include *Tribalism and Society in Islamic Iran* .

GARY REMER is assistant professor in the political science department at Tulane University, where he teaches courses on the history of political thought. He received his doctorate from UCLA; his dissertation topic was "Classical Rhetoric and the Humanist Defense of Religious Toleration."

RICHARD L. RUBENSTEIN is the Robert O. Lawton Distinguished Professor of Religion at Florida State University. Author of *After Auschwitz* (1966, 1992), *The Cunning of History* (1975), and *The Age of Triage* (1983), he is the editor of *In Depth*, a public policy quarterly; chairman of the Editorial Advisory Board of the *Washington Times*, and a regular columnist for *Sekai Nippo*, a Tokyo daily newspaper.

ROGER W. SMITH is professor of government at the College of William and Mary in Williamsburg, Virginia. He received his PhD from the University of California at Berkeley and is the editor and coauthor of *Guilt: Man and Society* as well as numerous articles and book reviews. In 1990 he attended the international conference on Genocide held in Yerevan.

FRANK A. STONE is professor of international education at the University of Connecticut and has directed the Isaac N. Thut World Education Center there for twenty-one years. A graduate of Heidelberg College, he holds doctoral degrees from Vanderbilt and Boston Universities. He taught at the American School in Tarsus, Turkey, from 1953 to 1966 and is the author of *Academies for Anatolia: A Study of the Rationale, Program and Impact of the Educational Institutions sponsored by the American Board in Turkey, 1830-1980*

YVES TERNON is the author of several books in French which have been translated into English, including *The Armenians: History of a Genocide*, *The Armenians: From Genocide to Resistance* (with Gérard Chaliand), and *The Armenian Cause*.

GEORGE WALD is professor emeritus of biology at Harvard University and winner of the Nobel Prize for Physiology and Medicine in 1967. He is a vice-president of the Permanent Peoples' Tribunal and was a member of the organization's 1984 Paris jury, which declared the Armenian Genocide an "international crime" for which the Turkish state must assume responsibility.

CHRISTOPHER J. WALKER is the author of *Armenia: The Survival of a Nation* and editor of *Armenia and Karabagh: The Struggle for Unity*. A frequent visitor to the communities in the Armenian diaspora, he was invited to Yerevan, Armenia, in September 1991 as an observer for the referendum and declaration of independence. Currently he is working on a biography of Oliver Baldwin.

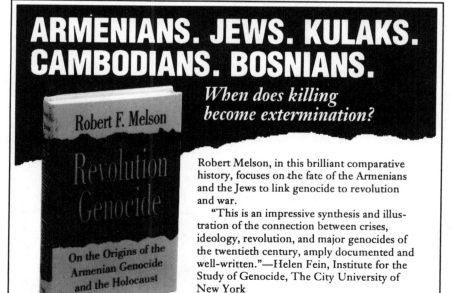